A special
SCIENCE
Compendium

ENERGY:
Use
Conservation
and Supply

Edited by

PHILIP H. ABELSON

American
Association
for the
Advancement
of
Science

Library of Congress Catalog Number 74-29004

Printed in the United States of America

The material in this book originally appeared in *Science*, the weekly journal of the American Association for the Advancement of Science. Many of the articles were first published in a special issue devoted to energy, dated 19 April 1974. Other articles were published in other issues over a period ranging from March 1973 to July 1974.

International Standard Book Number (CB) 0-87168-213-3; (PB) 0-87168-223-0
AAAS Miscellaneous Publication 74-15

Table of Contents

Foreword

The United States faces an extensive adjustment to living under circumstances in which energy is expensive and some forms are in short supply. The manner in which government, industry, academia, and the public cope with this adjustment will determine much of the shape of future society.

The staff and members of the American Association for the Advancement of Science have been aware of the significance of the energy problem, and many articles touching on it have been published in *Science*. Some of these articles have dealt with scientific and engineering research. They have been collected, supplemented with additional material, and published as a book with the title *Energy and the Future* (AAAS, Washington, D.C., 1973). This book has been translated into German and published with additional data from European experience [*Energie für die Zukunft* (Umschau, Frankfurt, 1974)]; also, arrangements have been made for publication of Japanese, Portuguese, and Hebrew translations early in 1975. In addition, an unusual issue of *Science* (19 April 1974) was devoted to a series of more general energy articles. Most of the articles were characterized by enduring and readable content. The special issue was well received, and, by September 1974, an overrun of 24,000 copies had been distributed to academic, industrial, and government establishments. Because of demand for this material, some of the articles from the Energy Issue, together with a few additional items that appeared in *Science* at other times, have been selected to form this compendium.

In a lead article entitled "Low-Cost, Abundant Energy: Paradise Lost?" Hans Landsberg provides a historical and general overview of the energy problem. He examines "the fundamental trends and forces that have brought this country to its present pass and that can be expected to persist."

The people of Western Europe and Japan live relatively comfortable lives, utilizing an energy per capita of half or less than that of the United States. Is there really a great loss in quality of life when one drives a one-ton rather than a two-ton automobile? Four articles devoted to conservation and to efficient use of energy make it clear that large quantities could readily be saved.

In an article entitled "Efficiency of Energy Use in the United States," transportation, space heating, and air conditioning are singled out as good targets for large energy savings. For example, the energy necessary per ton mile for railroad transportation is about one-fourth that for trucks.

Industrial consumption represents the largest factor in the use of energy in the United States. In general, processes have been selected and developed on the assumption of unlimited availability of cheap forms of energy. In engineering design such simple matters as heat insulation have been skimped on to save small capital investments while incurring large long-term dollar and energy costs.

Some thoughtful observers have lamented the fact that the oil embargo of 1973 ended so quickly. Had it lasted longer, everyone would have had a more thorough grounding in the need for conservation. We cannot be certain what form the next sharp crisis will take, but one will come. The thoughtful citizen should consider ways of providing against the next episode. Hammond has outlined some of the things that individuals can do, both for conservation and for cushioning the impact of future shortages.

Many of the methods of conserving energy involve simple measures that do not basically impinge on the way of life of the average citizen. But high prices and shortages of energy have hit the world in a place where it really hurts—the stomach. For years the people of the United States have enjoyed food that was comparatively cheap and even embarrassingly abundant. Production and subsequent processing and distribution were carried out by methods based on the availability of cheap and abundant amounts of hydrocarbons.

Two articles on the use of energy in food production and distribution outline how deeply our way of life and even our existence depend on the use of hydrocarbons. The question rises: Will there be enough hydrocarbons for agriculture? In September 1974 the United States was importing 40 percent of its consumption of petroleum and its products. Reserves of oil and natural gas were declining. Two articles in this volume are devoted to prospects of discovering additional supplies of these hydrocarbons. There is little basis for hope that enough petroleum can be found to sustain the present level of consumption. Either new sources of hydrocarbons must be developed or the United States must face an eventual return to horse-and-buggy agriculture, with all that it entails in the form of a large movement of people back to the farm and to hard manual labor.

For the next 10 to 20 years, four courses are available—conservation, obtaining oil from shale, obtaining oil from coal, and substitution of coal for applications in which hydrocarbons are burned under boilers merely in their heating values. If the people of this country understood what is at stake, it is likely that they would accept conservation measures aimed at ensuring a future food supply. However, in the absence of meaningful conservation, the possibilities inherent in other sources of hydrocarbons must be examined. A major potential source is oil from shale. The great deposits in Colorado, Utah, and Wyoming contain enough oil to supply the needs of the United States for a period of about 200 years. However, the oil can be produced only at considerable cost in money and with hazard to the environment. In an article on the extraction of oil from shale and in one on the problems of expanding production of coal, it is evident that, if energy is to be consumed at its present or expanded levels, substantial damage to the environment will be incurred. As long as most energy is obtained from oil and natural gas, environmental damage is nominal and not very evident, confined largely to oil spills. However, exploitation of shale, coal, and nuclear energy raises new kinds of problems of a magnitude not encountered previously.

In addition to the environmental consequences of mining coal, substantial damage results from sulfur dioxide created during combustion. If coal is to play its full role in sparing hydrocarbons for high priority tasks, practical ways must be found to minimize the sulfur problem. Two major methods—pretreatment of coal and removal of sulfur dioxide from stack gases—are discussed in separate articles.

The use of nuclear energy is increasing sharply; shortages and high prices of fossil fuels have increased the urgency for technology to go nuclear. Capital costs of nuclear plants are higher than those of coal-fired installations. However, operating costs are much lower. There are, of course, the counterbalancing problems of radioactivity, waste disposal, and possible illicit use of stolen plutonium. In an article on nuclear energy, Rose provides a broad analysis of the status of nuclear technology and its various problems. High prices for petroleum have hit in other countries even more heavily than in the United States: Western Europe and Japan are even more dependent on imported oil. Häfele discusses the situation faced by Western Europe, particularly by Germany, and concludes that the leading choice is "going nuclear."

For the longer term, there are a number of optional energy sources. One of these is geothermal energy, which today supplies the heat necessary to generate a substantial part of the electricity needs of San Francisco. At the moment commercial interest in such sources is considerable. Four of the articles discuss means of capturing energy that was initially generated by the sun—photosynthesis, solar panels, windmills, and heat engines working with seawater. For now and the next decade, their contribution other than for food and production will be modest.

Safe liquid fuels make possible great flexibility in small engine driven devices. If gasoline should become unavailable or scarce, a possible substitute is methanol, which can also be blended with gasoline. An article is devoted to this interesting chemical. Another intriguing chemical form of energy is hydrogen. Hydrogen can be used in place of petroleum or coal in many applications. If the United States goes nuclear instead of depending on coal, oil shale, or solar energy, hydrogen will have a central role as a secondary source of energy.

A final pair of articles is devoted to energy storage. Most power plants, and especially those utilizing nuclear reactors, operate most satisfactorily when carrying a steady load. However, electrical demand undergoes wide daily variations, and consequently there is need for energy storage.

The knowledge embodied in this collection of articles can be of considerable help in understanding the problems and in pointing the way toward practical solutions to the modes of supply and utilization of energy.—PHILIP H. ABELSON

Introduction

Low-Cost, Abundant Energy: Paradise Lost?

Hans H. Landsberg

The United States has entered an era of profound alteration in traditional patterns and trends in the field of energy. Price relationships, rates of use, sources of supply, and, in its broadest sense, national security, all have become areas affected with uncertainty and conflict.

With supplies likely to remain tight and prices up, the changes are widespread and painful. Although the Arab oil embargo has greatly aggravated the crisis, the underlying causes lie farther back in the past and hopes of long-term remedies lie well into the future. It would be fruitless here to describe the immediate situation or report on day-to-day efforts to improve it. Events are moving so fast that any up-to-the-minute account would be out-of-date before it could be gotten into print. Instead, let us examine the fundamental trends and forces that have brought this country to its present pass and that can be expected to persist. Although no clear answer can as yet be given, there is reason at least to ask whether we are witnessing the closing of still another frontier—the end of a low-cost, reliable energy supply in the United States.

If the answer should be unfavorable, we would have plenty of company. For many years relative prices of energy have been far higher in Europe, as every tourist who has pulled up at a gas pump knows. Western Europe and, to an even greater degree, Japan are vastly more dependent on energy imports than is the United States, which even for oil produces two-thirds of its own requirements (Tables 1 and 2).

The author is director, Energy and Minerals Program, Resources for the Future, Inc., Washington, D.C. This article is adapted from an essay in the Annual Report for 1973 of RFF.

Uncertainty of energy supply, both in availability at any given time and in quality of service, prevails through much of the world. Most of industrialized Europe, Japan, and in fact all but a handful of countries get along on one-half the per capita supply, or less, of what has seemed to be a necessity for Americans, although their growth rates in recent years have far exceeded that of the United States (Table 3).

Early Signs of Trouble

Energy problems did not hit the country full-blown in 1973. There were much earlier hints of impending trouble. Among them were the refusal of numerous natural gas utilities to connect new residential customers and voltage reductions and load shedding instituted by a number of eastern electric utilities during peak load periods in each of the past two summers.

In the late fall of 1972, shortages of heating oil prompted the closing of schools and other public buildings, and farmers in the Midwest began to worry about securing enough fuel to dry wet crops and power their implements. By the summer of 1973, distillate and fuel oil and gasoline, as well as crude, were in short supply. Sunday or early weekday closings of service stations or "sold out" signs on the pumps began to make their appearance before becoming routine matters late in the year. Beyond the borders of this country there were ever more frequent confrontations between the major exporters, banded together in the Organization of Petroleum Exporting Countries (OPEC), and their customers, until the seemingly unending string of short-term revisions in long-term basic compacts reached their climax in reduction or denial of access to supplies and drastic, unilateral price boosts, with grave economic and political ramifications.

At the end of the product line, the consumer's energy bill began to rise. Long a bargain, electric utility rates, as well as petroleum product prices, have started a rapid upward climb. Predictable reactions followed. There was increasing pressure for relaxation of environmental standards and controls. Both the automobile industry and numerous municipalities pressed for deferment of automotive emission standards; utilities sought temporary waivers of stack emission controls, largely in order to enable generating facilities to burn fuel of higher sulfur content; and high government officials asked environmentalists to be "reasonable," lest a backlash develop. (How many of these pressures were bona fide responses to the energy pinch and how many were a grasping of the opportunity to resist environmentalism is a warmly debated question.) Government action began to replace voluntarism; variances in and postponement of achieving prescribed standards had come to be official late in 1973.

Surging sales of compact cars were the consumer's first adjustment to fears of higher prices and uncertain availability of gasoline. In the booming auto market of 1973, sales of small cars during the first half of the calendar year reportedly constituted 40 percent of sales, up from 35 percent during the same period 1 year ago. More recently the news has been mixed, with an intensified small car boom followed by a resurgence of the standard automobile.

For both the executive and the legislative branches of government, energy policy has become a major concern. It has produced a rising swell of presidential messages, public addresses, research, and proposals for legislation. Organizational regrouping has been frequent but as yet unsuccessful in the search for Administration "coordination," although Project Independence provides at least a focus. Long-cherished policies like import quotas have been abandoned with little opposition. The flow of government energy research funds has steadily mounted. In fiscal 1975 they stand just short of $1 billion, mostly for nuclear reactor development, and are projected to rise to an annual $2 billion during the next 5 years, with more emphasis on nonnuclear energy sources.

The Congress, for its part, is considering a wide variety of measures to cope with energy problems. There is hardly a day on the congressional calendar that does not list hearings on one or more energy bills.

An animated search for the villain is under way. In a country as rich as the United States, few are willing to believe that the consumer suddenly faces shortages simply because demand has run up against a serious problem of supply. It must be someone's fault. Three convenient targets present themselves: the energy industry, the federal government, and the environmentalists. As seen by their adversaries, the first conspires, the second bungles, and the third obstructs. The first is a knave, the second a fool, and the third a dreamer. *Industry* is accused of withholding supplies—and information on their magnitude, alleged to be much greater than reported; thus it creates shortages, higher prices, and, as a bonus, is able to squeeze out independent refiners and service stations. *Government* is charged with holding down prices (or, by consumers, with not holding them down), reducing incentives, cutting subsidies, and enmeshing industry in a thicket of agencies, standards, and regulations, causing profits to decline, capital to become scarce, and initiative to evaporate. *Environmentalists* are held guilty of halting the wheels of progress, of following elitist aspirations, and of shunning the "facts of life."

Few of these accusations can be taken at face value. Neither can they all be dismissed.

It is obvious that demand has outrun supply at prices which have either been regulated or have risen only with some lag in time, so that quite likely considerably higher prices would be needed to bring about balance. The nature of the energy industry is such that, once its reserve margins of productive capacity have been exhausted, output can expand only slowly—that is, over a period of a few years rather than months. Anticipating the magnitude of future demand is thus of crucial importance, and, given the time lag between planning and operation, such estimates must be pushed substantially into the future to be useful.

Let us take oil demand as an exam-

Table 1. U.S. petroleum demand and imports (*3*).

Year	Domestic demand (10^3 barrel/ day)	Gross import (%)
1950	6,507	13.1
1955	8,460	14.8
1960	9,661	18.8
1965	11,303	21.8
1970	14,709	23.2
1971	15,213	25.8
1972	16,367	29.0
1973	17,248	35.7

Table 2. Significance of oil imported from the Middle East and North Africa during 1972 (*1*).

Area	Imports (gross) as percent of		
	Oil imports	Consumption	
		Oil	Energy
United States	14.9	4.4	2.1
West Europe	80.4	79.5	50.6
Japan	78.9	78.6	60.5
World	67.9	38.8	18.5

Table 3. Per capita energy consumption in selected countries during 1968 and 1971 (*2*).

Area	Coal equivalent (kg) per capita		Increase (%)
	1968	1971	
United States	10,398	11,244	8.1
France	3,282	3,928	19.7
Germany	4,488	5,223	16.4
Italy	2,267	2,682	18.3
United Kingdom	4,961	5,507	11.0
West Europe	3,313	3,878	17.1
U.S.S.R.	4,050	4,535	12.0
Japan	2,519	3,267	29.7
World	1,734	1,927	11.1

Table 4. Selected data on automobiles, United States, 1960 to 1971 (*4*).

Year	Passenger cars			
	Regis- tration ($\times 10^6$)	FIAC* (%)	Average use (mi/ car)†	Fuel (mi/ gallon)†
1960	61.7	6.9	9,446	14.28
1965	75.2	23.3	9,286	14.15
1968	83.6	43.3	9,448	13.91
1969	86.9	54.0	9,633	13.75
1970	89.2	60.9	9,783	13.58
1971	92.8	61.0	9,926	13.73
1972	96.9	68.6	10,184	13.49

* FIAC, factory-installed air conditioning. † 1 mile = 1.6 km; 1 gallon = 3.8×10^{-3} m³.

ple. Under 1958 limitations, approximately 12 percent of consumption was to be contributed by imports, but by 1973 imports represented closer to 36 percent (Table 2).

What has pushed imports up so far and so fast? One item has been the shift of electric utilities to oil, highly notable along the Atlantic Coast, and evident in the most spectacular manner in the Greater New York City area, where Consolidated Edison and Long Island Lighting relied on oil for 22 percent of their fuel input in 1960 and for nearly 80 percent in 1971. Controls imposed on emissions from plants that burn fossil fuel, the absence of a commercially viable technology for removing sufficient sulfur compounds from stack gases, and the tightness of natural gas supplies have caused utilities to shift to oil, which enables them to meet the restrictions imposed. The effect on prices is not surprising. In the Middle Atlantic region, cost to utilities of oil "as burned" rose 54 percent per barrel between 1969 and 1971, in constant dollars. Various industrial users have turned to oil and, within that category, to the less polluting, lighter distillates. This in turn has caused a tightening of oil available for heating.

At the same time, automobiles, which account for nearly 40 percent of oil consumed in this country, have become less efficient converters of gasoline into vehicle-miles. More power-consuming accessories on more cars (power steering, power brakes, air conditioners, and, more recently, emission control devices) are diverting part of the power produced from the drive shaft. These devices also have added to the car's weight, so that the same number of gallons will pull the car fewer miles, and there are more automobiles. Moreover, miles traveled per car per year have shown a moderate increase, after years of stability and despite the emergence on a rising scale of the two- and three-car family. Congestion in city streets and on highways adjacent to metropolitan areas could well have been another factor in lowering mileage per gallon (Table 4).

These factors have boosted demand for petroleum products. Gasoline demand rose by 2.6 percent per year from 1960 to 1965; it has risen at 4.5 percent since. From 1967 to 1972 it rose by 27 percent, or 4.9 percent per year. Consumption of residual fuel oil, the one-time Cinderella of refinery products that had risen by barely 1 percent per year from 1960 to 1965,

Small cars have increased in popularity.

shot up by an annual 7.2 percent over the latest 5-year span. This is the story for 1972, in percentage increases over 1971: gasoline, 6.0 percent; distillate, 8.5 percent; residual fuel oil, 10.1 percent; and total product demand, 7.3 percent.

The recent increases in consumption have no match on the domestic supply side. Through 1972 the trend of exploration activity and drilling was down, while refinery construction increased only slowly. Well completion, for example, had by the early 1970's declined to the level of 1946, after a sharply rising trend that began in 1948 and persisted through 1956 (Table 5). As a result, reserves, as defined in the industry statistics, have declined absolutely, and even more drastically as a multiple of production. The steep 1973 increase in gas drilling activities is encouraging, but too recent to evaluate as a guide to future events.

Promising new avenues of supply expansion have narrowed or closed altogether. Leading oil states like Texas and Louisiana now are lifting oil at essentially 100 percent of capacity, calculated at a rate of extraction designed to result in maximum economic recovery. Offshore drilling received a heavy setback from the Santa Barbara Channel spill. Existing wells in the area had to be throttled, and new ones could not be drilled. Moreover, the event cast a shadow over offshore drilling as a whole, a significant drag on future supply in view of the richness of the offshore fields and their rising relative role in recent years (from 4.5 percent of total crude and condensate production in 1960 to 16.4 percent in 1972) (Table 6). No less significant

has been the delay of production of the northern Alaska field. Had offshore drilling and producing continued as foreseen and had North Slope oil come into operation, these two sources could have contributed about 2 million barrels per day by now—substantially more than 10 percent of demand, or more than a third of current U.S. oil imports and thus roughly the equivalent of direct and indirect imports from Middle East sources. Moreover, production of North Slope natural gas on the heels of that of oil would have eased the demand that oil make up for the natural gas shortage. (These conclusions are offered strictly from the viewpoint of energy supply, with no intention of passing judgments on objections of environmentalists to both offshore drilling and the trans-Alaska pipeline.)

Caribou graze nonchalantly on the Arctic tundra within sight of one of the operating drilling rigs at Prudhoe Bay, Alaska. This photograph was taken during the animals' annual migration across the North Slope. [Courtesy Alyeska Pipeline Service Company, Bellevue, Washington]

5

The recent upturn in energy prices results not only from the failure of domestic production to expand as expected, but also from the fact that some of the costs of environmental damages are being taken into account. More such external costs will go into future concepts of "abundant, reliable, low-cost energy." Moreover, the price increases, for whatever reasons, are especially disconcerting because they follow a long period of declining *real* energy prices, which have been masked by price increases measured in current dollars. Thus a barrel of crude oil was worth $2.60 in 1948 and $3.39 in 1972, with only a slow upward trend until the very recent rise. In constant (1948) dollars, however, the 1972 price reached not $3.39 but $1.85, for a decline of about 30 percent during the quarter century. The price decline was even more pronounced in coal, whose price in constant dollars had declined by some 40 percent between the early postwar period and 1970, although it increased very sharply thereafter as a number of phenomena created a sudden shortage of coal, specifically of low-sulfur coal (here again the long slide in coal's real price must be taken into account when contemplating its subsequent rise). Only the price of natural gas had advanced in real terms, but that advance had been accomplished by the late 1950's, primarily because gas had been so drastically underpriced when it first came into use as a by-product of oil extraction. Even in 1972, its wellhead price of approximately 20 cents per million Btu (1 Btu $\sim$ 1.06 $\times$ 10³ joule) compared with 30 cents for coal (at the minemouth) and 60 cents for wellhead oil, although these differences are greatly reduced when costs of transportation to users are taken into consideration. Recent price behavior apparently marks the end of energy as one of the great postwar bargains.

Other factors have aggravated the situation. One of these is the slow pace in refinery construction, most pronounced along the East Coast, where no new refinery has been built in the last 15 years and capacity has been declining since 1961. This trend is frequently blamed on environmentalist opposition; but this cannot be the whole story if only because the slowdown antedates public environmental concern. Other factors—mostly within control of government—are: import limitations and uncertainties as to their duration and character; possibly capital tightness following the reduction in

Table 5. Number of oil and gas wells completed in the United States, 1945 to 1972.

Year	Reference	Wells (No.)*
1945	(5)	24,666
1950	(5)	42,039
1955	(5)	55,896
1960	(5)	44,018
1965	(5)	39,510
1970	(6)	28,120
1971	(6)	25,851
1972	(7)	27,291
1973	(8)	26,592

* Excludes service wells.

the depletion allowance; the suspension of the investment tax credit; tax advantages for location offshore; the uncertainties concerning the type of gasoline to be marketed; and the rising difficulties of obtaining low-sulfur oil, which most U.S. refineries are built to process. These factors have contributed to the failure of refining capacity to keep pace with rising demand. Actually, refining capacity has not stood still, even in the most recent past. It rose by about 4 percent annually, from 1967 to 1972, and by 1.2 percent, from 1971 to 1972. This limited expansion, however, was not nearly sufficient, and the wave of recently announced planned capacity growth cannot soon remedy this condition, even if fully implemented and supported by access to crude.

Furthermore, there have been substantial delays in the expansion of the electric power industry. Here, too, it would be wrong to hold environmentalists solely or even largely responsible. Rather the nuclear power industry has been plagued with childhood diseases, including unsuspected technical problems, poor workmanship, con-

Table 6. U.S. crude oil and condensate production, total and offshore (9).

Year	Production (10³ barrels)		Offshore as % of total
	Total*	Offshore†	
1960	2,574,933	116,763	4.5
1965	2,848,514	242,652	8.5
1966	3,027,763	300,270	9.9
1967	3,215,742	368,177	11.4
1968	3,329,042	471,191	14.2
1969	3,371,751	525,832	15.6
1970	3,517,450	575,714	16.4
1971	3,453,914	614,754	17.8
1972	3,455,000	569,206	16.4

* Total U.S. crude oil and condensate. † Total offshore "state" and "federal outer continental shelf" oil and condensate.

gested order books, strikes, and other delays not peculiar to the power equipment industry—slowness of the licensing process, multiplicity of agencies involved, and time-consuming tests in the courts. These, together with the concern of environmentalists about routine as well as accidental emission of radioactive substances, safe management of disposed material, thermal pollution of lakes and rivers, and the like, have slowed down the planned expansion of the industry.

Nor were there ready alternatives. Supplies of natural gas, the "clean fuel" par excellence, were becoming increasingly tight. Its use as boiler fuel once again was frowned upon, just as is had been some 20 years ago. Regulatory policies have played a part in perpetuating the price differential, keeping the price of gas below the level at which the market would be cleared without the "shortage" phenomenon that has emerged. Diminished regulatory control, most believe, would boost output from existing wells, while many expect, in addition, increased exploration and development.

As for coal-fired boilers, a reliable, commercial process for desulfurization has yet to be demonstrated, occasional reports to the contrary notwithstanding. Utilities have thus been reluctant to commit funds to coal-fired plants, an attitude strengthened by the judgment that problems attending nuclear generation will in time be solved and that the nuclear plant thus represents a wiser long-term investment. The overwhelming emphasis in R & D funding on nuclear energy has not helped matters. Current efforts at correcting it can bear fruit only in the years to come.

The evidence sketched above suggests no quick way out of the nation's energy bind, even though easing of gasoline supplies and rising oil inventories in the second half of 1974 have caused some observers to suggest—erroneously, in my judgment—that the crisis is over. In looking ahead, let us reexamine some familiar problems: import dependency, possibilities of curbing domestic demand and increasing domestic supply, and environmental impacts and trade offs that might be involved.

Until November 1973, nobody doubted continuance of the shift in supplies from indigenous to foreign sources, involving principally oil and, to a lesser degree, natural gas. The Magnitude and duration of the shift were less easily agreed on. Nor was it as-

Table 7. Percentage shares of primary energy sources in total consumption for selected countries in 1960 and 1970.

Country	Percentage shares of sources									
	Solid		Liquid		Gaseous		Hydro		Nuclear	
	1960	1970	1960	1970	1960	1970	1960	1970	1960	1970
United States	23.9	20.5	44.1	42.7	30.3	34.8	1.7	1.7		0.3
France	56.7	26.5	34.3	62.4	3.3	6.1	5.6	4.1	0.1	0.9
Germany	76.6	39.3	21.7	53.3	0.5	5.8	1.2	1.0		0.6
Italy	17.8	7.6	55.7	77.9	13.7	9.8	12.8	4.2		0.5
United Kingdom	73.6	48.0	25.8	44.2		5.0	0.2	0.2	0.4	2.6
Europe (OECD)	61.4	29.4	32.5	59.6	1.8	6.7	4.2	3.3	0.1	1.0
Japan	54.8	23.3	36.4	71.7	1.0	1.4	7.8	3.2		0.4

serted that there was no possibility of reversal. On the contrary, the new devotion to energy research and development was regarded as likely to provide the pivot on which the growing dependence could eventually turn around.

Concern over import dependency is not new. In its most conventional form it rests on considerations of national security. What degree of dependency, and therefore vulnerability, is tolerable, and what alternatives exist for ensuring adequate security in the face of growing dependency?

Such concern has gradually extended its scope. In the future, security is likely to be more broadly conceived as reliance on a minimum flow of energy materials to feed the economy as a whole, not just the defense machinery or the economy in times of war. Among the large issues at stake here are: (i) the impact on the nation's foreign trade and payments balance and (ii) the effect on U.S. foreign policy in a world where competition for fuel easily becomes a major disruptive influence among friends and a potent determinant of the formation and strength of new alliances.

Relations with OPEC countries located in the Middle East and along the southern shore of the Mediterranean have, for many years, been heavily affected by energy questions, but that was principally through the medium of security for Western Europe and the role of U.S. companies as operators in that part of the world. Henceforth, the far more direct impact of the oil (and gas) supply to the U.S. market and the impairment, if not the loss, of American ability to help Western Europe and Japan overcome sudden supply difficulties by reaching into current U.S. production will take on new importance and urgency, brought into sharp focus through recent U.S.-sponsored efforts at cooperation among consumer countries, and the difficulties associated

with them. At the same time, how and with what effects the exporting nations will use their growing oil revenues, assuming that large exports will take place even if not at rates desired by many potential customers, is an altogether new, and so far unanswered, question.

Of equal novelty is the idea that the U.S.S.R. might become a large-scale supplier of energy, in this instance natural gas, to the United States. Here security considerations of a different kind are bound to generate debate. Finally, rethinking the security concept will become necessary in the wake of recent evidence that Canada is reluctant to remain an unquestioned reserve pool for U.S. needs. The customary assumption that U.S. dependence on foreign supplies is acceptable as long as such supplies are located within strategically easy reach, could come in for review, modification, and perhaps abandonment.

From a purely economic viewpoint, the trend toward obtaining a growing share of energy supplies from abroad should not give rise to great concern. It is a familiar stage in the cycle of development and foreign trade. However, U.S. demand pressure coincides not only with precarious foreign trade and payments circumstances, but with similar pressures in the rest of the industrialized world. Moreover, the 1960's have witnessed a radical swing in both Western Europe and Japan to oil as the primary energy source (Table 7). Thus, plans for "sharing" were looked at askance by Europe and Japan even before the Middle East war. Now there is less to share and less willingness to do so, and the agreements among OECD countries remain to be tested when events call for implementation. As a result, the world's oil producers find themselves in an unprecedentedly strong bargaining position, which has enabled them to convert the

supply bind into spectacular price and revenue increases. Even if trade relations should become more normal, such revenue increases will have affected the economics of expanding production (why sell now if prices will continue to rise?) and reduced motivation to collect more revenue (what is to be done with the snowballing billions of dollars?). Thus, even sustained price increases may not bring a satisfactory expansion of crude oil supply from some foreign sources. High prices and moderate exports, if the cartel holds, could be an attractive alternative.

Boosting Efficiency and Output

One way to reduce dependency on imports (or, for that matter, relieve pressure on domestic supply) is to use energy more efficiently. Some results might come quickly, such as more car pooling and maximum use of available mass transit facilities. Higher gasoline prices, rationing, or a combination of both can assure reduction in consumption. Price increases alone can be expected to slow down demand, although our scant knowledge of price elasticities of energy as a whole and of its components suggests more about the direction of change than about its likely magnitude. We know that consumers purchase energy in driblets. This diminishes the demand-reducing effect of price increases. More potent deterrents, such as progressive taxes on energy-consuming durables, especially automobiles, have been discussed but have not as yet been put into operation. Increased capabilities for mass transportation, buildings that minimize heating and cooling requirements and other modifications of major living arrangements tend to have long incubation periods. Nonetheless, marginal adjustments are taking place even now, such as reductions in airplane cruising speeds, the buyers' shift to compact cars and increased use of buses and commuter lines. The effectiveness of admonitions to reduce driving speeds on highways, on the other hand, has quickly given way to mandatory reductions in official speed limits. However, gradual, socially motivated changes in behavior are not to be discounted. Setting the thermostat a few degrees higher in summer and lower in winter, or doing with less illumination in offices and at home could well be contagious responses to social pressure, especially as steeply higher utility bills begin to hit homeowners.

In designing policies and programs to increase the contribution of domestic sources, careful attention should be given to the relative costs for the economy as a whole. Attainment of a greater degree of self-sufficiency could be self-defeating if it imposed excessive burdens on the rest of the economy. Although the nation has lived with almost total import dependence for materials like nickel, manganese, chromium, and bauxite, and has carried on only modest research to probe potential domestic sources or new substitutes, one cannot realistically expect a similar attitude when the phenomenon shows up in basic energy materials.

⌐In exploring avenues for expansion of domestic sources, it is well to distinguish between short- and long-run means, with the next decade considered as the short term.⌐ In the latter context, resumption of oil and gas leasing of offshore sources, under appropriate environmental safeguards and guided by the lessons of past accidents and their consequences, comes immediately to mind. So does the completion in one way or another of the effort that will bring Alaskan oil and gas to the West Coast or the Midwest (or both).

Often neglected in the search for new zones of production are advances in the art of finding and recovering oil and gas. In recent years, we have witnessed a decline in exploration and drilling and little progress in bringing a larger proportion of discovered oil to the surface. Much of the liveliness of research in the mid- and late-1950's, when new recovery methods were engineered and tried and hopes were high for bringing 50 percent and more of oil in place to the wellhead, seems to have gone.

Since U.S. coal reserves are measured in hundreds of years, even at

rising annual rates of consumption, achievement of a "clean-burning" coal is of utmost importance. Technology has lagged in developing a process that would make such coal less costly than desulfurized oil or natural gas. Success is well within the focus of the short term as here defined, although not an instant remedy as is sometimes casually assumed.

Hand in hand with greater emphasis on technologies that promise short-term gains go incentives and policies designed to make the search for and use of such innovations attractive to producers. Whether there should be a more relaxed—and perhaps even positive—attitude toward price increases that reflect changing supply and demand relationships and must thus be distinguished from "inflationary" factors proper; whether, and what kinds of, special tax treatment, credit, allowances, and the like are indicated; whether there should be, as in the case of natural gas, less public regulation; whether and how federal funds are to be used to supplement private efforts —these are just a few of the questions that will be in the forefront of discussion.

In the Distance: True Innovation

Truly new energy sources or conversion methods to replace those approaches now narrowed or closed altogether by environmental problems are apparently not just around the corner. There is little dissent from the judgment that coal conversion to either gaseous or liquid form will not make much of a contribution before the early or mid-1980's. Moreover, should drastically higher prices elicit a correspondingly drastic supply response from oil and gas producers, the early need for producing liquefied or gasified coal would greatly diminish.

The technique of extracting oil from bituminous sands is now well advanced, though the largest operation, begun in 1967 in Canada, has only just begun to break even financially. No sand zones comparable to those of Alberta have been identified for early development in the United States. Expansion will come in Canada, if at all, and its benefit for the U.S. energy economy will at best be indirect.

Such indicators as rising crude oil prices, ongoing lease sales of rich shale oil land by the Department of Interior for construction of prototype

shale oil plants, and various economic studies suggest that the start of a shale oil industry could be in the offing. Similar indications in the past, however, have come to nothing. Moreover, there are still unresolved environmental issues concerning the development of oil shale. A cautiously optimistic view appears warranted at present. In the long run, lack of processing water may limit the size of a Rocky Mountains shale oil industry.

Any impact on the nation's total energy supply by most remaining technologies is probably even further in the future, not excepting advanced nuclear reactors—specifically, the breeder. Given the time it has taken non-breeding reactors to come into their own and that even "shelf-item" reactors now have a lead time of 8 years or more, as well as the fact that a breeder prototype is only now beginning to be engineered and put in place, a significant contribution within the next 15 to 20 years is excluded. The timetable for the emergence of commercially effective power derived from fusion is likely to take us into the next century. Nor is success a foregone conclusion. This does not, of course, say anything about either the timing, magnitude, or provenance of research and development funds. Uncertainty of eventual success and a long lead time are merely two factors to be considered in setting priorities; others are the likely impact of success and the capacity of the research community effectively to digest rising funds at each stage of work.

Both geothermal and solar energy are properly considered "new sources," since their present use is spotty; geothermal production now takes place under unusual circumstances, and solar energy is produced on a more or less experimental basis. Though these two approaches are technically feasible today, they are likely to be important supplemental sources only in the more distant future. Greater attention to the untapped potential of the earth's inner heat has already given life to a wholly new concept of exploiting it: the sinking of deep shafts, possibly blasting the holes with nuclear devices, and utilizing the heat of the rock masses to turn injected water into steam, to be raised and used in conventional generation. As a new technology, it is not likely to have an early payoff equaling that of shale, tar, or coal conversion, but, if commercially viable, it should come into play during this century. In several respects it is more attractive than traditional geothermal energy.

For good reason, solar energy has drawn increasing attention. At least on a global basis, its use would essentially free us of the thermal discharge penalty. It would thus get around atmospheric and climate problems and obviate limitations of energy use as an ultimate "limit to growth." Present prospects, however, are far behind the expectations aroused by popular writers. Even the more feasible applications of solar energy for heating and cooling residential and other structures would require major changes in building design, practices, and associated institutions. If adopted, it would gain importance slowly with the accretion of new housing to the existing stock, and probably not without a determined governmental drive to assure a mass market. As for electric power from solar energy, the conversion efficiency of the various devices so far designed is still exceedingly low and economic feasibility is correspondingly remote. To sum up, expansion of domestic capability in the near future will depend principally on (i) establishing effective incentives for exploration and discovery of oil and gas resources as yet unidentified, and for more complete recovery of those known and developed; (ii) bringing into operation, with acceptable environmental safeguards, Alaskan and offshore resources, and whatever other occurrences might be revealed; and (iii) expanding the use of coal as coal within acceptable limits of environmental impact.

Beyond lies resort to oil shale; to tar sands, provided Canada is willing to export; to coal conversion; to the breeder reactor; and eventually to geothermal, solar, and fusion energy. Not all of these are technically proven technologies, nor will demonstrated feasibility necessarily lead to utilization. A strong and quick response of oil and gas producers could slow down the emergence of coal conversion and shale oil production. Successful shale oil extraction might push coal conversion into the background, or vice versa. Thus, which items will be picked from the offered menu is as yet uncertain.

Reconciling Conflicting Values

Because environmental concern and action are so highly visible, it is easy to exaggerate their constraining impact in the current energy situation. For example, a nuclear power plant's schedule delayed by careless manufacturing methods is much less dramatic than court action by an advocate group. Yet available data suggest that fewer delays are caused by advocate groups than by technological and engineering problems. Again, automobile emission control devices tend to be blamed for higher gasoline consumption and, therefore, for shortages, when body weight, air conditioning and other add-ons, speed, and congestion are greater reducers of efficiency.

This is not to say that legislation during the 1960's, the administrative machinery now in place at the federal, state, and local levels, and the intervention of the courts have not significantly slowed the execution of energy-producing facilities; in this sense, the energy scene is probably the segment of the economy most heavily affected by environmental policies and considerations. Safeguards, risk-reducers, delays, and stopgap solutions add to cost. How far to carry these trade offs is a matter of legitimate disagreement. Value judgments prevail, the more so as even the underlying data regarding damage attributable to environmental impacts are often in controversy. The effect of the resulting cost and price (or rate) increases on income distribution and on competitiveness of given industries or activities, in both domestic and foreign markets, is calculable up to a point, but what to do about them is a political decision. Questions abound. How safe is safe, and how costly is costly?

Frequently, the advice given in these matters is to act "prudently," or to "preserve the maximum number of options." How does society conform to the prescription? And how does it choose among options? The choice is hard enough when only technological alternatives are at issue: coal versus nuclear energy, supertankers versus pipelines, or power parks versus plant dispersal. But comparison must also be made between benefits that accrue because of abstention from action and the cost of shortfalls that might result —between this generation and the next, between this country and others. In a much broader framework and over the long run, the two big questions are (i) how we can agree on the point up to which we wish to trade additional, or lower-cost, energy for environmental quality and (ii) in what proportion various groups in society will share the costs that inevitably flow from trade-off decisions, no matter where along the line they are made.

Low-cost energy has been an integral part of American economic history; but European experience suggests that not greatly lower levels of per capita income can be reached with much lower per capita energy consumption. One can contemplate with equanimity a prolonged period during which U.S. energy costs will be higher, utilization more efficient, and consumption patterns somewhat different, all without a profound sacrifice of welfare, although surely with temporarily painful adjustments and crisislike phenomena. Possibly such a period may be followed once again by one of low-cost and abundant energy, if and when the technologies of either nuclear fusion or solar energy have been solved. Environmentally attractive and basically unconstrained by "fuel availability," solar energy would eliminate even the problem of excessive discharges of heat to the atmosphere; fusion might ease it. What new technological and environmental problems we might encounter we do not yet know; but experience has taught us to expect them. The first priority is to manage the energy problems now crowding in, and likely to be with us for some years at least, in ways that will not impede long-term solutions and will give due recognition to the necessity of reconciling other aspirations of society with provision of abundant energy.

References and Notes

1. Testimony by J. Darmstadter and M. Searl, Resources for the Future, before Senate Committee on Foreign Relations, 30 May 1973.
2. United Nations, *Statistical Yearbook, 1972* (United Nations, New York, 1973).
3. U.S. Bureau of Mines, several issues of *Minerals Yearbook* (Government Printing Office, Washington, D.C.); news release, 13 March 1974.
4. U.S. Department of Commerce, Bureau of Public Roads, *Highway Statistics*; and Bureau of the Census, *Statistical Abstract, 1973*; also 1972 data from Bureau of Public Roads, personal communication.
5. American Petroleum Institute, *Petroleum Facts and Figures* (American Petroleum Institute, Washington, D.C., 1971), p. 24.
6. U.S. Bureau of Mines, *Minerals Yearbook, 1971* (Government Printing Office, Washington, D.C., 1973), pp. 88–89.
7. American Petroleum Institute, *Quarterly Review of Drilling Statistics for the United States* 6 (4), 15 (1973).
8. American Petroleum Institute spokesman, personal communication.
9. U.S. Geological Survey, *Outer Continental Shelf Statistics* (June 1973), pp. 73 and 75, and telephone communication.
10. *Oil, The Present Situation and Future Prospects* (Organization for Economic Cooperation and Development, Paris, 1973).
11. The assistance of Henry Jarrett in shortening and otherwise adapting the essay from which this article is derived is gratefully acknowledged. The work on which the unabridged essay was based was supported by the National Science Foundation.

People and Institutions

Efficiency of Energy Use in the United States

Transportation, space heating, and air conditioning provide opportunities for large energy savings.

Eric Hirst and John C. Moyers

Conflicts between the demand for energy and environmental quality goals can be resolved in several ways. The two most important are (i) development and use of pollution control technologies and of improved energy-conversion technologies and (ii) the improvement in efficiency of energy use. Increased efficiency of energy use would help to slow energy growth rates, thereby relieving pressure on scarce energy resources and reducing environmental problems associated with energy production, conversion, and use.

Between 1950 and 1970, U.S. consumption of energy resources (coal, oil, natural gas, falling water, and uranium) doubled (1), with an average annual growth rate of 3.5 percent—more than twice the population growth rate.

Energy resources are used for many purposes in the United States (2) (Table 1). In 1970, transportation of people and freight consumed 25 percent of total energy, primarily as petroleum. Space heating of homes and commercial establishments was the second largest end-use, consuming an additional 18 percent. Industrial uses of energy [process steam, direct heat, electric drive, fuels used as raw materials (3), and electrolytic processes] accounted for 42 percent. The remaining 15 percent was used by the commercial and residential sectors for water heating, air conditioning, refrigeration, cooking, lighting, operation of small appliances, and other miscellaneous purposes.

The authors are research staff members in the Oak Ridge National Laboratory–National Science Foundation environmental program, Oak Ridge National Laboratory, Oak Ridge, Tennessee 37830. The work reported here was sponsored by the National Science Foundation RANN program under Union Carbide Corporation contract with the U.S. Atomic Energy Commission.

During the 1960's, the percentage of energy consumed for electric drive, raw materials, air conditioning, refrigeration, and electrolytic processes increased relative to the total. Air conditioning showed the largest relative growth, increasing its share of total energy use by 81 percent, while the other uses noted increased their shares of the total by less than 10 percent in this period.

The growth in energy consumption by air conditioners, refrigerators, electric drive, and electrolytic processes—coupled with the substitution of electricity for direct fossil fuel combustion for some space and water heating, cooking, and industrial heat—accounts for the rapid growth in electricity consumption. Between 1960 and 1970, while consumption of primary energy (1) grew by 51 percent, the use of electricity (4) grew by 104 percent. The increasing use of electricity relative to the primary fuels is an important factor accounting for energy growth rates because of the inherently low efficiency of electricity generation, transmission, and distribution which averaged 30 percent during this decade (1, 4). In 1970, electrical generation (1) accounted for 24 percent of energy resource consumption as compared to 19 percent in 1960.

Industry, the largest energy user, includes manufacturing; mining; and agriculture, forestry, and fisheries. Six manufacturers—of primary metals; of chemicals; of petroleum and coal; of stone, clay, and glass; of paper; and of food—account for half of industrial energy consumption (5), equivalent to 20 percent of the total energy budget.

Energy consumption is determined by at least three factors: population, afflu-

ence, and efficiency of use. In this article we describe three areas in which energy-efficiency improvements (the third factor) might be particularly important: (i) transportation of people and freight, (ii) space heating, and (iii) space cooling (air conditioning).

Energy efficiency varies considerably among the different passenger and freight transport modes. Shifts from energy-intensive modes (airplanes, trucks, automobiles) to energy-efficient modes (boats, pipelines, trains, buses) could significantly reduce energy consumption. Increasing the amount of building insulation could reduce both space-heating and air-conditioning energy consumption in homes and save money for the homeowner. Energy consumption for air conditioning could be greatly reduced through the use of units that are more energy efficient.

Transportation

Transportation of people and goods consumed 16,500 trillion British thermal units (6) in 1970 (25 percent of total energy consumption) (1). Energy requirements for transportation increased by 89 percent between 1950 and 1970, an average annual growth rate of 3.2 percent.

Increases in transportation energy consumption (7) are due to (i) growth in traffic levels, (ii) shifts toward the use of less energy-efficient transport modes, and (iii) declines in energy efficiency for individual modes. Energy intensiveness, the inverse of energy efficiency, is expressed here as British thermal units per ton-mile for freight and as British thermal units per passenger-mile for passenger traffic.

Table 2 shows approximate values (8) for energy consumption and average revenue in 1970 for intercity freight modes; the large range in energy efficiency among modes is noteworthy. Pipelines and waterways (barges and boats) are very efficient; however, they are limited in the kinds of materials they can transport and in the flexibility of their pickup and delivery points. Railroads are slightly less efficient than pipelines. Trucks, which are faster and more flexible than the preceding three modes, are, with respect to energy, only one-fourth as efficient as railroads. Airplanes, the fastest mode, are only 1/60 as efficient as trains.

The variation in freight prices shown in Table 2 closely parallels the variation in energy intensiveness. The in-

13

creased prices of the less efficient modes reflect their greater speed, flexibility, and reliability.

Table 3 gives approximate 1970 energy and price data for various passenger modes (8). For intercity passenger traffic, trains and buses are the most efficient modes. Cars are less than one-half as efficient as buses, and airplanes are only one-fifth as efficient as buses.

For urban passenger traffic, mass transit systems (of which about 60 percent are bus systems) are more than twice as energy efficient as automobiles. Walking and bicycling are an order of magnitude more efficient than autos, on the basis of energy consumption to produce food. Urban values of efficiency for cars and buses are much lower than intercity values because of poorer vehicle performance (fewer miles per gallon) and poorer utilization (fewer passengers per vehicle).

Passenger transport prices are also shown in Table 3. The correlation between energy intensiveness and price, while positive, is not as strong as for freight transport. Again, the differences in price reflect the increased values of the more energy-intensive modes.

The transportation scenario for 1970 shown in Table 4 gives energy savings that may be possible through increased use of more efficient modes. The first calculation uses the actual 1970 transportation patterns. The scenario—entirely speculative—indicates the potential energy savings that could have occurred through shifts to more efficient transport modes. In this hypothetical scenario, half the freight traffic carried by truck and by aiplane is assumed to have been carried by rail; half the intercity passenger traffic carried by airplane and one-third the traffic carried by car are assumed to have been carried by bus and train; and half the urban automobile traffic is assumed to have been carried by bus. The load factors (percentage of transport capacity utilized) and prices are assumed to be the same for both calculations. The scenario ignores several factors that might inhibit shifts to energy-efficient transport modes, such as existing land-use patterns, capital costs, changes in energy efficiency within a given mode, substitutability among modes, new technologies, transportation ownership patterns, and other institutional arrangements.

The hypothetical scenario requires only 78 percent as much energy to move the same traffic as does the actual calculation. This savings of 2800 tril-

lion Btu is equal to 4 percent of the total 1970 energy budget. The scenario also results in a total transportation cost that is $19 billion less than the actual 1970 cost (a 12 percent reduction). The dollar savings (which includes the energy saved) must be balanced against any losses in speed, comfort, and flexibility resulting from a shift to energy-efficient modes.

To some extent, the current mix of transport modes is optimal, chosen in response to a variety of factors. However, noninternalized social costs, such as noise and air pollution and various

Table 1. End-uses of energy in the United States.

Item	1960* (%)	1970† (%)
Transportation	25.2	24.7
Space heating	18.5	17.7
Process steam	17.8	16.4
Direct heat	12.9	11.0
Electric drive	7.4	8.1
Raw materials	5.2	5.6
Water heating	4.0	4.0
Air conditioning	1.6	2.9
Refrigeration	2.1	2.3
Cooking	1.5	1.2
Electrolytic processes	1.1	1.2
Other‡	2.7	4.9

* Data for 1960 obtained from Stanford Research Institute (SRI) (2). † Estimates for 1970 obtained by extrapolating changes in energy-use patterns from SRI data. ‡ Includes clothes drying, small appliances, lighting, and other miscellaneous energy uses.

Table 2. Energy and price data for intercity freight transport.

Mode	Energy (Btu/ ton-mile)	Price (cents/ ton-mile)
Pipeline	450	0.27
Railroad	670	1.4
Waterway	680	0.30
Truck	2,800	7.5
Airplane	42,000	21.9

Table 3. Energy and price data for passenger transport.

Mode	Energy (Btu/pas- senger-mile)	Price (cents/pas- senger-mile)
*Intercity**		
Bus	1600	3.6
Railroad	2900	4.0
Automobile	3400	4.0
Airplane	8400	6.0
Urban†		
Mass transit	3800	8.3
Automobile	8100	9.6

* Load factors (percentage of transport capacity utilized) for intercity travel are about: bus, 45 percent; railroad, 35 percent; automobile, 48 percent; and airplane, 50 percent. † Load factors for urban travel are about: mass transit, 20 percent; and automobile, 28 percent.

government activities (regulation, subsidization, research), may tend to distort the mix, and, therefore, present modal patterns may not be socially optimal.

Present trends in modal mix are determined by personal preference, private economics, convenience, speed, reliability, and government policy. Emerging factors such as fuel scarcities, rising energy prices, dependence on petroleum imports, urban land-use problems, and environmental quality considerations may provide incentives to shift transportation patterns toward greater energy efficiency.

Space Heating

The largest single energy-consuming function in the home is space heating. In an average all-electric home in a moderate climate, space heating uses over half the energy delivered to the home; in gas- or oil-heated homes, the fraction is probably larger because the importance of thermal insulation has not been stressed where these fuels are used.

The nearest approach to a national standard for thermal insulation in residential construction is "Minimum Property Standards (MPS) for One and Two Living Units," issued by the Federal Housing Administration (FHA). In June 1971, FHA revised the MPS to require more insulation, with the stated objectives of reducing air pollution and fuel consumption.

A recent study (9) estimated the value of different amounts of thermal insulation in terms both of dollar savings to the homeowner and of reduction in energy consumption. Hypothetical model homes (1800 square feet) were placed in three climatic regions, each representing one-third of the U.S. population. The three regions were represented by Atlanta, New York, and Minneapolis.

As an example of the findings of the study, Table 5 presents the results applicable to a New York residence, including the insulation requirements of the unrevised and the revised MPS, the insulation that yields the maximum economic benefit to the homeowner, and the monetary and energy savings that result in each case. The net monetary savings are given after recovery of the cost of the insulation installation, and would be realized each year of the lifetime of the home. A mortgage interest rate of 7 percent was assumed.

The revised MPS provide appreciable savings in energy consumption and in the cost of heating a residence, although more insulation is needed to minimize the long-term cost to the homeowner. A further increase in insulation requirements would increase both dollar and energy savings.

The total energy consumption of the United States (1) in 1970 was 67,000 trillion Btu, and about 11 percent was devoted to residential space heating and 7 percent to commercial space heating (2). Table 5 shows reductions in energy required for space heating of 49 percent for gas-heated homes and 47 percent for electric-heated homes in the New York area by going from the MPS-required insulation in 1970 to the economically optimum amount of insulation. The nationwide average reductions are 43 percent for gas-heated homes and 41 percent for electric-heated homes. An average savings of 42 percent, applied to the space heating energy requirements for all residential units (single family and apartment, gas and electric), would have amounted to 3100 trillion Btu in 1970 (4.6 percent of total energy consumption). The energy savings are somewhat understated—as insulation is added, the heat from lights, stoves, refrigerators, and other appliances becomes a significant part of the total heat required. The use of additional insulation also reduces the energy consumption for air conditioning as discussed later.

Electrical resistance heating is more wasteful of primary energy than is direct combustion heating. The average efficiency for electric power plants (1) in the United States is about 33 percent, and the efficiency (4) of transmitting and distributing the power to the customer is about 91 percent. The end-use efficiency of electrical resistance heating is 100 percent; so the overall efficiency is approximately 30 percent. Thus, for every unit of heat delivered in the home, 3.3 units of heat must be extracted from the fuel at the power plant. Conversely, the end-use efficiency of gas- or oil-burning home heating systems is about 60 percent (claimed values range from 40 to 80 percent), meaning that 1.7 units of heat must be extracted from the fuel for each unit delivered to the living area of the home. Therefore, the electrically heated home requires about twice as much fuel per unit of heat as the gas- or oil-heated home, assuming equivalent insulation.

The debate about whether gas, oil, or electric-resistance space heating is better from a conservation point of view may soon be moot because of the shortage of natural gas and petroleum. The use of electricity generated by nuclear plants for this purpose can be argued to be a more prudent use of resources than is the combustion of natural gas or oil for its energy content. Heating by coal-generated electricity may also be preferable to heating by gas or oil in that a plentiful resource is used and dwindling resources are conserved.

The use of electrical heat pumps could equalize the positions of electric-, oil-, and gas-heating systems from a fuel conservation standpoint. The heat pump delivers about 2 units of heat energy for each unit of electric energy that it consumes. Therefore, only 1.7 units of fuel energy would be required at the power plant for each unit of delivered heat, essentially the same as that required for fueling a home furnace.

Heat pumps are not initially expensive when installed in conjunction with central air conditioning; the basic equipment and air handling systems are the same for both heating and cooling. A major impediment to their widespread use has been high maintenance cost associated with equipment failure. Several manufacturers of heat pumps have carried out extensive programs to improve component reliability that, if successful, should improve acceptance by homeowners.

Table 4. Actual and hypothetical energy consumption patterns for transportation in 1970.

| | Total traffic | Percentage of total traffic | | | | | | Total energy (10¹² Btu) | Total cost (10⁹ $) |
		Air	Truck	Rail	Waterway and pipeline	Auto	Bus*		
		Intercity freight traffic							
Actual	2210†	0.2	19	35	46			2400	45
Hypothetical	2210	0.1	9	44	46			1900	33
		Intercity passenger traffic							
Actual	1120‡	10		1		87	2	4300	47
Hypothetical	1120	5		12		58	25	3500	45
		Urban passenger traffic							
Actual	710‡					97	3	5700	68
Hypothetical	710					49	51	4200	63
		Totals							
Actual								12,400	160
Hypothetical								9600	141

* Intercity bus or urban mass transit.   † Billion ton-miles.   ‡ Billion passenger-miles.

Table 5. Comparison of insulation requirements and monetary and energy savings for a New York residence.

| Insulation specification | Unrevised MPS* | | Revised MPS* | | Economic optimum | |
	Gas	Electric	Gas	Electric	Gas	Electric
Wall insulation thickness (inches)	0	1⅞	1⅞	1⅞	3½	3½
Ceiling insulation thickness (inches)	1⅞	1⅞	3½	3½	3½	6
Floor insulation	No	No	Yes	Yes	Yes	Yes
Storm windows	No	No	No	No	Yes	Yes
Monetary savings ($/yr)	0	0	28	75	32	155
Reduction of energy consumption (%)	0	0	29	19	49	47

* Minimum property standards (MPS) for one and two living units.

Space Cooling

In all-electric homes, air conditioning ranks third as a major energy-consuming function, behind space heating and water heating. Air conditioning is particularly important because it contributes to or is the cause of the annual peak load that occurs in the summertime for many utility systems.

In addition to reducing the energy required for space heating, the ample use of thermal insulation reduces the energy required for air conditioning. In the New York case, use of the economically optimum amount of insulation results in a reduction of the electricity consumed for air conditioning of 26 percent for the gas home or 18 percent for the electric home, compared to the 1970 MPS-compliance homes.

The popularity of room air conditioners is evidenced by an exponential sales growth with a doubling time of 5 years over the past decade; almost 6 million were sold in 1970. The strong growth in sales is expected to continue since industry statistics show a market saturation of only about 40 percent.

There are about 1400 models of room air conditioners available on the market today, sold under 52 different brand names (10). A characteristic of the machines that varies widely but is not normally advertised is the efficiency with which energy is converted to cooling. Efficiency ranges from 4.7 to 12.2 Btu per watt-hour. Thus the least efficient machine consumes 2.6 times as much electricity per unit of cooling as the most efficient one. Figure 1 shows the efficiencies of all units having ratings up to 24,000 Btu per hour, as listed in (10).

From an economic point of view, the purchaser should select the particular model of air conditioner that provides the needed cooling capacity and the lowest total cost (capital, maintenance, operation) over the unit's lifetime. Because of the large number of models available and the general ignorance of the fact that such a range of efficiencies exists, the most economical choice is not likely to be made. An industry-sponsored certification program requires that the cooling rating and wattage input be listed on the nameplate of each unit, providing the basic information required for determining efficiency. However, the nameplate is often hard to locate and does not state the efficiency explicitly.

The magnitude of possible savings that would result from buying a more efficient unit is illustrated by the following case. Of the 90 models with a capacity of 10,000 Btu per hour, the lowest efficiency model draws 2100 watts and the highest efficiency model draws 880 watts. In Washington, D.C., the average room air conditioner operates about 800 hours per year. The low-efficiency unit would use 976 kilowatt-hours more electricity each year than the high-efficiency unit. At 1.8 cents per kilowatt-hour, the operating cost would increase by $17.57 per year. The air conditioner could be expected to have a life of 10 years. If the purchaser operates on a credit card economy, with an 18 percent interest rate, he would be economically justified in paying up to $79 more for the high-efficiency unit. If his interest rate were 6 percent, an additional purchase price of $130 would be justified.

In the above example, the two units were assumed to operate the same number of hours per year. However, many of the low-priced, low-efficiency units are not equipped with thermostats. As a result, they may operate almost continuously, with a lower-than-desired room temperature. This compounds the inefficiency and, in addition, shortens the lifetime of the units.

In addition to the probable economic advantage to the consumer, an improvement in the average efficiency of room air conditioners would result in appreciable reductions in the nation's energy consumption and required generating capacity. If the size distribution of all existing room units is that for the 1970 sales, the average efficiency (10) is 6 Btu per watt-hour, and the average annual operating time is 886 hours per year, then the nation's room air conditioners consumed 39.4 billion kilowatt-hours during 1970. On the same basis, the connected load was 44,500 megawatts, and the annual equivalent coal consumption was 18.9 million tons. If the assumed efficiency is changed to 10 Btu per watt-hour, the annual power consumption would have been 23.6 billion kilowatt-hours, a reduction of 15.8 billion kilowatt-hours. The connected load would have decreased to 26,700 megawatts, a reduction of 17,800 megawatts. The annual coal consumption for room air conditioners would have been 11.3 million tons, a reduction of 7.6 million tons, or at a typical strip mine yield of 5000 tons per acre, a reduction in stripped area of 1500 acres in 1970.

Other Potential Energy Savings

Energy-efficiency improvements can be effected for other end-uses of energy besides the three considered here. Improved appliance design could increase the energy efficiency of hot-water heaters, stoves, and refrigerators. The use of solar energy for residential space and water heating is technologically feasible and might some day be economically feasible. Alternatively, waste heat from air conditioners could be used for water heating. Improved design or elimination of gas pilot lights and elimination of gas yard lights would also provide energy savings (11). Increased energy efficiency within homes would tend to reduce summer air-conditioning loads.

In the commercial sector, energy savings in space heating and cooling such as those described earlier are possible. In addition, the use of total energy systems (on-site generation of electricity and the use of waste heat for space and water heating and absorption air conditioning) would increase the overall energy efficiency of commercial operations.

Commercial lighting accounts for about 10 percent of total electricity consumption (12). Some architects claim that currently recommended lighting levels can be reduced without danger to eyesight or worker performance (13). Such reduction would save energy directly and by reducing air-conditioning loads. Alternatively, waste heat from lighting can be circulated in winter for space heating and shunted outdoors in summer to reduce air-conditioning loads.

Changes in building design practices might effect energy savings (13). Such changes could include use of less glass and of windows that open for circulation of outside air.

Waste heat and low temperature steam from electric power plants may be useful for certain industries and for space heating in urban districts (14). This thermal energy (about 8 percent of energy consumption in 1970) (15) could be used for industrial process steam, space heating, water heating, and air conditioning in a carefully planned urban complex.

The manufacture of a few basic materials accounts for a large fraction of industrial energy consumption. Increased recycle of energy-intensive materials such as aluminum, steel, and paper would save energy. Savings could also come from lower production of certain materials. For example, the production of packaging materials (paper, metal, glass, plastic, wood) requires about 4 percent of the total energy budget. In general, it may be possible to design products and choose materials to decrease the use of packaging and to reduce energy costs per unit of production.

Implementation

Changes in *energy prices*, both levels and rate structures, would influence decisions concerning capital versus life costs, and this would affect the use of energy-conserving technologies. *Public education* to increase awareness of energy problems might heighten consumer sensitivity toward personal energy consumption. Various local, state, and federal *government policies* exist that, directly and indirectly, influence the efficiency of energy use. These three routes are not independent; in particular, government policies could affect prices or public education (or both) on energy use.

One major factor that promotes energy consumption is the low price of energy. A typical family in the United States spends about 5 percent of its annual budget on electricity, gas, and gasoline. The cost of fuels and electricity to manufacturers is about 1.5 percent of the value of their total shipments. Because the price of energy is low relative to other costs, efficient use of energy has not been of great importance in the economy. Not only are fuel prices low, but historically they have declined relative to other prices.

The downward trend in the relative price of energy has begun to reverse because of the growing scarcity of fuels, increasing costs of both money and energy-conversion facilities (power plants, petroleum refineries), and the need to internalize social costs of energy production and use. The impact of rising energy prices on demand is difficult to assess. According to one source (*16*):

. . . In the absence of any information, we assume a long-run price elasticity of demand of − 0.5 (meaning that in the long-run a doubling of energy prices will reduce demand by a factor of the square root of 2, namely to about 70 percent of what it would have been otherwise).

The factors cited above (fuel scarcity, rising costs, environmental constraints) are likely to influence energy price structures as well as levels. If these factors tend to increase energy prices uniformly (per Btu delivered), then energy price structures will become flatter; that is, the percentage difference in price between the first and last unit purchased by a customer will be less than that under existing rate structures. The impact of such rate structure changes on the demand for energy is unknown, and research is needed.

Increases in the price of energy should decrease the quantity demanded and this is likely to encourage more efficient use of energy. For example, if the price of gasoline rises, there will probably be a shift to the use of smaller cars and perhaps to the use of public transportation systems.

Public education programs may slow energy demand. As Americans understand better the environmental problems associated with energy production and use, they may voluntarily decrease their personal energy-consumption growth rates. Experiences in New York City and in Sweden with energy-conservation advertising programs showed that the public is willing and able to conserve energy, at least during short-term emergencies.

Consumers can be educated about the energy consumption of various appliances. The energy-efficiency data for air conditioners presented here are probably not familiar to most prospective buyers of air conditioners. If consumers understood energy and dollar costs of low-efficiency units, perhaps they would opt for more expensive, high-efficiency units to save money over the lifetime of the unit and also to reduce environmental impacts. Recently, at least two air-conditioner manufacturers began marketing campaigns that stress energy efficiency. Some electric utilities have also begun to urge their customers to use electricity conservatively and efficiently.

Public education can be achieved through government publications or government regulation, for example, by requiring labels on appliances which state the energy efficiency and provide estimates of operating costs. Advertisements for energy-consuming equipment might be required to state the energy efficiency.

Federal policies, reflected in research expenditures, construction of facilities, taxes and subsidies, influence energy consumption. For example, the federal government spends several billion dollars annually on highway, airway, and airport construction, but nothing is spent for railway and railroad construction. Until recently, federal transportation research and development funds were allocated almost exclusively to air and highway travel. Passage of the

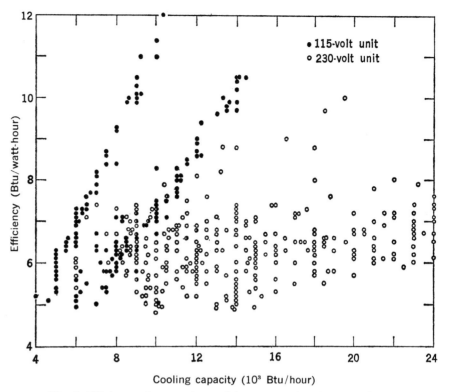

Fig. 1. Efficiency of room air conditioners as a function of unit size.

Urban Mass Transportation Act, establishment of the National Railroad Passenger Corporation (AMTRAK), plus increases in research funds for rail and mass transport may increase the use of these energy-efficient travel modes.

Similarly, through agencies such as the Tennessee Valley Authority, the federal government subsidizes the cost of electricity. The reduced price for public power customers increases electricity consumption over what it would otherwise be.

Governments also influence energy consumption directly and indirectly through allowances for depletion of resources, purchase specifications (to require recycled paper, for example), management of public energy holdings, regulation of gas and electric utility rate levels and structures, restrictions on energy promotion, and establishment of minimum energy performance standards for appliances and housing.

The federal government spends about $0.5 billion a year on research and development for civilian energy, of which the vast majority is devoted to energy supply technologies (16):

. . . Until recently only severely limited funds were available for developing a detailed understanding of the ways in which the nation uses energy. . . . The recently instituted Research Applied to National Needs (RANN) Directorate of the National Science Foundation . . . has been supporting research directed toward developing a detailed understanding of the way in which the country utilizes energy. . . . This program also seeks to examine the options for meeting the needs of society at reduced energy and environmental costs.

Perhaps new research on energy use will reveal additional ways to reduce energy growth rates.

Summary

We described three uses of energy for which greater efficiency is feasible: transportation, space heating, and air conditioning. Shifts to less energy-intensive transportation modes could substantially reduce energy consumption; the magnitude of such savings would, of course, depend on the extent of such shifts and possible load factor changes. The hypothetical transportation scenario described here results in a 22 percent savings in energy for transportation in 1970, a savings of 2800 trillion Btu.

To the homeowner, increasing the amount of building insulation and, in some cases, adding storm windows would reduce energy consumption and provide monetary savings. If all homes in 1970 had the "economic optimum" amount of insulation, energy consumption for residential heating would have been 42 percent less than if the homes were insulated to meet the pre-1971 FHA standards, a savings of 3100 trillion Btu.

Increased utilization of energy-efficient air conditioners and of building insulation would provide significant energy savings and help to reduce peak power demands during the summer. A 67 percent increase in energy efficiency for room air conditioners would have saved 15.8 billion kilowatt-hours in 1970.

In conclusion, it is possible—from an engineering point of view—to effect considerable energy savings in the United States. Increases in the efficiency of energy use would provide desired end results with smaller energy inputs. Such measures will not reduce the *level* of energy consumption, but they could slow energy growth *rates*.

References and Notes

1. Bureau of Mines, *U.S. Energy Use at New High in 1971* (News Release, 31 March 1972).
2. Stanford Research Institute, *Patterns of Energy Consumption in the United States* (Menlo Park, Calif., November 1971).
3. In this article all fuels used as raw materials are charged to the industrial sector, although fuels are also used as feedstocks by the commercial and transportation sectors.
4. Edison Electric Institute, *Statistical Yearbook of the Electric Utility Industry for 1970* (Edison Electric Institute, New York, 1971).
5. U.S. Bureau of the Census, *1967 Census of Manufactures, Fuels and Electric Energy Consumed* (MC67 (S)-4, Government Printing Office, Washington, D.C., 1971).
6. Conversion factors are: from British thermal units to joules (1055), from miles to meters (1609), from inches to meters (0.0254), from acres to square meters (4047), and from tons to kilograms (907).
7. E. Hirst, *Energy Consumption for Transportation in the U.S.* (Oak Ridge National Laboratory Report ORNL-NSF-EP-15, Oak Ridge, Tenn., 1972); R. A. Rice, "System energy as a factor in considering future transportation," presented at American Society of Mechanical Engineers annual meeting, December 1970).
8. Energy efficiency and unit revenue values for 1970 are computed in E. Hirst, *Energy Intensiveness of Passenger and Freight Transport Modes: 1950–1970* (Oak Ridge National Laboratory Report ORNL-NSF-EP-44, Oak Ridge, Tenn., 1973).
9. J. C. Moyers, *The Value of Thermal Insulation in Residential Construction: Economics and the Conservation of Energy* (Oak Ridge National Laboratory Report ORNL-NSF-EP-9, Oak Ridge, Tenn., December 1971).
10. Association of Home Appliance Manufacturers, *1971 Directory of Certified Room Air Conditioners*, 15 June 1971.
11. Hittman Associates, *Residential Energy Consumption—Phase I Report*, No. HUD-HAI-1, (Columbia, Md., March 1972).
12. C. M. Crysler, General Electric Company, private communication.
13. R. G. Stein, "Architecture and energy," presented at the annual meeting of the American Association for the Advancement of Science, Philadelphia, 29 December 1971.
14. A. J. Miller *et al.*, *Use of Steam-Electric Power Plants to Provide Thermal Energy to Urban Areas* (Oak Ridge National Laboratory Report ORNL-HUD-14, Oak Ridge, Tenn., 1971).
15. R. M. Jimeson and G. G. Adkins, "Factors in waste heat disposal associated with power generation," presented at the American Institute of Chemical Engineers national meeting, Houston, Texas, March 1971).
16. National Science Foundation RANN Program, *Summary Report of the Cornell Workshop on Energy and the Environment*, 22 to 24 February 1972, Senate Committee on Interior and Insular Affairs, No. 92-23, May 1972 (Government Printing Office, Washington, D.C., 1972).

Energy Conservation

Some challenges are proposed for science and technology.

G. A. Lincoln

As the energy crisis looms ever larger, energy conservation is beginning to receive increasing attention (1, 2). Energy conservation can make a substantial contribution in ameliorating or postponing the potential energy shortages faced by the United States over the next several decades. To realize this contribution, however, will require not only the political will to implement the necessary conservation measures but also the imagination and intellectual resources of the scientific community to develop new technologies to increase the efficiency of energy use.

This article is directed to provoking thought on how to attain economic, social, and other objectives while using less energy resources. Its purpose is not so much to answer questions of energy conservation as to raise them. The discussion is provocative in places, deliberately so. It is not intended to suggest any policy commitments on the part of the author or any of those whose advice and suggestions have contributed to the discussion. Rather, the objective is to enlist the interest of thinking people, and particularly the scientific community, in the energy conservation effort.

The history of civilization is, to a large extent, the story of man's progress in harnessing energy. Discovery of the controlled use of fire was certainly a major milestone in man's emerging domination of other forms of life. Development of the sail to utilize the energy of wind to propel watercraft opened up the rest of the world to curious and acquisitive societies around the Mediterranean basin. Windmills

and watermills represented early attempts to harness energy sources for direct work. The industrial revolution, one of the great landmarks of our present culture, consisted essentially of the large-scale replacement of muscle power by controlled mechanical energy derived, in turn, from thermal energy.

A less noted, but equally significant, impact of the industrial revolution was the general introduction of available energy when and where it was needed. In previous ages man used energy largely when and where it was found: he sailed when the wind blew, he forged his metals by the forests where firewood was plentiful. With the advent of combustion engines, however, man was freed to travel without (or even against) the wind, and at speeds which animals could not match. He could transmit large amounts of controlled mechanical power throughout a mill by use of shafts and pulleys. And finally, the understanding of electricity completed the revolution by permitting not only mechanical power but also information to be made available far from the originating source.

First wood, and then coal was used to satisfy the increasing demands for manageable sources of thermal energy. Both served the purpose admirably. But both wood and coal presented certain problems. Then came the discovery of oil and gas and how to use them with greatly increased versatility and flexibility in conversion of fuel to thermal energy. The internal combustion engine arrived and flourished, automatically fired boilers became the norm, and our modern mechanized society was at hand.

Increases in the convenience and economy of harnessed energy have led to additional applications, which in turn have increased the demand and, coming full circle, fostered further technological advances in the convenience and economy of harnessing energy. The use of energy in the United States today is not only growing but accelerating. With only 5 percent of the world's population, this nation already consumes about one-third of the world's energy production. And the current annual appetite for about 70×10^{15} British thermal units (Btu) is projected to double within 20 years to 140 quadrillion Btu (that is, from 1.7×10^{19} to 3.5×10^{19} calories) (3). Unfortunately, the finding and production of domestic energy supplies is not keeping pace with this rapidly growing demand. Thus, careful attention must now be addressed to the adequacy of our remaining domestic energy resources. More than 10 percent of our present requirements are met by importing foreign oil (about 4.6×10^6 barrels per day). Even the more conservative projections indicate that the level of imports of oil, and also of some gas in liquefied form, must increase a great deal within the next decade alone to compensate for the projected shortfall of available domestic fuels. This situation suggests serious problems both for the national security and for the balance of payments.

Furthermore, recent practices and trends in methods of fuel extraction, energy conversion, and energy utilization have caused pollution problems affecting the nation's health and natural environment. Yet because of extensive interdependence among these important national concerns—problems related to energy and problems related to the environment—measures to alleviate one can easily aggravate another. For example, estimates derived from a recent study indicate that the removal of lead from gasoline for pollution control as presently planned will cause an increase of about 1 million barrels per day in our gasoline needs by 1975, thus worsening the nation's supply situation (4). Some of the state implementation plans to meet the requirements of the 1970 Clean Air Act (5) provide other examples of such conflicting demands. Several of these plans project a demand for quantities of fuels of low sulfur content (gas, oil, coal, nuclear power) which will simply not be available on the time schedule envisaged. In addition, the shifts in equipment and fuel types and the processing costs to

The author is professor of economics and international studies at the University of Denver, Denver, Colorado.

19

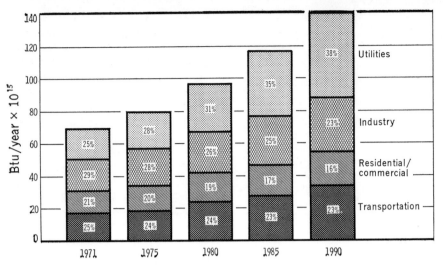

Fig. 1. Energy consumption in the United States by consuming sectors (6); 1 Btu = 0.259 cal; 10^{15} Btu $\cong$ 172 $\times 10^6$ barrels of oil, 970 $\times 10^9$ cubic feet of natural gas, 41.7 $\times$ 10^6 tons of coal.

manufacture such quality fuel can impose a severe economic penalty for the consumer. Shifts in types of fuel and their timing can have severe impacts on our industrial and economic structure; our foreign economic arrangements, including our balance of payments; our relations with other countries; and our own country's security. For energy security is now a critical component of our national security and overall foreign policy. ⌈Clearly, no one of these problems can be addressed apart from, or to the neglect of, the others; any reasonable solution must take all into account.

In order to lessen our potential dependence on foreign supply, we must increase our domestic energy supplies.⌋ Increased field exploration and extraction of oil and gas, including shale oil, are necessary. Measures should include expanded coal mining and the gasifica-

tion and liquefaction of coal, more rapid introduction of electrical power generated from nuclear fuels, and greater emphasis on the development and exploitation of unconventional energy sources such as solar radiation and geothermal power. All of these will be undertaken as the demand for energy rises in relation to the supply, and fuel prices inevitably follow suit. But most of these measures take years, even decades, and even though successful, may leave a continuing energy gap. Certainly that energy gap is going to exist for a long while.

⌈Although the increasing of energy supplies is essential, it is also important to reduce consumption or at least to ease its growth rate.⌋ This approach is intuitively appealing from the standpoint of assuaging those problems of environmental pollution which are related to energy consumption. Neverthe-

less, some of the potential approaches to reduced energy demand call for technology which, if available at all, is not yet advanced to an economically viable level. Equally or more difficult, ⌈some of the approaches may depend on fundamental changes in national attitudes toward living style, and even if the process of mass application of social incentives were well understood —which it is not—its ethical implications would require careful attention.

Energy conservation needs to be viewed both from the standpoint of the consumer and from the standpoint of broad national policy. The viewpoints are not necessarily conflicting, but at times may be.⌋ The useful but simplistic approach of achieving the same economic and social objectives with less energy needs to be combined with an approach of using the types of fuels which best further our national objectives while emphasizing the conservation of those fuels creating policy problems. For example, the consumption of oil is now beginning to pose policy problems. So also is the consumption of gas, since our domestic shortfall in production is made up by imported oil and gas. Hence, that conservation which holds back on consumption of oil and gas is most broadly useful. The most desirable way is through absolute reduction in consumption of energy from gas and oil. But just the substitution of more domestically available fuels, such as coal and nuclear fuel, is a plus in solving our energy problems and a logical component of an energy conservation endeavor.

Unfortunately, the concept of energy conservation through substitution of domestically more abundant fuels for the less abundant does run directly into the continuing friction, and sometimes direct confrontation, between environmental programs and energy utilization programs. Coal, for example, is abundant but often does not conform to environmental objectives. Coal now poses a challenge to science and technology of the same importance as that posed by oil and gas in the early period of their utilization for producing thermal energy.

The issue of energy conservation is an important and complex one. To provide the appropriate setting for its discussion, the general patterns of U.S. energy supply and demand will be outlined, and then the four major categories of energy consumption—transportation, residential/commercial, in-

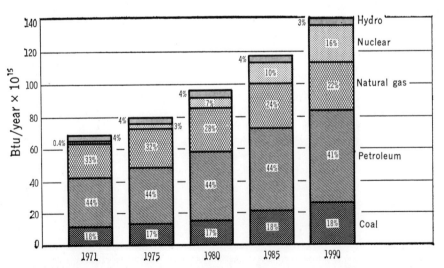

Fig. 2. Energy consumption in the United States by source (6). See Fig. 1 caption.

dustry, and electric utilities—will be examined somewhat more closely to reveal present trends and suggest possibilities for improved conservation. Finally, the complex problems of environmental pollution and economic investment will be introduced briefly.

Patterns of U.S. Energy
Supply and Demand

The Bureau of Mines, Department of the Interior, has made careful projections of energy consumption by consuming sector (Fig. 1) and by source (Fig. 2) for the period 1971 to 1990 (6). The major projected change between now and 1990 in the consuming sector is a tripling in the energy used in generating electric power in order to meet increases in projected demand. Electrical generation is expected to increase by 72 percent from 1971 to 1980 and by 78 percent from 1980 to 1990. Transportation is expected to hold its current share of the market, with projected increases of 35 percent from 1971 to 1980 and 41 percent from 1980 to 1990. For the entire period 1971 to 1990, industrial use of fossil fuel is expected to increase by 53 percent and residential/commercial use by 41 percent. The major projected change in the sources of energy between now and 1990 is that nuclear power will significantly increase its proportionate contribution, but the consumption of fossil fuels will also increase a great deal. Projections to 1990 indicate that the sources of U.S. energy in that year will be distributed as follows: coal, 18 percent; petroleum, 41 percent; natural gas, 22 percent; nuclear power, 16 percent; hydropower, 3 percent.

In terms of dollar expenditures for energy, the patterns and trends differ considerably between intermediate demand and final demand. The final demand consists of purchases for end uses such as automobile fuel, residential heating, and exports, while the intermediate demand consists of industrial and commercial purchases to produce products and services for end consumers. Intermediate demand expenditures for energy are related very closely to the gross national product (GNP); the ratio of the two has varied less than a quarter of a percent over more than a decade. Although not correlated as closely with the GNP, the final demand for energy has grown substantially during the same period. About 85 percent

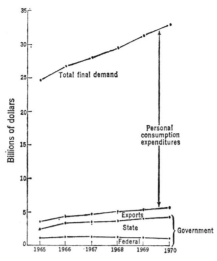

Fig. 3. Final demand expenditures for energy consumption according to the category of the consumer (7).

of the energy final demand during the last 5 years (Fig. 3) has consisted of personal consumption expenditures, which represent domestic consumption of fuel for such uses as private cars, home heating and air conditioning, and electric appliances (7).

Transportation

In 1970, transportation consumed 16.4×10^{15} Btu—one quarter of the total energy used in this country, a share which is expected to continue. Petroleum accounted for 96 percent of the fuel consumed for transportation in 1970. This amounted to 2,830,000,000 barrels of crude oil, or a rate of about 7,750,000 barrels per day

(roughly equivalent to daily dissipation of a dozen 100,000-ton tanker loads). Automobiles are the leading consumer, using 55 percent of the transportation energy in 1970 (14 percent of total national energy consumption), with trucks second at 21 percent, and aircraft third at 7.5 percent. The remaining 16 percent is made up of rail, bus, waterway, pipeline, and other categories (8).

Major trends among transportation modes include railroads and waterways giving way to pipelines and trucks for intercity freight movement; buses and railroads giving way to aircraft and automobiles for intercity passenger traffic; and mass transit, especially buses and trains, giving way to private automobiles for urban passenger traffic.

As Table 1 shows, enormous differences exist in the energy efficiencies of these transportation modes (9). For passenger travel, airplanes are less efficient users of energy than automobiles, which are in turn less efficient than buses and railroads. For freight movement, airplanes are less energy efficient than trucks and considerably less efficient than pipelines, waterways, and railroads.

Energy efficiency within transportation modes also varies substantially and, unfortunately, has tended to decrease with time. The quest for ever-increasing speed and convenience has been succeeding at the cost of increased energy consumption. The low average occupancy of commuter cars combines with short distances traveled and traffic congestion to lower drastically the energy efficiency of the automobile. In

Table 1. Transportation propulsion efficiency (22). Conversions are: 1 foot $\cong$ 0.305 m; 1 mile = 1.609 km; 1 horsepower (hp) = 746 watts; 1 knot $\cong$ 1.85 km/hr.

Passenger		Freight	
Transport type	Passenger miles per gallon	Transport type	Cargo ton miles per gallon
Large jet plane (Boeing 747)	22	One-half of a Boeing 707 (160 tons, 30,000 hp)	8.3
Small jet plane (Boeing 704)	21	One-fourth of a Boeing 747 (360 tons, 60,000 hp)	11.4
Automobile (sedan)	32	Sixty 250-hp, 40-ton trucks	50.0
Cross-country train*	80	Fast 3000-ton, 40-car freight train	97.0
Commuter train†	100	Three 5000-ton, 100-car freight trains	250.0
Large bus (40 foot)	125	Inland barge tow, 60,000 gross tons	220.0
Small bus (35 foot)	126	Large pipeline, 100 miles, two pumps	500.0
Suburban train (two-deck)‡	200	100,000-ton supertanker, 15 knots	930.0

*One 150-ton locomotive and four 70-seat coaches plus diner lounge and baggage coach.   †Ten 65-ton cars and two 150-ton 2000-hp diesel locomotives.   ‡A ten-car gallery-car commuter train, 160 seats per car.

21

1971, for example, 55 percent of automobile energy consumption went for urban trips of 10 miles (16 km) or less, and 56 percent of all commuting was by automobiles containing only one occupant (*10*). Emission controls also contribute significantly to lower energy efficiency; those currently being installed and projected will result in an additional gasoline consumption by 1980 of the order of 2 million barrels per day.

A large number of factors, including government policy, social and environmental concerns, the low cost of energy, uncontrolled urban growth, and the demand for increased mobility and transportation service (speed, comfort, reliability, and convenience) have contributed to a continuing shift toward the use of less energy efficient modes and to a continuing decline in the energy efficiency of all transportation modes.

Furthermore, this discouraging trend shows every indication of persisting. Projections of growth in aircraft and automobile use show that these two modes alone will account for 22×10^{15} Btu in 1985, more than 73 percent of the total transportation energy consumption for that year.

Several actions could be taken over the short and midterm periods (within 3 years and within 10 years) to increase energy efficiency, improve the balance between transportation modes, and decrease total demand for transportation. Incentives for using smaller automobiles, subsidized mass transit, and improved traffic flow through traffic metering systems and priority bus lanes, would encourage greater use of more energy efficient transportation modes. Improved communications facilities, the development of urban clusters, and the construction of attractive walkways and bicycle paths will all help to reduce total transportation demand for energy.

Estimates indicate that the implementation of short and midterm conservation measures could result in savings of 15 to 25 percent of the projected transportation energy demand by the early 1980's (*11*). These estimates are predicated on the assumption that curtailment of passenger and freight movement is largely unacceptable, so that emphasis is placed not on restrictions but on approaches designed to improve energy efficiency relative to present standards. Even though many of the measures have been tried to some extent, experience is insufficient to allow a full analysis of the effects of all plausible actions. Nevertheless, these short and midterm estimates assume no significant advances in technology.

Over the long term, however, technology and urban design stand out as the areas of greatest promise in reducing transportation energy demands. For example, the development of practical hybrid energy storage systems, such as a system combining a gas turbine with electricity, could significantly increase the operating efficiency of urban automobiles (*12*). Similarly, the quest for solutions to urban social, economic, and environmental problems is yielding concepts that have important implications for transportation. For example, the development of urban clusters can reduce drastically the need for transportation. In general, transportation energy efficiency could be greatly increased by providing incentives to separate people from automobiles, for example, rapid transit trunk lines between clusters, moving walkways, and bicycle paths. Increased understanding and appropriate coordination in transportation and urban planning can yield enormous dividends not only for energy conservation but also for the environment, and for the health and mobility of the American people.

Many of these conservation measures have costs—economic, political, and social. Government, industry, and consumers, however, must come to grips with some of the difficult choices that will have to be made over the next several decades. For example, should the federal government institute financial disincentives to encourage the use of small automobiles, as through higher use taxes on large automobiles or taxes on engine size or automobile weight? The advantages of promoting the use of smaller automobiles are numerous—savings approaching 3 million barrels per day in 1985, reduced import costs, and less pollution. On the other hand, by forcing consumers to choices they may not desire, such measures may be highly unpopular. Moreover they could produce serious, adverse economic consequences for the automobile industry and related industries.

Another hard question concerns the extent to which the federal government should encourage or subsidize mass transit. With a much greater efficiency on a passenger-mile basis, effective mass transit systems would not only materially reduce fuel consumption but also significantly ameliorate our balance of payments and environmental and traffic problems. On the other hand, to make such systems effective would probably require restrictions on consumers in the form of bans on automobile use in the inner city or high parking taxes. Moreover, adequate efforts would require an enormous capital outlay, and mass transit would have to compete with other important social needs for these funds.

Transportation serves a number of national and social goals that must be balanced against the objective of energy conservation. Nevertheless, energy efficiency must be given proper emphasis in the design, development, and utilization of our transportation systems. Any truly practical program will require a blend of actions carefully balanced and timed to avoid disruption of needed traffic flows, upheavals in life styles, damage to industries dependent on transportation, and aggravation of problems concerning the international balance of payments.

Residential and Commercial Sectors

Private residences and commercial establishments account for about one-fifth of the total U.S. energy consumption. Space heating and cooling, water heating, refrigeration, and cooking represent somewhat more than 75 percent of the commercial energy use and more than 85 percent of the residential use (*13*). By far the largest portion of this is due to space heating and cooling.

By 1980 the annual energy requirement for household space heating and cooling is expected to reach about 11×10^{15} Btu, or about 63 percent of the total projected residential and commercial energy consumption.

Some reduction in residential energy consumption could be achieved through a nationwide educational program encouraging good energy conservation practices in the home. For example, the setting of all residential thermostats 2 degrees higher during summer and 2 degrees lower during winter could produce in 1980 energy savings of about 1.3×10^{15} Btu.

The National Bureau of Standards estimates that improvements in insulation and construction can reduce the energy consumed in heating and air conditioning by 40 to 50 percent from present norms. Improved insulation technology can be readily adopted in new homes. Unfortunately, the high cost of introducing such improvements into existing homes by present methods makes widespread introduction there less likely (except for storm windows). The discovery and development of inexpensive insulating techniques for reducing the energy loss from existing houses is therefore an urgent need. Furnaces of higher efficiency, with provision for easy periodic cleaning by the homeowner, can and should be developed also.

An important step was taken in 1971 with the revision to the minimum property standard of the Federal Housing Authority (FHA), which significantly tightened insulation requirements for single-family houses. Unfortunately, many apartment houses and single-family homes which were built under conventional loans do not meet desirable minimum standards. Further tightening of insulation requirements for single- and multiple-family homes, offices, and other buildings would provide an additional and important contribution in reducing unnecessary energy consumption.

Higher fuel costs may make economically feasible the wider use of common district heating, total energy systems, and heat pumps. More urban buildings could be heated and cooled by using the steam rejected by a central power generating station. Municipal waste could be burned in power plant boilers along with coal, thus reducing fossil fuel requirements for power generation by an estimated 8 percent (14) (and also helping in solid waste disposal). One consulting engineer has estimated that a saving of 15 to 20 percent can be achieved in the amount of energy normally used in office and commercial buildings by such energy conservation measures as using better insulation to recover the heat in winter and the cooling effect in summer from the building's exhaust air, recovering heat from lighting, reducing heating (or cooling) and lighting levels in corridors and certain other spaces, and reducing the amount of outdoor air drawn into the building (15).

All of this suggests that by 1990 the nation's overall space heating and cooling requirements could be reduced by perhaps 30 percent from the projected demand levels in that year. Even within 10 years a more modest 20 percent re-

duction (about 2×10^{15} Btu) should be possible, most of it through improved insulation. Additional energy savings in water heating, refrigerating, cooking, and lighting systems and in air conditioning equipment are also possible. But improved technology is necessary in most cases to make the introduction and operation of the improvements economically feasible.

Industry

Industrial energy consumption constituted about 29 percent of the total domestic energy consumption in 1971 (16). The primary metal industries, chemicals and allied products, and petroleum refining and related industries together accounted for more than half of that. Natural gas was the most rapidly growing and largest source of industrial energy used (46.5 percent), followed by coal (26.0 percent), petroleum (16.8 percent), and electricity (10.6 percent).

There will undoubtedly be a change in the relative amounts of the various energy sources used by industry in the future. Many gas pipelines are now having to curtail shipments or existing contracts as a result of the developing shortage of natural gas. Gas prices will increase, especially as the pipelines seek to turn to such expensive sources as liquefied natural gas and synthetic natural gas. Natural gas usage certainly cannot continue to increase its share of the industrial market, and most likely will be cut back.

Today, however, plans for new petrochemical complexes call for the use of heavy oil feedstocks, primarily naphtha, and a new regulation of the mandatory oil import program will assist petrochemical producers to acquire naphtha produced from imported oil. This should enable these producers to remain competitive with foreign producers who have traditionally used these feedstocks.

The major industrial sectors have all achieved a general decline in energy used per unit output over the last decade (13). Nevertheless, more rapid improvement could almost certainly be effected by focusing attention on energy conservation.

Given a sufficient incentive, industry as a whole could probably cut energy demand by 5 to 10 percent of projected demand by 1980, primarily by replacing old equipment, demand-

ing more energy-conscious design, and increasing maintenance on boilers, heat exchangers, and so forth. Underpriced energy does not help in encouraging efficient energy use and results in inadequate exploration of avenues for improvement. Any deliberate economic incentive designed to cut energy demand would be made more effective by an accompanying "energy awareness" information program directed at trade associations, professional societies, equipment advertisers, and engineering design companies.

The general introduction of planning for the total life cycle in the use of resources, to include energy-conserving recycling or reusing, could also make noticeable contributions to energy conservation as well as conservation of other resources. Secondary recovery of materials is often less energy consuming than primary extraction and production; for many nonferrous metals, recycling energy requirements are only 20 percent or less of primary processing requirements. This approach is also a prime target for research and development.

Elimination of wasteful practices is of course important. Energy is a sufficiently large expense for the major industrial energy consumers that they already try to use it as economically as possible. Thus, wasteful practices are likely to be found primarily in marginal operators or in industries for which energy is a relatively minor expense.

Electric Utilities

Electric utilities represent the most rapidly growing consumer of energy among the four major groups. Their 1971 use of about 17×10^{15} Btu is projected to expand by a factor of almost 4 within 20 years, representing an increase from 25 to 38 percent of the growing national energy consumption. Thus, any improvements which can be achieved in the energy efficiency of electric power generation are of major importance.

Utilities already concentrate heavily on efficient use of fuel because it constitutes a major operating expense. Over the past quarter of a century, industry efficiency has improved by more than 30 percent; that is, the national average for energy input (in British thermal units) per kilowatt-hour output has declined from nearly 16,000 to about 11,000 (*17*). Nevertheless, efficiency has undergone a slight decline recently, a trend which the National Coal Association attributes partly to the heavy use of inefficient, old plants and peaking generators and partly to the use of more environmentally acceptable fuels with lower energy contents (*18*). An additional factor is the increasing installation of energy-consuming pollution control equipment.

It is sometimes argued that electrical power generation as a whole is a wasteful use of energy because of the large energy conversion losses involved (the overall conversion efficiency is about one-third). This alleged wastefulness must properly be measured against the alternative of direct fuel use. Except in some large industrial applications such as aluminum production, electrical power is distributed from large central generating plants to many small customers. Thus, the comparison is between one large energy consumer and many small ones. Aside from efficiencies due to the economics of size—which are substantial—the central generating plant generally offers much better equipment maintenance, a factor which bears directly on efficiency (a half-millimeter of soot in an oil burner can reduce its efficiency by 50 percent). Power distribution by electric transmission grids is generally more efficient than transportation of coal and oil by trucks (*14*), the usual method for small consumers. Furthermore, large electric power plants permit centralized pollution control, which is both more efficient and more easily monitored. On balance, it is not at all clear that electric power generation and distribution is as wasteful from an overall point of view as some of its detractors would claim.

Regardless of its relative efficiency, electrical power is increasingly in demand because of its cleanliness, convenience, and ease of control. An important question, then, is how to increase the energy efficiency of the centralized generation of electrical power by the utilities. Certainly, increased rates of replacement for obsolete equipment and reduced delays in bringing more efficient new plants on-stream would help. Accelerated introduction of nuclear plants would ameliorate substantially the demand on fossil fuels, whether from domestic or foreign sources. Smoothing the daily demand cycle in order to reduce heavy peak loads would significantly lessen the use of inefficient peaking generators.

The mechanisms for implementing these various measures are primarily economic, and perhaps also regulatory, in nature. But in electric power generation there are also long-term opportunities for significant improvements from new technology, some of it requiring extensive research and development. Historically, the electric utility industry has lacked an organized industry-wide research program. Equipment manufacturers have performed most of the research and development that has been carried out, and this has been limited. In recognition of this problem, the Electric Research Council, representing all segments of the electric utility industry, recently established a research corporation to be supported financially on a shared basis. This corporation is intended to address critical electric power problems at both applied and fundamental levels.

The more promising approaches to long-range improvement in the efficiency of generating electrical power include advanced power cycles, magnetohydrodynamics, various types of nuclear reactors, geothermal sources, cryogenic transmission, improved "waste heat" utilization, and total energy systems. The advanced power cycle, involving the combination of coal gasification with a gas turbine–steam turbine power plant, is currently under study by the Environmental Protection Agency. It promises improved flexibility in plant size and location, relatively low cost, and potentially high efficiency. Nevertheless, full benefits depend on the development of an efficient coal gasification process. Magnetohydrodynamic techniques offer greater efficiency as well as low maintenance and substantially reduced cooling requirements. The practical realization of any of several breeder reactor principles under study would reduce not only fossil fuel demands but also nuclear fuel demands—a factor of equal importance in the long run. Geothermal power already enjoys some limited use, but large-scale exploitation (which would make available a huge new energy source) awaits extensive investigation of several alternative approaches. Cryogenic transmission systems suggest exceedingly high distribution efficiencies but present difficult problems in practical realization beyond the laboratory scale. Various uses suggested for the waste heat dissipated from electrical power plants (two-thirds of the energy value of the fuel) include district heating for nearby residential or commercial installations, hothouse support for increased agricultural production, and prevention of ship channel freezing. All require considerable additional investigation.

A particularly appealing idea is the total energy system—an integrated package for electrical generation, air conditioning, water heating, steam generation, and any other energy functions required by a residential complex or shopping center. The greatest deterrent appears to be the problem of balancing demand among the various functions, but the potential is sufficiently promising that the National Bureau of Standards is conducting a carefully controlled experiment with a pilot total energy system in an apartment-shopping complex (*19*).

Some Thorny Issues—
Pollution, Investment

Most energy sources can have significant environmental impacts, for example, strip mining and the disposal of heated water from power generating plants. But conversely, pollution controls have significant impacts on energy consumption. They can and do result in the additional use of energy, and may contribute to shortages of desired fuels. For example, motor vehicle exhaust systems have been proposed to reduce automobile pollution by over 90 percent; when implemented, they will introduce fuel penalties of 5 percent or more (under 1970 performance) for *each* technique needed to control different emissions; a fully equipped car will probably experience at least a 15 percent fuel penalty (*20*). To meet environmental quality standards industry invested some $9.3 billion in pollution control in 1970, and this investment rate is expected to double by 1975. The percentages of total annual capital expenditures invested in pollution control ranged from a high of 10 percent for the iron and steel industries down to 0 percent for the communications industry, with 2.6 percent for transportation and 3.8 percent for electric utilities (*21*). It is not clear, however, that all these investments produce energy-efficient pollution control systems. Firms whose energy costs are significant with respect to profits have probably installed efficient pollution controls. For other firms, federal standards may need to be considered.

Relating traditional profit incentives to efficient pollution control will be difficult until the principle of pollution control itself has become common practice. The capital investment and the institutional policies (such as environmental protection and licensing polices) take substantial time to implement on a regional or a national basis.

In some cases energy conservation is the fortuitous result of investment in other programs. For example, urban mass transit systems promoted to shorten commuter time and reduce highway costs also produce several times less pollutants per passenger mile than the automobile and reduce energy consumption considerably. But effective urban mass transit, for whatever goals, remains experimental in scope for lack of the capital necessary to modernize and integrate such systems as a substitute for the ubiquitous private automobile.

At any rate, environmental studies and programs should now have the included task of considering energy costs (and benefits). An explicit treatment should provide decision-makers with the tradeoffs which are the needed bases for thinking and actions by all of us.

We must begin to ask whether a slight relaxation in environmental standards, many of which may have been arbitrarily set with little thought to their full ramifications, could permit significant energy savings. For example, we should carefully examine the question of whether the nation's environment would be better served by obtaining emission reduction through policies designed to reduce automobile use and to increase mass transit use rather than by maintaining current strict emission standards which increase engine inefficiency (1). We also have to balance the extremely high costs which consumers are paying to obtain the last small increment of environmental protection against the potential energy and dollar savings from more energy efficient pollution control systems.

In summary, the close interdependence of these issues makes it essential that programs be coordinated in meeting where possible the objectives of both pollution control and energy conservation. The needed objectives include making pollution control systems more energy efficient and encouraging greater energy conservation by choice of those options (applications) which

limit both energy consumption and pollution.

Improvements to energy conservation could also have significant implications for the national economy. Capital investment in the U.S. energy industry has been projected at $566 billion (in 1971 dollars) for the period 1971 to 1985. This enormous capital investment requirement raises several potentially serious problems with respect to all areas of our economy. The amount of money available for capital investment is rather inflexible—it depends strongly on the rate of savings, which tends to be very stable. An increase in capital needs for one sector, that is, the energy industry, could significantly affect the money market through increased interest rates. Hence, if conservation can reduce energy consumption, the sizable capital requirement in this area would also be lessened. One estimate indicates that the savings in energy consumption, as a result of conservation measures, could lead to potential savings of $97 billion or 17 percent of the projected capital investment of $566 billion during the 15-year period from 1971 to 1985 (11).

Summary

We can no longer afford to ignore the serious potential consequences of our lavish use of energy. Continuation of the present rate of increase, particularly with the trend to imported fuels, will lead in short order to a level of dependency on imports which is disturbing for both the national security and the balance of payments.

The inevitable rise in the price of energy will presumably lead to some increases in the domestic energy supply. But our reserves, particularly in the preferred forms of petroleum, gas, and even low-sulfur coal, are finite. Thus, the energy problem must also be attacked from the standpoint of energy conservation. The forthcoming rise in fuel prices will, of course, make more attractive some forms of conservation which at present are economically marginal. Nevertheless, consumers, industry, and government will have to make difficult choices in the years ahead: between greater convenience and lower energy bills, between the high capital costs of energy conservation measures and the long-term dollar savings from increased energy efficiency, and between environmental protection and the

availability of needed energy supplies.

Existing capabilities and technology, on which short- and midterm improvements must be based, appear to offer substantial possibilities for reducing U.S. energy consumption within the next decade (11). Long-term solutions to the energy problem, however, will depend to a considerable extent on the continuing appearance of new technological capabilities for increased efficiency of energy utilization and increased integration of energy applications. The capacity for continuing technological advances is, of course, dependent in turn on a strong relevant scientific base.

I still consider the foregoing analysis substantially sound a year and a half later. There is a need, however, for greater emphasis on the possibilities for energy conservation in the field of "business."

The Department of Commerce states that, broadly speaking, 70 percent of energy is consumed by business. Higher prices provide the economic incentive to buy (or remodel) for lower fuel consumption and also to produce more fuel efficient items for sale. There is a study needed of trade-offs to appraise the merits of applying time, and particularly limited capital, to conservation as compared to expanding supply. If we rebuild all our plants to be more energy efficient we may not be able to sustain and expand enough energy to keep them running.

While the National Academy of Engineers in its *Future Energy Prospects* (23) report speaks of only 10 percent industrial savings, the Secretary of Commerce, in his 13 May 1974 testimony to the Senate Commerce Committee, stated:

Realizable energy savings, even using current technology, therefore throughout the business community are quite large— 15 percent in industrial operations; 25 percent in commercial buildings; 15 percent in business-controlled transportation. Were one as a nation to achieve these improvements, the savings in terms of 1973 usage would be equivalent of nearly 5 million barrels of oil a day.

The Secretary noted that these goals required a considerable effort and also noted that there are theoretical savings of 35 to 40 percent in industrial savings, but such would require major revision to a large segment of America's manufacturing facilities.

Business has a double potential to improve its own efficiency and to provide conservation impetus to employees, customers, suppliers, and the community at large.

Finally, energy conservation should be viewed and analyzed in the same way as any other source of energy—coal, oil, gas, and so forth—for cost trade-offs, comparative environmental impacts, timing, and other factors. It cannot do the job alone; it can help a lot.

A word of caution is necessary. Recent experience has shown that technological advances alone will not solve the problem. The problem spans not only the traditional physical and engineering sciences but also those sciences which deal with human attitudes and actions, that is, the social sciences, and includes a more fundamental understanding of underlying economic principles. The challenge to all sectors of American science should be clear.

References and Notes

1. P. H. Abelson, *Science* **178**, 355 (1972).
2. A. L. Hammond, *ibid.*, p. 1079.
3. Energy industries generally employ the British thermal unit (Btu) as a common denominator among the various specialized fuel and energy units of measure. Approximate conversion factors between the major measures are: 1 barrel of oil $= 5.8 \times 10^6$ Btu $= 1.5 \times 10^9$ cal; 1000 cubic feet of gas $= 1.0 \times 10^6$ Btu $= 2.5 \times 10^8$ cal; 1 ton of bituminous coal $= 2.5 \times 10^7$ Btu $= 6.3 \times 10^9$ cal; 1 kilowatt-hour of electricity $= 3.4 \times 10^3$ Btu $= 9.6 \times 10^5$ cal.
4. "An economic analysis of proposed schedules for removal of lead additives from gasoline," a study prepared by Bonnor and Moore Associates, Inc., Houston, Texas, for the Environmental Protection Agency in June 1971, They estimate that lead removal would cause a 12 percent increase in gasoline consumption. Since refinery output is approximately 50 percent gasoline, and 1975 crude runs are estimated by the National Petroleum Council [Committee on U.S. Energy Outlook, *U.S. Energy Outlook* (National Petroleum Council, Washington, D.C., 1971), vol. 1, p. 27] at 18.4 million barrels per day, the resulting increase in gasoline would be approximately $0.5 \times 0.12 \times 18.4 = 1.1$ million barrels per day in 1975.
5. Public Law 91-604.
6. Bureau of Mines, *U.S. Energy Through the Year 2000* (Department of the Interior, Washington, D.C., December 1972). For the purposes of this article, electric energy is accounted for solely in the electric utility sector and is not distributed to the other sectors. In addition to extrapolating current trends in energy consumption, the Bureau of Mines projections assume continued improvements of the efficiency of fossil fuel plants, improved insulation in new home construction based on raised FHA standards, and a continued increase in the proportion of steel produced by the more energy-efficient basic oxygen furnace process.
7. A. A. Schulman, *DITT Data Estimates and Input-Output Review* (OEP Report IST-103, Office of Emergency Preparedness, Executive Office of the President, Washington, D.C., 1972). Values are derived by the use of the demand impact transformation tables (DITT).
8. E. Hirst, *Energy Consumption for Transportation in the U.S.* (Report ORNL-NSF-EP-15, Oak Ridge National Laboratory, Oak Ridge, Tenn., 1972).
9. R. A. Rice, *Technol. Rev.* **74**, 31 (January 1972).
10. Automobile Manufacturers Association, *Automobile Facts and Figures* (Automobile Manufacturers Association, Detroit, Mich., 1971), p. 53.
11. Office of Emergency Preparedness, *The Potential for Energy Conservation: A Staff Study* (Government Printing Office, Washington, D.C., 1972).
12. W. E. Fraize and R. K. Lay, *A Survey of Propulsion Systems for Low Emission Urban Vehicles* (Report No. M70-45, MITRE Corporation, McLean, Va., September 1970). Hybrid energy storage systems allow constant maximum efficiency load to be placed on the engine, for example, by combining a heat engine, storage batteries, and electric drive.
13. "Patterns of energy consumption in the United States," a study prepared by Stanford Research Institute, Menlo Park, Calif., for the Office of Science and Technology in 1972.
14. Federal Power Commission, *The 1970 National Power Survey* (Government Printing Office, Washington, D.C., 1971).
15. F. S. Dubin, professional engineer, Dubin-Mindell-Bloome Associates, New York, personal communication.
16. Electrical power is excluded.
17. National Economic Research Associates, *Energy Consumption and Gross National Product in the U.S.* (National Economic Research Associates, Washington, D.C., 1971).
18. National Coal Association, *Steam-Electric Plant Factors* (National Coal Association, Washington, D.C., 1971).
19. Department of Commerce, *The Application of Total Energy Systems to Housing Developments* (Department of Commerce, Washington, D.C., March 1972).
20. Environmental Protection Agency, *The Economics of Clean Air* (Environmental Protection Agency, Washington, D.C., February 1972).
21. Council on Environmental Quality, *Second Annual Report* (Government Printing Office, Washington, D.C., August 1971).
22. R. A. Rice, "System energy as a factor in considering future transportation," *Am. Soc. Mech. Eng. Pap. 70-WA/ENER-8* (1971).
23. Task Force on Energy, National Academy of Engineers, *U.S. Energy Prospects: An Engineering Viewpoint* (National Academy of Engineers, Washington, D.C., 1974).
24. I thank Robert H. Kupperman of the Office of Emergency Preparedness, chairman of the interagency working group on energy conservation. This article draws heavily from the findings of that group's report. I am also grateful to Felix Ginsburg, Frederick McGoldrick, and Richard Wilcox for their review and thoughtful observations and to Philip Essley and Robert Shepherd for their critical reading of the article.

Conservation in Industry

Charles A. Berg

A little more than a year and a half ago, the Office of Emergency Preparedness undertook a staff study on *The Potential for Energy Conservation.* At the outset of this effort, the then somewhat novel idea was advanced that one might conserve fuels simply by using them more efficiently. One of the staff members working on the study asked knowledgeable persons in industry about that possibility, and was told that at the prevailing price of fuel, industry made the most efficient use of fuel possible. The implication was that economic justification had been considered in the various trade-offs that can be made to reduce fuel consumption, and further improvements in equipment to gain fuel efficiency would not have been justified.

However, a small group of industrial spokesmen began to tell quite a different story. For example, Dow Chemical began to publicize its internal energy management programs, which had resulted in steadily decreasing fuel consumption per unit of production for several years—years in which fuel prices had been declining relative to other prices. The measures applied to gain this improved efficiency of fuel use were economically justifiable, according to Dow.

Other spokesmen from industry, including representatives of Du Pont, Union Carbide, Thermo Electron, Surface Combustion, Bloom Engineering, Consolidated Natural Gas, and the American Gas Association, to mention only a few, told the same story: that there was significant latitude to improve the efficiency of fuel use in industry through measures that were economically justifiable at prevailing fuel prices.

On the basis of this preliminary information and some further staff study, the final report issued by the OEP included the possibility that, in some instances, industry might conserve fuels through more efficient use.

The potential for conservation of fuel through effective utilization began to attract the attention of numerous investigators, some of whom followed further the line of investigation of the OEP study. In conference after conference, university researchers, industrial engineers, business executives, and government scientists adduced evidence that it would be possible to save fuel and to save money too, in many industrial operations.

Today, in rereading the OEP report and the proceedings of the conferences that followed it, one can detect that the possible existence of economically justifiable measures to reduce industrial fuel requirements was given rather circumspect treatment. In fact, some of those who wrote and spoke on this subject confessed to a feeling of puzzlement. Their evidence indicated that many economically attractive measures to reduce industrial fuel consumption had been available, but had not been applied. This did not conform with the teachings of classical economics, that corporations would necessarily use all such measures to reduce their costs of operation.

As more evidence was brought out, those investigating fuel utilization in industry began to suspect that procedures of economic justification used in industry—particularly in small businesses and light industry—might depart significantly from the classical economic procedure advocated in textbooks and management schools, and upon which the economic justification of many fuel saving measures was based. In addition, investigators began to wonder whether there were factors in addition to technical feasibility or straightforward economic justification, which might exert an overriding influence on industrial decisions to adopt —or not to adopt—fuel saving equipment. Influences including those of political and institutional character may require examination if one is to explain why seemingly economically attractive fuel saving measures were not adopted in the past. It may, in fact, be necessary to find an explanation in order to plan for fuel conservation efforts in the future. If the influence of fuel price alone was not sufficient in the past to promote optimally efficient use of fuels, one may reasonably question the theory that the influence of higher fuel price will be sufficient to promote fuel efficiency to newly optimized levels. This will be considered further, below.

Present Measures

Nearly every newspaper, magazine, and professional journal one picks up today has an article on energy, and many of these articles concern improved fuel utilization in industry. For example, the 24 February *New York Times* carried an article by Gene Smith summarizing fuel conservation efforts by American Telephone & Telegraph, Litton Industries, TRW, Upjohn, Pfizer, General Electric, and other large corporations. An article in the *Wall Street Journal* on 11 March by Urban Lehner also dealt with efforts to improve efficiency of fuel utilization in such large corporations as Westinghouse, Dow, Du Pont, Greyhound, and RCA. The examples cited in these and other recent articles involved tuning up plant equipment, diligent management practices in plant operation, careful use of lighting and air conditioning, and other similar measures to eliminate outright waste of energy. The measures were said not to interfere with production, not to reduce worker safety or performance, and not to entail unjustifiable cost; in fact, in many instances, the fuel conservation measures were said to be accompanied by significant cost savings.

The quantity of fuel saved through the measures cited in current reports is impressive, especially in view of the simplicity of the measures themselves. For example, after requiring a daily report of the energy used by each department in its plants one corporation found that its energy consumption declined by 15 percent. Simple, straightforward steps such as adjusting combustion equipment and controlling plant ventilation have yielded fuel savings of 10 percent or more in many industrial plants. It appears that those who earlier expressed their belief that

---

The author is chief engineer at the Federal Power Commission, Washington, D.C. 20426.

27

Fig. 1. A large heat-treating furnace, with the insulated water-cooled skid rails used to convey material through the furnace.

substantial quantities of fuel might be conserved through more effective use of energy in industrial processes have been sustained.

However, the present concern with fuel efficiency in industry follows a wave of unprecedented oil price increases and comes in a time when oil and natural gas may be temporarily unavailable to industry at any price. Thus, it can be argued that what one is seeing in present industrial fuel conservation efforts is simply a readjustment to increase the efficiency of fuel utilization to a new and higher level which is justified at new and higher fuel prices. That is, today's fuel conservation efforts merely illustrate

the power of fuel price to promote efficient utilization.

But the measures being applied in the industrial fuel conservation efforts today could just as well have been applied in the past, to save both fuel and overall costs of operation. For example, in one large manufacturing plant in the southeastern United States, the first major step in an overall fuel conservation program was to replace several hundred broken windows through which heated or refrigerated air had been leaking for years. An executive from this plant stated that at the outset of his firm's conservation program no one knew just how many broken windows there were. In a small plant located in northeast

New England, a major fuel saving was attained through careful loading dock operations. The plant ships large goods, and to load cargo the trucks had to be pulled into the plant building. It was common practice to park trucks in the doorway to the plant, which, of course, required that the large loading door remain open. During the period of several hours required to load the truck, the heated air from the plant was allowed to escape freely to the outside. The correction of the major heat leak from this small plant cost nearly nothing, but saved significant quantities of fuel.

Many of the industrial fuel saving measures reported in the press (and cited above) fall in the category of housekeeping, and as such can be adopted at little or no cost. These actions do save appreciable amounts of fuel and thus offer examples of economically attractive—but previously unapplied—measures for fuel savings in industry. However, the general tightening up of industrial maintenance, housekeeping, and energy management which has taken place recently—with highly salubrious effect—does not provide a measure of the full potential for the improvement of fuel utilization which might be gained through investment in improved equipment, and other capital projects. Nor does the history of housekeeping measures indicate the sort of influences which factors other than fuel price might exert on the decisions involving capital projects to improve fuel efficiency.

One of the first things industry might do to improve fuel efficiency would be to reexamine technical measures that have been available in the past. This is, in fact, taking place today, and at a vigorous pace. A few examples of some capital projects are offered here as an indication of the significance, range, and economic attractiveness of the fuel savings they offer.

Insulation of Heat-Treating Furnaces

Figure 1 shows a large heat-treating furnace used in the steel industry. Steel slabs are conveyed through the furnace on skid rails. These rails must be water-cooled so that they will not soften and collapse. The water-cooled skid rail system is an excellent way to remove heat from the inside of the furnace. Insulation can be applied to these rails to reduce heat losses, as the rails shown

Table 1. Costs and benefits of insulating water-cooled skids in a reheat furnace. The furnace capacity is 160 tons per day; insulation reduces heat input by 40.3 million Btu per hour. Fuel, at $0.72 per thousand cubic feet, is reduced by 40.3 thousand cubic feet per hour. Data are from Powell (2).

Item	Annual amount (dollars)
Capital cost	100,000
Operating cost analysis	
Maintenance, 5 percent of capital cost	5,000
Taxes and insurance, 2 percent of capital cost	2,000
Interest, 4.5 percent of capital cost	4,500
Depreciation in 1 year	100,000
Total annual operating cost	111,500
Economic benefit of fuel use reduction	
Annual fuel cost reduction*	243,734
Annual cost	111,500
Annual benefit	132,234

* Calculated on the basis of 40.3 thousand cubic feet per hour, at $0.72 per thousand cubic feet, for 8400 hours per year.

in Fig. 1 demonstrate. The insulation wears out as the furnace is used: One type of insulation currently marketed will last about 4 months with normal use, while a newer form of insulation is expected to give a year of service. Industrial experts estimate that approximately 50 percent of the water-cooled skid rails in heat-treating furnaces in the United States are fully insulated, while approximately 90 percent of those used in the major steel producing countries abroad are fully insulated. Further, industrial studies of the use of such insulation indicate that if insulation were applied to the presently uninsulated skid rail systems in the United States, the total saving of fuel would be equivalent to approximately 30,000 barrels of oil per day (1 barrel = 0.16 m³) (1).

Now, the essential question about such a measure is, does it pay? Powell (2) has considered this question, and his data (Table 1) show that the expenditure of approximately $100,000 on insulation can save approximately $234,000 worth of natural gas per year. Whether one wishes to use the same tax or interest rates as Powell, the economic justification of furnace rail insulation is clear.

Many similar studies of furnace insulation, combustion control, burner positioning, and similar capital improvements in heat-treating furnaces have been carried out. Some of the more notable studies have been conducted by J. D. Nesbitt of the Institute of Gas Technology (3). Nearly all the studies available reach the same conclusions. Small additional investments in furnace insulation and similar capital projects yield significant savings of fuel and are very attractive economically.

The price of natural gas used in the studies cited here, $0.72 per thousand cubic feet (1 cubic foot = 0.028 m³), is not exceptionally high. Some plants were paying this for firm gas contracts well before the present fuel crisis. The economic justification of the measures considered here was established well before the present trend of rapidly increasing fuel prices set in.

Industrial Furnace Efficiency and Heat Recuperation

A large part of the heat of combustion of the fuel used in high temperature industrial furnaces is lost in the

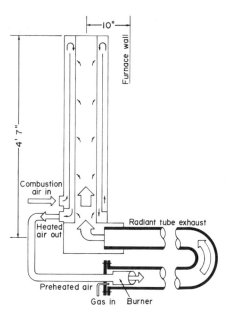

Fig. 2. A heat recuperator suitable for recapturing stack gas heat from a radiant fired tube and using it to preheat combustion air.

exhaust. Table 2 gives data assembled by Hemsath (4), showing the efficiency of various types of industrial furnaces. Note that in many furnaces 50 percent or more of the energy used goes up the chimney.

There are no data in Table 2 for one important industrial furnace—the glass melting furnace. As a rule, these are large installations and involve regenerative heat recovery stages which are several times larger than the melting chamber (tank) of the furnace itself. These furnaces are generally designed to have extremely long lives, as industrial equipment goes, and careful economic justification is applied to their construction. The result is that large glass melting furnaces may be the most efficient of large high temperature industrial furnaces—the only possible rival being some steel furnaces.

For the rest of the furnaces listed in Table 2, it would be possible to use heat recovery equipment, such as heat recuperators, to recapture some of the heat normally lost in stack gases. One type of heat recuperator is illustrated in Fig. 2. This is designed for use with a radiant tube furnace, in which combustion is used to heat a tube through which the combustion products flow from the burner tip to the exhaust

Table 2. Efficiences of various types of industrial furnaces; D, directly fired; ID, indirectly fired. Data are from Hemsath (4).

Industry and process	Operating temperature (°F)	Type of heating	Heat distribution (%)	
			Process	Exhaust
Steel and alloys				
Annealing	1450–1650	ID	35	56
Normalizing	1575–1700	D	43	46
Hardening	1400–1600	ID	36	38
Tempering	400–1200	D	54	32
Gas carburizing	1650–1700	ID	34	58
Carbonitriding	1300–1650	ID	35	57
Gas nitriding	950–1050	ID	45	40
Reheating	2200–2300	D	30	65
Sintering	2000	D	38	53
Brazing	2000	D	38	53
Aluminum				
Ingot heating	1100	ID	44	41
Coil annealing	800	ID	47	36
Solution heat treating	900–1025	ID	45	38
Strip heating	1000	ID	45	38
Copper and brass				
Ingot (coke) heating	1700	D	43	46
Annealing	600–1200	ID	44	41
Billet heating	1700–1800	ID	32	61
Solution heat treat	1700	ID	35	58
Strip heating	1300	D	51	36
Glass				
Annealing	100–1050	D, ID	45	38
Tempering	1250	D	53	34
Decorating	1200	D, ID	43	43
Bending	1250	D	54	32
Fabrication	1000–1400	D	47	41
Carbon				
Carbon baking	1600–1800	D	42	48
Rebaking	1600–1800	D	42	48

29

stack. The hot tube then radiates heat to the charge in the furnace. The recuperator in Fig. 2 draws fresh combustion air down over the outside of the exhaust stack, and thus uses part of the heat normally lost in the exhaust to preheat the combustion charge.

The effectiveness of using heat recuperation for such purposes is indicated by the data of Fig. 3, which were assembled by Kemsath. The data may be interpreted as follows. The process being executed in the furnace sets the flue gas exit temperature. Thus, for a process at, say 2500°F, the fuel to be saved by preheating combustion air to various temperatures can be determined directly from Fig. 3. For example, preheating the combustion air to 1000°F reduces the total fuel consumption in the furnace by more than 30 percent (5).

Direct heating operations in industry, such as heat treating, smelting, and glass melting, account for approximately 11 percent of the total fuel consumption in the United States (6). It appears possible that as much as 30 percent of the fuel in certain direct heating operations can be saved through the use of devices similar to the one in Fig. 2.

As for the use of such devices on radiant tubes alone, there are approximately 900,000 radiant tubes in heat-treating furnaces in U.S. plants, and very few of them are equipped with heat recuperators. Heat recuperators are being introduced to the market now for this purpose. Industrial estimates indicate that each recuperator can save fuel equivalent to ½ barrel of oil per day. Recuperators cost $1000 to $1500 per unit. The total potential (equivalent) fuel saving for all the radiant tubes in operation today is of the order of 450,000 barrels of oil per day. Furthermore, a device costing $1000 to $1500, which will eliminate the need for ½ barrel of oil per day (equivalent) is economically rather attractive now (7).

On-Line Computer Controls

The use of computer controls in the operation of large thermal processing plants is a most attractive way to save fuel and reduce costs. In one European steel plant, the use of on-line computer controls to execute a carefully devised program of operation for steel reheat-

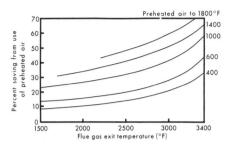

Fig. 3. Effectiveness of combustion air preheating as a measure for saving fuel. The data are from K. Hemsath.

ing resulted in a 25 percent reduction in fuel consumption per ton of production, and was accompanied by a 12 percent increase in the plant's rate of production (8). The functions monitored by the computer included the furnace idling temperatures, the temperature of the charge in the furnace and in passage from furnace to furnace, and the speed of passage of the charge. One of the virtues of using the computer control system was that once a planned schedule of operation was programmed it could be met. This was a key element in increasing the productivity of the plant. The investment in the computer control system was clearly justifiable for the steel company.

On-line computer controls are also very useful for combustion equipment. Regulation of combustion air is most important for the efficient operation of high temperature industrial furnaces; excess air quenches the flame temperature and reduces the efficiency of heat transfer to the furnace. Combustion equipment, particularly oil-fired equipment, can be thrown out of adjustment by rapid changes in atmospheric conditions, and by other phenomena, such as progressive fouling, which might be thought to be of minor importance by anyone except a combustion expert. Industrial experts have studied the significance of proper burner adjustment and maintenance (9), and many have concluded that, in the case of burner units which are not equipped with on-line continuous stack gas analysis and feedback control, diligent application of exacting adjustment procedures could save 5 to 10 percent of the fuel consumed. Some field measurements have shown fuel savings of as much as 30 percent. The wider application of combustion control systems would appear to be an economically attractive avenue to promote industrial fuel efficiency (10).

Accelerated Adoption of
Improved Equipment

The examples discussed above involve capital improvements of existing plants or new plants of conventional design. It is also possible to adopt new plant design to improve industrial fuel efficiency.

One often hears speculations that it might take 15 years or more to effect substantial changes in large industrial plant equipment. But it would be a mistake to underestimate just how rapidly industry can change, when the incentives involved are sufficiently strong. For example, the Pilkington float glass process for producing flat glass received its large international marketing push in the middle and late 1960's. In the early and middle 1960's most flat glass produced in the United States was made in plate glass plants. The Pilkington process, although significantly more costly to set up as a rule, is much more efficient in its use of all factors of production, including fuel. The result of the introduction of the float glass process has been that, in somewhat less than 10 years, flat glass production in the United States has been converted from plate glass production to a state in which only one plate glass plant remains in operation, and the remainder of the country's flat glass is made as float glass. In one major flat glass plant, a new plate glass furnace costing somewhat more than $15 million was operated only 1 year, and was then shut down because it could not compete with the float glass equipment installed next to it. Industry can indeed move very rapidly when the incentives are attractive. Far from requiring 15 years or more for significant changes to be brought about, industrial production can be revolutionized in less than a decade if the incentives are sufficiently strong.

Cement making is an industry in which one might see rapid changes in plant equipment. The average fuel consumption in U.S. cement kilns today is 1.2 million Btu per barrel of cement (11). The most efficient U.S. cement kilns, operating on a dry process, use approximately 750,000 Btu per barrel.

In European cement making, advances in heat transfer technology have been applied to reduce fuel consumption to significantly lower levels. The use of heat recuperation is the principal measure by which higher efficiency of fuel use in cement calcination has been achieved. Reject heat from a kiln is used to preheat the limestone charge before it is introduced into the kiln. A large, modern European cement kiln, equipped with several preheating units, is shown in Fig. 4. This type of kiln, which is being installed in Europe today, uses only 550,000 Btu per barrel of cement. This represents an efficiency of somewhat more than 55 percent.

There are further advances which can be introduced to cement kiln operations. Fluidized bed processing, for example, offers not only some further gains in fuel efficiency but some additional gains in flexibility of operation and speed of processing.

With fuel prices climbing and with energy purchases representing as much as 20 percent of the total operating costs of some cement plants, one should not be surprised to see the rapid application of new and more efficient equipment in this field.

Longer-Range Possibilities

Having looked at improvement of existing plants and at plant equipment of superior efficiency that is now available, we turn to the possible future use of equipment still under development. An example of such equipment is the heat pipe vacuum furnace (12).

The conventional design of a vacuum furnace calls for energy to be supplied via electrical resistance radiators inside the furnace. This means that for every Btu of heat delivered to the charge in the furnace approximately 3 Btu of fuel must be consumed at the electrical power plant that energizes the furnace. The temperature required in the furnace is often less than the adiabatic temperature of combustion of the fuel used at the power plant. In a prototype model, a heat pipe has been used to supply energy to the interior of the vacuum furnace from a local combustion chamber. In addition, certain modifications of insulation were applied to the vacuum furnace, to take advantage of the fact that the heat transfer from the charge to the furnace wall takes place entirely by radiation. The combined effects of using specially designed antiradiative insulation and a local direct combustion–heat pipe system to supply energy to the furnace reduced the fuel requirements for oper-

Fig. 4. A modern European cement kiln with multiple preheaters.

ation of the furnace by 75 percent, as compared with a conventional electric vacuum furnace. The elimination of the electric power generation was responsible for most of this saving. The principle on which this step is based is the use of energy at the quality required by the process (direct heat) rather than energy of excess quality (electricity). Figure 5 shows the Shefsiek-Lazaridis prototype vacuum furnace (12); note the combustion chamber at the rear of the device.

Another method of improving industrial fuel efficiency in the future is to combine industrial production of process steam (which accounts for approximately 17 percent of the total fuel consumption in the United States) with electric power generation. Many steam raising operations such as paper pulping, paper drying, and vulcanizing require low-quality steam (13). If one were to use additional fuel, and raise the steam to somewhat higher quality, it would be possible to pass the steam through a power generation plant and produce electricity, and to use the steam rejected by the steam turbines to operate the process for which the steam was originally required. Electric power is thus generated by using only the extra fuel required to increase the quality of the steam above that needed for normal operations. In this manner, power can be generated with very high efficiencies: heat rates as low as 4500 Btu per kilowatt-hour can be obtained.

Fig. 5. The heat pipe vacuum furnace of Shefsiek and Lazaridis.

This compares very favorably with the most optimistic expectations for advanced technologies of power generation, such as magnetohydrodynamics.

An average paper plant could produce three to four times as much electrical power as it could consume. Thus, thermal integration of paper plants (and other similar steam raising operations) with electrical power generation could provide highly efficient growth in electrical generating capacity.

Is it actually technically feasible or economically attractive to build thermally integrated steam raising power generation plants? This scheme is but a minor variation on the currently popular notion of waste heat utilization at power plants. Instead of building a power plant and trying to find some use for the waste heat, one builds a steam raising plant and tries to find a use for the surplus electrical power generated. In addition, the idea is neither new nor economically uncertain. In the 1920's and early 1930's, several major paper companies used exactly the idea considered here. It proved to be a very profitable way to generate electrical power—so much so that in the 1930's the Department of Justice took an interest in the matter. In a series of court suits the paper companies were required to decide whether they were in the paper business or the electric power business, and most opted for the paper business, leaving power generation behind.

The technical feasibility and economic attractiveness of thermally integrated steam raising and power generation has long been established. The fact that the measure saves fuel is well established. The essential problem in trying to adopt such a measure is to find a way to do so which does not abridge other requirements of society, such as preserving open competition in industry. Much the same can be said of integrating power generation with direct heat processes in industry.

Corporate Policy

We have seen that there are technically effective and economically attractive measures for conserving fuel in industry. If the measures are both technically effective and economically justifiable, should there be anything left to consider? Should not the influence of increasing fuel price alone stimulate their adoption to the economically optimal level? As some of the above examples indicate, this did not happen in the past. There may be some important problems left to consider after one has resolved all those of a straightforward technical and economic nature.

In a recent meeting between business executives and government officials, called to discuss energy use in industry, it was suggested that if the technical and economic problems of industrial fuel conservation were not serious, and yet industrial adoption of fuel conservation measures had not been rapid, problems of an institutional or political nature might be of overriding importance. The reception of this idea was less than enthusiastic: Several executives expressed doubt that researchers outside industry understand the real world in which industry functions (14). But one senior executive of a corporation which has been a leader in fuel conservation efforts acknowledged the validity of the question.

His answer (to which I subscribe) was that the problem was one of awareness. Senior industrial management in the past had not been fully aware of the economic potential of industrial fuel conservation. The recent oil embargo served to get management's attention more effectively than either the past entreaties of inventors of fuel conservation measures or forecasts of future fuel price increases ever could have done. Having become aware, the executive contended, industry would move, and more rapidly. He concluded by saying that his corporation expected to make a lot of money out of energy conservation. He is probably right, and this may be the biggest boost conservation could have.

But the executive was indicating that a major obstacle to adoption of fuel conservation measures in the past had been the institutional and political aspects of corporate policy and management. No matter how comprehensive human intellect might be, only so many things can be taken into consideration at any one time. Business executives are continually faced with a broad spectrum of problems to resolve (labor, material supply marketing, sales, and so forth), and only a few resources apply to controlling them. Until something happens to persuade the executive that control of energy use (or any one of a number of other considerations) must be taken into account, it probably will not be. The problems of controlling the use of increasingly costly labor or of expanding plant capacity on increasingly costly money, or other problems which, if unattended, are certain to lead to crisis, are likely to occupy the executive's attention fully. This is particularly true of small business and light industry, where margins of error are small. This is the classical mechanism by which opportunities are missed—not because the things considered were not well considered, but because not enough things were considered. After the recent oil embargo and price increases, control of energy use will be taken into consideration in almost every business decision.

Some other factors affecting business decisions should also be taken into account. The economic justification of capital projects is considered in the process of budgeting. While the ideal model of budgeting would have one establish all projects in terms of a base budget, this rule is honored in the breach. It seems to be more common for yearly changes in the budget to be examined than the base budget itself. Thus, changes in the costs in various sectors of a production operation provide the signals by which the framework of budgeting actually is worked out in many corporations (and at many levels of government, too). An area in which costs are going up rapidly receives a great deal of attention; an area of declining costs may be viewed as a problem which is solving itself. This may help to explain why many measures for fuel conservation were not adopted in the past, because over the last decade or two energy prices have declined relative to other prices. If this view of budgeting, which has been expressed by numerous persons, is in any way correct, the fact that fuel prices are now rising may be an even more powerful stimulus to improving fuel efficiency than the present high level of fuel prices.

Lending policy also influences decisions, especially in small businesses. Most industrial fuel saving measures will require some capital projects, necessarily financed with borrowed money. With a very large part of the heat-treating equipment in the United States located in small corporations specializing in that field, the adoption of heat recuperators, furnace insulation, and other similar measures will require loans and will be influenced by policy governing loans. Businessmen and bankers who have discussed this subject seem to agree that loans for expanding plant capacity are usually given a higher priority than loans for improving existing plant performance. One consideration is that expansion of plant capacity promotes local employment. This has usually been given high priority in lending decisions, particularly in the recent past. Lending policies of this type may help to solve local unemployment, but loans to help improve fuel efficiency can have significant indirect effect on employment and can help control the consumption of natural resources in the process. One should also consider the influence of technological risk—the risk that a new installation or new piece of equipment may not work as well as expected. This risk seems to loom largest in large-scale thermal processing equipment. In many instances, the laws of scaling used by engineers and scientists are simply not adequate to permit one to scale up a new type of cement kiln or a multifuel furnace from laboratory model to full production size, with sufficient accuracy to satisfy the economic constraints of the industry concerned. It is not a question of whether the scaled-up plant will work or not. But if the rate of production of some types of large thermal processing plants were to turn out to be several percent less than predicted, the owner of the installation might find himself in serious trouble. And, to repeat, the engineering scaling laws on which one must rely may not be sufficiently accurate, especially with regard to circumvention of instabilities. Anyone who has attempted to scale up a fluidized bed apparatus or a large ceramic structure will recognize the difficulty.

A basic problem here is that one is required to scale up the laboratory model to a full-scale facility. If one

were able to experiment, modify, tune, and adjust one full-scale facility (say a large inclined fluidized cement processor or a large ceramic gas turbine) one could undoubtedly debug the full-size apparatus so that others could be reproduced from it and put into production without major difficulty. But few industries can justify putting up a large production facility on which experiments and debugging efforts are to be conducted.

The cement kiln of Fig. 4 runs well in Europe, but the limestone and aggregate used there differ from those found in the United States. Where dry process cement making is practicable in the United States such kilns could most probably be used, once some adjustments were made (15). But to say to a prospective owner of such a plant that it probably can be made to work here is to dampen his enthusiasm considerably.

In other countries, large-scale demonstration plants have been built to permit experimentation, tuning, and debugging of large-scale thermal processing equipment. Such demonstrations would be very helpful in U.S. efforts to resolve energy problems.

Finally, institutional, regulatory, and legal barriers can constrain the adoption of technology to improve fuel efficiency. The earlier example of integration of industrial steam raising and power generation illustrates this. Legal barriers have been erected for good reasons—they safeguard certain things which society deems essential. With fuel and other natural resources becoming progressively more precious to society, it may be necessary to reexamine some of the legal and institutional constraints established in the past. It may be possible to find ways to preserve competition, and other such valuable aspects of society, and to conserve fuels and other natural resources too.

Conclusion

There is a wide range of technical measures to improve the efficiency of fuel use in industry. The economic justification for adopting these measures can, as a rule, be readily established. If one can resolve the nontechnoeconomic constraints which affect the adoption of these measures, one can look forward to substantial reductions in the fuel required to operate many important industrial processes.

References and Notes

1. Most of these furnaces are fired by natural gas.
2. A. S. Powell, paper presented at the Cleveland State University Conference on Energy Utilization, Cleveland, Ohio, 24 October 1973.
3. J. D. Nesbitt, paper presented at the East Ohio Gas Company Seminar on Fuel Conservation in the Steel Industry, 20 April 1972.
4. K. H. Hemsath, paper presented at the American Flame Research Committee meeting at the Massachusetts Institute of Technology, Cambridge, 4 June 1973.
5. To convert temperatures to degrees Celsius, subtract 32 and divide the result by 1.8.
6. "Patterns of energy consumption in the United States," report to the President's Office of Science and Technology by Stanford Research Institute, January 1972.
7. Most radiant tubes are fired on natural gas, and most heat treating furnaces can be assumed to operate 8000 hours a year.
8. F. Hollander and R. L. Huisman, paper presented at the annual convention of the Association of Iron and Steel Engineers, Chicago, 1971.
9. H. C. Hottel and T. B. Howard, *New Energy Technology—Some Facts and Assessments* (MIT Press, Cambridge, 1971).
10. A number of large glass furnaces have been equipped with on-line computer control of combustion. Typically, these systems permit about 1 percent excess oxygen in the stack gases, which represents very efficient combustion conditions. However, some of the largest furnaces are not yet equipped, and manual adjustment procedures are used.
11. One British thermal unit (Btu) $= 1.06 \times 10^3$ joules; 1 barrel of cement weighs 150 kilograms.
12. P. K. Shefsiek and L. J. Lazardidis, *Proceedings of the Second Natural Gas Research and Technology Conference* (Atlanta, Georgia, 5 to 7 June 1972).
13. The term quality is used here in the engineering sense: high-temperature dry steam is high quality.
14. It seems increasingly fashionable among public and private executives to describe one's own area of endeavor as the "real world."
15. Different aggregates react differently with cements having different processing histories. If dry processed cement is not properly controlled in the kiln, it can undergo deterioration in service through alkaline reactions with certain aggregates.

Individual Self-Sufficiency in Energy

Allen L. Hammond

Project Independence is supposed to free the United States from dependence on imports of energy by 1980. Well before that time, some Americans, harking back to an earlier tradition of individual self-reliance, will have become partially or completely independent of utilities and oil companies for their energy supplies. Not for them the blackouts, heating oil shortages, and frustrations of gasoline lines. Of course, not everyone would care to do his or her commuting on a bicycle, pioneer a solar-heated house, or return to an entirely gadgetless style of life. Still, the concept of an autonomous house has considerable appeal, especially for those who live in rural areas. Urban and suburban dwellers might find attractive the prospect of buffering their dependence on conventional energy sources. The possibilities range from the eminently practical to the absurd. In this article, I will look at both kinds of suggestions in the areas of individual lifestyles, food, housing, and transportation.

The revival of interest in self-sufficiency did not start with the energy shortage, but dates back at least to the 1960's search for alternative life-styles and to the concern with the individual's ability to control his own destiny that produced *The Whole Earth Catalogue* and similar volumes. The energy crisis has provided a new focus for these concerns and has spawned a raft of small businesses that sell information on, and sometimes hardware for, everything from windmills and solar-heated houses to methane digestors and household composters. The energy shortage has also brought to the fore a small army of backyard technologists and would-be entrepreneurs promoting electric cars and energy-saving cookware. Other contributors to the growing array of wood stoves, solar collectors, and

The author is head of the Research News section of *Science*.

energy-conserving appliances have proceeded from more purely commercial motives, although some manufacturers, such as the bicycle and long underwear industries, have literally had success thrust upon them. Most of the big companies are actively studying the potential market for solar heating systems and similar equipment and are stepping-up production of heat pumps and other energy-conserving devices, but it is the newcomers who are responsible for most of what is available so far.

What could an individual or a family do now or in the near future to be more self-sufficient in energy? One facile answer is to change personal habits, lifestyles, and philosophies, to adopt what an environmentalist might call "right thinking"—making do with less. The President's request to turn down the thermostat belongs in this category. So do other suggestions, such as wearing warmer clothes, shopping less frequently, and reverting to the old-fashioned ways of doing things by hand—mowing the lawn, mixing batter, brushing teeth. (Many of these, it is true, have a trivial impact on overall energy consumption but may have a significant effect on one's attitudes. Lawns, for example, require energy to cut them and usually fertilizer, produced with natural gas, to make them grow. And there is no better way to appreciate the esthetics of alternative forms of ground cover or of vegetable gardens than mowing a large lawn by hand.) The standard conservation ideas—turning out lights, putting up storm windows, servicing the furnace—deserve mention here, as do some of the less standard ideas, such as the counterculture's injunction to "save water, shower with a friend." Of course, some of the dozens of electrical appliances found in most homes not only save time and effort, but are difficult to replace. Hand-powered washing machines, for example, are rare today. Brooms and nonelectric blankets, how-

ever, are not. Clearly, some rethinking of what is essential and what is peripheral in our energy needs will help edge us toward self-sufficiency.

Recreation is another energy consumer. If we could not afford the energy for our television sets, would reading aloud, playing music, and meditation enjoy a revival? Can participation replace spectatorship as the country's major sport? And as for the American custom of traveling every weekend and holiday, perhaps a major effort to improve urban environments would make local recreations more attractive.

Agriculture is an energy-intensive industry in the United States, and whereas the individual consumer does not himself use the large amounts of fertilizer, tractor fuel, and process heat that go into making the supermarket product, he nonetheless pays for it. Hence the suggestion, hinted at above, to turn lawns into "independence gardens" that are a source, not a sink, of energy. Cooking also takes energy, and here enthusiasts point out that Chinese methods of preparing food—rapid cooking of small pieces—is preferable from an energy standpoint to the steak on the grill. Finally, for the truly dedicated energy conserver, there is the recipe that appeared in a New England paper some years ago for cooking a roast, wrapped in aluminum foil, on the engine block of the family car while enroute to Grandmother's house.

Solar Heated Houses

Reducing energy use is not the same as having an independent supply, and more autonomous means of providing a house with heat and electricity are being developed, and in some cases revived. Perhaps a score of experimental houses heated with solar energy have been built in this country over the past 20 years, with half a dozen more under construction this year and the beginnings of a minor boom in sight. The advantage of heating with sunlight, of course, is that it is free. (One Southern California utility did approach the Federal Power Commission a couple of years ago to ask if it could secure rights to sunlight in that state.) The equipment to capture and store heat from the sun, however, is relatively costly and can be unsightly. It need not be sophisticated: Some solar collectors consist of a blackened sheet of metal covered with panes of glass.

Harry Thomason's house near Washington, D.C., is a good example of what can be done. Water is circulated over corrugated aluminum collectors on the roof of his house and is stored, along with the solar heat it has picked up, in a 1600-gallon tank in his basement. Surrounding the tank are 50 tons of stones, which also store heat and provide a large heat-transfer surface. Air is blown over the rocks and circulated to heat the house. A key to the system's success is its use of large volumes of low velocity, low-temperature air (temperatures as low as 75° to 80°F) compared to conventional heating systems (140° to 160°F). Low-temperature operation means fewer heat losses, more efficient operation of the solar collectors, and more hours of use. Backup heat is provided by an oil furnace, which, according to Thomason, is needed only a few hours per week. A heat exchanger in the storage tank provides hot water. In summer, Thomason cools the storage reservoir at night with a conventional air conditioner and circulates cool air through the house during the day. One of the more effective of the older solar houses, it was designed and built by Thomason himself, a former patent attorney, and it illustrates many of the characteristics of any solar house—good insulation, collectors, thermal storage, and a variety of automatic controls not found in conventional homes (2). A measure of the interest in solar houses is that George Washington University, in Washington, D.C., now offers a course for potential builders and contractors of solar houses, taught by Thomason.

Several companies now offer solar collectors for a variety of purposes, and more sophisticated collectors (based on selective surfaces that absorb more sunlight, while emitting less thermal radiation than black paint) are being readied for market. Horace McCracken of the Sunwater Company in El Cajon, California, reports a brisk demand for his solar stills, which compete as a water supply with bottled water in arid parts of the Southwest. He is beginning to sell larger units as swimming pool heaters, now that natural gas for that purpose is being shut off (3). The Australian Beasley Solapak and the Israeli Miromit companies manufacture solar water heaters and either have or are seeking U.S. outlets for their collectors (4). Sunworks, a newly formed Connecticut company; Solar Systems, Incorporated, in Texas; Intertechnology

Early reports indicate that the demand for motorcycles and other energy-saving forms of transportation may outstrip the supply this summer. [Source: Eric Poggenpohl, *Science*]

Corporation in Virginia; and AAI, Incorporated, in Maryland all manufacture advanced solar collectors suitable for heating houses and commercial buildings (5). Even the big guys are getting into the act—both General Electric and Honeywell have produced collectors in experimental quantities and are exploring the prospects for commercialization. A word of caution to the venturesome—the collectors available today cost $6 to $25 per square foot, mostly in the higher range for small orders, and the durability of the selective surfaces on advanced collectors has yet to be established. All of the manufacturers report a deluge of mail, however, and if interest turns into hard orders, the cost of collectors may go down substantially.

There are other ways of heating a house. Wood stoves are back in fashion, and well-designed fireplaces can lessen heating loads for those who have an ample supply of firewood. Heating with gas is not such a bad idea if you grow your own, and, while methane digesters (which produce the gas by anaerobic decomposition of organic matter) are not commercially available in the United States yet, several groups will sell you plans and instructions for building a system (6). The catch is that one family's organic waste does not produce enough methane to heat a house, although it may be enough for cooking purposes. If you own a pig farm, however, or live near a feedlot that is will-

ing to dispose of its animal wastes, it may be worth looking into.

To be truly autonomous, of course, a house needs a source of electricity as well. Indeed, most heating systems depend on electrically driven fans or pumps. Short of putting a generator on the treadwheel in your gerbil cage, as one wag suggested, coming up with alternative sources of electricity is not easy. Photovoltaic cells generate electricity directly from sunlight, and an experimental house at the University of Delaware gets part of its electricity that way. But solar cells are still prohibitively expensive for household use. Small water-powered turbines are available for those fortunate enough to live beside a flowing brook (7). Windmills, long a forgotten technology in this country, are now experiencing a revival. The Davey-Dunlite Company of Australia and Elektro G.M.b.H. of Switzerland both manufacture wind generators suitable for home power application, and their products are available from the Solar Wind company in East Holden, Maine (8). Plans for home-built wind generators are also available (9).

Because winds, like sunlight, are irregular, some means of storing electricity is necessary. In practice, a self-sufficient wind-generating system needs a wind generator, a tower to place it on, a bank of storage batteries, direct current to alternating current inverters, and a variety of control equipment—

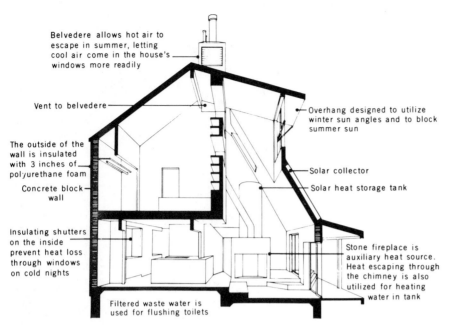

Belvedere allows hot air to escape in summer, letting cool air come in the house's windows more readily

Vent to belvedere

The outside of the wall is insulated with 3 inches of polyurethane foam

Concrete block wall

Insulating shutters on the inside prevent heat loss through windows on cold nights

Filtered waste water is used for flushing toilets

Overhang designed to utilize winter sun angles and to block summer sun

Solar collector

Solar heat storage tank

Stone fireplace is auxiliary heat source. Heat escaping through the chimney is also utilized for heating water in tank

A solar-heated semiautonomous house being built for Everett Barber in Guilford, Connecticut. [Source: Sunworks, Inc.]

all of which makes the system expensive. Although wind systems compete well with gasoline-powered generators (especially in reliability) for remote installations, the cost of electricity from present commercial units is probably four to six times as much as the local power company charges. Power costs are rising dramatically, however, and less expensive American-made units may be on the market within a few years. It is also possible to hook a windmill system in tandem with the power company's supply, with automatic switching from one to the other when needed. (Reportedly, it is possible, with such an arrangement, to put excess wind-generated electricity back onto the power lines, thus running the meter in reverse, cutting the power bill, and using the utility as the storage battery for the system.)

Autonomous or nearly autonomous houses built recently include the Bob Reines house near Albuquerque, New Mexico, and the Henry Clews house near East Holden, Maine, both designed and built by their owners. The New Mexico house is a hemispherical dome, heavily insulated, heated by solar panels, and powered by windmills. A butane stove is the only conventional source of energy. The Maine house is of more conventional design. It is heated by three wood-burning stoves that consume about 8 cords of firewood a winter. Windmills provide power for lighting, small kitchen appliances, television, and a pump that supplies running water from a well. Propane gas is used for cooking and running a refrigerator, while gasoline is used for driving a chain saw to cut wood. Neither house is connected to utility services. Although these houses do not have all the comforts of a modern suburban development, they are not primitive.

The Modern Autonomous House

More elegant examples are under construction. The house of Nicky Wilson, near Martinsburg, West Virginia, will be an architectural showcase. It will include solar heating and both photovoltaic and windmill power generators, as well as conventional oil heating and utility connections for backup (10). The house will also have two built-in greenhouses, one for a small garden and the other for plants that will filter and refresh the air that is circulated through the house. Kitchen and human wastes will be composted with a Swedish clivus system, which converts them aerobically to compost and eliminates the need for a sewer hookup. Everett Barber's house, near Gilford, Connecticut, will get about 80 percent of its heat and electricity from built-in solar collectors and a pair of windmills, with backup by an oversized, oil-fired water heater and an electrical utility connection (11). A thick layer of polyurethane foam insulation will be sprayed on the outside of the concrete block walls, making

the house extremely resistant to heat loss and giving it something of an adobe appearance. Barber's house will also incorporate a number of energy-saving features—heat from the refrigerator coil and the kitchen sewer is used to warm up water for the water heater; the fireplace draws air from outside the house rather than inside; insulated shutters for the windows are closed at night; and, in summer, air will be circulated through the house convectively, rather than blown by a fan.

Short of full autonomy, still another way to use solar energy is in combination with a heat pump. Heat pumps transfer heat by evaporating and condensing a working fluid—much like an air-conditioner or refrigerator run in reverse—and can pump two or three units of heat into a house for every unit of electricity required to drive the unit, depending on operating conditions. Most of the heat pumps available today are designed for air-to-air heat transfer and are sized for cooling rather than heating purposes. Even these would markedly reduce the cost of electric heating, which in some all-electric homes in the New York City area is reportedly running as high as $300 a month. Heat pumps designed for heating and for water-to-air transfer will soon be available from most major manufacturers. When used in combination with solar collectors, as, for example, in the condominium townhouses being designed for Richard Blazej, a Vermont builder, by Fred Dubin of Dubin, Mindell, Bloome Associates in New York City, the solar system provides a reservoir of lukewarm water. Even in the middle of a Vermont winter, a relatively small collector can provide 50°F water. Both the collectors and the heat pump can run efficiently under these conditions. Dubin expects the condominiums to use less than half the energy (in the form of electricity and backup oil heat) of conventional houses.

Solar air conditioners that run on a heat-driven absorption cycle are under development by a variety of companies, and commercial units are just becoming available (12). Reductions in the use of water (and thus, ultimately, energy at the treatment plant) can also be achieved. Most major plumbing manufacturers have faucet and toilet designs that cut back on water use. The Swedish clivus unit, which provides complete autonomy in sewage disposal, is now being manufactured by an American firm (13). The unit is essentially a tilted fiberglass box that accepts organic wastes, digests them aerobically by circulating air through the box, and produces at the end of a 2- to 3-year turnover period a dry mulch that is excellent fertilizer.

Housing design and construction techniques are another area in which there is considerable room for energy-saving improvements. According to David Hartman of Dubin, Mindell, Bloome Associates, a study the firm did in association with the National Bureau of Standards for the General Services Administration showed that heavier construction, and the resultant increase in thermal mass of a building, reduces the peak loads for thermal conditionings. They also found that insulation was more effective on the outside of the structure than on the inside. The incorporation of these and other energy-conserving features in new housing will not greatly help those who now live in drafty older houses, but most areas have companies that specialize in retrofitting existing housing with blown-in insulation.

Transportation—How Far on Foot?

Although the home is where most Americans use the majority of the energy they consume, transportation runs a close second. Here the principle villain—the family car or cars—is more easily identified, and the alternatives, unfortunately, far fewer. The typical American car converts gasoline to motive force with an efficiency of less than 20 percent and gets 12 to 15 miles per gallon. The readily available choices for reducing one's dependence on gasoline, in order of descending energy consumption, include a smaller car, a motorcycle, walking, and bicycling. Sales of bicycles in the United States have doubled since 1970 and for the past 2 years have surpassed automobiles in the number sold. Some 15 states are now financing construction of bikeways, although most cyclists must still face the risks of competing with automobiles. Sales of motorcycles are also booming, as are those of small cars.

Buses, subways, and cable cars, for those fortunate enough to live in a community with good mass transportation, also seem to be making a comeback. Several cities are experimenting with free or reduced fare service. The

return of car pooling and of hitchhiking as means of getting to work offer obvious advantages from an energy-independence point of view. An energy-conscious transportation strategy may call for making fewer trips and living near places of work or mass transit lines.

Several other methods of travel are available, ranging from methane- and alcohol-powered cars and electric vehicles to a gas-powered pogo stick that is reported to get 500,000 hops per gallon. Converting an internal combustion engine to methane or methanol is not difficult. If you have a private still or one of the methane-producing

digestors mentioned earlier and a supply of organic feedstock, you have the wherewithal for at least local transportation independent of the gas station. Neither methane nor alcohol is readily available along the highway, however, and methane-powered vehicles in particular (because of storage limitations) have a short range. Nonetheless, several municipalities are looking into the possibilities of operating fleet vehicles on methanol made from sewage sludge.

Electric vehicles are not new, but their reemergence from the world of the private hobbyist into the commercial marketplace is. Electric golf carts

Self-sufficiency in energy does not have to mean a return to drudgery and discomfort, although it may mean a return to a simpler style of life. [Source: U.S. Department of Agriculture]

and forklift trucks are no longer a novelty, and nearly three dozen manufacturers have built prototype urban cars, delivery trucks, and buses (some of these vehicles are in limited production) (14). Electric motors are several times heavier than internal combustion engines of the same power, and lead-acid batteries add additional weight. Most electric car bodies are therefore built of fiber glass and aluminum to reduce weight. Few electric vehicles can go farther than 50 miles before the batteries must be recharged, and few are suitable for freeway driving. Nonetheless, electric cars are more efficient users of energy than present automobiles—electric motors are between 85 and 90 percent efficient, and electricity is generated and transmitted with an efficiency of about 30 percent, for a combined efficiency of 25 percent or more. Tests of an electric mail van in Cupertino, California, showed that its average fuel costs per mile were half those of a standard, 4-cylinder mail truck over the same route. The Post Office is ordering 350 electric vehicles for more extensive tests. The Avis Company will also be testing electric rent-a-cars in Chicago this year.

Fuel costs of less than 1¢ a mile are claimed for some lightweight electric cars, as is the advantage of almost no maintenance. Batteries, however, must be replaced every year or so, and they are expensive. Still, by charging-up his vehicle regularly at night, an electric car owner could commute right past gas station lines. What may be the prototype of networks of service and recharge stations for electric vehicles has been opened in the suburbs of Boston, Massachusetts. *Electric Vehicle News* (15) estimates that nearly 1000 home-built electric cars will be on the road in 1974, in addition to those commercially produced. There is even a small boom in electric motorbikes—a German company, Solo Motors, and a Massachusetts firm, Auranthetic Corporation, are both producing about 2000 bikes a month and selling them readily at prices in excess of $500 (16). It is only a matter of time before someone couples a windmill generator and an electric vehicle to demonstrate that autonomous commuting is possible even for those too lazy to ride a bicycle.

For most of us, there is not much that can be done to completely alleviate our dependence on centralized sources of energy. Indeed, many would argue on the grounds of overall efficiency that centralization is by far the preferable means of generating and supplying energy, that dependency on large industrial organizations for the essentials of life is the hallmark of technologically advanced societies. This may well be true, but gasoline lines, brownouts, and shortages of natural gas are reminders that the system is far from perfect. The consumer is surprisingly vulnerable, not just to the ice storm that can down power lines, but to the mistakes of planners over whom he has little control and to the whims of the oil-exporting nations. Under the circumstances, a little self-reliance is not necessarily a foolish policy. It is encouraging that there are individuals who wish to increase their autonomy of energy supply and who, in the process, may provide the rest of us with more options of the same kind.

References and Notes

1. If you can't find long johns and other warm clothes at your neighborhood department store, try some of the mail-order houses patronized by hikers and hunters.

2. Plans for Thomason's solar house can be ordered from Edmund Scientific Co., 555 Edscorp Building, Barrington, N.J. 08007, for $10.

3. A solar still with a capacity of 2 gallons per day costs between $150 and $500, depending on how automated it is; solar swimming pool heaters average $1000. Write Sunwater Co., 1112 Pioneer Way, El Cajon, Calif. 92020.

4. Information on Beasley collectors can be obtained from Bill Edmunds of the Solar Energy Digest, P.O. Box 17776, San Diego, Calif.

5. Addresses for information are Sunworks, Inc., 669 Boston Post Road, Guilford, Conn. 06437; Solar Systems, Inc., P.O. Box 807, Tyler, Tex. 75701; Intertechnology Corp., Box 340, Warrenton, Va. 22186; AAI, Inc., P.O. Box 6767, Baltimore, Md. 21204.

6. Mother's Bookshelf, P.O. Box 70, Henderson, N.C. 28739, sells a methane information package for $8. A subscription to *The Mother Earth News* (available from the same address) will keep you up to date on what's new in self-sufficient living ($8 a year for six issues). The New Alchemy Institute East, P.O. Box 432, Woods Hole, Mass. 02543 also has information on methane digesters.

7. See *Pamphlet A, Hints on the Development of Small Water Power*, available from James Leffel and Co., Springfield, Ohio 45501. Leffel also manufactures suitable turbines.

8. Solar Wind Co., East Holden, Me. 04429. Their pamphlet, *Electric Power from the Wind* (price: $2), provides general information on wind power systems.

9. Available from Sencenbaugh Wind Electric, P.O. Box 11174, Palo Alto, Calif. 94306 (this company also sells the Australian Dunlite equipment) and Windworks, Box 329, Route 3, Mukwonago, Wisc. 53149. Other companies with plans to manufacture windpower equipment are Environmental Energies, Inc., 11350 Schaefer St., Detroit, Mich. 48227 and ILS Laboratories, Star Route 103, Tijeras, N.M.

10. The house was designed by Richard Rittelmann of the architectural firm of Burt, Hill Associates, 610 Mellon Bank Building, Butler, Pa. 16001.

11. The house was designed to Barber's specifications by the New Haven architectural firm of Charles W. Moore Associates.

12. Arkla Industries, 930 East Virginia St., Evansville, Ind. 47701 sells one of the first suitable units.

13. For more information, contact Clivus Multrum, Inc., 14A Eliot St., Cambridge, Mass. 02138. They cost about $1000.

14. Several of the largest U.S. firms are Otis Elevator Co., Special Vehicles Division, P.O. Box 8600, Stockton, Calif. 95204; Battronic Truck Corp., Third and Walnut Streets, Boyertown, Pa. 19512; Electromotion, Inc., P.O. Box 323, Bedford, Mass. 01730; and Sebring-Vanguard, Inc., P.O. Box 1479, Sebring, Fla. 33870.

15. For those who want to follow the electric vehicle industry, this quarterly magazine is published by Porter Corp., P.O. Box 533, Westport, Conn. 06880, and costs $10 per year.

16. The North American distributor is Solo Klinmotoren GmbH, Burlington, Ontario, Canada. Auranthetic Corp. is located at 706 Adams St., Quincy, Mass.

Energy and Food

Food Production and the Energy Crisis

David Pimentel, L. E. Hurd, A. C. Bellotti,

M. J. Forster, I. N. Oka, O. D. Sholes, R. J. Whitman

By 1975 the world population is expected to reach 4 billion humans (*1*). As it continues to grow, there is increasing concern about ways to prevent wholesale starvation (*2*). Concurrently, an energy crisis (due to shortages and high prices) is expected as finite reserves of fossil fuels are rapidly depleted (*3, 4*). The energy crisis is expected to have a significant impact on food production technology in the United States and the "green revolution," because both systems of crop production depend upon large energy inputs.

Both the U.S. type of agriculture and the "green revolution" type of agriculture have been eminently successful in increasing crop yields through improved technology. The ratio of persons not on farms to each farm worker in the United States increased from 10 in 1930 to 48 persons in 1971 (*5, 6*). This has lead to great social change as numbers of unemployed, untrained farm laborers migrated to our cities (*7*). In addition, the costs to the natural environment have been great, as is reflected in depleted soils, pollution, disruption of natural plant and animal populations, and natural resource shortages. One nonrenewable resource fast being depleted is fossil fuel—the most important element in the impressive yields and quality of agriculture in the United States. Energy is used in mechanized agricultural production for machinery, transport, irrigation, fertilizers, pesticides, and other management tools. Fossil fuel inputs have, in fact, become so integral and indispensable to modern agriculture that the anticipated energy crisis will have a significant impact upon food production in all parts of the world which have adopted or are adopting the Western system.

As agriculturalists, we feel that a careful analysis is needed to measure energy inputs in U.S. and green revolution style crop production techniques. Our approach is to select a single crop, corn (maize), which typifies the energy inputs for crops in general, and to make a detailed analysis of its production energy inputs. With the data on input and output for corn as a model, an examination is then made of energy needs for a world food supply that depends on modern energy intensive agriculture. Using corn as an example, we consider alternatives in crop production technology which might reduce energy inputs in food production. Other than recognizing the high costs of U.S. energy intensive agriculture, we make no effort to examine any of the projected economic, sociological, or political "trade-offs" in the United States or other countries when the energy crisis upsets the world community (*8*).

Energy Resources

As fossil fuel resources decline, the costs of obtaining fuels both from domestic and foreign sources will rapidly increase. If current use patterns continue, fuel costs are expected to double or triple in a decade (*4*) and to increase nearly fivefold by the turn of the century (*9, 10*). When energy resources become expensive, significant changes in agriculture will take place.

High energy use correlates closely with high gross national product (GNP) (*11*). In 1970, the United States consumed a total of 1.6×10^{16} kilocalories, or more than one-third of the total world energy consumption (*3*) and 35 percent of the world's petroleum (*12*)— for only one-seventeenth of the world population. This country's energy use has doubled during the past 20 years. In some types of agricultural production, the rate of energy use has increased more than threefold during the same period.

Hammond (*3*) reported that about 96 percent of the United States' energy "comes from fossil fuels: petroleum, 43 percent, mostly for transportation; natural gas, 33 percent; and coal, 20 percent. Hydroelectric energy accounts for about 3 percent of present production, and nuclear energy for about 1 percent." Peak petroleum consumption is expected to occur by the end of the century (*13*). Hammond (*3*) estimated that, if the United States were to use petroleum exclusively to provide all of its energy needs at present rates of consumption, the known, recoverable U.S. reserves would be depleted in only 5 years.

As was mentioned, crop production depends heavily on energy inputs just to produce the raw product. In addition, large amounts of energy are consumed as the raw products are transported to centers to be processed, frozen, canned, dehydrated, ground, baked, and so forth. Farmers process little of their own food, being dependent themselves upon the food processing, wholesaling, and retailing industries. They also depend on a multitude of other industries to supply machinery, fertilizers, pesticides, improved crop varieties, and other supplies. For every farm worker, it is estimated there are two farm-support workers (*14*). Thus, about 20 percent of the nation's work force and industries are involved in supplying food (*14*). The farm-support and food processing industries may use more energy than farming itself, further emphasizing the dependence of our food system upon energy. The oft-quoted statistic that one farm worker feeds 48 persons (*5*) is misleading because the farmer depends on a complex of support industries.

Corn Production and Energy Inputs

To investigate the relationship of energy inputs to crop production, we selected corn for the following reasons. (i) Corn generally typifies the energy inputs in U.S. crop production for it is intermediate in energy inputs between the extremes of high energy-

D. Pimentel and L. E. Hurd are members of the faculty of the New York State College of Agriculture and Life Science, and A. C. Bellotti, M. J. Forster, I. N. Oka, O. D. Sholes, and R. J. Whitman are graduate students, Cornell University, Ithaca, New York 14850.

demand fruit production and low energy-demand tame hay and small grain production. (ii) Corn is one of the leading grain crops in the United States and the world. (iii) More data are available on corn than on other crops. Concerning corn data, we have had to rely heavily on Department of Agriculture survey data and estimates provided by various other studies. Although the best available, some of these data have inherent limitations. Despite these shortcomings, this analysis provides a valuable perspective concerning the large energy inputs in U.S. agriculture.

Corn, the most important grain crop grown in the United States, ranks third in world production of food crops (15). In terms of world cereal grains, it ranks second to wheat. During 1971, world corn production on 279 million acres was 308 million metric tons (16).

Corn yield per acre (1 acre = 0.405 hectare) in the United States has increased significantly from 1909 to 1971 (Fig. 1). During 1909, the corn yield averaged 26 bushels per acre, and during 1971 it averaged 87 bushels per acre. A sharp rise in production per acre started about 1950—a time when many changes, including the planting of hybrid corn, were taking place in corn culture (17–19). The planting of hybrid corn probably accounts for 20 to 40 percent of the increased corn yields since the 1940's with energy resource inputs accounting for 60 to 80 percent (17, 20, 21). Hybrid corn and energy inputs toward increased yields overlap because corn plants are often selected for characteristics that make the plant perform well under specific environmental conditions as, for example, with high fertilizer inputs. Without the appropriate genetic background, the corn plant will not respond to the fertilizer inputs and, of course, the corn plant cannot respond if fertilizer is absent.

While corn yields increased about 240 percent from 1945 to 1970, the labor input per acre decreased more than 60 percent (Table 1). Intense mechanization reduced the labor input and, in part, made possible the increased corn yield.

Machinery in agriculture has increased significantly during the past 20 years; the mean rate of horsepower per farm worker has increased from 10 in 1950 to 47 in 1971 (5). The number of tractors increased (88 percent) from 2.4 million in 1945 to 4.5 million in 1972 (6, 22). Concurrently, the rated horsepower of these tractors increased 2.6-fold from 18.0 to 46.6 horsepower (6, 22). The mean number of acres farmed per tractor was 62 in 1963 (22). In our estimates we assumed that tractors and other machinery were used to farm 62 acres and assumed to function for 10 years (Table 1).

Fuel consumption for all farm machinery rose from slightly more than 3.3 billion gallons (1 gallon = 3.8 liters) in 1940 to about 7.6 billion gallons in 1969 (22, 65). For total U.S. corn production, fuel consumption for all machinery rose from an estimated 15 gallons per acre in 1945 to about 22 gallons per acre in 1970 (Table 1). Indeed, farming uses more petroleum than any other single industry (24).

The use of fertilizer in corn production has been rising steadily since 1945 (Fig. 2). An estimated 7 pounds (i pound = 0.4 kilogram) of nitrogen, 7 pounds of phosphorus, and 5 pounds of potassium were applied per acre to the acres fertilized in 1945 (25). By 1970 the application of fertilizers had risen to 112 pounds of nitrogen, 31 pounds of phosphorus, and 60 pounds of potassium per acre (26). The increase in nitrogen alone has been about 16-fold.

Table 1. Average energy inputs in corn production during different years (all figures per acre).

Inputs	1945	1950	1954	1959	1964	1970
Labor*	23	18	17	14	11	9
Machinery (kcal $\times 10^3$)†	180	250	300	350	420	420
Fuel (gallons)‡	15	17	19	20	21	22
Nitrogen (pounds)§	7	15	27	41	58	112
Phosphorus (pounds)§	7	10	12	16	18	31
Potassium (pounds)§	5	10	18	30	41	60
Seeds for planting (bushels)‖	0.17	0.20	0.25	0.30	0.33	0.33
Irrigation (kcal $\times 10^3$)¶	42	52	60	69	76	76
Insecticides (pounds)#	0	0.10	0.30	0.70	1.00	1.00
Herbicides (pounds)**	0	0.05	0.10	0.25	0.38	1.00
Drying (kcal $\times 10^3$)††	4	14	30	66	100	120
Electricity (kcal $\times 10^3$)‡‡	32	54	100	140	203	310
Transportation (kcal $\times 10^3$)§§	20	30	45	60	70	70
Corn yields (bushels per acre)‖‖	34	38	41	54	68	81

* Mean hours of labor per crop acre in United States (6, 25). † An estimate of the energy inputs for the construction and repair of tractors, trucks, and other farm machinery was obtained from the data of Berry and Fels (63), who calculated that about 31,968,000 kcal of energy was necessary to construct an average automobile weighing about 3400 pounds. In our calculations we assumed that 244,555,000 kcal (an equivalent of 13 tons of machinery) were used for the production of all machinery (tractors, trucks, and miscellaneous) to farm 62 acres of corn. This machinery was assumed to function for 10 years. Repairs were assumed to be 6 percent of total machinery production or about 15,000,000 kcal. Hence, a conservative estimate for the production and repair of farm machinery per corn acre per year for 1970 was 420,000 kcal. A high for the number of tractors and other farm machinery on farms was reached in 1964 and continues (64, 65). The number of tractors and other types of machinery in 1945 were about half what they are now. ‡ DeGraff and Washbon (66) reported that corn production required about 15 gallons of fuel per acre for tractor use—intermediate between fruit and small grain production. Because corn appeared to be intermediate, the estimated mean fuel (gallons) burned in farm machinery per harvested acre was based on U.S. Department of Agriculture (22, 64) and U.S. Bureau of Census (65) data. § Fertilizers (N, P, K) applied to corn are based on USDA (25, 26, 61, 62) estimates. ‖ During 1970, relatively dense corn planting required about one-third of a bushel of corn (25,000 kernels or 34,000 kcal) per acre; the less dense plantings in 1945 were estimated to use about one-sixth of a bushel of seed. Because hybrid seed has to be produced with special care, the input for 1970 was estimated to be 68,000 kcal. ¶ Only about 3.8 percent of the corn grain acres in the United States were irrigated in 1964 (67), and this is not expected to change much in the near future (68). Although a small percentage, irrigation is costly in terms of energy demand. On the basis of the data of Smerdon (69), an estimated 1,992,375 kcal is required to irrigate an acre of corn with an acre-foot of water for one season. Higher energy costs for irrigation water are given by The Report on the World Food Problem (2). Since only 3.8 percent of the corn acres are irrigated (1964–1970), it was estimated that only 76,000 kcal were used per acre for corn irrigation. The percentage of acres irrigated in 1945 was based on trends in irrigated acres in agriculture (55, 67) # Estimates of herbicides applied per acre of corn are based on the fact that little or no insecticide was used on corn in 1945, and this reached a high in 1964 (28, 51). ** Estimates of herbicides applied per acre of corn are based on the fact that little or no herbicides were used on corn in 1945 and that this use continues to increase (28, 51). †† When it is dried for storage to reduce the moisture from about 26.5 percent to 13 percent, about 408,204 kcal are needed to dry 81 bushels (70). About 30 percent of the corn was estimated to have been dried in 1970 as compared to an estimated 10 percent in 1945. ‡‡ Agriculture consumed about 2.5 percent of all electricity produced in 1970 (24) and an estimated 424.2 trillion British thermal units of fossil fuel were used to produce this power (71); on croplands this divides to 310,000 kcal per acre for 1970 (6, 51). The fuel used to produce the electrical energy for earlier periods was estimated from data reported in Statistical Abstracts (72). §§ Estimates of the number of calories burned to transport machinery and supplies to corn acres and to transport corn to the site of use is based on data from U.S. Department of Commerce (73), U.S. Bureau of the Census (65, 67, 71), Interstate Commerce Commission (74), and U.S. Department of Transportation (75). For 1964 and 1970 this was estimated to be about 70,000 kcal per acre, it was about 20,000 kcal per acre in 1945. ‖‖ Corn yield is expressed as a mean of 3 years, 1 year previous and 1 year past (55, 59, 60).

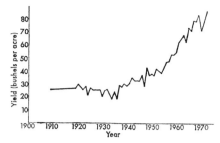

Fig. 1. Corn production (bushels per acre) in the United States from 1909 to 1971 (55, 59, 60).

Other inputs in corn production include seeds, irrigation, and pesticides (Table 1). The use of pesticides in corn has been increasing rapidly during the past 20 years and this parallels the general increase in pesticide use in the United States (27) (Table 1). About 41 percent of all herbicides and 17 percent of all insecticides used in agriculture are applied to corn (28).

Hybrid corn that is currently harvested has a higher moisture content because the newer varieties have growing seasons which extend further into the fall when drying conditions are poor (19). Moisture content above 13 percent (the maximum suitable for long-term storage) causes spoilage, and a drying process is used to reduce moisture (Table 1).

Agriculture consumed about 2.5 percent of all electricity produced (Table 1). The energy input for transportation is an important feature of modern intensive agriculture (Table 1). Machin-

ery, pesticides, seeds, gasoline, and other supplies must be transported to the farm. Then the corn harvest must be transported to the place of use for animal feed or processing.

To gain an idea of the changes occurring over a period of time in corn production energy inputs, the years 1945, 1950, 1954, 1959, 1964, and 1970 were selected for a detailed analysis (Tables 1 and 2). Exact 5-year intervals were not selected because more complete data were available on these specific years than on others.

In 1970 about 2.9 million kcal was used by farmers to raise an acre of corn (equivalent to 80 gallons of gasoline) (Table 2). From 1945 to 1970, mean corn yields increased from about 34 bushels per acre to 81 bushels per acre (2.4-fold); however, mean energy inputs increased from 0.9 million kcal to 2.9 million kcal (3.1-fold) (Table 2). Hence, the yield in corn calories decreased from about 3.3 kcal per one fuel kilocalorie input in 1945 to a yield of about 2.5 kcal from the period of 1954 to 1970, a 24 percent decrease.

The 2.9 million kcal input of fossil fuel represents a small portion of the energy input when compared with the solar energy input. During the growing season, about 2043 million kcal reaches a 1-acre cornfield; about 1.26 percent of this is converted into corn and about 0.4 percent in corn grain (at 100 bushels per acre) itself (29). The 1.26 percent represents about 26.6 million kcal. Hence, when solar energy input

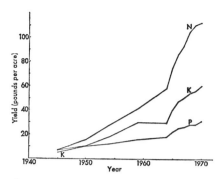

Fig. 2. Fertilizer (nitrogen, phosphorus, and potassium) applied per acre in corn production (25, 26, 61, 62).

is included, man's 2.9-million-kcal fossil fuel input represents about 11 percent of the total energy input in corn production. The important point is that the supply of solar energy is unlimited in time, whereas fossil fuel supply in finite.

The trends in energy inputs and corn yields confirm several agricultural evaluations which conclude that the impressive agricultural production in the United States has been gained through large inputs of fossil energy (8, 30).

Alternatives

Some alternatives may be needed to reduce energy inputs in agricultural food production when conventional energy resources become in short supply and costs soar. Some of the practical alternatives which might be employed

Table 2. Energy inputs in corn production (all figures in kilocalories).

Input	1945	1950	1954	1959	1964	1970
Labor*	12,500	9,800	9,300	7,600	6,000	4,900
Machinery†	180,000	250,000	300,000	350,000	420,000	420,000
Fuel‡	543,400	615,800	688,300	724,500	760,700	797,000
Nitrogen§	56,000	120,000	216,000	328,000	464,000	896,000
Phosphorus‖	10,150	14,500	17,400	23,200	26,100	44,950
Potassium¶	5,000	10,000	18,000	36,000	41,000	60,000
Seeds for planting#	30,464	35,840	44,800	53,760	59,136	59,136
Irrigation†	42,000	52,000	60,000	69,000	76,000	76,000
Insecticides**	0	1,100	3,300	7,700	11,000	11,000
Herbicides††	0	600	1,100	2,800	4,200	11,000
Drying†	4,000	14,000	30,000	66,000	100,000	120,000
Electricity†	32,000	54,000	100,000	140,000	203,000	310,000
Transportation†	20,000	30,000	45,000	60,000	70,000	70,000
Total inputs	935,514	1,207,640	1,533,200	1,868,560	2,241,136	2,879,986
Corn yield (output) ‡‡	3,046,400	3,404,800	3,673,600	4,838,400	6,092,800	7,257,600
Kcal return/input kcal	3.26	2.82	2.40	2.59	2.72	2.52

* It is assumed that a farm laborer consumes 21,770 kcal per week and works a 40-hour week. For 1970: (9 hours/40 hours) × 21,770 kcal = 4,900 kcal. † See Table 1. ‡ Gasoline, 1 gallon = 36,225 kcal (76). § Nitrogen, 1 pound = 8,000 kcal, including production and processing (77). ‖ Phosphorus, 1 pound = 1,450 kcal, including mining and processing (77). ¶ Potassium, 1 pound = 1,000 kcal, including mining and processing (77). # Corn seed, 1 pound = 1,600 kcal (78). This energy input was doubled because of the effort employed in producing hybrid seed corn. ** Insecticides, 1 pound = 11,000 kcal including production and processing (similar to herbicide; see ††). †† Herbicides, 1 pound = 11,000 kcal including production and processing (31). ‡‡ Each pound of corn was assumed to contain 1,600 kcal (78) and a bushel of corn was considered to be 56 pounds.

in corn and other crop production are reviewed below.

The energy input from farm labor in corn production is the smallest of all inputs, only 4,900 kcal (Table 2). Increasing some labor inputs can significantly reduce some energy inputs. For example, one application of herbicide to corn requires about 18,000 kcal/acre if applied by tractor and sprayer (31) but less than 300 kcal if applied by hand sprayer. Although 1/60 as much energy is used, the labor cost of hand application today is about four times that of the tractor application. Hand application might become economically profitable when fuel costs increase and if herbicides are used in spot treatment only.

Machinery and gasoline comprise a large energy input in corn production (Table 2). A viable alternative for reducing this fuel use would be to use machinery precisely scaled for its job and operate it at efficient speeds (32). Some of the extremely large tractors and other machinery will do more work per unit time, but this efficiency is offset by greater fuel requirements during operation. In addition, increasing the number of acres tended by a tractor or other machinery (currently about 62 acres per tractor) would help reduce this input. Horses and mules are not satisfactory substitutes for machinery because of the large quantity of energy they consume in feed (33).

The single largest input in corn production is fertilizer; nitrogen requires the largest quantity of energy to produce (Tables 1 and 2). A potential fertilizer source is the small percentage of livestock manure that is not now being used in crop production.

We mentioned that chemical fertilizer is applied to corn at a rate of 112 pounds of nitrogen, 31 pounds of phosphorus, and 60 pounds of potassium (Table 1). A like amount of nitrogen is available from manure produced during one year by either 1 dairy cow, 2 young fattening beef cattle, 9 hogs, or 84 chickens (34). In addition to the nutrients manure adds to the soil, it adds organic matter which increases the number of beneficial bacteria and fungi in the soil, makes plowing easier, improves the water-holding and percolation capacity of soil, reduces soil erosion, and improves the ratio of carbon to nitrogen in the soil (35).

The major costs of using manure for crop production are hauling and spreading. Hauling and spreading manure

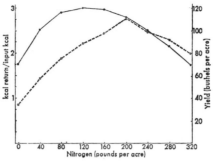

Fig. 3. Corn yields (bushels per acre, dashed line) with varying amounts of nitrogen (phosphorus = 34 pounds per acre) applied per acre (45). The kilocalorie return per kilocalorie of input (solid line) was calculated from the data of Munson and Doll (45) and from the 1970 input data in Tables 1 and 2.

within a radius of ½ to 1 mile (1 mile = 1.6 kilometers) is estimated to require 1.1 gallons of gasoline per ton [calculated from data of Linton (36)]. If the average manure application is 10 tons (production by 1 cow for 1 year) per acre, an estimated 398,475 kcal (11 gallons of gasoline) per acre is necessary to apply the manure and hence to fertilize corn with manure. Producing chemical fertilizer (112 pounds of nitrogen, 31 pounds of phosphorus, 60 pounds of potassium) for 1 acre requires a total of 1,000,950 kcal (Table 2). One gallon of gasoline is used for tractor application, therefore a total of 1,037,175 kcal for chemical fertilizer application is used. Hence, if manure were substituted for chemical fertilizer, the savings in energy would be a substantial 600,000 kcal per acre.

Current U.S. livestock manure production is estimated to be 1.7 billion tons per year, over 50 percent of which is produced in feedlots and confinement rearing situations (37). If 20 percent of the manure produced in feedlots and confinement rearing situations (0.17 billion tons) were available for use in corn production, 17.0 million acres of corn could be fertilized at an average manure application rate of 10 tons per acre. The above acreage would be 30 percent of the 1970 harvested grain corn acreage (38). In addition to saving valuable fuel energy, applying this manure to crop land would effectively recycle these animal wastes (39).

If some of the livestock manure from feedlots and confinement rearing situations is to be used, then these livestock production facilities would have to be moved closer to cropland where the

manure is to be used. Redistributing livestock facilities would itself require a careful analysis of associated costs.

Nitrogen fertilizer inputs can also be reduced by planting legumes or other alternate crops in rotation with corn. For example, planting sweet clover in the fall and plowing it under 1 year later will add about 150 pounds of nitrogen per acre to the soil (40). Rotating corn with a legume would also effectively control the corn rootworm (41), would reduce corn disease problems (42), and would reduce weed problems (43).

When rotations are not feasible, it is possible to plant legumes between corn rows in late August and to plow this green manure under in early spring. In the northeast, Sprague (44) reports that seeding corn acreage to winter vetch in late August and plowing the vetch under in late April yielded about 133 pounds of nitrogen per acre. A cover crop also protects the soil from wind and water erosion during the winter and has the same advantages as manure in adding organic matter to the soil.

The energy cost of seeding a legume, we estimate, would require about 90,000 kcal/acre (fuel and seeds). For the commercial production of 133 pounds of nitrogen, 1.06 million kcal are needed; thus the energy saved by planting a legume for green manure would be substantial or 970,000 kcal/acre. Hence, green manure offers a greater saving than livestock manure.

With fertilizer and other alternative inputs, a measure should be made to determine the maximum benefit per input in combination with all other inputs. In an investigation of fertilizer inputs in Iowa, Munson and Doll (45) reported that with 34 pounds of phosphorus per acre and 200 pounds of nitrogen per acre, they calculated mean corn yields of about 101 bushels per acre with all other inputs held constant (Fig. 3). Combining most of the 1970 energy input data from Tables 1 and 2 with the nitrogen, phosphorus, and corn yield data of Munson and Doll, we calculated the kilocalorie return per kilocalories input (Fig. 3). Maximum return was 3.0 kcal for 1 kcal input at 120 pounds of nitrogen per acre. A return of 2.5 for 1 was estimated for 1970 with the use of 112 pounds of nitrogen and 31 pounds of phosphorus per acre (Table 2). On the basis of only nitrogen inputs combined with the other inputs listed for 1970, it would appear that 112 pounds of nitrogen per acre provide nearly a maximum kilocalorie return per input kilocalorie.

Weeds can be controlled effectively and economically by either mechanical cultivation, herbicides, or a combination (46). On the basis of the energy expenditure, herbicidal weed control requires more energy than mechanical cultivation. For example, using 2 pounds of preemergence and 2 pounds of postemergence herbicides per acre requires a total energy input of about 80,225 kcal/acre (11,000 kcal per pound of herbicide plus 1 gallon of gasoline for two applications) (31). The use of three cultivations (rotary hoe twice) would require an estimated 2 gallons of gasoline or 72,450 kcal/acre. Although the saving is not as large as some, alternatives do exist for reducing energy inputs for weed control. With postemergence herbicides under certain conditions, it might be possible to spot-treat and therefore reduce the total quantity of herbicide used. To be done effectively, more labor would be necessary. In general, today's high labor and low energy costs would prohibit this, but with high energy costs, spot treatments could become economically feasible.

Rotating corn with other crops such as legumes and small grains may significantly reduce weed problems (47) and, therefore, reduce energy inputs for weed control.

Minimum tillage may also offer some opportunity to reduce energy inputs in plowing and disking, but this must be balanced against increased pest problems. A more complete analysis would be necessary to determine the precise costs and benefits of this alternative.

The protein content of corn has changed little since 1910, averaging about 9 percent (48, 49). However, the protein content of corn could be increased by selection to 12 to 15 percent (50). The value of increasing the quantity of protein in corn by even 1 percent is clear when it is calculated that this would reduce the need for 2 million tons of soybean meal in U.S. mixed feeds (48). Some increased energy inputs, such as nitrogen, would be necessary for cultivars of high protein corn, but the benefits would more than offset the costs.

Breeding corn for insect, disease, and bird resistance would in itself reduce the energy inputs of pesticides. At the same time this would reduce problems from pesticide pollution. Also, less energy would be needed for corn production if new corn varieties could be developed for faster maturity, reduced moisture content, greater water efficiency, and improved fertilizer response.

While only a small percentage (3.8 percent) of corn acres is irrigated, transporting water is an operation that demands lots of energy. The only alternative to reduce irrigation costs is to raise corn in regions where irrigation is seldom necessary. In the future, high energy costs may automatically reduce the percentage of corn acres irrigated.

The energy input for transportation of equipment and supplies to and from the farm is considerable. A real opportunity to reduce this input would be to move more of the materials and goods by train than by truck, because trains are significantly more efficient for transport (8).

Most of the alternatives mentioned would probably not fit easily into current corn management programs; however, when energy becomes costly, some or all of the alternatives may become practical and necessary. Furthermore, it should be emphasized that in some cases the partial use of one or more alternatives may prove to be the most economical procedure. By employing combinations of several of these alternatives, we estimate that it would be possible to reduce energy inputs by about a half and still maintain present yields. The economic feasibility of this depends of course upon many factors—including future energy costs.

World Food Supply

The shortages of food supplies in some nations (2) have prompted the United States to develop various international agricultural programs to aid in the "green revolution." Green revolution agricultural technology requires high energy inputs especially in fertilizers, pesticides, and hybrid seeds. Obviously, as energy shortages occur and costs increase, the success of the green revolution will be affected. For this reason, the problems of food production and energy demand on a worldwide basis are briefly examined.

In estimating the fuel energy needs to feed 4 billion humans, modern crop production technology similar to U.S. and green revolution agriculture is assumed. Energy data on U.S. corn will be used since it approximates average inputs and outputs in modern crop production. Our analysis indicated that about 2.9 million kilocalories of energy was used to raise an acre of corn in 1970—the equivalent of 80 gallons (1.9 barrels) of gasoline per acre (Table 2).

An estimated 330 million acres were planted in crops in 1970 (excluding cotton and tobacco) (6, 51). With about 200 million people in the United States, this averages about 1.7 acres per capita; but since about 20 percent of our crops is exported, the estimated acreage is about 1.4 acres per capita. In terms of fuel per person for food, employing modern intensive agriculture, this is the equivalent of 112 gallons of gasoline per person (80 gallons per acre × 1.4 acres per person = 112 gallons). Including the energy for food processing, distribution, and preparation, the total is estimated to be an equivalent of about 336 gallons of gasoline equivalents. Using U.S. food system and technology to feed a world population of 4 billion on an average U.S. diet for 1 year would require the energy equivalents of 1,464 billion gallons of fuel.

To gain some idea about what the energy needs would be for different diets if U.S. agricultural technology were employed, an estimate is made of how long it would take to deplete the known and potential world reserves of petroleum. The known reserves have been estimated to be 546 billion barrels (52). If we assume that 76 percent of raw petroleum can be converted into fuel (52), this would equal a usable reserve of 415 billion barrels. If petroleum were the only source of energy and if we used all petroleum reserves solely to feed the world population, the 415-billion-barrel reserve would last a mere 12 years [[(415 billion barrels)/(1,464 billion gallons/42 gallons per barrel) = 12 years]. The estimate would be 57 years if all potential reserves (2,000 billion barrels) (53) of petroleum were used for food production. However, if the world population were willing to eat nothing but corn grain, potential petroleum reserves could feed a projected 10 billion humans for about 300 years.

Contrary to popular belief, U.S. food production costs are high (54). Although only 16.6 percent of a person's total disposable mean income of $3595 in the United States was spent for food in 1970 (5, 23), the percentage is small only because U.S. per capita earnings are high. The 16.6 percent of U.S. per capita income of $3595 for food is $597. Since a third of food retail prices is production costs (55), it costs about $199 to produce $597 worth of food or 3110 kcal per person per day per year [including 66 g of animal protein and 18 g of animal fat (2, (56)]. This is the equivalent of 5280 plant kcal per person per day per year (assuming that 7 kcal of plant product is needed to produce 1 kcal of animal protein and fat with 1 g of animal protein = 4 kcal and 1 g of fat = 9 kcal). Thus, the cost of 1000 kcal of plant product is about $38.

In India about 77 percent of a person's income is spent for food with expenditures per capita averaging about $23 (includes marketing costs) per year (2). The calorie intake per person per day averages 2000 kcal, with animal protein being about 7 g per day and animal fats assumed to be 2 g (2). This is the equivalent of 2280 plant kcal per person per day per year. Thus the cost for 1000 plant kcal is about $10. Hence, the cost of producing 1000 plant kcal per day per year in India is significantly less than the $38 costs in the United States. This is in part due to the difference between nations in the plant crops used for food.

Conclusions

The principal raw material of modern U.S. agriculture is fossil fuel, whereas the labor input is relatively small (about 9 hours per crop acre). As agriculture is dependent upon fossil energy, crop production costs will also soar when fuel costs increase two- to fivefold. A return of 2.5 kcal of corn per 1 kcal of fuel input may then be uneconomical.

Green revolution agriculture also uses high energy crop production technology, especially with respect to fertilizers and pesticides. While one may not doubt the sincerity of the U.S. effort to share its agricultural technology so that the rest of the world can live and eat as it does, one must be realistic about the resources available to accomplish this mission. In the United States we are currently using an equivalent of 80 gallons of gasoline to produce an acre of corn. With fuel shortages and high prices to come, we wonder if many developing nations will be able to afford the technology of U.S. agriculture.

Problems have already occurred with green revolution crops, particularly problems related to pests (57). More critical problems are expected when there is a world energy crisis. A careful assessment should be made of the benefits, costs, and risks of high energy-demand green revolution agriculture in order to be certain that this program will not aggravate the already serious world food situation (58).

To reduce energy inputs, green revolution and U.S. agriculture might employ such alternatives as rotations and green manures to reduce the high energy demand of chemical fertilizers and pesticides. U.S. agriculture might also reduce energy expenditures by substituting some manpower currently displaced by mechanization.

While no one knows for certain what changes will have to be made, we can be sure that when conventional energy resources become scarce and expensive, the impact on agriculture as an industry and a way of life will be significant. This analysis is but a preliminary investigation of a significant agricultural problem that deserves careful attention and greater study before the energy situation becomes more critical.

References and Notes

1. National Academy of Sciences, *Rapid Population Growth*, I–II (Johns Hopkins Press, Baltimore, 1971).
2. President's Science Advisory Committee, *Report of the Panel on the World Food Supply*, I–III (The White House, Washington, D.C., 1967).
3. A. L. Hammond, *Science* **177**, 875 (1972).
4. P. H. Abelson, *ibid.* **178**, 355 (1972).
5. U.S. Department of Agriculture, *Misc. Publ.* No. 1063 (1972).
6. ———, *Stat. Bull.* No. 233 (1972).
7. T. L. Smith, *International Labour Review* **102**, 149 (1970).
8. L. Rocks and R. P. Runyon, *The Energy Crisis* (Crown, New York, 1972), pp. 12 and 131.
9. G. V. Day, *Futures* **4**, 331 (1972).
10. M. Slesser, *Report to Program on Policies for Science and Technology in Developing Nations* (Univ. of Strathclyde, Glasgow, 1972).
11. E. Cook, *Sci. Am.* **225**, 135 (1971).
12. J. Darmstadter, P. D. Teitelbaum, J. G. Polach, *Energy in the World Economy* (Johns Hopkins Press, Baltimore, 1971).
13. P. E. Glaser, *Science* **162**, 857 (1968).
14. K. L. Robinson, personal communication.
15. Food and Agriculture Organization of the United Nations, *Production Yearbook* **25**, 35 (1972).
16. ———, *Monthly Bull. Agr. Econ. Stat.* No. 20 (1971).
17. C. V. Griliches, *Econometrica* **25**, 501 (1957).
18. R. W. Allard, *Principles of Plant Breeding* (Wiley, New York, 1960), p. 265.
19. S. R. Aldrich and E. R. Leng, "Modern corn production," *Farm Quarterly* (1966), p. 296 and figure 150.
20. C. Grogan, personal communication.
21. H. L. Everett, personal communication.
22. U.S Department of Agriculture, *Stat. Bull.* No. 344 (1964).
23. U.S. Department of Commerce, *Survey of Current Business* **52**, table 10 (1972).
24. *Committee on Agriculture, House of Representatives* (92nd Congress, 1971), p. 20.
25. U.S. Department of Agriculture, *Changes in*

Farm Production and Efficiency (Agricultural Research Service, Washington D.C., 1954).
26. ———, *Fertilizer Situation* (Economics Research Service, FS-1, 1971).
27. ———, *The Pesticide Review 1970* (Agricultural Stabilization and Conservation Service, Washington, D.C., 1971).
28. ———, *Agricultural Economics Report* No. 179 (Economics Research Service, 1970).
29. E. N. Transeau, *Ohio J. Sci.* **26**, 1 (1926).
30. P. Handler, *Biology and the Future of Man* (Oxford Univ. Press, New York, 1970), p. 462; H. T. Odum, *Environment, Power, and Society* (Wiley, New York, 1971), p. 115; R. A. Rappaport, *Sci. Am.* **225**, 117 (1971); G. Borgström, *Hungry Planet* (Macmillan, New York, 1972), p. 513; K. E. F. Watt, *Principles of Environmental Science* (McGraw-Hill, New York, 1973), p. 216.
31. D. Pimentel, H. Mooney, L. Stickel, *Panel Report for Environmental Protection Agency*, in preparation.
32. W. H. Johnson and B. J. Lamp, *Principles, Equipment, and Systems for Corn Harvesting* (Agricultural Consulting Associates, Inc., Wooster, 1966), p. 95.
33. F. B. Morrison, *Feeds and Feeding* (Morrison, Ithaca, N.Y., 1946), pp. 50 and 429.
34. E. J. Benne, C. R. Hoglund, E. D. Longnecker, R. L. Cook, *Mich. Agr. Exp. Sta. Cir. Bull.* No. 231 (1961); R. S. Dyal, *National Symposium on Poultry Industry Waste Management* (Nebraska Center for Continuing Education, Lincoln, 1963); R. C. Loehr and M. Asce, *J. San. Eng. Division* 2 (1969), p. 189; L. W. McEachron, P. J. Zwerman, C. D. Kearl, R. B. Musgrave, *Animal Waste Management* (College of Agriculture, Cornell University, Ithaca, N.Y., 1969), pp. 393–400; T. C. Surbrook, C. C. Sheppard, J. S. Boyd, H. C. Zindel, C. J. Flegal, *Proc. Int. Symp. Livestock Wastes* (American Society of Agricultural Engineers, St. Joseph, Mo., 1971), p. 193.
35. N. B. Andrews, *The Response of Crops and Soils to Fertilizers and Manures* (Mississippi State University, State College, ed. 2, 1954); R. I. Cook, *Soil Management for Conservation and Production* (Wiley, New York, 1962), pp. 46–61; S. L. Tisdale and W. L. Nelson, *Soil Fertility and Fertilizers* (Macmillan, New York, 1966).
36. R. E. Linton, *Cornell Ext. Bull.* No. 1195 (1968).
37. J. R. Miner, *Iowa Agr. Exp. Sta. Spec. Rep.* No. 67 (1971).
38. U.S. Department of Agriculture, *Crop Production* (Crop Report Board, Washington, D.C., 1970).
39. President's Science Advisory Committee, *Report of the Environmental Pollution Panel* (White House, Washington, D.C., 1965), p. 172.
40. C. J. Willard, *Ohio Agr. Exp. Sta. Bull.* No. 405 (1927).
41. H. D. Tate and O. S. Bare, *Nebr. Agr. Exp. Sta. Bull.* No. 381 (1946); pp. 1–12; R. E. Hill, E. Hixon, M. H. Muma, *J. Econ. Entomol.* **41**, 392 (1948); C. L. Metcalf, W. P. Flint, R. L. Metcalf, *Destructive and Useful Insects* (McGraw-Hill, New York, 1962), p. 510; E. E. Ortman and P. J. Fitzgerald, *Proc. Ann. Hybrid Corn Ind. Res. Conf.* **19**, 38 (1964); R. E. Robinson, *Agron. J.* **58**, 475 (1966).
42. L. C. Pearson, *Principles of Agronomy* (Reinhold, New York, 1967), pp. 73–84.
43. National Academy of Sciences, *Principles of Plant and Animal Pest Control* II, Publication 1597 (National Academy of Sciences, Washington, D.C., 1968), pp. 256–257.
44. H. B. Sprague, *N.J. Agr. Exp. Sta. Bull.* **609**, 1 (1936).
45. R. D. Munson and J. P. Doll, *Advan. Agr.* **11**, 133 (1959).
46. J. S. Drew and R. N. Van Arsdall, *Ill. Agr. Econ.* **6**, 25 (1966); D. L. Armstrong, J. K. Leasure, M. R. Corbin, *Weed Sci.* **16**, 369 (1968); F. W. Slife, personal communication.
47. R. J. Delroit and H. L. Ahlgren, *Crop Production* (Prentice-Hall, Englewood Cliffs, N.J., 1953), pp. 572–573; P. W. Michael, *Herbage Abst.* **39**, 59 (1969).
48. G. F. Sprague, *Corn and Corn Improvement* (Academic Press, New York, 1955), pp. 643 and 663.
49. National Academy of Sciences, *National Research Council Publication* No. 1232 (Na-

tional Academy of Sciences, Washington, D.C., 1964), pp. 77–89; *ibid.*, No. 1684 (1969), pp. 38–45.
50. D. D. Harpstead, *Sci. Am.* **225**, 34 (1971).
51. U.S. Department of Agriculture, *Agr. Econ. Rep.* No. 147 (1968).
52. H. Jiler, *Commodity Yearbook* (Commodity Research Bureau, Inc, New York, 1972), pp. 252–253.
53. National Academy of Sciences, *Resources and Man* (Freeman, San Francisco, 1969), p. 143.
54. G. Borgström, *Principles of Food Science* (Macmillan, New York, 1968), vol. 2, p. 376.
55. U.S. Department of Agriculture, *Agricultural Statistics 1970* (Government Printing Office, Washington, D.C., 1970), pp. 28 and 430.
56. ———, *Fats and Oils Situation* (Economics Research Service, FOS-257, Washington, D.C., 1971).
57. G. R. Conway, *Environment, Resources, Pollution, and Society* (Sineurer Associates, Inc., Stamford, 1971), pp. 302–325; S. Pradhan, *World Sci. News* **8**, 41 (1971).
58. J. N. Black, *Ann. Appl. Biol.* **67**, 272 (1971).
59. U.S. Department of Agriculture, *Agricultural Statistics 1967* (Government Printing Office, Washington, D.C., 1967), pp. 34–35.
60. ———, *Crop Production, 1971 Annual Summary* (State Report Service, 1972).
61. ———, *Agr. Res. Ser. Stat. Bull.* No. 216 (1957).
62. ———, *Stat. Rep. Serv. Bull.* No. 408 (1967).
63. R. S. Berry and M. F. Fels, *The Production and Consumption of Automobiles. An Energy Analysis of the Manufacture, Discard, and Reuse of the Automobile and its Component Materials* (Univ. of Chicago, Chicago, 1973).
64. U.S. Department of Agriculture, *Bur. Agron. Econ. Bull.* No. FM 101 (1953).
65. U.S. Bureau of the Census, *Statistical Ab-stract of the U.S., 93rd Edition* (Government Printing Office, Washington, D.C., 1972), pp. 600–601.
66. H. F. DeGraff and W. E. Washbon, *Agr. Econ.* No. 449 (1943).
67. U.S. Bureau of the Census, *Census of Agriculture 1964 II* (1968), pp. 909–955.
68. E. O. Heady, H. C. Madsen, K. J. Nicol, S. H. Hargrove, *Report of the Center for Agriculture and Rural Development*, prepared at Iowa State University, for the National Water Commission, (National Technical Information Service, Springfield, Va., 1972).
69. E. T. Snerdon, "Energy conservation practices in irrigated agriculture," Sprinker Irrigation Association Annual Technical Conference, Denver, Colo., 24 February 1974.
70. *Corn Grower's Guide* (W. R. Grace and Co., Aurora, Ill., 1968), p. 113.
71. U.S. Bureau of the Census, *Statistical Abstract for the United States, 92nd Edition* (Government Printing Office, Washington, D.C., 1971), p. 496.
72. ———, *Statistical Abstract of the United States 86th Edition* (Government Printing Office, Washington, D.C., 1965), p. 538.
73. U.S. Department of Commerce, *Census of Transportation*, III (3) (Government Printing Office, Washington, D.C., 1967), pp. 102–105.
74. Interstate Commerce Commission, *Freight Commodity Statistics, Class I Motor Carriers of Property in Intercity* (Government Printing Office, Washington, D.C., 1968), p. 97; ———, *Freight and Commodity Statistics Class I Railroads* (Government Printing Office, Washington, D.C., 1968); ———, *Transportation Statistics*, I, V, VII (Government Printing Office, Washington, D.C., 1968).
75. U.S. Department of Transportation, *Highway Statistics* (Government Printing Office, Washington, D.C., 1970), p. 5.
76. *Handbook of Chemistry and Physics* (Chemical Rubber Company, Cleveland, 1972), Table D-230.
77. G. Leach and M. Slesser, *Energy Equivalents of Network Inputs to Food Producing Processes* (Univ. of Strathclyde, Glasgow, 1973).
78. U.S. Department of Agriculture, *Composition of Foods,* Agriculture Handbook No. 8 (Consumer and Food Economics Research Division, Agriculture Research Service, Washington, D.C., 1963).
79. We thank the following specialists for reading an earlier draft of the manuscript and for their many helpful suggestions: Georg Borgström, Department of Food Science and Geography, Michigan State University; Harrison Brown, Foreign Secretary, National Academy of Sciences; Gordon Harrison, Ford Foundation; Gerald Leach, Science Policy Research Unit, University of Sussex; Roger Revelle, Center for Population Studies, Harvard University; Malcolm Slesser, Department of Pure and Applied Chemistry, University of Strathclyde; and, at Cornell University: R. C. Loehr, Department of Agricultural Engineering; W. R. Lynn and C. A. Shoemaker, Department of Environmental Engineering; K. L. Robinson, Department of Agricultural Economics; C. O. Grogan, Department of Plant Breeding; R. S. Morison, Program of Science, Technology and Society; N. C. Brady and W. K. Kennedy, Department of Agronomy; and L. C. Cole and S. A. Levin, Section of Ecology and Systematics. Any errors or omissions are the authors' responsibility. Supported in part by grants from the Ford Foundation and NSF (GZ 1371 and GB 19239).

Energy Use in the U.S. Food System

John S. Steinhart and Carol E. Steinhart

In a modern industrial society, only a tiny fraction of the population is in frequent contact with the soil, and an even smaller fraction of the population raises food on the soil. The proportion of the population engaged in farming halved between 1920 and 1950 and then halved again by 1962. Now it has almost halved again, and more than half of these remaining farmers hold other jobs off the farm (1). At the same time the number of work animals has declined from a peak of more than 22×10^6 in 1920 to a very small number at present (2). By comparison with earlier times, fewer farmers are producing more agricultural products and the value of food in terms of the total goods and services of society now amounts to a smaller fraction of the economy than it once did.

Energy inputs to farming have increased enormously during the past 50 years (3), and the apparent decrease in farm labor is offset in part by the growth of support industries for the farmer. With these changes on the farm have come a variety of other changes in the U.S. food system, many of which are now deeply embedded in the fabric of daily life. In the past 50 years, canned, frozen, and other processed foods have become the principal items of our diet. At present, the food processing industry is the fourth largest energy consumer of the Standard Industrial Classification groupings (4). The extent of transportation engaged in the food system has grown apace, and the proliferation of appliances in both numbers and complexity still continues in homes, institutions, and stores. Hardly any food is eaten as it comes from the fields. Even farmers purchase most of their food from markets in town.

Present energy supply problems make this growth of energy use in the food system worth investigating. It is our pur-

pose in this article to do so. But there are larger matters at stake. Georgescu-Roegen notes that "the evidence now before us—of a world which can produce automobiles, television sets, etc., at a greater speed than the increase in population, but is simultaneously menaced by mass starvation—is disturbing" (5). In the search for a solution to the world's food problems, the common attempt to transplant a small piece of a highly industrialized food system to the hungry nations of the world is plausible enough, but so far the outcome is unclear. Perhaps an examination of the energy flow in the U.S. food system as it has developed can provide some insights that are not available from the usual economic measures.

Measures of Food Systems

Agricultural systems are most often described in economic terms. A wealth of statistics is collected in the United States and in most other technically advanced countries indicating production amounts, shipments, income, labor, expenses, and dollar flow in the agricultural sector of the economy. But, when we wish to know something about the food we actually eat, the statistics of farms are only a tiny fraction of the story.

Energy flow is another measure available to gauge societies and nations. It would have made no sense to measure societies in terms of energy flow in the 18th century when economics began. As recently as 1940, four-fifths of the world's population were still on farms and in small villages, most of them engaged in subsistence farming.

Only after some nations shifted large portions of the population to manufacturing, specialized tasks, and mechanized food production, and shifted the prime sources of energy to move society to fuels that were transportable and usable for a wide variety of alternative activities, could energy flow be used as a measure of societies' activities. Today

it is only in one-fifth of the world where these conditions are far advanced. Yet we can now make comparisons of energy flows even with primitive societies. For even if the primitives, or the euphemistically named "underdeveloped" countries, cannot shift freely among their energy expenditures, we *can* measure them and they constitute a different and potentially useful comparison with the now traditional economic measures.

What we would like to know is: How does our present food supply system compare, in energy measures, with those of other societies and with our own past? Perhaps then we can estimate the value of energy flow measures as an adjunct to, but different from, economic measures.

Energy in the U.S. Food System

A typical breakfast includes orange juice from Florida by way of the Minute Maid factory, bacon from a midwestern meat packer, cereal from Nebraska and General Mills, eggs and milk from not *too* far away, and coffee from Colombia. All of these things are available at the local supermarket (several miles each way in a 300-horsepower automobile), stored in a refrigerator-freezer, and cooked on an instant-on stove.

The present food system in the United States is complex, and the attempt to analyze it in terms of energy use will introduce complexities and questions far more perplexing than the same analysis carried out on simpler societies. Such an analysis is worthwhile, however, if only to find out where we stand. We have a food system, and most people get enough to eat from it. If, in addition, one considers the food supply problems present and future in societies where a smaller fraction of the people get enough to eat, then our experience with an industrialized food system is even more important. There is simply no gainsaying that many nations of the world are presently attempting to acquire industrialized food systems of their own.

Food in the United States is expensive by world standards. In 1970 the average annual per capita expenditure for food was about $600 (3). This amount is larger than the per capita gross domestic product of more than 30 nations of the world which contain the majority of the world's people and a vast majority of those who are under-

Dr. J. S. Steinhart is professor of geology and geophysics, and professor in the Institute for Environmental Studies, University of Wisconsin-Madison. Dr. C. E. Steinhart, formerly a biologist with the National Institutes of Health, is now a science writer and editor.

fed. Even if we consider the diet of a poor resident of India, the annual cost of his food at U.S. prices would be about $200—more than twice his annual income (3). It is crucial to know whether a piece of our industrialized food system can be exported to help poor nations, or whether they must become as industrialized as the United States to operate an industrialized food system.

Our analysis of energy use in the food system begins with an omission. We will neglect that crucial input of energy provided by the sun to the plants upon which the entire food supply depends. Photosynthesis has an efficiency of about 1 percent; thus the maximum solar radiation captured by plants is about 5×10^3 kilocalories per square meter per year (3).

Seven categories of energy use on the farm are considered here. The amounts of energy used are shown in Table 1. The values given for farm machinery and tractors are for the manufacture of new units only and do not include parts and maintenance for units that already exist. The amounts shown for direct fuel use and electricity consumption are a bit too high because they include some residential uses of the farmer and his family. On the other hand, some uses in these categories are not reported in the summaries used to obtain the values for direct fuel and electricity usage. These and similar problems are discussed in the references. Note the relatively high energy cost associated with irrigation. In the United States less than 5 percent of the cropland is irrigated (1). In some countries where the "green revolution" is being attempted, the new high-yield varieties of plants require irrigation where native crops did not. If that were the case in the United States, irrigation would be the largest single use of energy on the farm.

Little food makes its way directly from field and farm to the table. The vast complex of processing, packaging, and transport has been grouped together in a second major subdivision of the food system. The seven categories of the processing industry are listed in Table 1. Energy use for the transport of food should be charged to the farm in part, but we have not done so here because the calculation of the energy values is easiest (and we believe most accurate) if they are taken for the whole system.

After the processing of food there is

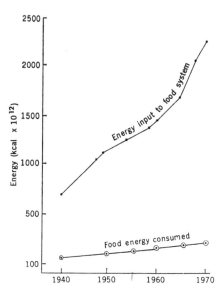

Fig. 1. Energy use in the food system, 1940 through 1970, compared to the caloric content of food consumed.

further energy expenditure. Transportation enters the picture again, and some fraction of the energy used for transportation should be assigned here. But there are also the distributors, wholesalers, and retailers, whose freezers, refrigerators, and very establishments are an integral part of the food system. There are also the restaurants, schools, universities, prisons, and a host of other institutions engaged in the procurement, preparation, storage, and supply of food. We have chosen to examine only three categories: the energy required for refrigeration and cooking, and for the manufacture of the heating and refrigeration equipment (Table 1). We have made no attempt to include the energy used in trips to the store or restaurant. Garbage disposal has also been omitted, although it is a persistent and growing feature of our food system; 12 percent of the nation's trucks are engaged in the activity of waste disposal (1), of which a substantial part is related to food. If there is any lingering doubt that these activities—both the ones included and the ones left out—are an essential feature of our present food system, one need only ask what would happen if everyone should attempt to get on without a refrigerator or freezer or stove? Certainly the food system would change.

Table 1 and the related references summarize the numerical values for energy use in the U.S. food system, from 1940 to 1970. As for many activities in the past few decades, the story is one of continuing increase. The totals are displayed in Fig. 1 along with the energy value of the food consumed by the public. The food values were obtained by multiplying the daily caloric intake by the population. The differences in caloric intake per capita over this 30-year period are small (1), and the curve is primarily an indication of the increase in population in this period.

Omissions and Duplications for Food System Energy Values

Several omissions, duplications, and overlaps have been mentioned. We will now examine the values in Table 1 for completeness and try to obtain a crude estimate of their numerical accuracy.

The direct fuel and electricity usage on the farm may be overstated by some amounts used in the farmer's household, which, by our approach, would not all be chargeable to the food system. But about 10 percent of the total acreage farmed is held by corporate farms for which the electrical and direct fuel use is not included in our data. Other estimates of these two categories are much higher [see Table 1 (15, 16)].

No allowance has been made for food exported, which has the effect of overstating the energy used in our own food system. For the years prior to 1960 the United States was at times a net importer of food, at times an exporter, and at times there was a near balance in this activity. But during this period the net flow of trade was never more than a few percent of the total farm output. Since 1960 net exports have increased to about 20 percent of the gross farm product (1, 3). The items comprising the vast majority of the exports have been rough grains, flour, and other plant products with very little processing. Imports include more processed food than exports and represent energy expenditure outside the United States. Thus the overestimate of energy input to the food system might be 5 percent with an upper limit of 15 percent.

The items omitted are more numerous. Fuel losses from the wellhead or mineshaft to end use total 10 to 12 percent (6). This would represent a flat addition of 10 percent or more to the totals, but we have not included this item because it is not customarily charged to end uses.

We have computed transport energy

for trucks only. Considerable food is transported by train and ship, but these items were omitted because the energy use is small relative to the consumption of truck fuel. Small amounts of food are shipped by air, and, although air shipment is energy-intensive, the amount of energy consumed appears small. We have traced support materials until they could no longer be assigned to the food system. Some transportation energy consumption is not charged in the transport of these support materials. These omissions are numerous and hard to estimate, but they would not be likely to increase the totals by more than 1 or 2 percent.

A more serious understatement of energy usage occurs with respect to vehicle usage (other than freight transport) on farm business, food-related business in industry and commercial establishments, and in the supporting industries. A special attempt to estimate this category of energy usage for 1968 suggests that it amounts to about 5 percent of the energy totals for the food system. This estimate would be subject to an uncertainty of nearly 100 percent. We must be satisfied to suggest that 1 to 10 percent should be added to the totals on this account.

Waste disposal is related to the food system, at least in part. We have chosen not to charge this energy to the food system, but, if one-half of the

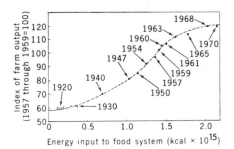

Fig. 2. Farm output as a function of energy input to the U.S. food system, 1920 through 1970.

waste disposal activity is taken as food-related, about 2 percent must be added to the food system energy totals.

We have not included energy for parts and maintenance of machinery, vehicles, buildings, and the like, or lumber for farm, industry, or packaging uses. These miscellaneous activities would not constitute a large addition in any case. We have also excluded construction. Building and replacement of farm structures, food industry structures, and commercial establishments are all directly part of the food system. Construction of roads is in some measure related to the food system, since nearly half of all trucks transport food and agricultural items [see Table 1 (27)]. Even home construction could be charged in part to the food system since space, appliances, and plumbing

are, in part, a consequence of the food system. If 10 percent of housing, 10 percent of institutional construction (for institutions with food service), and 10 percent of highway construction is included, about 10 percent of the total construction was food-related in 1970. Assuming that the total energy consumption divides in the same way that the Gross National Product does (which overstates energy use in construction), the addition to the total in Table 1 would be about 10 percent or 200×10^{12} kcal. This is a crude and highly simplified calculation, but it does provide an estimate of the amounts of energy involved.

The energy used to generate the highly specialized seed and animal stock has been excluded because there is no easy way to estimate it. Pimentel et al. (3) estimate that 1800 kcal are required to produce 1 pound (450 grams) of hybrid corn seed. But in addition to this amount, some energy use should be included for all the schools of agriculture, agricultural experiment stations, the far-flung network of county agricultural agents [one local agent said he traveled over 50,000 automobile miles (80,000 kilometers) per year in his car], the U.S. Department of Agriculture, and the wide-ranging agricultural research program that enables man to stay ahead of the new pest and disease threats to our highly specialized

Table 1. Energy use in the United States food system. All values are multiplied by 10^{12} kcal.

Component	1940	1947	1950	1954	1958	1960	1964	1968	1970	References
On farm										
Fuel (direct use)	70.0	136.0	158.0	172.8	179.0	188.0	213.9	226.0	232.0	(13–15)
Electricity	0.7	32.0	32.9	40.0	44.0	46.1	50.0	57.3	63.8	(14, 16)
Fertilizer	12.4	19.5	24.0	30.6	32.2	41.0	60.0	87.0	94.0	(14, 17)
Agricultural steel	1.6	2.0	2.7	2.5	2.0	1.7	2.5	2.4	2.0	(14, 18)
Farm machinery	9.0	34.7	30.0	29.5	50.2	52.0	60.0	75.0	80.0	(14, 19)
Tractors	12.8	25.0	30.8	23.6	16.4	11.8	20.0	20.5	19.3	(20)
Irrigation	18.0	22.8	25.0	29.6	32.5	33.3	34.1	34.8	35.0	(21)
Subtotal	124.5	272.0	303.4	328.6	356.3	373.9	440.5	503.0	526.1	
Processing industry										
Food processing industry	147.0	177.5	192.0	211.5	212.6	224.0	249.0	295.0	308.0	(13, 14, 22)
Food processing machinery	0.7	5.7	5.0	4.9	4.9	5.0	6.0	6.0	6.0	(23)
Paper packaging	8.5	14.8	17.0	20.0	26.0	28.0	31.0	35.7	38.0	(24)
Glass containers	14.0	25.7	26.0	27.0	30.2	31.0	34.0	41.9	47.0	(25)
Steel cans and aluminum	38.0	55.8	62.0	73.7	85.4	86.0	91.0	112.2	122.0	(26)
Transport (fuel)	49.6	86.1	102.0	122.3	140.2	153.3	184.0	226.6	246.9	(27)
Trucks and trailors (manufacture)	28.0	42.0	49.5	47.0	43.0	44.2	61.0	70.2	74.0	(28)
Subtotal	285.8	407.6	453.5	506.4	542.3	571.5	656.0	787.6	841.9	
Commercial and home										
Commercial refrigeration and cooking	121.0	141.0	150.0	161.0	176.0	186.2	209.0	241.0	263.0	(13, 29)
Refrigeration machinery (home and commercial)	10.0	24.0	25.0	27.5	29.4	32.0	40.0	56.0	61.0	(14, 30)
Home refrigeration and cooking	144.2	184.0	202.3	228.0	257.0	276.6	345.0	433.9	480.0	(13, 29)
Subtotal	275.2	349.0	377.3	416.5	462.4	494.8	594.0	730.9	804.0	
Grand total	685.5	1028.6	1134.2	1251.5	1361.0	1440.2	1690.5	2021.5	2172.0	

food crops. These are extensive activities but we cannot see how they could add more than a few percent to the totals in Table 1.

Finally, we have made no attempt to include the amount of private automobile usage involved in the delivery system from retailer to home, or other food-related uses of private autos. Rice (7) reports 4.25×10^{15} kcal for the energy cost of autos in 1970, and shopping constitutes 15.2 percent of all automobile usage (8). If only half of the shopping is food-related, 320×10^{12} kcal of energy use is at stake here. Between 8 and 15 percent should be added to the totals of Table 1, depending on just how one wishes to apportion this item.

It is hard to take an approach that might calculate smaller totals but, depending upon point of view, the totals could be much larger. If we accumulate the larger estimates from the above paragraphs as well as the reductions, the total could be enlarged by 30 to 35 percent, especially for recent years. As it is, the values for energy use in the food system from Table 1 account for 12.8 percent of the total U.S. energy use in 1970.

Performance of an Industrialized Food System

The difficulty with history as a guide for the future or even the present lies not so much in the fact that conditions change—we are continually reminded of that fact—but that history is only one experiment of the many that might have occurred. The U.S. food system developed as it did for a variety of reasons, many of them not understood. We would do well to examine some of the dimensions of this development before attempting to theorize about how it might have been different, or how parts of this food system can be transplanted elsewhere.

Energy and Food Production

Figure 2 displays features of our food system not easily seen from economic data. The curve shown has no theoretical basis but is suggested by the data as a smoothed recounting of our own history of increasing food production. It is, however, similar to most growth curves and suggests that, to the extent that the increasing energy

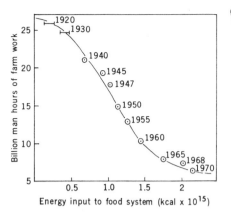

Fig. 3. Labor use on farms as a function of energy use in the food system.

subsidies to the food system have increased food production, we are near the end of an era. Like the logistic growth curve, there is an exponential phase which lasted from 1920 or earlier until 1950 or 1955. Since then, the increments in production have been smaller despite the continuing growth in energy use. It is likely that further increases in food production from increasing energy inputs will be harder and harder to come by. Of course, a major change in the food system could change things, but the argument advanced by the technological optimist is that we can always get more if we have enough energy, and that no other major changes are required. Our own history—the only one we have to examine—does not support that view.

Energy and Labor in the Food System

One farmer now feeds 50 people, and the common expectation is that the labor input to farming will continue to decrease in the future. Behind this expectation is the assumption that the continued application of technology—and energy—to farming will substitute for labor. Figure 3 shows this historic decline in labor as a function of the energy supplied to the food system, again the familiar S-shaped curve. What it implies is that increasing the energy input to the food system is unlikely to bring further reduction in farm labor unless some other, major change is made.

The food system that has grown in this period has provided much employment that did not exist 20, 30, or 40 years ago. Perhaps even the idea of a reduction of labor input is a myth when the food system is viewed as a whole,

instead of from the point of view of the farm worker only. When discussing inputs to the farm, Pimentel *et al.* (3) cite an estimate of two farm support workers for each person actually on the farm. To this must be added employment in food-processing industries, in food wholesaling and retailing, as well as in a variety of manufacturing enterprises that support the food system. Yesterday's farmer is today's canner, tractor mechanic, and fast food carhop. The process of change has been painful to many ordinary people. The rural poor, who could not quite compete in the growing industrialization of farming, migrated to the cities. Eventually they found other employment, but one must ask if the change was worthwhile. The answer to that question cannot be provided by energy analysis anymore than by economic data, because it raises fundamental questions about how individuals would prefer to spend their lives. But if there is a stark choice between long hours as a farmer or shorter hours on the assembly line of a meat-packing plant, it seems clear that the choice would not be universally in favor of the meat-packing plant. Thomas Jefferson dreamed of a nation of independent small farmers. It was a good dream, but society did not develop in that way. Nor can we turn back the clock to recover his dream. But, in planning and preparing for our future, we had better look honestly at our collective history, and then each of us should closely examine his dreams.

The Energy Subsidy to the Food System

The data in Fig. 1 can be combined to show the energy subsidy provided to the food system for the recent past. We take as a measure of the food supplied the caloric content of the food actually consumed. This is not the only measure of the food supplied, as the condition of many protein-poor peoples of the world clearly shows. Nevertheless, the comparison between caloric input and output is a convenient way to compare our present situation with the past, and to compare our food system with others. Figure 4 shows the history of the U.S. food system in terms of the number of calories of energy supplied to produce 1 calorie of food for actual consumption. It is interesting and possibly threatening to note that there is no real suggestion that this curve is leveling off. We appear to be increasing

Giant grain elevators are only a first step in the storage, processing, and distribution portions of the food system. [Source: Marine Studies Center, University of Wisconsin]

the energy input even more. Fragmentary data for 1972 suggest that the increase continued unabated. A graph like Fig. 4 could approach zero. A natural ecosystem has no fuel input at all, and those primitive people who live by hunting and gathering have only the energy of their own work to count as input.

Some Economic Features of the U.S. Food System

The markets for farm commodities in the United States come closer than most to the economist's ideal of a "free market." There are many small sellers and many buyers, and thus no individual is able to affect the price by his own actions in the marketplace. But government intervention can drastically alter any free market, and government intervention in the prices of agricultural products (and hence of food) has been a prominent feature of the U.S. food system for at least 30 years. Between 1940 and 1970, total farm income has ranged from $4.5 to $16.5 billion, and the National Income originating in agriculture (which includes indirect income from agriculture) has ranged from $14.5 to $22.5 billion (1). Meanwhile, government subsidy programs, primarily farm price supports and soil bank payments, have grown from $1.5 billion in 1940 to $6.2 billion in 1970. In 1972 these subsidy programs had grown to $7.3 billion, despite

foreign demand of agricultural products. Viewed in a slightly different way, direct government subsidies have accounted for 30 to 40 percent of the farm income and 15 to 30 percent of the National Income attributable to agriculture for the years since 1955. This point emphasizes once again the striking gap between the economic description of society and the economic models used to account for that society's behavior.

This excursion into farm price supports and economics is related to energy questions in this way: first, so far as we know, government intervention in the food system is a feature of all highly industrialized countries (and, despite the intervention, farm incomes still tend to lag behind national averages); and, second, reduction of the energy subsidy to agriculture (even if we could manage it) might decrease the farmer's income. One reason for this state of affairs is that the demand for food quantity has definite limits, and the only way to increase farm income is then to increase the unit price of agricultural products. Consumer boycotts and protests in the early 1970's suggest that there is considerable resistance to this outcome.

Government intervention in the functioning of the market in agricultural products has accompanied the rise in the use of energy in agriculture and the food supply system, and we have nothing but theoretical suppositions to suggest that any of the present system can be deleted.

Some Energy Implications for the World Food Supply

The food supply system of the United States is complex and interwoven into a highly industrialized economy. We have tried to analyze this system on account of its implications for future energy use. But the world is short of food. A few years ago it was widely predicted that the world would suffer widespread famine in the 1970's. The adoption of new high-yield varieties of rice, wheat, and other grains has caused some experts to predict that the threat of these expected famines can now be averted, perhaps indefinitely. Yet, despite increases in grain production in some areas, the world still seems to be headed toward famine. The adoption of these new varieties of grain—dubbed hopefully the "green revolution"—is an attempt to export a part of the energy-intensive food system of the highly industrialized countries to nonindustrialized countries. It is an experiment, because, although the whole food system is not being transplanted to new areas, a small part of it is. The green revolution requires a great deal of energy. Many of the new varieties of grain require irrigation where traditional crops did not, and almost all the new crops require extensive fertilization.

Meanwhile, the agricultural surpluses of the 1950's have largely disappeared. Grain shortages in China and Russia have attracted attention because they have brought foreign trade across ideological barriers. There are other countries that would probably import considerable grain, if they could afford it. But only four countries may be expected to have any substantial excess agricultural production in the next decade. These are Canada, New Zealand, Australia, and the United States. None of these is in a position to give grain away, because each of them needs the foreign trade to avert ruinous balance of payments deficits. Can we then export energy-intensive agricultural methods instead?

Energy-Intensive Agriculture Abroad

It is quite clear that the U.S. food system cannot be exported intact at present. For example, India has a population of 550×10^6 persons. To feed the people of India at the U.S. level of about 3000 food calories per day (instead of their present 2000) would require more energy than India now uses for all purposes. To feed the entire world with a U.S. type food system, almost 80 percent of the world's annual energy expenditure would be required just for the food system.

The recourse most often suggested to remedy this difficulty is to export methods of increasing crop yield and hope for the best. We must repeat as plainly as possible that this is an experiment. We know that our food system works (albeit with some difficulties and warnings for the future). But we cannot know what will happen if we take a piece of that system and transplant it to a poor country, without our industrial base of supply, transport system, processing industry, appliances for home storage, and preparation, and, most important of all, a level of industrialization that permits higher costs for food.

Fertilizers, herbicides, pesticides, and in many cases machinery and irrigation are needed for success with the green revolution. Where is this energy to come from? Many of the nations with the most serious food problems are those nations with scant supplies of fossil fuels. In the industrialized nations, solutions to the energy supply problems are being sought in nuclear energy. This technology-intensive solution, even if successful in advanced countries, poses additional problems for underdeveloped nations. To create the bases of industry and technologically sophisticated people within their own countries will be beyond the capability of many of them. Here again, these countries face the prospect of depending upon the goodwill and policies of industrialized nations. Since the alternative could be famine, their choices are not pleasant and their irritation at their benefactors—ourselves among them—could grow to threatening proportions. It would be comfortable to rely on our own good intentions, but our good intentions have often been unresponsive to the needs of others. The matter cannot be glossed over lightly. World peace may depend upon the outcome.

Choices for the Future

The total amount of energy used on U.S. farms for the production of corn is now near 10^3 kcal per square meter per year (3), and this is more or less typical of intensive agriculture in the United States. With this application of energy we have achieved yields of 2 ×

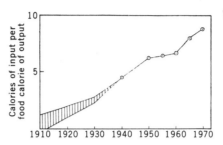

Fig. 4. Energy subsidy to the food system needed to obtain 1 food calorie.

10^3 kcal per square meter per year of usable grain—bringing us to almost half of the photosynthetic limit of production. Further applications of energy are likely to yield little or no increase in this level of productivity. In any case, no amount of research is likely to improve the efficiency of the photosynthetic process itself. There is a further limitation on the improvement of yield. Faith in technology and research has at times blinded us to the basic limitations of the plant and animal material with which we work. We have been able to emphasize desirable features already present in the gene pool and to suppress others that we find undesirable. At times the cost of the in-

creased yield has been the loss of desirable characteristics—hardiness, resistance to disease and adverse weather, and the like. The farther we get from characteristics of the original plant and animal strains, the more care and energy is required. Choices need to be made in the directions of plant breeding. And the limits of the plants and animals we use must be kept in mind. We have not been able to alter the photosynthetic process or to change the gestation period of animals. In order to amplify or change an existing characteristic, we will probably have to sacrifice something in the overall performance of the plant or animal. If the change requires more energy, we could end with a solution that is too expensive for the people who need it most. These problems are intensified by the degree to which energy becomes more expensive in the world market.

Where Next to Look for Food?

Our examination in the foregoing pages of the U.S. food system, the limitations on the manipulation of ecosystems and their components, and the

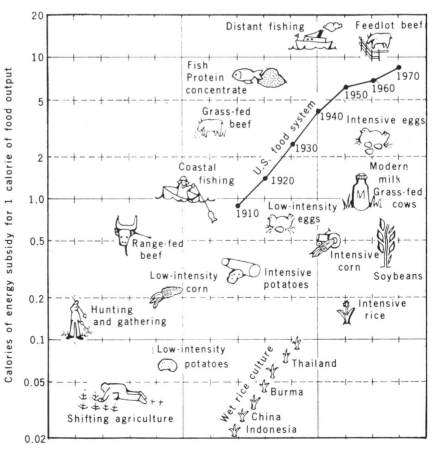

Fig. 5. Energy subsidies for various food crops. The energy history of the U.S. food system is shown for comparison. [Source of data: (31)]

A Wisconsin farm about 1910. Extensive changes in food production and farm life are part of the food system. [Source: Wisconsin Historical Society]

risks of the green revolution as a solution to the world food supply problem suggests a bleak prospect for the future. This complex of problems should not be underestimated, but there are possible ways of avoiding disaster and of mitigating the severest difficulties. These suggestions are not very dramatic and may be difficult of common acceptance.

Figure 5 shows the ratio of the energy subsidy to the energy output for a number of widely used foods in a variety of times and cultures. For comparison, the overall pattern for the U.S. food system is shown, but the comparison is only approximate because, for most of the specific crops, the energy input ends at the farm. As has been pointed out, it is a long way from the farm to the table in industrialized societies. Several things are immediately apparent and coincide with expectations. High-protein foods such as milk, eggs, and especially meat, have a far poorer energy return than plant foods. Because protein is essential for human diets and the amino acid balance necessary for good nutrition is not found in most of the cereal grains, we cannot take the step of abandoning meat sources altogether. Figure 5 does show how unlikely it is that increased fishing or fish protein concentrate will solve the world's food problems. Even if we leave aside the question of whether the fish are available—a point on which expert opinions differ somewhat—it would

be hard to imagine, with rising energy prices, that fish protein concentrate will be anything more than a by-product of the fishing industry, because it requires more than twice the energy of production of grass-fed beef or eggs (9). Distant fishing is still less likely to solve food problems. On the other hand, coastal fishing is relatively low in energy cost. Unfortunately, without the benefit of scholarly analysis fisherman and housewives have long known this, and coastal fisheries are threatened with overfishing as well as pollution.

The position of soybeans in Fig. 5 may be crucial. Soybeans possess the best amino acid balance and protein content of any widely grown crop. This has long been known to the Japanese who have made soybeans a staple of their diet. Are there other plants, possibly better suited for local climates, that have adequate proportions of amino acids in their proteins? There are about 80,000 edible species of plants, of which only about 50 are actively cultivated on a large scale (and 90 percent of the world's crops come from only 12 species). We may yet be able to find species that can contribute to the world's food supply.

The message of Fig. 5 is simple. In "primitive" cultures, 5 to 50 food calories were obtained for each calorie of energy invested. Some highly civilized cultures have done as well and occasionally better. In sharp contrast, industrialized food systems require 5 to

10 calories of fuel to obtain 1 food calorie. We must pay attention to this difference—especially if energy costs increase. If some of the energy subsidy for food production could be supplied by on-site, renewable sources—primarily sun and wind—we might be able to continue an energy-intensive food system. Otherwise, the choices appear to be either less energy-intensive food production or famine for many areas of the world.

Energy Reduction in Agriculture

It is possible to reduce the energy required for agriculture and the food system. A series of thoughtful proposals by Pimentel and his associates (3) deserves wide attention. Many of these proposals would help ameliorate environmental problems, and any reductions in energy use would provide a direct reduction in the pollutants due to fuel consumption as well as more time to solve our energy supply problems.

First, we should make more use of natural manures. The United States has a pollution problem from runoff from animal feedlots, even with the application of large amounts of manufactured fertilizer to fields. More than 10^6 kcal per acre (4×10^5 kcal per hectare) could be saved by substituting manure for manufactured fertilizer (3) (and, as a side benefit, the soil's condition would be improved). Extensive expansion in the use of natural manure will require decentralization of feedlot operations so that manure is generated closer to the point of application. Decentralization might increase feedlot costs, but, as energy prices rise, feedlot operations will rapidly become more expensive in any case. Although the use of manures can help reduce energy use, there is far too little to replace all commercial fertilizers at present (10). Crop rotation is less widely practiced than it was even 20 years ago. Increased use of crop rotation or interplanting winter cover crops of legumes (which fix nitrogen as a green manure) would save 1.5×10^6 kcal per acre by comparison with the use of commercial fertilizer.

Second, weed and pest control could be accomplished at a much smaller cost in energy. A 10 percent saving in energy in weed control could be obtained by the use of the rotary hoe twice in cultivation instead of herbicide application (again with pollution abatement as a side benefit). Biologic pest control

—that is, the use of sterile males, introduced predators, and the like—requires only a tiny fraction of the energy of pesticide manufacture and application. A change to a policy of "treat when and where necessary" pesticide application would bring a 35 to 50 percent reduction in pesticide use. Hand application of pesticides requires more labor than machine or aircraft application, but the energy for application is reduced from 18,000 to 300 kcal per acre (3). Changed cosmetic standards, which in no way affect the taste or the edibility of foodstuffs, could also bring about a substantial reduction in pesticide use.

Third, plant breeders might pay more attention to hardiness, disease and pest resistance, reduced moisture content (to end the wasteful use of natural gas in drying crops), reduced water requirements, and increased protein content, even if it should mean some reduction in overall yield. In the longer run, plants not now widely cultivated might receive some serious attention and breeding efforts. It seems unlikely that the crops that have been most useful in temperate climates will be the most suitable ones for the tropics where a large portion of the undernourished peoples of the world now live.

A dramatic suggestion, to abandon chemical farming altogether, has been made by Chapman (11). His analysis shows that, were chemical farming to be ended, there would be much reduced yields per acre, so that most land in the soil bank would need to be put back into farming. Nevertheless, output would fall only 5 percent and prices for farm products would increase 16 percent. Most dramatically, farm income would rise 25 percent, and nearly all subsidy programs would end. A similar set of propositions treated with linear programming techniques at Iowa State University resulted in an essentially similar set of conclusions (12).

The direct use of solar energy farms, a return to wind power (modern windmills are now in use in Australia), and the production of methane from manure are all possibilities. These methods require some engineering to become economically attractive, but it should be emphasized that these technologies are now better understood than the technology of breeder reactors. If energy prices rise, these methods of energy generation would be attractive alternatives, even at their present costs of implementation.

Energy Reduction in the U.S. Food System

Beyond the farm, but still far from the table, more energy savings could be introduced. The most effective way to reduce the large energy requirements of food processing would be a change in eating habits toward less highly processed foods. The current aversion of young people to spongy, additive-laden white bread, hydrogenated peanut butter, and some other processed foods could presage such a change if it is more than just a fad. Technological changes could reduce energy consump-

Commercial and institution food service has grown by almost 20 percent in the past decade. [Source: Marine Studies Center, University of Wisconsin]

Use of electricity in the food system has been growing at least as rapidly as for the United States as a whole. This nuclear power plant control room is another part of the food system. [Source: Marine Studies Center, University of Wisconsin]

Behind the food system at every stage is the fuel production, refining, and distribution system. [Source: Marine Studies Center, University of Wisconsin]

tion, but the adoption of lower energy methods would be hastened most by an increase in energy prices, which would make it more profitable to reduce fuel use.

Packaging has long since passed the stage of simply holding a convenient amount of food together and providing it with some minimal protection. Legislative controls may be needed to reduce the manufacturer's competition in the amount and expense of packaging. In any case, recycling of metal containers and wider use of returnable bottles could reduce this large item of energy use.

The trend toward the use of trucks in food transport, to the virtual exclusion of trains, should be reversed. By reducing the direct and indirect subsidies to trucks we might go a long way toward enabling trains to compete.

Finally, we may have to ask whether the ever-larger frostless refrigerators are needed, and whether the host of kitchen appliances really means less work or only the same amount of work to a different standard.

Store delivery routes, even by truck, would require only a fraction of the energy used by autos for food shopping. Rapid transit, giving some attention to the problems with shoppers with parcels, would be even more energy-efficient. If we insist on a high-energy food system, we should consider starting with coal, oil, garbage—or any other source of hydrocarbons—and producing in factories bacteria, fungi, and yeasts. These products could then be flavored and colored appropriately for cultural tastes. Such a system would be more efficient in the use of energy, would solve waste problems, and would permit much or all of the agricultural land to be returned to its natural state.

Energy, Prices, and Hunger

If energy prices rise, as they have already begun to do, the rise in the price of food in societies with industrialized agriculture can be expected to be even larger than the energy price increases. Slesser, in examining the case for England, suggests that a quadrupling of energy prices in the next 40 years would bring about a sixfold increase in food prices (9). Even small increases in energy costs may make it profitable to increase labor input to food production. Such a reversal of a 50-year trend toward energy-intensive

agriculture would present environmental benefits as a bonus.

We have tried to show how analysis of the energy flow in the food system illustrates features of the food system that are not easily deduced from the usual economic analysis. Despite some suggestions for lower intensity food supply and some frankly speculative suggestions, it would be hard to conclude on a note of optimism. The world drawdown in grain stocks which began in the mid-1960's continues, and some food shortages are likely all through the 1970's and early 1980's. Even if population control measures begin to limit world population, the rising tide of hungry people will be with us for some time.

Food is basically a net product of an ecosystem, however simplified. Food production starts with a natural material, however modified later. Injections of energy (and even brains) will carry us only so far. If the population cannot adjust its wants to the world in which it lives, there is little hope of solving the food problem for mankind. In that case the food shortage will solve our population problem.

References and Notes

1. *Statistical Abstract of the United States* (Government Printing Office, Washington, D.C., various annual editions).
2. *Historical Statistics of the United States* (Government Printing Office, Washington, D.C., 1960).
3. D. Pimentel, L. E. Hurd, A. C. Bellotti, M. J. Forster, I. N. Oka, O. D. Scholes, R. J. Whitman, *Science* **182**, 443 (1973).
4. A description of the system may be found in: *Patterns of Energy Consumption in the United States* (report prepared for the Office of Science and Technology, Executive Office of the President, by Stanford Research Institute, Stanford, California, Jan. 1972), appendix C. The three groupings larger than food processing are: primary metals, chemicals, and petroleum refining.
5. N. Georgescu-Roegen, *The Entropy Law and the Economic Process* (Harvard Univ. Press, Cambridge, 1971), p. 301.
6. *Patterns of Energy Consumption in the United States* (report prepared for the Office of Science and Technology, Executive Office of the President, by Stanford Research Institute, Stanford, Calif., Jan. 1972).
7. R. A. Rice, *Technol. Rev.* **75**, 32 (Jan. 1972).
8. Federal Highway Administration, Nationwide Personal Transportation Study Report No. 1 (1971) [as reported in Energy Research and Development, hearings before the Congressional Committee on Science and Astronautics, May 1972, p. 151].
9. M. Slesser, *Ecologist* **3** (No. 6), 216 (1973).
10. J. F. Gerber, personal communication (we are indebted to Dr. Gerber for pointing out that manures, even if used fully, will not provide all the needed agricultural fertilizers).
11. D. Chapman, *Environment (St. Louis)* **15** (No. 2), 12 (1973).
12. L. U. Mayer and S. H. Hargrove [*CAED Rep. No. 38* (1972)] as quoted in Slesser (9).
13. We have converted all figures for the use of electricity to fuel input values, using the average efficiency values for power plants given by C. M. Summers [*Sci. Am.* **224** (No. 3), 148 (1971)]. Self-generated electricity was converted to fuel inputs at an efficiency of 25 percent after 1945 and 20 percent before that year.
14. Purchased material in this analysis was con-

verted to energy of manufacture according to the following values derived from the literature or calculated. In doubtful cases we have made what we believe to be conservative estimates: steel (including fabricated and castings), 1.7×10^7 kcal/ton (1.9×10^4 kcal/kg); aluminum (including castings and forgings), 6.0×10^7 kcal/ton; copper and brass (alloys, millings, castings, and forgings), 1.7×10^6 kcal/ton; paper, 5.5×10^6 kcal/ton; plastics, 1.25×10^6 kcal/ton; coal, 6.6×10^6 kcal/ton; oil and gasoline, 1.5×10^6 kcal/barrel (9.5×10^3 kcal/liter); natural gas, 0.26×10^3 kcal/cubic foot (9.2×10^3 kcal/m³); petroleum wax, 2.2×10^6 kcal/ton; gasoline and diesel engines, 3.4×10^6 kcal/engine; electric motors over 1 horsepower, 45×10^3 kcal/motor; ammonia, 2.7×10^7 kcal/ton; ammonia compounds, 2.2×10^6 kcal/ton; sulfuric acid and sulfur, 3×10^6 kcal/ton; sodium carbonate, 4×10^6 kcal/ton; and other inorganic chemicals, 2.2×10^6 kcal/ton.
15. Direct fuel use on farms: Expenditures for petroleum and other fuels consumed on farms were obtained from *Statistical Abstracts* (1) and the *Census of Agriculture* (Bureau of the Census, Government Printing Office, Washington, D.C., various recent editions) data. A special survey of fuel use on farms in the 1964 *Census of Agriculture* was used for that year and to determine the mix of fuel products used. By comparing expenditures for fuel in 1964 with actual fuel use, the apparent unit price for this fuel mix was calculated. Using actual retail prices and price indices from *Statistical Abstracts* and the ratio of the actual prices paid to the retail prices in 1964, we derived the fuel quantities used in other years. Changes in the fuel mix used (primarily the recent trend toward more diesel tractors) may understate the energy in this category slightly in the years since 1964 and overstate it slightly in years before 1964. S. H. Schurr and B. C. Netschert [*Energy in the American Economy, 1850–1975* (Johns Hopkins Press, Baltimore, 1960), p. 774], for example, using different methods, estimate a figure 10 percent less for 1955 than that given here. On the other hand, some retail fuel purchases appear to be omitted from all these data for all years. M. J. Perelman [*Environment (St. Louis)* **14** (No. 8), 10 (1972)] from different data, calculates 270×10^{12} kcal of energy usage for tractors alone.
16. Electricity use on farms: Data on monthly usage on farms were obtained from the "Report of the Administrator, Rural Electrification Administration" (U.S. Department of Agriculture, Government Printing Office, Washington, D.C., various annual editions). Totals were calculated from the annual farm usage multiplied by the number of farms multiplied by the fraction electrified. Some nonagricultural uses are included which may overstate the totals slightly for the years before 1955. Nevertheless, the totals are on the conservative side. A survey of on-farm electricity usage published by the Holt Investment Corporation, New York, 18 May 1973, reports values for per farm usage 30 to 40 percent higher than those used here, suggesting that the totals may be much too small. The discrepancy is probably the result of the fact that the largest farm users are included in the business and commercial categories (and excluded from the U.S. Department of Agriculture tabulations used).
17. Fertilizer: Direct fuel use by fertilizer manufacturers was added to the energy required for the manufacture of raw materials purchased as inputs for fertilizer manufacture. There is allowance for the following: ammonia and related compounds, phosphatic compounds, phosphoric acid, muriate of potash, sulfuric acid, and sulfur. We made no allowance for other inputs (of which phosphate rock, potash, and "fillers" are the largest), packaging, or capital equipment. Source: *Census of Manufactures* (Government Printing Office, Washington, D.C., various recent editions).
18. Agricultural steel: Source, *Statistical Abstracts* for various years (1). Converted to energy values according to (14).
19. Farm machinery (except tractors): Source, *Census of Manufactures*. Totals include direct energy use and the energy used in the manufacture of steel, aluminum, copper, brass, alloys, and engines converted according to (14).
20. Tractors: numbers of new tractors were de-

rived from *Statistical Abstracts* and the *Census of Agriculture* data. Direct data on energy and materials use for farm tractor manufacture was collected in the *Census of Manufactures* data for 1954 and 1947 (in later years these data were merged with other data). For 1954 and 1947 energy consumption was calculated in the same way as for farm machinery. For more recent years a figure of 2.65×10^6 kcal per tractor horsepower calculated as the energy of manufacture from 1954 data (the 1954 energy of tractor manufacture, 23.6×10^{12} kcal, divided by sales of 315,000 units divided by 28.7 average tractor horsepower in 1954). This figure was used to calculate energy use in tractor manufacture in more recent years to take some account of the continuing increase in tractor size and power. It probably slightly understates the energy in tractor manufacture in more recent years.

21. Irrigation energy: Values are derived from the acres irrigated from *Statistical Abstracts* for various years; converted to energy use at 10^6 kcal per acre irrigated. This is an intermediate value of two cited by Pimentel *et al.* (*3*).

22. Food processing industry: Source, *Census of Manufacturers*; direct fuel inputs only. No account taken for raw materials other than agricultural products, except for those items (packaging and processing machinery) accounted for in separate categories.

23. Food processing machinery: Source, *Census of Manufactures*. Items included are the same as for farm machinery [see (*13*)].

24. Paper packaging: Source, *Census of Manufactures* for various years. In addition to direct energy use by the industry, energy values were calculated for purchased paper, plastics, and petroleum wax, according to (*14*). Proportions of paper products having direct food usage were obtained from *Containers and Packaging* (U.S. Department of Commerce, Washington, D.C., various recent editions). [The values given include only proportional values from Standard Industrial Classifications 2651 (half), 2653 (half), 2654 (all).]

25. Glass containers: Source, *Census of Manufactures* for various years. Direct energy use and sodium carbonate [converted according to (*14*)] were the only inputs considered. Proportions of containers assignable to food are from *Containers and Packaging*. Understatement of totals may be more than 20 percent in this category.

26. Steel and aluminum cans: Source, *Census of Manufactures* for various years. Direct energy use and energy used in the manufacture of steel and aluminum inputs were included. The proportion of cans used for food has been nearly constant at 82 percent of total production (*Containers and Packaging*).

27. Transportation fuel usage: Trucks only are included in the totals given. After subtracting trucks used solely for personal transport (all of which are small trucks), 45 percent of all remaining trucks and 38 percent of trucks larger than pickup and panel trucks were engaged in hauling food or agricultural products, or both, in 1967. These proportions were assumed to hold for earlier years as well. Comparison with ICC analyses of class I motor carrier cargos suggests that this is a reasonable assumption. The total fuel usage for trucks was apportioned according to these values. Direct calculations from average mileage per truck and average number of miles per gallon of gasoline produces agreement to within ± 10 percent for 1967, 1963, and 1955. There is some possible duplication with the direct fuel use on farms, but it cannot be more than 20 percent considering on-farm truck inventories. On the other hand, inclusion of transport by rail, water, air, and energy involved in the transport of fertilizer, machinery, packaging, and other inputs of transportation energy could raise these figures by 30 to 40 percent if ICC commodity proportions apply to all transportation. Sources: *Census of Transportation* (Government Printing Office, Washington, D.C., 1963, 1967); *Statistical Abstracts* (*1*); *Freight Commodity Statistics of Class I Motor Carriers* (Interstate Commerce Commission, Government Printing Office, Washington, D.C., various annual editions).

28. Trucks and trailers: Using truck sales numbers and the proportions of trucks engaged in food and agriculture obtained in (*27*) above, we calculated the energy values at 75×10^6 kcal per trucks for manufacturing and delivery energy [A. B. Makhijani and A. J. Lichtenberg, *Univ. Calif. Berkeley Mem. No. ERL-M310* (revised) (1971)]. The results were checked against the *Census of Manufactures* data for 1967, 1963, 1958, and 1939 by proportioning motor vehicles categories between automobiles and trucks. These checks suggest that our estimates are too small by a small amount. Trailer manufacture was estimated by the proportional dollar value to truck sales (7 percent). Since a larger fraction of alumi-

num is used in trailers than in trucks, these energy amounts are also probably a little conservative. Automobiles and trucks used for personal transport in the food system are omitted. Totals here are probably significant, but we know of no way to estimate them at present. Sources: *Statistical Abstracts*, *Census of Manufactures*, and *Census of Transportation* for various years.

29. Commercial and home refrigeration and cooking: Data from 1960 through 1968 (1970 extrapolated) from *Patterns of Energy Consumption in the United States* (*6*). For earlier years sales and inventory in-use data for stoves and refrigerators were compiled by fuel and converted to energy from average annual use figures from the Edison Electric Institute [*Statistical Year Book* (Edison Electric Institute, New York, various annual editions] and American Gas Association values [*Gas Facts and Yearbook* (American Gas Association, Inc., Arlington, Virginia, various annual editions] for various years.

30. Refrigeration machinery: Source, *Census of Manufactures*. Direct energy use was included and also energy involved in the manufacture of steel, aluminum, copper, and brass. A few items produced under this SIC category for some years perhaps should be excluded for years prior to 1958, but other inputs, notably electric motors, compressors, and other purchased materials should be included.

31. There are many studies of energy budgets in primitive societies. See, for example, H. T. Odum [*Environment, Power, and Society* (Wiley, Interscience, New York, 1970)] and R. A. Rappaport [*Sci. Am.* **224** (No. 3), 104 (1971)]. The remaining values of energy subsidies in Fig. 5 were calculated from data presented by Slesser (*9*), Table 1.

32. This article is modified from C. E. Steinhart and J. S. Steinhart, *Energy: Sources, Use, and Role in Human Affairs* (Duxbury Press, North Scituate, Mass., in press) (used with permission). Some of this research was supported by the U.S. Geological Survey, Department of the Interior, under grant No. 14-08-0001-G-63. Contribution 18 of the Marine Studies Center, University of Wisconsin–Madison. Since this article was completed, the analysis of energy use in the food system of E. Hirst has come to our attention ["Energy Use for Food in the United States," *ONRL-NSF-EP-57* (Oct. 1973)]. Using different methods, he assigns 12 percent of total energy use to the food system for 1963. This compares with our result of about 13 percent in 1964.

Oil, Coal, Gas, and Uranium

Prognosis for Expanded U.S. Production of Crude Oil

R. R. Berg, J. C. Calhoun, Jr., R. L. Whiting

The future production of crude oil will depend upon a variety of parameters, some of which relate to the geology of the earth and to the techniques for oil production but many of which are dependent upon economics, governmental regulations, material supply, and similar factors. A prediction of future oil suppliers will be found in a composite assessment of several questions, namely: (i) How much oil is there to be found? (ii) How fast can unfound oil be located? (iii) How much of the oil that has been found or will be found will be produced? and (iv) How fast can known oil be produced? The answer to every one of these questions is an estimate, and the uncertainties in the estimates arise from both nonphysical and physical elements.

Since its beginning in 1859 the U.S. oil industry has produced 100×10^9 barrels (1.6×10^{13} liters) of crude oil, and of the total oil discovered to date only about 38×10^6 barrels remain as proved reserves. Meanwhile, consumption has increased markedly until today domestic production of crude oil supplies only a little more than one half of the demand for all liquid petroleum.

To place this problem in proper perspective, it is necessary to recognize that for approximately 20 years the U.S. petroleum industry has experienced diminishing activity. During this period certain trends have been observed. (i) The percentage of the world crude oil reserves in the United States has decreased from 14 to 7 percent while that of the Middle East has decreased from 66 to 56 percent, although the U.S. crude oil reserves have increased from 30×10^9 barrels to 38×10^9 barrels. (ii) The percentage of the world crude oil produced in the United States has decreased from 44 to 19 percent while that of the Middle East has increased from 24 to 40 percent, although the U.S. production rate has increased from 2.2×10^9 to 3.3×10^9 barrels per year. (iii) The U.S. demand for crude oil in this period has increased from 2.56×10^9 to 4.30×10^9 barrels per year, an increase of 70 percent. The U.S. domestic crude oil reserves based on the latest demand rate have decreased from an equivalent 12-year supply to an equivalent 7-year supply. (iv) The total number of producing oil wells has declined from 594,000 to 504,000. (v) The total number of wells drilled per year has decreased from 57,000 to 27,000, but of more consequence is the fact that the number of exploratory wells has decreased from 16,000 to 8,000 per year and the total footage drilled has decreased from 235×10^6 feet (71×10^6 meters) to 140×10^6 feet. Unquestionably, the net effort of all the forces acting on petroleum exploration and production has not provided the impetus to develop a continuing reserve and productivity.

The Oil-Finding Process

The finding of oil in the past has depended upon a complex industry which has been dominated by small business interests and individuals who may have owned a drilling rig, who may have dealt in real estate holdings and mineral interests, who may have been geological consultants, or who may have had investment capital. Inasmuch as the risks were high, the system was sensitive to economic factors, tax incentives, and governmental regulations which may have changed the probabilities of financial return. Over the past 20 years, the number of independents engaged in drilling and production operations has decreased from 40,000 to less than 4,000 and the total number of drilling rigs has decreased from 5,300 to 1,400.

Geophysical tools are available which make it possible to interpret the structure of the earth from its surface and geological analyses provide for establishing the probability that petroleum may be found in a given situation, but the oil is not found except by drilling. It order to drill a well, there are two minimal requisites: first, the right to drill, and, second, the hardware to drill. The right to drill for oil must be obtained from the owner, usually in the form of a lease which conveys the power to explore and produce oil in exchange for monetary compensations and a share of the oil that is subsequently produced.

The most attractive areas for leasing are the large unleased government lands, principally on the continental shelf. Land held onshore and in nongovernmental hands is not so likely to be in large parcels. It takes time to assemble small leases into sufficiently large groups to make the risk of exploratory drilling worth the cost, and it is becoming increasingly difficult to assemble such tracts.

In the most favorable economic and political climate, the implementation of petroleum resource development requires at least a 5-year lead time. Geological and geophysical surveys must be conducted to identify favorable prospects; adequate funding and participations must be arranged; lands must be leased; drilling equipment must be acquired (or designed and built for special conditions); adequate manpower must be acquired and trained; well drilling and completion must be accomplished; and production and transportation facilities must be installed and product sales contracted.

A desirable strategy would be to commence exploratory drilling in all favorable areas simultaneously. However, this is not possible because of the limited number of drilling rigs and the limited manpower presently available. The alternate strategy is to evaluate and rate undeveloped resource areas according to their potential for success. Decisions must also be made on the assignment of drilling rigs to exploratory or development drilling, or both, because there is a great need for development drilling in fields already dis-

Dr. Berg is professor of geology and director of university research, Texas A & M University, College Station 77843. Dr. Calhoun is professor of petroleum engineering and vice president for academic affairs, Texas A & M University. Dr. Whiting is professor of petroleum engineering and head of the Department of Petroleum Engineering, Texas A & M University.

covered. All of the 1400 U.S. drilling rigs are committed for the next 18 months, and it is difficult for these rigs to operate efficiently because of the shortage of metal goods used in drilling and production.

Without question, any breakthrough in drilling technology could accelerate the rate of discovery of petroleum. Although drilling technology has steadily improved, there have been no major innovations in the past 50 years, in spite of the expenditure of hundreds of millions of dollars in drilling research. Although many exotic drilling techniques have been proposed and are being investigated, the rotary drilling technique still remains the most efficient and economic method for drilling in the earth's crust.

Domestic Oil Reserves

How much oil is there in the unexplored parts of the earth to attract the discoverer and developer? Studies indicate that thus far approximately half of the oil in place in the United States and its territorial waters has been discovered. More than half of this remaining oil is expected to be found in the offshore areas and Alaska, but it is to be expected that drilling will proceed at a slower rate in these hostile environments.

Rather widely known are the estimates of total oil production for the United States made by Hubbert (1, 2) and illustrated in Fig. 1. The basic assumptions of his approach are that the total amounts of oil resources are finite and that constantly increasing demand results in maximum annual production, Q. Consequently, the annual production curve accurately reflects, at any given time, a percentage of the total reserves that can be produced. When the rate of change, dQ/dt, decreases and then becomes negative, projection of the curve becomes increasingly more reliable for the prediction of the total ultimate oil resource.

For U.S. oil production it is seen that the curve has recently changed slope and that the rate of change is decreasing. If the rate of change has reached zero, then half of the total ultimate reserve will have been produced and the remaining curve will be essentially a mirror image of past production. The total ultimate recovery, Q_u, of oil may be estimated as the area under the curve. This recovery, according to Hubbert, will be about 200×10^9 barrels. Therefore, about 100×10^9 barrels remain as a combination of oil already discovered and oil that remains to be discovered. Of this amount it is estimated that 38×10^9 barrels are identifiable as recoverable reserves from known reservoirs. Consequently, there would be about 62×10^9 barrels of oil remaining to be discovered.

Hubbert's estimates of ultimate production are among the lowest, and the depletion concept on which they are based has been soundly defended, as, for example, by Cook (3). Other estimates are larger. The National Petroleum Council (4) has estimated that there are 727×10^9 barrels of oil in place, and, if we use their average recovery figure of 31.4 percent, the ultimate recoverable oil should be 228×10^9 barrels (Table 1). This would mean an undiscovered resource of about 90×10^9 barrels.

The American Association of Petroleum Geologists (5) has estimated a total resources of 824×10^9 barrels in place, with an ultimate recoverable supply of 258×10^9 barrels at 30 percent recovery. This would mean that the recoverable oil to be found is 120×10^9 barrels. These estimates were based on detailed evaluations of producing areas by geologists who are intimately familiar with the various aspects of exploration and production potential of their areas. But none of these estimates includes undiscovered resources of some of the more speculative land and offshore areas that remain largely unexplored.

The U.S. Geological Survey (6) has estimated a larger amount of discoverable oil in place, which yields an ultimate recoverable volume of 568×10^9 barrels if recovery averages 30 percent. This estimate is based largely on volumes of sedimentary rock available for exploration in the land and offshore areas of the United States and on the amount of expected oil that can be obtained from such volumes, based on past production experience.

The total area of the U.S. continental shelf and slope to a water depth of 8000 feet is approximately equal to the land area from which most of our past and present production has come, and it is logical to assume that the Hubbert figures should be extended for this reason. On the basis of geological similarities, it may be assumed that the shelves will yield about the same amount of oil as has already been produced or is expected to be produced from our land areas, that is, an additional 200×10^9 barrels of oil. The total estimate of 400×10^9 barrels of oil as the ultimate amount of producible oil falls within the range of estimates of other recent studies.

If the exploration effort for new oil is expanded immediately, particularly on the continental shelf and in Alaska, it is estimated that at least 5 years

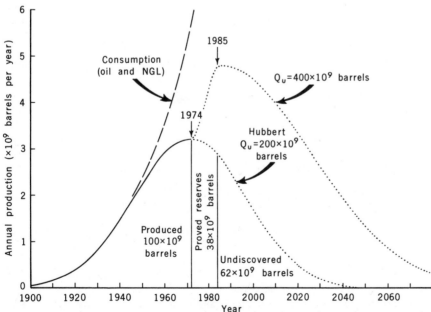

Fig. 1. Total oil production history for the United States, including Alaska, of ultimate recovery, $Q = 200 \times 10^9$ barrels [Hubbert (1)] and a possible recovery, $Q_u = 400 \times 10^9$ barrels. The consumption curve includes not only crude oil but also natural gas liquids (NGL), which account for about 15 percent of consumption.

will be required before significant production can be established, and 10 years until peak production is achieved. Superimposing the additional resources of 200×10^9 barrels of oil on the Hubbert production curve (Fig. 1), therefore, shows that the total annual production for the United States might be increased to nearly 5×10^9 barrels per year in about 10 years. If these estimates are reasonable, the United States can become self-sufficient in oil production only if the demand for crude oil also decreases sharply. Even if the estimated figure of 400×10^9 barrels is somewhat low, this conclusion is not altered significantly.

It is generally conceded that virtually all of the giant onshore U.S. oil fields have been discovered and that future inland discoveries will be confined to small stratigraphic trap fields which are located most efficiently by drilling. Such field additions are expected to add ultimately to U.S. reserves and productivity, but what is needed now is a giant oil field discovery which could complement immediately the petroleum reserve and productivity. The best prospect for such fields lies in the U.S. offshore territorial waters and in Alaska. These areas remain relatively unexplored and should be the subject for accelerated geological and geophysical reconnaissance.

Additional oil from continental shelves or from deeper strata on dry land will be most difficult and expensive to find and produce. The professional exploration talent is available, however. About 15,000 geologists are now engaged in petroleum exploration, 5,000 geophysicists interpret the required geophysical surveys, and more than 20,000 engineers apply the technology for oil production. (These figures are based on various society memberships.) To this pool of imaginative and experienced manpower can be added in future years the thousands of students now being trained in our universities.

Future Oil Recovery

Once new oil has been found, many factors determine how much of it is available to us. Our history of oil production to date demonstrates that we will recover about 30 percent of what we have found. The reasons for this lie in the nature of oil occurrence, in the efficiency of recovery systems, in economic factors, and in government regulations.

An oil reservoir occurs in those favorable geological situations which permit oil to accumulate in the interstices of rocks. The reservoir container is the rock itself, and its containing capacity (porosity) is expressed as a percentage of the total rock volume. It is unusual to find a reservoir with a porosity of more than 30 percent, and it is common to find commercially productive reservoirs with porosities of less than 10 percent.

Not all of the containing capacity of

Offshore drilling drifting platform, Gulf of Mexico, 1974. [Courtesy Tenneco Inc., Houston, Texas]

the reservoir will be filled with oil, however. Generally, water coexists with the oil. It is unusual to find a reservoir with less than 15 percent of its pore spaces filled with water, and some reservoirs may have in excess of 50 percent water. Consequently, in a reservoir with 15 percent porosity and 30 percent water, each cubic foot of oil found requires about 10 cubic feet of rock volume (1 cubic foot = 0.028 cubic meter). A reservoir having sufficient oil to make it economically attractive to spend large amounts of money to find therefore represents a large rock volume.

Reservoirs which produce oil in commercial quantity in the continental United States may range from a few thousand barrels to several billion barrels of oil in place. Historically, only one exploratory well in ten has found oil in sufficient quantities to justify production at all (that is, to justify the further costs of completing the well after it has been drilled). Only about one well in 50 has found an oil reservoir of sufficient size to repay its total costs.

An oil reservoir is not only a container, it is also a conduit through which the fluid must move. The well is a cylindrical hole in the reservoir rock, perhaps 6 inches (15.2 centimeters) in diameter, and oil may move into the well from an areal extent of thousands of feet depending upon the physical parameters of the rock and the oil. The rate at which oil will move through the reservoir rock to the well is dependent upon the capacity of the reservoir rock to transmit fluid (its permeability), upon the viscosity of the oil, and upon the pressure differentials that are available for movement. Many oils are very viscous even at the elevated temperatures of most oil reservoirs and often cannot be commercially

Table 1.

Table 1. Some estimates of ultimate oil recovery in the United States. Undiscovered recoverable reserves have been estimated by subtracting the present cumulative production of 100×10^9 barrels and the expected reserves of 38×10^9 barrels from the ultimate recoverable reserves.

Reference	Oil in place ($\times 10^9$ barrels)	Ultimate recoverable reserves ($\times 10^9$ barrels)	Undiscovered recoverable reserves ($\times 10^9$ barrels)
Hubbert (1, 2)		190	62
National Petroleum Council (4)	727	228 (31%)	90
American Association of Petroleum Geologists [Cram (5)]	824	258 (30%)	120
U.S. Geological Survey [Theobald et al. (6)]	1895	568 (30%)	430

Cranes used in the unloading of barges which bring bulk supplies to Prudhoe Bay during the summer from Houston, Seattle, and other points. The ice moves off the Arctic coast for less than 2 months each summer and the barges have to slip through the moving ice and hurriedly deliver their supplies to avoid being frozen in for the winter. [Courtesy BP Alaska, Inc., Anchorage, Alaska]

produced for this reason. Techniques of heating have been used successfully in some instances, and attempts have been made to produce heavy oils through a process in which part of the oil is burned in place in order to provide heat for producing the remainder.

Whatever may be the physical nature of the reservoir rock, its oil, or its producing pressures, the removal of oil from a reservoir is a process that ordinarily extends over a number of years. The Bradford oil field which was discovered in the late 1800's is still producing some oil, as is the East Texas oil field which was discovered in 1930. Both of these are large oil fields, but it is not the size which leads to long production periods. The long periods are a result of (i) the relatively low capacity of most reservoir rocks to transmit fluid, (ii) the geometry of the well producing system whereby the fluids must flow to a small hole from a wide area, (iii) the declining amounts of driving energy that are available as the oil is produced, and (iv) the physics of fluid flow in porous materials.

Although a reservoir may be discovered and its potential may be estimated from a single discovery well, the true extent of the reservoir, its form, and its capacity to produce will not have been determined until many wells have been drilled. It is not unusual for development to proceed over a 2- or 3-year period before the reservoir has been adequately delineated and an appropriate number of wells have been drilled and completed to drain the reservoir efficiently. The reservoir's structural features (areal extent and thickness), rock properties (porosity and permeability), and fluid content (oil, water, and gas) must be ascertained in order to estimate the volume of petroleum in place. Each oil field is unique not only with respect to these characteristics but also with respect to the natural forces which will be effective in displacing the oil from the reservoir into wells. These natural forces may produce a very efficient or very inefficient recovery of oil, and it is necessary to identify them in order to achieve the most effective utilization of this natural energy. Often it is necessary to supplement the natural energy in the reservoir through fluid injection.

Oil recovery technology has passed through a period in which secondary recovery techniques have been and are being applied to reservoirs which were produced only with the native energy available in the reservoir. These techniques require the introduction of fluids, usually water or gas, to provide a driving force to move additional oil to producing wells. Such procedures require the drilling of injection wells to introduce fluid into the reservoir. New oil reservoirs are being produced in which the best recovery techniques are used from the start so that in more recently discovered reservoirs the secondary recovery phase will not need to be incorporated.

Since oil production is a dynamic process, it is rate-sensitive. There is not only an optimum rate of production to achieve maximum oil recovery but also an optimum rate of production to achieve maximum economic return. These rates are seldom the same. In general, oil production rates are not established at either of these extremes but lie somewhere between and most frequently closer to those corresponding to the optimum for maximum economic return.

The fraction of oil that can be taken from reservoirs will be quite variable, ranging from essentially zero to as high as 80 percent, but, overall, the average has been about 30 percent. Many fundamental problems which might be solved by technology could increase the amount of oil that can be recovered from a given reservoir. One problem is the "efficiency of displacement." This efficiency is the amount of oil that is moved out when the pores of a rock are swept by water or gas. Attempts to increase this efficiency have included the use of detergents, foams, high-velocity displacement agents, solvents, and combustion.

Another problem is "sweep efficiency." This is a measure of the oil that is bypassed in a reservoir because of the geometry of the reservoir and the location of wells at which withdrawals and injections are made. Attempts to increase this efficiency include high-viscosity displacement fluids, fracturing techniques, and well location arrangements. A third problem is "reservoir heterogeneity." Geological formations in many situations are layered with interconnecting and interlocking strata that may vary markedly in their characteristics for fluid flow. It is important in the development of a reservoir to recognize these variables as early as possible and to take them into consideration in the well location and completion decisions.

In all instances of production, however, the continuation of production and the application of new techniques are

(Left) Tank battery with crude oil manifold lines and old style pumping jack in foreground. (Right) Stock tanks, pump building, and electric pumping unit in the background. [Courtesy Pennzoil Company, Bradford, Pennsylvania]

sensitive to regulations and to economic conditions. It is convenient to classify oil fields as (i) producing or (ii) abandoned. Simply stated, this means that for producing fields it is economical to continue to produce oil whereas for abandoned fields it is not. Abandoned fields may be reactivated to producing status if economics—such as an increase in the price of oil—are favorable.

The conditions which contribute to the abandonment of a producing field are directly associated with the costs of producing and treating the oil and the selling price of the oil. As an oil field is depleted and loses its energy, the oil must be lifted to the surface by various means. The oil becomes contaminated with other fluids or materials and must be treated to provide an oil which will comply with pipeline quality standards. All of the factors which impact on the cost of lifting and treating the oil will influence the rate at which oil will be produced. Of primary importance are the costs of equipment, energy, treating materials, and labor. A producing oil field, for example, that is being stimulated by water injection may become uneconomical and the field may be abandoned when the produced ratio of water to oil becomes 5 to 1 and the price of oil is $3 per barrel. However, this same field might be reactivated to producing status if the price of oil increases to $4 or $5 per barrel.

Unquestionably, over one half of the oil discovered in past years in the United States remains economically un-

recoverable at this time. Oil recovery technology is highly developed and sophisticated, and secondary or tertiary oil recovery methods capable of recovering a high percentage of the oil remaining in abandoned fields are known. Many remain untried on a field basis because of the lack of economic incentives.

Summary and Conclusions

It is estimated that less than one half of the oil in place has been discovered to date in the United States and its territorial waters. Although some new oil will be discovered inland, it is anticipated that most new oil will be found offshore and in Alaska. Estimates of the total vary, but from all the evidence there appears little probability that within the next 10 years the United States can produce enough crude oil to meet our liquid hydrocarbon needs, unless there is a change in the life-style of its people.

The drilling rate (footage drilled annually), the finding rate (volume of petroleum discovered per unit of drilling), and access to favorable petroleum provinces are the principal factors controlling the discovery of petroleum. Hence, oil will not be found unless an oil-finding capacity is maintained and further developed. There is a long time lag in the finding of oil because of the need for geological and geophysical evaluations, for leasing arrangements, and for hardware to do the drilling. The risks of oil finding are especially sensitive to the marketplace.

The immediate exploration effort that is needed for the discovery and development of new reserves on the continental shelves will be expensive, perhaps even beyond the means of the largest oil companies. Furthermore, this exploration effort should be made in the public interest for the eventual benefit of the entire nation. For these reasons, a committee of geologists (7) has proposed that the federal government consider assuming the burden of initial exploration costs, primarily those of geophysical surveys of the continental shelves, and that the data so obtained be made available to the public.

Of the oil that is found, not all can be produced. The development of technology for improving oil recovery efficiency will require much research and much fieldwork. If techniques could be developed to raise the recovery average to 60 percent, this would double the estimated reserves we would have at our disposal. The reserves available will be produced over an extended number of years because the depletion of an oil reservoir requires time. Producing rates must be balanced between the maximum which the reservoir will allow and the maximum for achieving the most efficient oil recovery. For the next 10 years, domestic production will be obtained primarily through a continuation of the production methods that we have used heretofore. However, oil production by secondary and tertiary techniques is expected to constitute an ever-increasing percentage of the total domestic production of oil.

If we assume the current continuing downtrend in both drilling rate and finding rate, it is expected that domestic crude oil production 10 years hence will provide less than one half of the U.S. demand if demand continues to increase linearly. If it is assumed that the drilling rate will grow linearly for the next 10 years and equal the maximum achieved in 1956, that the finding rate will increase to correspond to the higher finding rates of the past, and that economic and political conditions will be favorable, it is expected that the U.S. domestic production could provide approximately 75 percent of the demand if that demand continues to increase linearly. Any technological breakthrough in exploration, drilling, production, or oil recovery; the discovery of a giant field; or substantial improvement in the economic incentives will reduce the gap between domestic crude oil production and demand.

There is a need, therefore, for urgency and commitment by government and industry to cooperate to solve this problem. It is essential to have a stable, satisfactory economic and governmental regulatory climate. Positive incentives are needed to expand exploration activities and to apply improved oil recovery techniques. More specifically, risk capital is needed to expand activities. This requires a fair return on total investment as well as anticipation of attractive earnings on current and future investments. Price incentives may provide part of the stimulus for such capital.

Complementing and supplementing these incentives, the government should provide a consistent and stable policy directed to encourage accelerated development of oil reserves and increased productivity. Of particular importance are policy issues relating to leasing, including government lands; to environmental conservation and ecological impairment; to production and product regulation; to import quotas; to price regulation, including petroleum, materials, and labor; and to taxation.

The seriousness of the energy crisis necessitates practical "trade-offs" which must be instituted to stimulate activity and which can be modified as the solution to the problem evolves.

References and Notes

1. M. K. Hubbert, *Am. Ass. Petrol. Geol. Bull.* **51**, 2207 (1967).
2. ———, in *Resources and Man* (Freeman, San Francisco, 1969), pp. 157–242.
3. E. Cook, U.S. Senate Committee on Public Works (93rd Congr., 1st sess., 1973), serial No. 93-12, pp. 47–138.
4. *U.S. Energy Outlook* (National Petroleum Council, Washington, D.C., December 1972).
5. I. H. Cram, Ed., *Future Petroleum Provinces of the United States—Their Geology and Potential* (American Association of Petroleum Geologists Memoir 15, Tulsa, Oklahoma, 1971), vol. 1, pp. 1–34.
6. P. K. Theobald, S. P. Schweinfurth, D. C. Duncan, *U.S. Geol. Surv. Circ. No. 650* (July 1972).
7. The proposal to explore the continental shelves through establishment of a National Petroleum Resource Assessment Commission resulted from a meeting of a Geological Committee on Petroleum Resources in December 1973 at the California Institute of Technology, Pasadena, under the leadership of Harrison H. Schmitt, chairman. The committee members included Robert R. Berg, James Boyd, Daniel A. Busch, Mason L. Hill, Michael T. Halbouty, Barclay Kamb, Thane H. McCullough, Grover E. Murray, Richard P. Shelton, Caswell Silver, and Leon P. Silver.

Oil and Gas Resources:
Did USGS Gush Too High?

yes.

Robert Gillette

If the U.S. Geological Survey is right, the United States is at least a decade away from seriously depleting its domestic oil and gas resources. But if several distinguished disbelievers of the Geological Survey are right, the United States is running out of oil and gas right now.

In a dispute that a committee of the National Academy of Sciences is trying to mediate, the Survey is striving to defend its oil and gas estimates and protect its century-old reputation as the nation's most authoritative mapper and measurer of natural resources. A lot more than the reputation of a government agency hangs in the balance, though. If the critics—who include top exploration authorities in two major oil companies and one of the Survey's own resource experts—are right, the outlook for increased domestic oil production based on new discoveries is dim, and President Nixon's Project Independence could be in deep trouble.

The controversy does not involve "proved reserves"—the amounts of oil and gas the industry knows it has found and can produce at current prices. At issue instead are estimates of the "unknowns"—the undiscovered oil and gas that may eventually be found and produced.

Both sides in the controversy think there is still a great deal of oil and gas left in the ground. The question is whether these resources are plentiful enough for the economists' rule of price-supply elasticity to operate—for prices to drive up production significantly—or whether the United States is already bumping up against the physical limits of rapidly diminishing fossil fuel resources.

Among those challenging the Survey's resource estimates is John D. Moody, the Mobil Oil Corporation's senior vice president for exploration and producing. Moody says that Mobil researchers have calculated national oil and gas resources by three different methods, all of which lead to the conclusion that the Geological Survey's estimates are far too high. On the strength of Mobil's research, Moody contends that the United States has already dug so deeply into its petroleum and gas resources that the industry will be lucky to maintain oil production at its present level of 8.9 million barrels a day. This is 375,000 barrels a day behind the U.S. output at the same time last year.

As for the possibility of increasing production enough to reduce reliance on foreign oil, Moody says, "There's just no way. . . . We're going to have to conserve wherever we can, and make the necessary political accommodations with the producing countries."

If his attitude seems uncharacteristically pessimistic for an oilman, Moody says it's simply realism. Moreover, in a day-long meeting organized on 5 June by the Academy's Committee on Mineral Resources and Environment (of which Moody is a member), two other well-respected researchers presented the results of their own independent studies that appear to corroborate Mobil's conclusions.

The two researchers were Richard Jodry, a senior scientist with the Sun Oil Company, and M. King Hubbert, a former president of the Geological Society of America and a research geophysicist with the Geological Survey. For more than a decade, Hubbert has maintained that the Survey's oil and gas estimates were erroneously high, and he now appears to have gained influential support.

In addition, Hubbert believes that he has found a crucial error in the Survey's method of estimation that could account for the differences currently in contention; Moody and Jodry think Hubbert is right.

The Survey, for its part, is standing by its numbers, but is leaving open the possibility that it might revise them later this year. In an interview, Vincent E. McKelvey, the USGS director, said that from what he understands of Mobil's method of analysis, its results may not fully account for many small reservoirs of oil and gas. As for the error alleged by Hubbert, McKelvey says he's "mulling it over."

Estimates of ultimate resources have always been inherently vague and subject to argument, especially when they involved areas like the continental shelves where very little drilling has been done. The vagueness, moreover, has been compounded by a tangle of terminology and conflicting assumptions that make comparisons among estimates a bookkeeper's nightmare.

One indisputable feature of oil and gas figures, however, is that, for the past 10 years, the Geological Survey's have been head and shoulders higher than almost everyone else's.

According to the Survey's latest estimates, published on 26 March, somewhere between 200 billion and 400 billion barrels of oil and between 1000 trillion and 2000 trillion cubic feet of natural gas remain to be found and recovered in Alaska and the lower 48 states and along continental shelves. (By comparison, the United States has produced about 115 billion barrels of oil and 437 trillion cubic feet of gas since the 1860's.)

The new oil figures represent a substantial drop from the Survey's 1972 prediction that about 477 billion barrels would eventually be found and recovered; much of the difference resulted from a nearly 50 percent reduction in estimates of offshore oil.

Still, Survey officials are convinced that, with record prices driving an exploration boom, these vast resources should permit a rise in domestic production that will take the nation a substantial stride toward self-sufficiency in energy—unless the oil and gas left in the ground is not so vastly plentiful as the Survey thinks it is.

In a 29 March letter to McKelvey, Moody said his company's best estimate was that about 88 billion barrels of oil and 443 trillion cubic feet of natural gas remained to be produced

Mobil

Table 1.

Location	Undiscovered recoverable oil and natural gas liquids (billions of barrels)			Undiscovered recoverable natural gas (trillions of cubic feet)		
	Mobil expected value	USGS Low	USGS High	Mobil expected value	USGS Low	USGS High
Onshore						
Alaska	21	25	50	104	105	210
Lower 48 states	13	110	220	65	500	1000
Subtotal onshore	34	135	270	169	605	1210
Offshore						
Atlantic	6	10	20	31	55	110
Alaska	20	30	60	105	170	340
Gulf of Mexico	14	20	40	69	160	320
Pacific Coast	14	5	10	69	10	20
Subtotal offshore	54	64	130	274	395	790
Total United States	88	200	400	443	1000	2000

Mobil estimates include water depths to 6000 feet, whereas USGS now stops at 660 feet. Mobil's numbers represent the median value of a probability distribution. For instance, there is a 90 percent that total U.S. oil is greater than 50 billion barrels and less than 150 billion; the expected value is 88 billion.

from the whole of the United States, onshore and offshore to a water depth of 6000 feet. Oddly enough, the greatest discrepancies occurred where they might have been least expected: onshore in the lower 48 states. More than 2 million wells have been drilled in the conterminous states in the past 100 years, making this region one of the most thoroughly explored on earth. Yet here, Mobil predicted less than a tenth of the oil and gas that the Survey estimated to exist. Moody said the higher figures were "inconceivable."

How to account for such huge disparities? The answer must lie in the methods used. Either some are right and some are wrong, or not everyone is measuring the same thing. The Survey, for its part, thinks Mobil's method is perfectly natural for an oil company but inappropriate for measuring the entire resource base. And the Survey's critics think its approach uses erroneous assumptions.

Mobil's technique employs an elaborate computer program to combine the geologic and production characteristics of known (and possible) oil and gas reservoirs with the instincts of Mobil's explorationists in the field. The result is a series of "probability profiles" that project the output of known and suspected deposits in each of the nation's 14 oil provinces.

One drawback of the system is that someone, somewhere in the company, must at least conceive of a "play" or prospect of oil before it enters the calculations. But Moody says the technique is "as sophisticated as we know how to

make it" and that it covers all U.S. territory, onshore and offshore.

McKelvey and other Survey experts are convinced, however, that Mobil's method must inevitably reflect the major oil companies' tendency to look for giant oil-bearing structures—like the one at Prudhoe Bay on Alaska's North Slope—while giving short shrift to small and scattered deposits that could add up to a lot of oil. Many geologists, McKelvey among them, firmly believe that immense volumes of oil are hidden in small and subtle "stratigraphic traps," sandwiched between otherwise undistinguished layers of impervious rock. "Our best hope," McKelvey says, is that improved seismic detection technology will soon begin finding these elusive traps.

Others in the Survey are less diplomatic about Mobil's method. One resource expert describes it as "computer frosting on subjective judgment. It's the old situation of garbage in and garbage out."

The Geological Survey arrives at its petroleum estimates in a simpler way, requiring nothing more sophisticated than a geologic map of the country and an adding machine.

The technique was first advanced in about 1960 by a Survey researcher named A. D. Zapp. Frustrated by resource estimates that invariably turned out to be ultraconservative (in 1918, for instance, the Survey said the U.S. was on the threshold of running out of oil), Zapp sought a method that broke away from the old practice of extrapolating from proved reserves, the size of

which had as much to do with economics as geology.

Zapp's new method led him to the conclusion that, since only 20 percent of the nation's sedimentary rock on and off shore had been thoroughly explored, 80 percent of the recoverable oil resource (or more than 460 billion barrels) remained to be discovered. Except for minor refinements this was the official position of the USGS—and, by implication, the government as a whole—from 1961 to this year.

Zapp's reasoning went like this: Thick sedimentary rock covers 1.86 million square miles of land and near-shore seabed. To explore this area thoroughly, if not completely, would require one well drilled to an average depth of 6000 feet every 2 square miles, for a total of 5 billion feet of exploratory drilling.

By the late 1950's, cumulative exploratory drilling added up to just under 1 billion feet or 20 percent of the necessary total, leaving 80 percent of the rock to be explored—and the same proportion of oil to be found.

With all that oil, Zapp wrote in 1962, shortly before his death, the size of the resource would not limit domestic production capacity "in the next 10 to 20 years at least, and probably [not] for a much longer time."

It is hard to tell just how this optimistic forecast affected federal energy policy during the 1960's. It may have contributed to Federal Power Commission decisions to hold down the price of natural gas, a contributing factor to the present shortage. A 1968 energy policy report by the Interior Department* noted that if the Survey's oil and gas estimates turned out to be too low "we certainly should know about it in time to decide intelligently among the available alternatives."

The report went on, however, to indicate that the Survey's estimates were probably valid. On the other hand, Harry Perry, a Washington energy analyst with long experience in the Interior Department, say the Survey's predictions were generally taken with a grain of salt. "I don't know anyone who used these estimates for planning public policy," Perry says.

They were, in any case, promptly questioned by Hubbert. Writing in a report on national energy resources produced by the Academy in 1962, Hubbert pointed out that Zapp's ap-

* *United States Petroleum Through 1980* (U.S. Department of the Interior, 1968).

proach implied that oil had been, and would continue to be, found at a uniform rate per foot of drilling. In fact, "finding rates" had fallen sharply since the late 1930's as oilmen skimmed the cream off the prospects in Texas, Oklahoma, and California. From a high of 276 barrels per foot of exploratory drilling, discoveries have fallen to about 35 barrels per foot by 1965 and to 30 in 1972.

Not until 1965, however, did the Survey concede Hubbert's point. That year, the USGS noted a "definite decline" in discoveries and postulated now that oil would, on the average, prove to be only half—not equally—as abundant in unexplored rock as in explored rock. Now this number is in contention, with Hubbert claiming that it's at least five times too large for onshore terrain. McKelvey acknowledges that the figure of one-half was largely a "subjective judgment" and another official describes it as "mostly a guess."

Hubbert is a man to be reckoned with. One of the Survey's more venerable researchers, he was among the crews that pioneered seismic technology in the Texas oil fields in the late 1920's. Since the late 1940's Hubbert has been refining his own novel technique for estimating oil and gas resources, and along the way he has acquired a reputation as something of an oracle.

In the long run, Hubbert reasons, the oil industry's growth and inevitable decline must follow a roughly bell-shaped curve dictated by a finite resource—first an exponential rise slowing to a peak, then an exponential decline tailing off to zero. The area under the curve would represent total U.S. oil production. Using past records of discovery, reserve growth, and production, Hubbert says that this total will be about 190 billion barrels (of which 143 billion have already been found).

In 1956 this conclusion led Hubbert to a prediction that was almost universally considered outrageous at the time: U.S. oil production, he said, would reach its peak between 1966 to 1971. Perhaps by coincidence and perhaps not, domestic oil production peaked in November 1970 and has slowly declined ever since. Hubbert has also predicted that natural gas production will peak this year or next.

No one disputes that the petroleum industry must inevitably follow some sort of growth-and-decline curve. Says McKelvey, "Hubbert can't possibly be wrong. In time we will reach a peak and start to decline. The question is when."

Hubbert says it happened 3½ years ago, and the Survey's numbers imply a peak sometime around 1985. The pessimistic view reinforces the oil industry's argument for accelerating offshore leasing. But, as energy policy analyst S. David Freeman notes, it also undercuts industry's case for still higher oil prices.

Whoever is right, the implications for energy policy beyond the mid-1980's are the same. The nation will urgently need dependable replacements for oil and gas. In the shorter term, Harry Perry observes, "The difference is whether the next 10 years will be tough or not."

It's possible, of course, to increase production by improving recovery techniques and by drawing down reserves. Much of the new drilling since last fall, in fact, seems aimed at the latter goal, rather than at extending known fields or finding new ones.

But the United States is down to about a 9-year reserve, whereas the industry has traditionally regarded a 12-year cushion as a rock-bottom minimum. Unless reserves are to be allowed to shrink further, the production rate will have to be keyed to the discovery of new oil, and that means reversing a 19-year slump in discoveries.

The possibility of an undersea Saudi Arabia off the Atlantic Coast, looms large according to the Survey. But almost no drilling has been done along the Atlantic shelf and the little that has occurred has been sorely disappointing. In the past 5 years half a dozen oil companies have spent upward of $200 million to drill 65 holes off the presumably oil-rich coast of Newfoundland. All but three of these were dry, and those contained too little oil to justify building a pipeline to shore.

In the meantime, the Geological Survey is working on a computerized model of fossil fuel resources that will take account of geologic conditions as they vary from one sedimentary basin to the next. But the new model and its more refined estimates probably won't be of much use to the Federal Energy Administration in drawing up its "blueprint" for Project Independence. The FEA's deadline is November.

Almost certainly the blueprint will call for a sharp increase in domestic oil production by 1980. But any expectation that the increase can come from newly discovered oil will be based on only the haziest assurance that the necessary oil really exists. It seems fair to say that a careful review of conflicting resource estimates is long overdue.

Oil Shale: A Huge Resource of Low-Grade Fuel

William D. Metz

The rich oil shale deposits on the western slope of the Rocky Mountains constitute a potential source of fuel several times as great as the identified reserves of U.S. oil, and processes for extracting synthetic crude oil from the thick seams of brown-black rock have been ready to go for 15 years. Technologically, the production of synthetic crude oil from shale is a simple process. When the shale is crushed and heated to 480°C, raw shale oil is released. Because it does not require special mineral preparation, high pressures, or difficult catalytic procedures, the process of oil shale recovery is easier than either coal gasification or coal liquefaction. Until October 1973, the principal limitation to oil shale recovery was its price, which was projected by the National Petroleum Council to be about $5.50 per barrel.

Now that the price of domestic crude oil is at least $7 per barrel, oil shale appears to be economically viable. But "it's not simply a question of raising the price of conventional oil high enough and shale oil will automatically appear—although much of the material on the subject blithely makes this assumption," according to James E. Akins, U.S. Ambassador to Saudi Arabia and formerly chief State Department advisor on fuels and energy. "There are severe ecological and mining problems in extracting shale oil which cannot and must not be ignored." Under the close scrutiny that energy alternatives have received since the October 1973 boycott, it is clear that shortages of water will probably limit shale oil production to a few percent of the U.S. petroleum consumption, no matter what the crude oil price.

Water Shortage Limits Development

According to studies by the Department of the Interior and the Atomic Energy Commission, that limit will probably be 1 million barrels per day,

a figure that pales beside the daily U.S. oil consumption, which is 18 million barrels. Not even oil shale enthusiasts seem to be proposing that shale oil can be squeezed out of the rock at a rate much higher than 1 million barrels per day, because 3 barrels of water will be required for each barrel of oil produced with the existing technology. The production rate could perhaps be doubled if in situ technology—the release of oil by cracking and burning the shale in place underground—were perfected, because water otherwise used to dispose of spent shale above ground could be saved. But in situ technologies have not been proved to be workable yet.

The actual amount of shale oil extracted will also depend heavily on government policies. The Department of the Interior, which controls 80 percent of the rich shale lands, is currently leasing six small (5120-acre) tracts for development. Estimates of the shale oil production from these tracts as well as from private lands range from a high of 300,000 barrels per day by 1980 to a low of 100,000 or 250,000 barrels per day by 1985. Private oil shale developers argue that production will not nearly reach 1 million barrels per day, even with an expanded leasing program, unless the government provides substantial economic incentives, such as guaranteed loans, rapid amortization of plants, import restrictions, or a price floor.

Oil shale is found in many areas of the contiguous 48 states and in Alaska, but almost all the shale that is rich enough to yield more than 15 gallons of oil per ton is in one geological formation, along the Green River in Colorado, Wyoming, and Utah (Fig. 1). About 1800 billion barrels of shale oil are buried in the three-state region, but almost all the prime shales, with at least 30 gallons of oil per ton in seams 30 feet or more thick, are in the

Piceance Creek basin in Colorado. Those are estimated at 117 billion barrels, about double the 52 billion barrels of oil that is identified and recoverable. Much of the high quality shale is in a formation called the Mahogany Zone, which is about 70 feet thick, and can be seen on the exposed faces of the canyon walls. The zone is a deposit from the sedimentation of Lake Uinta, a freshwater lake that covered the area during the Tertiary period. The burnable component of so-called oil shale, which is actually a marlstone rock, is an organic polymer called kerogen. Large quantities of nahcolite, $NaHCO_3$, and dawsonite, $NaAl(OH)_2CO_3$, are also found in parts of the Piceance basin, and they contribute to the natural alkalinity of the shale.

The people of western Colorado have heard recurring rumors that oil shale developers would start mining the region since before World War I. Oil shale was mined in Scotland for about 100 years after 1860, and 25 million tons of shale are now mined each year in Estonia, more than half for burning at mine-mouth generating stations rather than for conversion to oil. In 1957 the Union Oil Company of California tested a pilot plant that was built on privately held land along Parachute Creek, south of the major deposits in the Piceance Creek basin, which is predominantly federally owned. The Union plant successfully extracted oil from 300 to 1000 tons of shale per day, and was closed in 1958 because market prices for crude oil were too low to make the operation profitable. Union recently announced plans to build a full-size plant by 1979 that will produce 50,000 barrels per day with an improved version of the earlier process. The original version employs a large piston to continually pump rock upward through a retort where hot gases release shale oil; the oil drains out the bottom and spent shale is forced out the top in the form of large chunks or clinkers.

Also along Parachute Creek, only about 75 miles from the well-known ski center of Aspen, the Colony Development Corporation* owns 8000 acres of shale land, and has spent up to $55 million for research with a pilot plant that has processed 1000 tons of shale per day. The Colony operation is the source of much of the information currently available about the environ-

---

* Colony is a joint venture by the Atlantic Richfield Company, the Oil Shale Corporation (TOSCO), Ashland Oil and Refining, and Shell Oil Company.

mental effects of shale recovery, particularly in the environmental impact statement filed by the Department of the Interior for its oil shale leasing program. In the Colony process, ceramic balls are heated and then mixed with finely crushed oil shale to break down the kerogen to shale oil. Heat transfer is very efficient because two solids are in contact rather than a gas and a solid, and the yield of shale oil is virtually 100 percent. Colony has nearly completed the design of a large plant, to produce 50,000 barrels per day, which is scheduled to begin operation in 1977. Colony will almost certainly be the first company to market shale oil commercially.

Although strip mining has been suggested, the most likely method of removing shale from the Piceance basin is underground mining, since the overburden above the shale zone is generally at least 1000 feet thick. In the western portion of the basin, where tract C-a was leased, the overburden is considerably less, so that tract is a possible candidate for strip mining. A 100,000-barrel-per-day operation is projected. But for most of the region strip mining would be too expensive, so the shale will probably be removed by carving out underground rooms in the Mahogany Zone, leaving behind pillars of shale to hold up the roof. Since the height of the mine ceiling, determined by the shale zone thickness, will be 50 to 70 feet, an underground shale mine could accommodate very large equipment, such as trucks and front loaders. According to a study recently prepared by the Cleveland Cliffs Iron Company, the operation would be very similar to one in a large surface mine.

The alternative to mining would be in situ conversion of shale to oil, but true in situ processes appear to require at least 15 more years of development, if they ultimately prove feasible, in spite of much private and government research. The problem is to create enough void space in the shale, which is quite impermeable in its natural state, so that a flame front will burn evenly through a large underground region. The Bureau of Mines has tested hydraulic fracturing followed by chemical explosives. After the shale is ignited, air is pumped into the region at high pressure to sustain burning, and the resulting shale oil is pumped out. Although this process was promising in shallow shale beds, it has not yet worked in deeper zones.

A hybrid process, often called in situ, has been proposed by the research arm of the Occidental Petroleum Corporation. Up to the point of igniting the shale, the Occidental process requires conventional underground mining. A stope mining technique is used to tunnel into the shale, hollow out a low room, and then blast down the ceiling. Then the room is sealed off and ignited. Shale oil is drained out through a trough previously cut in the floor. From 20 to 35 percent of the shale would have to be removed from the mine to make the tunnels and rooms, and that shale would be processed above ground with the same problems of any shale extraction operation. Un-

der ground, the main uncertainties about the Occidental process are how large the rooms can be, how uniform the broken shale will be, and whether the process will work in shale that is susceptible to groundwater. Once ignited, a room would need to burn for several months to extract all the shale oil.

Occidental has successfully produced shale oil from a room 30 feet square and 70 feet high, and is now lighting a second room the same size. The yield is much lower than in aboveground processing. Experiments that simulated the Occidental in situ retorting with a large steel retort of the Bureau of Mines at Laramie, Wyoming, obtained a maximum of 60 percent shale

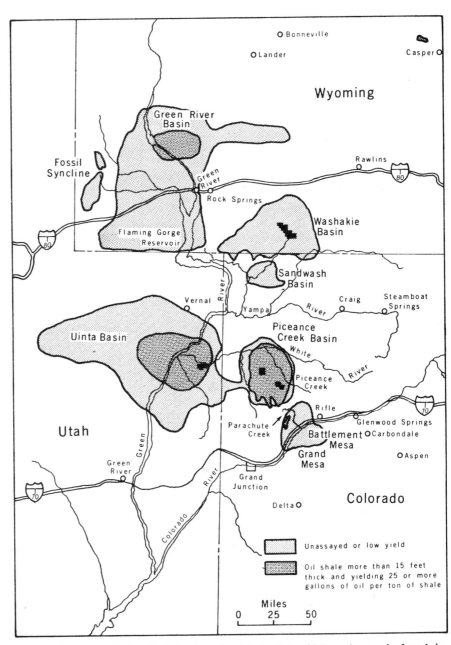

Fig. 1. The major U.S. oil shale deposits. Most of the high-grade ore is found in the Piceance Creek basin in western Colorado. Black areas indicate tracts of federal land leased for private development.

oil recovery. After testing a third small room, Occidental is proposing to mine a much larger room, about 250 feet high, to test the process on a commercial scale. To extract 30,000 barrels per day would require completing at least one such room each week, according to knowledgeable observers. Even if all four test rooms are successful, Occidental would probably require at least 4 years to begin commercial operation, in the opinion of Gerald Dinneen, director of the Bureau of Mines station at Laramie. Others, particularly competitors, predict that 10 years will be required for development.

Unless a true in situ process can be found, oil shale development will require a mining effort that can only be called gargantuan. Oil shale has less energy value per ton than practically any substance that has been used for commercial fuel. Even for the high-grade deposits, about 1.5 tons of shale will be required to produce each barrel of oil. With coal, only about 0.5 ton would be needed to produce a barrel of synthetic crude oil, if the technology for coal liquefaction were available. To get 1 million barrels of oil per day from shale would require mining, transporting, crushing, and retorting 1.5 million tons of oil shale, then disposing of 1.3 million tons of residue. Altogether, 2.8 million tons of material would be handled each day, or about 1 billion tons per year. Last year, the total coal production in the United States was 570 million tons. Even if the Occidental in situ process were used, about 250 million tons of rock would be minded and moved each year. In order to obtain 3 million barrels of oil per day from shale, these figures would have to be trebled. In the course of 3 months, as James Akins likes to note for perspective, the tonnage would be equivalent to the weight of earth and rocks excavated in constructing the Panama Canal. "This does not mean that extraction of oil from shale is impossible," says Akins, "It is just that it is very difficult."

Because of the low energy value of shale, which necessitates such massive mining, and the aridity of the region where shale naturally occurs, its development will inevitably alter the environment and has the potential for extensive damage. The growth of a mature oil shale industry could present problems with the disposal of spent shale, revegetation of affected areas, disturbance of natural habitats, increase in the salinity of the Colorado River, and release of dust and sulfur dioxide to the air. A true in situ process would eliminate some problems, but by no means all. According to Charles Prien, at the University of Denver, Denver, Colorado, in situ methods may just hide the environmental problems underground. Specifically, there are two major aquifers for return of water to the Piceance Creek—which eventually flows into the Colorado River. In the northern half of the basin, one aquifer is above the shale zone and one is below. Prien points out that in some areas of the basin mining could create communication between these two aquifers, and that water passing through the spent shale could leach salts out of it. He thinks that the problem could probably be better controlled in the course of conventional mining than by in situ methods. In the following discussion of environmental effects, conventional underground mining is assumed.

Environmental Changes

After processing, most companies plan to dispose of waste shale above ground, probably in nearby canyons, rather than store it back underground in the mines at a higher cost. Spent shale from the original Union Oil Company process is composed of large chunks at least 10 cm across, shale from a Bureau of Mines process is about 1 cm in average size, and spent shale from the TOSCO process is a fine powder about 0.07 mm in size. Characteristics such as permeability and alkalinity also vary significantly, so the shale disposal problems with one process may be different from the problems with another. The spent shale from a 50,000-barrel-per-day plant will fill a typical canyon in the region, such as Davis Gulch where Colony will dispose of its shale, to a depth of 250 feet in 7 years, leaving about 700 acres of bare shale exposed on top. To minimize the volume, each layer of shale will be compacted as the pile is built up, and the pile will be stable against sliding if the slope is less than 3:1, according to Colony. However, tests by John C. Ward at Colorado State University, Fort Collins, have shown that snowfall destroys the compaction of spent shale to a depth of at least 2 feet. So sliding could occur if the spent shale isn't protected with topsoil and vegetation, according to Ward.

How readily the native grasses and shrubs can grow on spent shale is a question that will largely determine the environmental effects of the shale industry. Of course, the aesthetic appeal of a canyon cannot be regained by growing grass on the false floor, but the success of revegetating spent shale will affect the quantity of salts leached out of the shale by rain and snowfall, and the reduction of the wildlife population in the area, as well as the stability of the pile against erosion. The Piceance basin is the winter range for one of the largest herds of migratory deer in the world, 30,000 to 60,000 mule deer, and is the home of at least a dozen nests of golden eagles. The Department of the Interior estimates that a mature shale industry would disturb 80,000 acres of land over 30 years.

Spent shale must be heavily watered to remove salts before most grasses will grow. The spent shale from the TOSCO process has a significant alkalinity (pH about 9) and contains essentially no nitrogen or phosphorus. In many small test plots, Colony has gotten at least three native grasses to grow profusely, after watering heavily for the first year, using commercial fertilizer, and mulching. Two native shrubs have also grown, but so far none of the woody species used as browse by deer. Colony does not readily distribute data on how much watering was necessary to achieve this. The annual rainfall in the Piceance Creek region is only 12 to 15 inches per year, and one of the major unanswered questions is whether vegetation growing on shale can survive several dry seasons. A test plot of spent shale from the Union Oil process grew grasses naturally, however, according to Harry Johnson at the Interior Department. Tests on a plot of TOSCO spent shale by Ward showed that after 41 inches of water had been applied, with no fertilizer or mulch, only tiny weeds appeared 2 years later. Ultimately, it may be necessary—and cheaper—to cover spent shale with topsoil than to revegetate it. Besides a shortage of natural water, the industry faces another problem for artificial seeding of shale piles: where can you buy four-winged saltbush seeds?

The residents of the Rocky Mountain region and the Far West could also experience a problem with increased salinity in the Colorado River. A mature shale industry (1 million barrels per day) would deplete the quantity of fresh water flowing into the Colorado enough that the salinity at Hoover Dam would increase by 1.5

percent, according to the Department of the Interior. But many observers think that the 1.5 percent effect could be dwarfed by the contributions of salts added to the Colorado River from saline underground aquifers and by leaching of spent shale. The environmental impact statement for prototype leasing did not try to estimate such salt loading, which has been estimated to increase the salinity at Hoover Dam as much as 50 percent.

There is no doubt that the runoff from bare shale is extremely salt-laden. Ward found that the concentration of dissolved inorganic solids to be as high as 5000 mg/liter, about five times the salinity of the Colorado River in the region. Colony plans to install a catch basin at the toe of the shale embankment to keep the runoff from reaching Parachute Creek and thence the Colorado. To evaporate water fast enough so that it didn't overflow, such a basin would have to be quite large. Further increases in the salinity of the Colorado River might require considerable expenditures for desalinization downstream, where there is heavy demand for municipal and agricultural water.

Besides the potential for polluting the Colorado River, an oil shale industry could pollute the air with dust from mining, crushing, and disposal operations, and with sulfur dioxide emission from the retorting process. Some local impact on plants would occur, and there is considerable doubt whether shale operations could meet the recent court ruling that air quality not be degraded when it is purer than environmental standards.

Environmental degradation is certain to occur with a mature oil shale industry, and there is the potential for a very serious impact, according to Harry Johnson, although only local degradation will occur with the prototype program. All parties, including the environmental groups, agree that not enough is known from small test plots to assess the environmental damage to be expected on a larger scale, and the Department of the Interior intends to monitor the prototype program closely and use the information to decide about expanding the industry.

Since most of the rich oil shale is on federal lands, the industry cannot grow to 1 million barrels per day without additional public land leasing. Critics of the prototype leasing operation argue, however, that 5120-acre leases were certainly not needed to determine the environmental effects, that there are many loopholes in the stipulation that all affected lands should be rehabilitated, and that the enforcement provisions are inadequate.

Perhaps one of the most important concerns is that the shale industry will grow up, prove unsuccessful, and be abandoned, leaving the western slope of the Rockies in somewhat the same condition as Appalachia. There is no doubt that a 1 million-barrel-per-day oil shale industry would alter the character of the region. The industry would bring in 115,000 people, more than double the population that now lives in the counties where oil shale is found. Towns would have to expand their municipal services, mobile home settlements would be wheeled in, and many rural aspects of life in the region would disappear. If the industry failed, it could leave the region environmentally desolated and economically broke.

Although oil shale is a bounteous reserve compared to oil, it is clear that it cannot be extracted from the earth without paying a far greater environmental cost. Even so, the rate at which oil can be fired out of shale will be more dependent on the water reserves than on shale reserves. Even the estimated ceiling of 1 million barrels per day may be high, because much of the available water in the region has reportedly been cornered for surface coal mining. One would think that the major reason for urgently developing shale oil would be to utilize its portability as a liquid fuel. But, more likely than not, the first use of raw shale oil will be to burn it, in place of sulfureous coal, for generating electricity in the far Southwest.

Problems of Expanding Coal Production

John Walsh

The author is a member of the News and Comment staff of *Science*.

Coal is dirty fuel, dangerous to mine underground, expensive to transport, and awkward to handle. It retains, in other words, the disadvantages that caused it to lose markets to oil and natural gas after World War II. In addition, a rapid increase in surface mining operations in recent years has inflicted environmental damage which has incited a campaign for effective controls that could limit expansion of strip mining. Now, of course, waning domestic supplies of oil and natural gas and rising international fuel costs have made coal relatively attractive again. If the United States is to gain energy self-sufficiency—however defined—by the end of the decade, a prodigious increase in the production and consumption of coal will be necessary. The country has huge reserves of good quality coal. Conservative estimates put at 150 billion tons the coal recoverable by current mining methods. Project Independence, the federal government's plan for becoming "reasonably self-sufficient" by 1980, calls for an increase in coal production from 602 million tons in 1973 to 962 million tons per year in 1980. However, expanding the supply and use of coal, particularly in the short run, requires the successful clearing of a formidable array of environmental, technical, social, and economic hurdles.

These problems have been exacerbated by a lag in research in the coal industry. Attainable technologies, for conversion of coal to synthetic fuels, for example, have not been brought to maturity because of indifferent research and development programs. A defeatist attitude has contributed to the

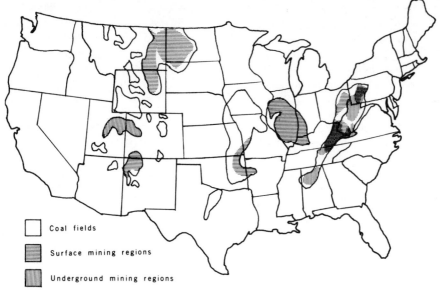

Major coal reserves and mining areas in the United States.

lag. Coal was dethroned by oil and natural gas after World War II, and the conventional wisdom was that nuclear energy was the long-term energy source. It is still hard to convince coal industry veterans that coal is the fuel of the future rather than the fuel of the past.

For the coal industry and for the electric power industry that uses about two-thirds of the coal consumed domestically, the major immediate issue is air pollution. One of the chief accomplishments of the environmental movement, which crested in the 1960's, was fostering the passage of the Clear Air Act of 1970. Provisions of the act scheduled to go into effect next year set standards for sulfur emissions which, in effect, would rule out the use of a major portion of the coal from the fields that now supply power plants in the East. The chances that the Clean Air Act would be fully enforced on schedule virtually vanished in the winter energy shortage. Several states have already relaxed their own air quality standards and federal energy administrator William E. Simon has called for the setting aside of some secondary air quality standards for a 5-year period. The real question now for the government seems to be how drastically and for how long to postpone effective air pollution controls.

The coal and power industries have been pushing hard for policies they say are necessary to permit the rapid expansion of coal production in the years immediately ahead. Coal industry spokesmen like Carl E. Bagge, president of the National Coal Association, recently have been most active in op-

posing tighter regulation of environmental damage as proposed in strip-mine legislation (H.R. 11500) now under discussion in Congress. But the industry also continues to exert strong pressure on government policy-makers to postpone air pollution controls.

The coal industry feels insecure about the firmness of the nation's new commitment to coal and argues that the industry needs solid guarantees from government before it can attract the investment capital that will be needed. What it asks is that coal be given status as a kind of most-favored fuel. The industry's two basic demands are (i) that relaxation of air quality controls be set for long enough to persuade Eastern power companies to convert to coal and for mining companies to invest the large sums required to expand supplies, and (ii) that strip-mine regulations not prevent large-scale surface mining in the Western coalfields.

Clean Air Act Levels

The practical possibilities of meeting Clean Air Act standards by preventing sulfur emissions that exceed the standards of the act are largely discounted by the power industry, at least for most of the rest of the 1970's. Industry generally takes a more pessimistic view of sulfur-removal technology than do other knowledgeable sources (a full discussion of sulfur removal follows in an article on page 83) but there seems to be genuine uncertainty about when fully reliable, commercially feasible equipment will be available for instal-

lation. Industry sources are also skeptical about the likelihood of achieving significant new energy sources by 1980 through conversion of coal to synthetic fuels. Development of synthetic fuels through coal gasification and by synthesizing liquid fuels from coal is a major element in Project Independence. Industry attitudes appear to be influenced by fears that contemplated use of Western coal for large-scale coal conversion operations may be undercut by restrictions on strip mining and by problems of securing the large supplies of water required in the conversion processes (*Science*, 2 November 1973).

Problems of the environment and of the state of the art are by no means the only ones that affect the expansion of coal production. Human factors will also exert strong influence. Higher coal production in the next few years will require increased output from existing underground mines and the opening of new mines. A major increase in the work force will occur at a time when the labor relations in the coal industry have entered a period of uncertainty. Productivity has declined in recent years. Industry attributes this in part to the requirements of the Coal Mine Health and Safety Act of 1969, but probably more significant is that coal mining, as much as any occupation in the United States, is being affected by deep currents of social change. These changes are symbolized as well as anything by the attempts to reconstruct the United Mine Workers of America (UMW) by a reform union administration which now faces its first contract negotiations with the bituminous coal industry. Many observers feel that the ingredients are present for a period of unrest in the coalfields unmatched since the turbulent years after World War II.

What all of this means is that devising a strategy for coal as a component of a national energy policy will not be easy. In the past, major coal industry decisions have been based on judgments of profitability. How and to what extent the federal government is to influence such decisions in the future has not been made clear. A key question which must be answered, for example, if Project Independence is to achieve a significant degree of reality, is, What will the government do to induce the coal industry to create a capacity for producing synthetic liquid fuels which are intensely vulnerable to price competition from oil?

A policy of increasing coal production entails hard decisions on what kind of coal to mine, where to mine it, and how to mine it. American coal varies greatly in accessibility, in heat values, and in geochemistry. The coal-fields of the United States can be grouped roughly into three regions with different kinds of coal, different mining problems, and different options for coal use. The oldest major mining region, which stretches along the line of the Appalachians from Pennsylvania to Alabama, has large deposits of good quality bituminous coal, including valuable metallurgical or coking coal marketed widely here and abroad. Appalachian coal generally has a high heat value, but only about 20 percent of available deposits is thought to meet the maximum 0.7 percent sulfur content which the Clean Air Act sets as a primary standard. Underground mines are characteristic of Appalachia, although there has also been extensive strip mining including destructive "contour stripping" on the region's steep hillsides.

The "midcontinent" region is comprised primarily of areas in western Kentucky, Indiana, Illinois, and Ohio. Surface mining is dominant here. Midwestern bituminous coal has a large market as a fuel for big power plants, but has a high sulfur content which has begun to limit its markets in areas where air pollution regulations are stiff.

The largest reserves of Western coal are subbituminous and lignite varieties found in the tier of Rocky Mountain states, although mining operations seem to be increasing in the Southwest. Western coal has a relatively low heat value compared to coal found east of the Mississippi, but it is low in sulfur. High transportation costs seem to make it unlikely that great quantities of Western coal will be shipped out of the region. Already, however, power companies are generating electricity from big plants literally in the coal-fields, and Western coal is regarded as logical raw material for a coal conversion industry. Opening of a real coal rush in the West has been delayed, however, at least until the debate on strip-mine reclamation is settled and until investment prospects on synthetic fuels are clearer. Government policy on leasing federal lands for mining will also be particularly significant in the West, where much coal land is federally owned.

In recent years, about two-thirds of the nation's coal has been mined in the Appalachian region, including Ohio, but production has been increasing more rapidly in the Midwest, which has accounted for about a quarter of production, and the West, which produces most of the rest.

Industry decisions are likely to continue to be influenced by a strain of caution and pessimism which is the legacy of the coal industry's experience since World War II. This period for coal was one of slump and partial recovery. Coal production last year was almost exactly what it was in 1947. Employment in bituminous coal mining, however, fell from about 400,000 to perhaps 150,000 last year. The loss of markets for coal occurred rapidly starting in the late 1940's, when oil and natural gas became widely available as a result of expanded production during the war and the coming of the big pipelines. Coal rapidly lost the markets for domestic heating and railroad fuel. The late 1940's were years of serious labor trouble in the industry. So severe did the disruptions become that the government at some points took over the mines. The dominant figure in this era was John L. Lewis, who had guided the UMW through the violent organizing campaigns of the 1930's and exercised virtually unquestioned authority over the union.

By the early 1950's unemployment was making deep inroads in the miners' ranks and Lewis abruptly changed tactics to accord with a fundamental change of policy. He decided to embrace mechanization of the mines, which meant a smaller but better-paid, unionized, work force with relatively secure employment. In a few years, typical mining methods changed from the traditional system in which miners blasted coal from the coalface and then loaded it by hand into carriers to a highly mechanized "continuous mining" operation. Productivity climbed, but demand for coal kept falling until it reached a low point of about 400 million tons in 1958. The industry pacesetters in this period were the so-called "captive" mines owned by major steel companies, utilities, and railroads which used the coal from their mines exclusively for their own use. These corporations had the resources to carry out mechanization and offer relative security to miners, while employment of miners continued to drop in the industry as a whole.

Coal production turned up in the early 1960's, if sluggishly, reaching 512 million tons in 1965 and 602 million tons in 1970. What mainly revived demand was the new, coal-using technology in big power plants.

Coal Industry Changes

The shape of the coal industry altered drastically in the 1960's. Surface mining produced a rapidly increasing proportion of coal output (coal production now is divided almost evenly between deep mines and surface mines) and a new pattern of ownership developed. Coal companies were taken over in growing numbers by conglomerates. Often, these were "integrated energy companies," in many cases oil industry "majors."* These corporations were aware that domestic fossil fuel supplies were dwindling and were astute and rich enough to hedge their bets. The big companies, especially, have been attracted by the prospect of converting low-sulfur Western coal to synthetic fuels and are said to control reserves of 25 billion tons of low-sulfur, strippable coal.

These takeovers by "outsiders" are deplored by some critics as creating the conditions for energy monopolies. (On 1 April the Supreme Court let stand a Federal Trade Commission decision that Kennecott Copper should divest itself of Peabody Coal on the grounds that the acquisition in 1972 violated antitrust laws.) It is usually conceded, however, that the new owners, particularly the oil companies, have both the inclination and the resources to bolster the coal research effort. The general industry explanation for its poor research record in the past is that profits on coal have been too low to finance a major research effort. Certainly, the industry was not attuned to seeking salvation in the laboratory, and this listlessness appears to have been reflected in government-sponsored research on coal as well. Relatively small sums have been available over the years for coal research administered by the Interior Department's Bureau of Mines and the record has not been brilliant. In the late 1950's the survival instinct did make the coal industry bestir itself and seek a fresh start on government-

---

* Some of the bigger acquisitions were Consolidation Coal (which produced 60 million tons of coal in 1973) by Continental Oil; Peabody Coal (69.5 million tons) by Kennecott Copper; Island Creek (24.5 million tons) by Occidental Petroleum; and Ayrshire Collieries (16.6 million tons) by American Metal Climax.

financed coal research. The result was establishment of the Office of Coal Research (OCR) which is part of the Interior Department, but separate from the Bureau of Mines. Starting with initial funding of $1 million in fiscal year 1961, OCR's budget rose relatively slowly during the halcyon days of research in the 1960's (the figure was $6.8 million in 1966) but entered its own period of exponential growth with the energy shortage. The budget for fiscal year 1973 was $43.5 million; in the current year it is $123 million, and the estimated budget for next year is $283 million.

Bureau of Mines research has characteristically been in-house research while most OCR research has been contract research with industry. Contributions by industry to cooperative research projects with OCR next year will amount to an estimated $100 million.

One of the explanations for the lackluster record of coal R & D is that moving from the laboratory and pilot plant stages to commercial application of a process is a difficult and expensive proposition. Federal research funding has until recently been inadequate to finance crucial pilot plants and demonstration plants. Coal gasification, for example, is the synthetic fuel process thought to be nearest to commercial application in the period between now and 1980. The basic technology was developed by the Germans to meet the necessities of World War II. (Coal gasification technology is discussed in the article on page 77.) Industry sources predict economic production of synthetic gas by 1978, although the prediction seems to be based on the assumption that surface mining in Western coalfields will be expanded to provide coal for gasification.

Prospects for production of liquid fuels from coal appear more distant. The consensus seems to be that considerable additional laboratory and pilot plant work will be necessary. The exception appears to be methanol, a clean-burning liquid fuel with about half the heat value of kerosene. Methanol can be produced by an adaptation of the technology for making high-Btu gas. The resulting methanol would be suitable, for example, for use as boiler fuel or perhaps jet fuel.

The crucial questions about synthetic fuels seem to be economic rather than scientific or engineering questions. To get through the demonstration plant stage into commercial production, it may be necessary for the government to pay producers in the synthetic fuel industry the difference between the market price and production costs. Formulation of federal policy on this point is in the very early stages, and there appears to be stiff resistance at top policy levels to a costly, long-term government support program for synthetic fuel producers. The alternative to such a program, however, may be no significant synthetic fuel production.

The main technical problem facing the coal industry is dealing with coal's sulfur content. It is theoretically possible to remove sulfur from coal before, during, or after burning. The present strong consensus is that the best hope for controlling sulfur emissions in this decade lies in the improvement of stack gas scrubbing processes now being developed (see page 83 for a discussion of sulfur-removal technology). One practical difficulty is that the power industry, which is the major user of high-sulfur coal, looks on stack gas scrubbers as expensive and unreliable. A National Academy of Sciences study panel in 1970 reported† that a "commercially proven technology for control of sulfur oxides from combustion processes does not exist." Despite substantial investment in development work since then, informed opinion is that 2 or 3 years more will be required before it will be possible to identify the best operational system. The word in the industry is that none of the available scrubbing equipment works for more than 2 months without a complete teardown, and that the need for self-cleaning hardware will not be met for at least several years.

A Mass of Uncertainties

Energy planners are faced with a mass of uncertainties similar to those that inhibit sulfur removal. If Project Independence is to be more than a slogan, however, effective long-term planning is obviously required. Until now, federal energy officials have dealt

---

† Ad Hoc Panel on Control of Sulfur Dioxide from Stationary Combustion Sources, *Abatement of Sulfur Oxide Emissions from Stationary Sources* (National Academy of Sciences–National Research Council, Washington, D.C., 1970).

mainly with allocation of existing fuel supplies, with conservation programs, and with efforts to increase the output of present energy sources. Particularly for the period between now and 1980, national energy policy means a national fuel policy. And it is widely agreed that coal will play an increasing role in such policy.

The extent of that role will be heavily influenced in the next year by decisions made on pending strip-mine legislation and on implementation of the Clean Air Act and the Coal Mine Health and Safety Act. These decisions will be made under heavy pressure from the coal and power industries for what amounts to an environmental moratorium. The industry attitude is expressed, for example, in the remark of the Coal Association's Bagge that the nation "can say goodbye to the idea of a synthetic fuels industry based on coal" if Congress sharply curtails surface mining.

Labor relations may be the unanticipated catch in expanding coal production. The new leaders of the UMW are fighting a two-front war. They are working to restructure the union on democratic lines. At the same time they are seeking to win a contract for their members in the bituminous coal industry with advances in wages, working conditions, and fringe benefits that would make up ground the leaders felt has been lost in past years. There is no reason, incidentally, to doubt the seriousness of the union's new president, Arnold Miller, in stating the view that coal should be mined safely or not at all. It seems very possible that contract negotiations between the union and the coal companies could produce a major confrontation which would soon involve the government.

Expanding coal production in the 1970's is not, therefore, just a matter of decisions by high-level federal officials about what share of needed energy should be supplied by coal, as compared with oil, natural gas, or nuclear power. Perhaps surprisingly, many informed people express greater doubts about attaining the energy goals of 1980 than reaching the higher levels of 1985, perhaps because prospective investments in R & D are expected to pay off by then. With respect to coal in a national energy policy, then, the questions remain elementary ones: Can we mine it and can we burn it?

Clean Fuels from Coal Gasification

Arthur M. Squires

Until 1972, the United States could produce more natural gas or petroleum on demand. When the chokes came off the wells in early 1972, marginal supplies of clean fuels were no longer available from a domestic source. Today, nuclear and coal-fired electricity remain the only margins against rising energy demand that are under domestic control. The former entails high capital costs and long construction times, often made longer by controversy. The latter entails environmental problems not yet resolved. Furthermore, electricity cannot be substituted for gas or oil in many applications. Today, Arab nations command the only practicable, quick margin against most of the world's energy needs. Owners of gas- and oil-burning equipment have experienced in recent months the interruptions of supply and skyrocketing costs that Arab decisions can create.

Synthetic fuels from coal could provide a new margin. Since even a small synthetic fuels industry could have a large effect upon the price of oil, speed is more important than the industry's initial size. What is the quickest path to synthetic fuels?

In considering this question, we must take stock both of technologies now in use (or in use recently) and also of engineering firms competent to reproduce and adapt these technologies quickly. We must consider how the technologies may be applied with maximum effect.

Some few coal-conversion procedures survived the worldwide shift to oil and natural gas in recent decades. They survived in small nations that wished to produce town gas (1) or ammonia or other chemicals from native coals. For example, coal is being gasified today in Turkey, India, South Africa, Scotland, Morocco, Yugoslavia, and Korea.

Substantially all surviving procedures include a step in which coal is reacted with either air or a mixture of oxygen and steam. By gasifying coal with air, the engineer can produce "power gas" (2), a mixture of carbon monoxide and hydrogen with nitrogen. Power gas has a relatively low heating value, about one-sixth that of natural gas. By gasifying with oxygen and steam, one obtains "blue water gas" or "synthesis gas," a mixture of carbon monoxide and hydrogen. In existing plants, this gas is being converted to ammonia or methanol or, in South Africa, to synthetic gasoline. The gas could also be used as a fuel and has a heating value about one-third that of natural gas. Here I will dub it "industrial gas."

Table 1 lists gasification systems that possess immediate commercial credibility (with some caution: see footnotes for Table 1).

Table 2 lists markets for clean fuel gases made from coal. We should promptly initiate projects for each of the markets based upon several gasifiers. Our immediate need is not for the best possible gasification systems but for experience on systems that are sure to work.

The projects might include conversion of industrial gas to methane for addition to the nation's natural gas pipelines, as well as conversion to methanol or liquid hydrocarbons for addition to the supply of liquid fuels. Each of these syntheses, however, entails an energy loss of at least about 20 percent as well as expensive hardware.

A quicker route to "new" gas and liquid fuel is to retrofit equipment now being fired with natural gas or oil, so that it can use either power gas or industrial gas made from coal. The Electric Power Research Institute of Palo Alto, California, has initiated studies to identify gas- and oil-fired utility boilers that are candidates for such retrofit. Comparable studies should get under way quickly for industrial boilers. One might expect to "liberate" some 3 to 4×10^{12} cubic feet (1 cubic foot = 0.028 cubic meter) of gas annually from utility and industrial boilers, and perhaps some 300 to 400×10^6 barrels of oil (1 barrel = 159 liters). It should be appreciated that much gas- and oil-fired equipment could not be altered to burn coal directly.

Even earlier visibility for a new energy margin can come from application of the historic gas producer. Our several opportunities are best considered in light of a review of available gasification techniques. Processes for making power gas or industrial gas are characterized by (i) the physical form and disposition of the carbonaceous material brought into contact with air or oxygen-steam mixture and (ii) the method of extracting inorganic ash matter from the reaction zone. For (i), there are gravitating-bed gasifiers of lump coal, suspension gasifiers of pulverized coal, and fluidized-bed gasifiers of crushed coal. For (ii), ash can be withdrawn as relatively free-flowing powder, clinkers or ash agglomerates, or molten slag. The form of the ash reflects the temperature to which it has been exposed. Almost every combination of (i) and (ii) has been operated, at least experimentally (3).

Gasification in Gravitating Beds

Air-blown producers have provided fuel gas continuously since 1836. In the mid-1920's, there were 150 manufacturers of producers in the world. There were nearly 12,000 producers in the United States consuming perhaps about 25×10^6 tons per year of coal (1 short ton = 0.907 metric ton) (4). By the 1960's, only a few producers in the Pennsylvania anthracite region were left; but the industrialist of South Africa, for example, has always recognized the gas producer as a competitive route to clean energy.

About a year ago, the Glen-Gery Corporation of Reading, Pennsylvania, reactivated a Wellman-Galusha producer to furnish fuel gas to a brick kiln. This company has placed an order for a new producer, to be supplied by McDowell-Wellman Engineering Company of Cleveland, and has three others on standby (5). Producers for anthracite should be revived, and probably

The author is professor of chemical engineering at the City College of the City University of New York, New York 10031.

will be, just as quickly as coal can be made available. Pennsylvania anthracite is low in sulfur, and only dedusting of the power gas will be needed to satisfy environmental concerns. The producers could, for example, serve manufacturers of brick, glass, ceramics, and baked foods, as well as those who melt or anneal metals.

The low heating value of power gas is not as much of a disadvantage as it might initially appear to be. The flow of combustion products determines many aspects of equipment for heat recovery and heat utilization. For the user, a better comparison with natural gas is the heating value per unit volume of combustion products. On this basis, the "worth" of power gas is only about 15 percent below that of natural gas (4).

Can-Do, Inc., of Hazleton, Pennsylvania, in the heart of the anthracite district, is examining the feasibility of an installation to provide power gas to some 80-odd energy customers in its two industrial parks. The initial installation might include up to eight producers. Yet to be resolved are engineering questions in regard to the distribution and utilization of the gas, but answers can be obtained quickly by analysis at the desk; the feasibility of making the gas is not in question. If the Can-Do gas works should prove a feasible and attractive development, it could provide quick visibility for a new margin against energy demand.

In a producer, humidified air is introduced into the bottom of a column of lump coal, to which fresh coal is continuously being supplied at the top. Oxygen in the air disappears, within a short distance of the air inlet, in a shallow combustion zone that separates a lower region of carbon-free ash matter and an upper region comprising lumps of carbon. These descend by gravity toward the combustion zone in a motion countercurrent to the flow of hot gases rising from this zone. Humidity in the air has the effect of controlling the temperature at the hottest point, by putting into play the endothermic reaction of steam and carbon. This reaction, as well as the endothermic reaction of carbon with carbon dioxide formed in the combustion zone, occurs as the hot gases pass upward through the bed of carbon. In an efficient design, a high conversion of steam to hydrogen and carbon monoxide, and of carbon dioxide to carbon monoxide, is achieved.

The ash must not form clinkers too

hard to be crushed readily. An eccentric grate is provided that can loosen weakly sintered ash as it advances. There are ports, however, through which an operator can insert a poker to break up hard clinkers that may form on occasion.

The flow of rising gases must be kept below a rate at which they would buoy the bed. Working on rice and buckwheat anthracite (about 5 to 15 millimeters), a 10-foot producer (1 foot = 30.5 centimeters) can gasify about 20 ton/day. The same producer, fitted with a stirrer to permit gasification of a caking bituminous coal, can handle up to about 80 ton/day of such coal at a size of 30 to 50 millimeters. Producers of this size in South Africa treat 80 tons of subbituminous coal per day at a size of 15 to 65 millimeters. A disadvantage of a producer gasifying bituminous or subbituminous coal is that tars appear in the gas and complicate its cleaning. The M. W. Kellogg Company of Houston and Pennsylvania State University are formulating plans to study the performance of a producer on caking bituminous coals, including the problems of removing sulfur and tar from fuel gas.

Although producers can supply the first new gas to U.S. industry, their long-range role is limited by their small capacity. Industrial boilers commonly burn the equivalent to hundreds of tons of coal per day; electricity boilers, thousands of tons. The scale-up of the historic producer to such capacities in a reasonable time is not credible.

Lurgi Mineraloeltechnik of Frankfurt (Main), West Germany, introduced nearly 40 years ago a producer blown with oxygen and steam at 20 atmospheres (6). South Africa has a plant with 13 Lurgi units that provide synthesis gas for the production of 5000 barrels of gasoline per day. Other Lurgi units furnish town gas and synthesis gas for ammonia. For these purposes, a gas of high hydrogen content is advantageous. It was no disadvantage, therefore, that the pressure producer required a steam flow roughly double that needed at atmospheric pressure to keep ash free-flowing and to guarantee against clinkers. (In a pressure producer, the operator cannot resort to a poker!)

Lurgi has recently adapted its pressure producer for blowing with air and steam to produce power gas at high pressure for use in a gas turbine (7, 8). No other pressure gasifier is commercially available, but the Lurgi has not been operated under U.S. conditions. Commonwealth Edison Company of Chicago has recognized the importance of gaining experience on such operation in an electricity-generation context, as well as experience on gas cleaning. Commonwealth will install three Lurgi units at its Powerton station, each gasifying about 500 tons of Illinois bituminous coal per day.

In tests sponsored by the American Gas Association, a Lurgi at Westfield, Scotland, has recently completed successful campaigns on run-of-mine Illinois No. 6 coal and on sized Pittsburgh No. 8 coal. The latter is a highly caking coal.

The air-blown Lurgi has the dis-

Table 1. Commercial gasification systems.

Blown with air to yield "power gas"	Blown with oxygen and steam to yield "industrial gas"
Historic gas producer	Gas producer
Winkler (East German)*	Winkler (East German)†
Ignifluid‡	Lurgi pressure gasifier§
Lurgi pressure gasifier§	Winkler (West German)
	Koppers-Totzek
	Babcock & Wilcox-duPont‖

* Air-blown Winkler gasifiers ran only for about 1 year in 1929.   † All East German Winkler experience has been with lignite.   ‡ The Ignifluid gasification system has not been operated as a "pure" gasifier but to supply power gas for prompt burning in a boiler directly above a gasification bed.   § The Lurgi is the only gasifier available for operation at elevated pressure.   ‖ The Babcock & Wilcox–duPont gasifier operated for only about a year.

Table 2. Markets for clean fuel gases produced from coal.

Power gas	Industrial gas	Pipeline-quality gas
Agriculture		Homes
Small industry		Small business
Industrial and utility boilers	Industrial and utility boilers	
Industrial furnaces	Industrial furnaces	
Service to industrial parks	Service to industrial parks	
Gas turbines and combined cycles*	Gas turbines and combined cycles*	
	Hydrogen production*	
	Chemical synthesis*	
	Liquid fuel synthesis*	

* For these uses, there is a large advantage in gasifying at elevated pressure.

advantage that its power gas contains a great deal of hydrogen (and steam besides) that causes an unnecessary loss of water latent heat to the atmosphere. The loss amounts to about 10 percent of the heating value of the coal gasified. In addition, it is not likely that the Lurgi could be scaled up quickly to sizes much beyond 500 ton/day.

Slagging-Bed Gasification

A path toward gravitating-bed gasifiers of higher capacity is the development of equipment in which ash is removed as molten slag. Indeed, the iron blast furnace is a slagging gasifier, and Japanese furnaces today gasify up to about 4000 tons of coke per day (9). It is no surprise, then, to find that hard coke has been gasified in experimental slagging gasifiers, blown with oxygen and steam, at capacities as high as 635 ton/day in Germany (10) and 230 ton/day in Russia (11). The gasifiers resembled the blast furnace: oxygen and steam were blown through a number of horizontal blowpipes or tuyeres into the bottom of a deep bed of coke.

The British Gas Council conducted trials of oxygen-blown gasification in similar equipment at 20 atmospheres at the 120 ton/day scale (12). Similar experiments were conducted at 4 atmospheres by the British Ministry of Power (13) and at 28 atmospheres by the U.S. Bureau of Mines at Grand Forks, North Dakota (14), the latter experiment gasifying lignite.

An overall impression left by these experiments is that tuyere-blown gasifiers working on anything other than hard coke will be difficult to scale upward to large capacities, especially for elevated pressures. Each tuyere creates a "raceway," that is, a cavity in the fuel bed in which coke particles are tumbled about in violent cyclonic motion, and thereby degraded in size. The raceway is larger at larger gas inputs, and the degradation is more troublesome.

The British Coal Utilisation Research Association has studied (15) a slagging grate invented by Secord (16) having the advantage that treatment of the lump coal is gentle. Weak and friable cokes were gasified successfully at a rate of 5 ton/day. Oxygen and steam entered the fuel bed across a grate consisting of horizontal, thin-walled, water-cooled, narrowly spaced steel

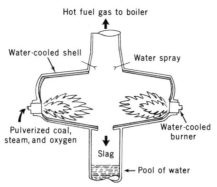

Fig. 1. Schematic cross section of the Koppers-Totzek gasifier.

tubes. Below the grate was a zone supplied with coal fines that burned to create slagging temperatures in this zone and at the grate.

Brief Russian trials (up to 4 hours) of a small air-blown gasifier (9 ton/day) at 5 atmospheres suggest that Secord's grate might accommodate at least one-half of the fuel as coal fines fed below the grate (17).

Slagging-bed gasifiers cannot make an early contribution to U.S. energy needs. The Secord grate is worth study.

Suspension Gasifiers

For the past 20 years, the Koppers Company, Inc., of Pittsburgh has marketed the Koppers-Totzek gasifier (Fig. 1), in which finely pulverized coal (70 percent smaller than 75 micrometers) reacts in a dilute suspension with oxygen and steam at atmospheric pressure (18). The gasifier

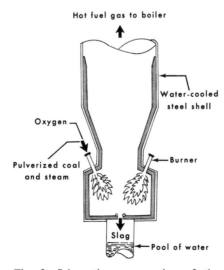

Fig. 2. Schematic cross section of the Babcock & Wilcox–duPont gasifier, operated on bituminous coal for about 1 year in the mid-1950's at Belle, West Virginia.

is a refractory-lined steel shell with a water jacket for producing steam. A design with two opposing burner heads can gasify over 400 tons of coal per day, whereas a four-headed gasifier, with burners 90 deg apart, can handle 850 ton/day. The reaction temperature is 1900° to 2000°C. For most coals, much of the ash matter drops out of the reaction zone as slag, but fine ash particles also leave with gas flowing upward into a boiler. Some reaction of carbon with steam and carbon dioxide occurs. These reactions are endothermic, and, if the coal is reactive, such as lignite or subbituminous, they may reduce the gas temperature to around 1200°C at the gasifier outlet. For less reactive coals, endothermic reactions do not come much into play, and the operator must spray water into the gas to lower its temperature so that ash matter will not stick to tubes in the boiler.

The Koppers-Totzek gasifier was exploited in the first instance to provide synthesis gas for ammonia. For this purpose, the gas preferably contained as little methane as possible. The high temperature afforded a gas that normally contained less than 0.1 percent (by volume) of methane. It also led to equipment of great flexibility, no doubt accounting for the commercial success of the Koppers-Totzek in a period during which little equipment was sold for coal gasification. All kinds of coal can be handled, including highly caking bituminous coals with no pretreatment as well as coals that have a high ash fusion temperature such as Pennsylvania anthracite. Many Koppers-Totzek gasifiers were retrofitted successfully to gasify heavy oil.

For present energy needs, the high temperature of this gasifier carries a price: the Koppers-Totzek needs expensive oxygen. If Koppers-Totzek gas is burned in an electricity boiler, for example, roughly 10 percent of the electricity will be needed to provide the oxygen.

It is probably not feasible to substitute air for the oxygen, since air would have to be preheated beyond about 900°C to achieve the high temperature of the Koppers-Totzek. One could employ air enriched in oxygen at less preheat, and this alternative should be explored.

The Koppers-Totzek is probably best suited for large installations that supply industrial gas to a pipe network or for large combined-cycle electricity equipment. Several systems are said to be at an advanced stage of negotiation, and the Koppers-Totzek appears to be the front-runner in the competition for providing new supplies of clean fuel gas in large applications.

The suspension gasifier is the particular choice of most steam power engineers familiar with pulverized-fuel combustion, and many efforts have sought to develop a suspension gasifier that brings endothermic gasification reactions more into play than the Koppers-Totzek design can do. Such efforts face the inherent problem that the carbon inventory is small, making it difficult to promote the slow endothermic reactions. Mixing of gases in the reaction zone tends to defeat an attempt to create a temperature gradient through agency of endothermic reactions, and the several approaches taken reflect different ways to reduce mixing (19).

In collaboration with duPont, Babcock & Wilcox developed an oxygen-blown design that operated commercially at the 400 ton/day scale for about 1 year at Belle, West Virginia, in the mid-1950's (Fig. 2) (20). The design directs flames from 12 burners toward a central slag taphole, to produce there a temperature of about 1500° to 1600°C. A narrow "waist" separates the hot zone from a cooler zone above, in which endothermic reactions reduce the temperature of the gases to about 1200° to 1300°C as they leave to enter a boiler. The waist prevents backward convection of heavier, cooler gases from the endothermic zone into the hot, slagging zone.

Between about 1961 and 1963, Babcock & Wilcox conducted air-blown tests at the 60 ton/day scale in equipment like that shown in Fig. 2 (21). With air preheated at 550°C, a gas having a heating value of 70 to 80 British thermal units (Btu) per cubic foot was obtained (1 Btu/cubic foot = 3.7×10^4 joule/cubic meter). The Babcock & Wilcox designers believed that a gas at 100 Btu could be achieved in an operation on a larger scale, with a lower heat loss. This is to be compared with a heating value of about 150 Btu for an atmospheric producer or an air-blown Lurgi.

Designers at Combustion Engineering, Inc., have performed studies for an air-blown gasifier like that shown in Fig. 2 and believe that a heating value of about 125 Btu can be achieved by feeding a portion of the raw coal to the upper zone, above the waist.

Operating gas producer at Shoemakersville, Pennsylvania, brick factory. [Source: Glen-Gery Corporation]

Char would be recovered from steps for cleaning the gas and fed to the lower zone.

The Szikla-Rozinek boiler incorporated a "suspension" gasification zone, although coal was fed at appreciably larger sizes than coal to other suspension gasifiers. In the Szikla-Rozinek boiler ash matter accumulated in the form of agglomerates suspended by gas rising through the gasification zone, until they grew to a size to fall upon an ingenious ash-discharge mechanism. Rozinek's paper (22) is valuable both for its description of this mechanism and other construction details. Unfortunately, so far as I am aware, the Szikla-Rozinek attained a scale of only about 40 ton/day. Further scale-up might not be easy. In any case, it could hardly be considered to be commercially available in the United States.

Gasification in Fluidized Beds

The first commercial fluidized bed was the air-blown Winkler gasifier producing power gas at Leuna, East Germany, for gas engines to run ammonia synthesis gas compressors. Five units operated in 1929 to provide gas for an impressive 130 megawatts of shaft power. The largest unit had a capacity of about 650 tons of dried lignite per day (23). The units were idle in the economic recession of 1930, and after that they were revised to blow oxygen and steam.

A disadvantage of the Winkler is that great amounts of carbon fines are produced, that blow out of the unit. To improve utilization of these fines, additional gasification medium (air or oxygen-steam) is blown into the overhead space above the fluidized bed, raising the temperature of this space. With this expedient, carbon gasification efficiency is, in general, about 80 to 85 percent.

Revision of the Leuna gasifiers to blow oxygen and steam allowed the temperature of the gasification bed to be lowered from 950° to 800°C, and that of the overhead space from 1000° to 850°C. The 150°C reduction in temperature reflects the greater reactivity and higher partial pressure of steam in a gasifier blown with oxygen and steam by comparison with the reactivity and especially the partial pressure of carbon dioxide in the air-blown unit (where a high partial pressure of nitrogen prevails). The reduction in temperature eliminated problems associated with formation of "bird's nests" near the gas exit—accumulations of loosely sintered ash matter.

Leuna accomplished major improvements in its Winklers over the years (24) but without building new units. The five original Winkler units were finally shut down in 1971.

A different path of development arose in West Germany (25) from Pintsch Bamag's (GmbH) desire to provide a gasifier blown with oxygen and steam that could handle bituminous coals less reactive than the lignite gasified at Leuna. The Bamag designers found it necessary to operate the fluidized bed at about 1000°C and to raise the temperature of the overhead space to about 1100°C. Taller reactors were provided, and boiler surface was situated within the reactor near the top to reduce the exit temperature to about 900°C to avoid the growth of troublesome ash deposits in the gas-outlet system. By analogy with the experience at Leuna, it would appear that air-blowing of a bituminous coal would require temperatures appreciably above 1000°C. Davy Power-gas, Inc., of Lakeland, Florida, has acquired rights to the Pintsch Bamag experience in Winkler gasification.

The Winklers operate at gas velocities between about 5 to 8 meter/second. Coal feed is coarse, generally 10 millimeters and smaller in size.

In the early 1940's, the U.S. petroleum industry introduced a catalytic fluidization technique in which much finer powders and much lower velocities (between about 20 and 75 centimeter/second) were used. This technique acquired better visibility, especially in academic research, than the high-velocity, coarse-powder approach. During the 1940's and 1950's, at least eight research groups worked upon low-velocity fluidized-bed gasification (26), and new efforts have been initiated in the 1960's and 1970's. Temperatures were generally limited to 1000°C, to avoid clinkers. Much of the work was carried out on chars or anthracites. In work on bituminous coal, tars did not appear in the make-gas if the temperatures were above 925°C.

An impression arising from this work is that the production of ultrafine particles of carbon is inherent in fluidized-bed gasification. Even at low velocities, carbon losses can be serious. Rayner (27) has reported careful experiments for several carbon feedstocks, including hard coke, and typically found carbon losses to run beyond 20 percent. He did not believe the losses could be reduced by circulating fines back to the bed. He determined that losses were associated with gasification itself and not with mechanical attrition by the action of the bed. Rayner believed that a gasifying carbon particle becomes vesicular and weak and tends to fall into bits, when about 80 percent of the carbon has been removed.

I was therefore surprised to learn that carbon utilization routinely exceeds 99 percent in the operation of the Ignifluid boiler, invented by Albert Godel and marketed by Fives-Cail Babcock of Paris (28). The Ignifluid incorporates an air-blown fluidized bed gasifying coarse particles of coke that arise from crushed coal supplied to the bed. Its performance is all the more impressive when one remembers that a Lurgi generally affords a carbon burnup of between about 95 and 98 percent, whereas utilization in a suspension gasifier can fall below 90 percent for less reactive coals and will approach 99 percent only for highly reactive lignites.

The Ignifluid bed operates at conditions that are a logical extrapolation from Winkler art, if one wished to devise an air-blown gasifier for relatively unreactive coal: velocities of 10 to 15 meter/second and temperatures of about 1200° to 1300°C. In spite of this logic, Godel deserves great credit for having shown the wit and courage to attempt such extreme conditions.

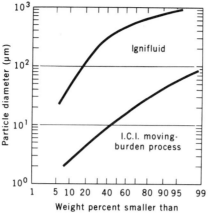

Fig. 3. Comparison of the size of "fly carbon" recovered by the second stage mechanical collectors of an Ignifluid boiler operating on bituminous coal (fluidizing velocity, about 20 meter/second) with that from a fluidized bed of the Imperial Chemical Industries, Ltd., "moving burden process" (velocity about 30 centimeter/second) (27). In the latter instance, the fly carbon represented a loss of more than 20 percent of the carbon fed. In the Ignifluid, reinjection of the fly carbon leads to 99 percent carbon utilization.

At these temperatures the ash matter of all coals is sticky, and one might expect the attempt to lead to a catastrophically huge clinker. On the contrary, Godel discovered that small clinkers appear throughout the bed and remain fluidized and grow in size without risk. Apparently the high fluidizing–gas velocity produces an effect much like the continuous action of a poker.

Air is introduced into the bed through an escalating grate. The edges of the grate are relatively stagnant, and clinkers that come to rest there tend to remain. They are sticky and capture other clinkers by collision, so that a continuous pad of clinkers, low in carbon, forms toward the upper end of

the grate, which dumps the clinkers into an ash pit. Secondary air is admitted above the fluidized bed to burn the power gas and supply heat to a boiler.

A team at City College has studied the Ignifluid (29). A major question has been: What accounts for its good carbon utilization? One possibility is that micrometer-size carbon particles do not survive passage through the secondary combustion zone above the bed. There is a large circulation of carbon particles upward through the boiler, into mechanical dust-collecting devices, and thence into a lance for reinjection at high velocity into the deep end of the fluidized bed. In one Ignifluid the rate of circulation was measured to be about one-half of the bituminous coal feed, and carbon utilization efficiency was stated to depend upon careful aim of the lance toward the deep end of the bed (30). This Ignifluid has two mechanical collectors in series, and the finer dust from the second collector was astonishingly coarse by comparison with carbon dust reported by Rayner (27) for a fluidized-bed gasifier running at low velocity (see Fig. 3). A fine particle injected about 1 meter below the surface of the deep end of the bed would remain in the bed for a number of minutes. The City College team's present view is that micrometer-size particles of the size seen by Rayner simply cannot survive for several minutes at the conditions of the Ignifluid bed. It will be important to put this view to a test.

One special capability of the Ignifluid is the combustion of dirty fuels of high ash content. It will be excellent for anthracite wastes, both culm banks and silts.

Pennsylvania Electric Company (a subsidiary of General Public Utilities) is considering the erection of an 80-

Table 3. Development activities deserving high priority.

Blown with air	Blown with oxygen and steam
Ignifluid	
Revamp to provide "pure" gasifier	Test revamp
Develop larger sizes	
Develop pressure version	Test at pressure
Koppers-Totzek	
	Develop pressure version
Babcock & Wilcox–duPont type of suspension gasifier	
Develop	Get more experience
Develop pressure version	Test at pressure
Gas cleaning	
Get experience with wet systems for removing dust and hydrogen sulfide in electricity-generation context	
Develop techniques for removing dust and sulfur species from hot fuel gas	

megawatt Ignifluid as a "high sulfur combustor" to serve its Seward station. The concept is to beneficiate bituminous coal to a reduced sulfur level for the larger boilers at the station, while burning tailings with 7 to 10 percent sulfur and 40 percent ash in the Ignifluid.

After the outbreak of war in the Middle East last October, the City College team recognized a role for a "quickie" revamp of the Ignifluid gasification system to provide a gas for retrofit of existing gas- or oil-fired boilers (31, 32). The largest present Ignifluids are two units in Casablanca, each capable of treating about 400 tons of a low-grade Moroccan anthracite per day. Quick scaling of the Ignifluid design to capacities of several thousands of tons per day, suitable for retrofitting boilers for several hundred megawatts, appears feasible.

During a recent visit to Paris, I learned that Fives-Cail Babcock has not been idle. A small test Ignifluid (13 ton/day) at La Corneuve is being modified (at Babcock's own expense!) as shown in Fig. 4. A baffle is being added to allow the depth of bed to be increased. With this change ports previously used for the admission of secondary combustion air can admit a portion of the gasification air, this portion preheated to a temperature above that at which air can be furnished through the grate. An arch is being added to separate the chamber into a gasification space below and a combustion space above. Fuel gas quality will be determined from samples taken from the pipe conveying fuel gas from the lower to the upper space.

A much larger experiment is both desirable and justified, and outside funding is urgently needed. The City College team expects that a gas of at least about 125 Btu/cubic foot can be provided.

The Ignifluid gasification system, housed in a circular vessel and with different means for removing ash clinkers, is a strong candidate for development for operation at high pressure. The presence of a significant inventory of carbon affords safety against an explosion that could result in a suspension gasifier if the coal feed is lost and air or oxygen supplies are not shut off at once. Typically, the gas residence time in a suspension gasifier is about 3 seconds, and an explosive mixture would develop in a few seconds if the air or oxygen supply is not instantly interrupted upon loss of fuel. The feed-

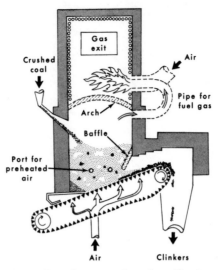

Fig. 4. Experiment on "pure" gasification in a revamp of a small test Ignifluid boiler at La Corneuve, France.

ing of fine coal at atmospheric pressure is a well-established art, but it is not established for high pressure. Development of a Koppers-Totzek or Babcock & Wilcox design for high pressure would need to be followed by an ample operating history before the design could be widely adopted. An Ignifluid for pressure could be certified for safety much more quickly. Fives-Cail Babcock are now engaged in an Ignifluid experiment (at Babcock's own expense!) at 4 atmospheres in a circular vessel fitted with an ingenious rotating grate invented recently by Godel (33).

Hydrocarbon Research, Inc., of Trenton, New Jersey, plans tests of a fast fluidized-bed gasifier suitable for pressure that uses the Godel technique for generating ash agglomerates (8, 34). Several approaches to removing the agglomerates will be tried.

Retrofit of Gas-Fired Boiler to Burn Power Gas

The City College team has examined the problem of retrofitting an existing gas-fired boiler to burn power gas from a revamped Ignifluid. It was assumed that the gasifier and coal pile could not be situated near the existing boiler. It appears possible to match operation of the gasifier and boiler so that steam-superheating and water-heating duties of the boiler are held substantially the same as in the present gas-fired operation. Fuel gas would be cooled to about 260°C for cleaning and would be supplied at this temperature to the existing boiler. Hot water would be sent from

the boiler to the gasifier and converted to steam, with about 40°C superheat, for return to the boiler. The effect of this steam is to reduce the fire box duty at the existing boiler by about 40 percent. Power gas at 125 Btu/cubic foot could sustain the reduced fire box duty. The temperatures of the combustion products entering the superheating and water-heating sections of the boiler would be close to present values. With use of New Mexican coal of low sulfur content (obviating the problem of sulfur controls) and containing 30 percent moisture, the overall effect of the retrofit is to reduce boiler efficiency by only 1 point, from 85 to 84 percent on a higher heating value basis.

Conclusions

The quickest way to establish a visible new margin against energy demand is the historic producer serving small industry and gasifying Pennsylvania anthracite. In 2 years many producers could be in operation.

The quickest way to obtain significant supplies of "new" gas or oil is to retrofit existing electricity and industrial boilers for power or industrial gas. Important results could be achieved in 6 years.

Table 3 identifies development activities deserving high priority to speed the capture of gas and oil now burned in boilers, and to speed realization of the advantages of combined-cycle equipment running on coal (8).

Obviously, these activities are not enough. Many exciting and worthwhile concepts at various stages of development can furnish improved techniques for converting coal to pipeline gas and liquid fuels for the long run. Reviews of these concepts are available (6, 32, 35). I have neglected them in this article not to deny their importance but to stress the earlier opportunities from technology that is ready now, or nearly ready.

The oil and gas industries might well consider the historical progression from Wells Fargo to Western Union to American Telephone and Telegraph to Radio Corporation of America. These industries will miss the boat if they regard themselves simply as purveyors of their historical fuels and not as purveyors of clean energy. The gas industry especially will be in trouble if it lets its major industrial customers, such as steel and electricity, provide their own supplies of power and industrial gas.

References and Notes

1. Town gas ("coal gas") comprises primarily hydrogen, methane, and carbon monoxide, and was made historically by heating bituminous coal in retorts in the absence of air. Modern town gas processes depend upon gasifying coal with oxygen and steam.
2. "Power gas" is the historical term introduced by Ludwig Mond in about 1890, when a preferred procedure for generating shaft power was to burn power gas in a gas engine. The term "low-Btu gas" has regrettably become current.
3. I am not aware of an experiment in which molten slag was withdrawn from a fluidized-bed gasifier.
4. G. M. Hamilton, paper presented at the meeting of American Institute of Mining, Metallurgical, and Petroleum Engineers, St. Louis, February 1961.
5. Ironically, the hiatus in producer operation was brief. Natural gas became generally available to industry in the heart of the anthracite district only about 5 years ago, and both Glen-Gery and Hazleton Brick Company operated producers until nearly 2 years ago.
6. For a diagram of a Lurgi, see H. Perry, *Sci. Am.* **230**, 19 (March 1974).
7. P. F. H. Rudolph, *Am. Chem. Soc. Div. Fuel Chem. Prepr.* **14** (No. 2) (May 1970), p. 13.
8. A. M. Squires, *Sci. Am.* **227**, 26 (October 1972).
9. M. Higuchi, M. Iizuka, T. Shibuya, *J. Iron Steel Inst. (Lond.)* **211**, 605 (1973).
10. F. Duftschmid and F. Markert, *Chem. Ing. Tech.* **32**, 806 (1960).
11. N. V. Kalmykov, *Gazov. Prom.* **7**, 8 (1956).
12. D. Hebden, J. A. Lacey, A. G. Horsler, *Gas Counc. (Gt. Brit.) Res. Commun. GC 112* (1964).
13. S. Masterman and W. A. Peet, paper presented at the Joint Conference on Gasification Processes, Hastings, Susex, England, 1962; *Gas J.* **312**, 19 (1962).
14. G. H. Gronhovd, A. E. Harak, M. M. Fegley, D. E. Severson, *U.S. Bur. Mines Rep. Invest.* 7408 (July 1970).
15. H. R. Hoy, A. G. Roberts, D. M. Wilkins, *J. Inst. Gas Eng.* **5**, 444 (1965).
16. C. H. Secord, U.S. Patent 3,253,906 (31 May 1966).
17. Kh. I. Kolodtsev and V. I. Babii, *Teploenergetika* **5**, 25 (May 1958).
18. J. F. Farnsworth, H. F. Leonard, D. M. Mitsak, R. Wintrell, *The Production of Gas from Coal through a Commercially Proven Process* (Koppers Company, Inc., Pittsburgh, August 1973).
19. In about 1958, Texaco conducted an experiment at the 100 ton/day scale on a suspension gasifier at elevated pressure with a downward flow of gas and takeoff of both gas and molten slag at the bottom of a tall reaction zone. The configuration caters to gradients in temperature and gas composition, but operability on coals of high ash-fusion temperature is doubtful. Both the Institute of Gas Technology and the U.S. Bureau of Mines tested downshot suspension gasifiers at elevated pressure on a smaller scale [C. G. von Fredersdorff, E. J. Pyrcioch, E. S. Pettyjohn, *Inst. Gas Technol. Res. Bull.* 7 (1957); J. H. Holden, K. D. Plants, G. R. Strimbeck, L. F. Willmott, *U.S. Bur. Mines Rep. Invest.* 5856 (1962)]. Panindco conducted downshot tests at atmospheric pressure with dry ash discharge [P. Foch and R. Loison, *Int. Conf. Complete Gasification Mined Coal* (Liege, Belgium, May 1954), p. 224]. Ruhrgas Company of West Germany experimented in about 1951 with an air-blown, upflow slagging gasifier of unusual height, provided in an effort to achieve a temperature gradient [K. Traeckner, *Trans. Am. Soc. Mech. Eng.* **75**, 1095 (1953)].
20. P. R. Grossman and R. W. Curtis, *Trans. Am. Soc. Mech. Eng.* **76**, 689 (1954).
21. E. A. Pirsh and W. L. Sage, *Am. Chem. Soc. Div. Fuel Chem. Prepr.* **14** (No. 2) (May 1970), p. 39.
22. A. Rozinek, *Feuerungstechnik (Leipzig)* **30**, 153 (1942).
23. [British] Ministry of Fuel and Power, *Report on the Petroleum and Synthetic Oil Industry of Germany* (His Majesty's Stationery Office, London, 1947), p. 21.
24. B. von Portatius, *Freiberg. Forschungsh. Reihe A* **69**, 5 (1957).
25. W. Flesch and G. Velling, *Edroel Kohle Erdgas Petrochem.* **15**, 710 (1962).
26. A. M. Squires, *Trans. Inst. Chem. Eng.* **39**, 3 (1961); *ibid.*, p. 10; *ibid.*, p. 16; *ibid.*, p. 22.
27. J. W. R. Rayner, *J. Inst. Fuel* **25**, 50 (1952).
28. A. M. Squires, *Science* **169**, 821 (1970); A. A. Godel, *Rev. Gen. Therm.* **5**, 349 (1966).
29. J. Yerushalmi *et al.*, in preparation. The Illinois State Geological Survey has kindly assisted with inspections of samples of carbon and clinker from Ignifluid beds.
30. Messrs. Loyez, Lejeune, Fillinger (Usines Solvay, 54110 Dombasle-sur-Meurthe, France), personal communication.
31. A. M. Squires, paper presented at the RANN Symposium, Washington, D.C., 19 November 1973; to appear in the proceedings of this conference.
32. ——, *Ambio* **3**, 1 (1974).
33. A. A. Godel, paper presented at the Third International Conference on Fluidized Bed Combustion, Houston Woods, Ohio, October 1972; to appear in the proceedings of this conference.
34. A. L. Hammond, W. D. Metz, T. H. Maugh II, *Energy and the Future* (AAAS, Washington, D.C., 1973), p. 22.
35. H. C. Hottel and J. B. Howard, *New Energy Technology: Some Facts and Assessments* (MIT Press, Cambridge, Massachusetts, 1971).
36. Coal gasification studies at the City College are supported by grant GI-34286 from the RANN Program ("Research Applied to National Needs") of the National Science Foundation. I thank G. R. Hill, S. B. Albert, B. Louks, and D. Teixeira of the Electric Power Research Institute, Palo Alto, California, for helpful discussions.

High-Sulfur Coal for Generating Electricity

James T. Dunham, Carl Rampacek, T. A. Henrie

The United States has an abundance of coal. Coal reserves economically recoverable by today's mining technology are estimated at 200 billion tons (1), and total domestic coal resources are of the order of 3 trillion tons, or enough to meet a large part of our energy needs for centuries (2). We are experiencing an energy shortage in the 1970's, despite such vast amounts of coal, because we have become overdependent on natural gas and oil to supply some of our increasing energy needs, among them that for electrical power.

Electricity provides about 25 percent of our total energy needs. According to a Department of the Interior study (3), per capita use of electricity increased from slightly more than 2000 kilowatt-hours in 1950 to 7800 kwh in 1971, and is projected to reach about 32,000 kwh by the year 2000.

Cheap, convenient low-sulfur oil and natural gas are competing with coal as the preferred fuel for the electric utility market (Table 1). While annual consumption of coal for power plants in the northeastern and east northcentral regions of the United States stayed approximately constant in the 6 years from 1966 to 1971, oil consumption has increased by factors of 3 and 25 in these regions, respectively, and gas consumption has increased by up to a factor of 3 (4–6). Continued use of petroleum and natural gas at the present rate will aggravate the serious supply problems for these fuels.

Programs under way to augment our oil and gas supplies and to diversify our energy base (7), such as coal gasification, extracting oil from western oil shales, harnessing solar energy, wind, and geothermal steam and brines, will have little impact on electricity generating needs for many years. Similarly, although nuclear reactor power plants are expected to provide up to 25 percent of the demand for electricity by 1985 and up to 50 percent by 2000, these optimistic estimates assume the timely development of the fast breeder reactor program and satisfactory solution of environmental problems in siting and operating nuclear reactors. In the meantime, fossil fuel–fired power plants must supply a large part of our electrical power demands, and only coal is available in the United States in sufficient quantity to provide this energy for the next 25 years.

The authors are at the U.S. Bureau of Mines, Washington D.C. 20240. James T. Dunham is staff metallurgist, Division of Solid Wastes; Carl Rampacek is Assistant Director–Metallurgy; and T. A. Henrie is Deputy Director–Mineral Resources and Environmental Development.

Air Pollution from Coal Combustion

An important factor influencing the change in the pattern of energy use in thermal electrical power generation from coal to oil or gas in recent years has been the limitation on the emission of pollutants to the atmosphere. Air pollution regulations affecting power plants are primarily concerned with three pollutants: particulates, nitrogen oxides, and sulfur oxides. Of these three, sulfur oxides are of the most concern from a regulatory standpoint. Ambient air quality standards (Table 2) limit the concentration of sulfur oxides in the atmosphere while emission standards (Table 3) limit the amount of sulfur oxides that can be discharged into the atmosphere (8, 9). Emission standards can generally be met only by burning coal containing 1 percent sulfur or less. In coal, sulfur occurs in both the inorganic and organic forms. Substantial amounts of inorganic sulfur, mostly pyrite, can be removed by mechanical cleaning, but the organic sulfur cannot. Because the sulfur in high-sulfur (3 to 6 percent) coal is often about half pyrite and half organic, mechanical cleaning alone does not reduce the sulfur content to the point that the coal can be burned without exceeding the emission standards for sulfur oxides.

Fuel trends in the heavily populated and industrialized regions reflect the impact of air pollution regulations on the use of coal. Burning low-sulfur oil or natural gas has been one method of controlling sulfur oxide emissions, but when switching to oil or gas has not been feasible, utilities have turned to low-sulfur coal, often at great expense because of high transportation costs. Most of the available low-sulfur coal in the United States is in the West, and much of that in the East is captive and used by the metallurgical industry. Accordingly, utilities in Chicago meet air pollution regulations by using low-sulfur coal mined in Montana and Wyoming and pay as much as $8.50 per ton for unit train rail haulage.

In his report to Congress on the energy situation on 23 January 1974, President Nixon urged postponement of the implementation date for air pollution standards to permit conversion of oil- and gas-fired electric generating plants to the use of coal. On 6 February 1974, a report issued by the Federal Energy Office (10) cited ten eastern plants that converted from oil to high-sulfur coal and several other

Table 1. Sources of energy for generating electricity in 1972 [from (5)].

Source	Electricity generated (percent of total)
Coal	42.2
Natural gas	22.1
Petroleum	16.9
Hydroelectric	15.7
Nuclear	3.1
Geothermal	Negligible

plants that were willing to convert if environmental, technical, transportation, and supply obstacles could be overcome. These actions have freed some oil and gas for other uses. In 1973, use of coal for generating electricity increased slightly at the expense of oil and natural gas (11). However, widespread conversions by established utilities or construction of new plants designed to burn high-sulfur coal are unlikely unless utilities can be assured that they can ultimately comply with air quality regulations.

Control of Sulfur Oxides at Power Plants

One of the major deterrents to the unlimited and widespread use of coal for generating electricity in the United States, particularly in the Midwest and East, is the quality of the combustion gases released to the atmosphere. If high-sulfur coal is burned, there are three alternatives for producing gaseous emissions meeting air quality standards: (i) Coal can be converted to a sulfur-free fuel; (ii) coal can be burned directly at a rate and under conditions that generate emissions meeting ambient air quality standards; or (iii) coal can be burned and the sulfur oxide gases removed during combustion or before discharge of flue gases to the atmosphere. In the near future, sulfur-free fuels derived from coal by gasification or liquefaction will, at best, have limited application in electrical power generation. The other alternatives are more likely for immediate and short-range use.

Tall Stacks and Curtailment

Before establishment of air quality standards, it was common practice to burn high-sulfur coal and vent the combustion gases to the atmosphere through tall stacks to disperse the sulfur oxides, nitrogen oxides, and particulates. By reducing the rate of coal burning and venting through the tall stacks, ambient air quality standards can be achieved in many cases, but under no conditions can emission standards be met.

The curtailment technique consists of monitoring concentrations of sulfur dioxide at ground level near the power plant and meteorologically forecasting unfavorable atmospheric conditions that might force the gas from the stack to ground level. When adverse conditions are indicated, electrical power generation is curtailed to the degree necessary to maintain the ground level sulfur dioxide content of the air below the ambient air quality limits. This control strategy, called the "closed-loop system" or "intermittent control system," has been used for controlling sulfur dioxide emissions at copper smelters in Tacoma, Washington, and El Paso, Texas. The Tennessee Valley Authority has demonstrated the technique at its Paradise steam plant in west central Kentucky (12). The Environmental Protection Agency (EPA) has recognized this method of control as supplemental to emission controls and suitable for some power plants (13).

Curtailment is simple and cheap, and can be implemented almost immediately for some degree of sulfur dioxide emission control from generating plants. However, extensive use of the procedure would reduce electricity generating capacity. This method of control should be considered a stopgap measure to permit burning of high-sulfur coal until positive methods for controlling sulfur oxides become available.

Removing Sulfur Dioxide from Flue Gases

Research to develop technology for removing sulfur dioxide from gases generated during coal combustion in electric utility boilers covers a span of 40 years in the United States and abroad. These processes include (i) injecting limestone or lime into the combustion chamber to produce a throwaway product; (ii) high-temperature regenerative systems (that is, those that recycle the absorbent) using solid absorbents to concentrate sulfur dioxide gas for conversion to sulfuric acid or sulfur; (iii) direct catalytic oxidation of the dilute flue gases to sulfur trioxide and then to sulfuric

84

acid; (iv) wet scrubbing of the cooled gases with alkaline solutions or slurries to yield throwaway products; and (v) wet scrubbing with regenerative solutions to produce either liquid sulfur dioxide, sulfuric acid, or elemental sulfur. This technology is still controversial, with opinions varying as to the reliability, operating and capital costs, and acceptability of the end products or byproducts of the various processes.

In a 1970 study of available technology for stack gas cleanup made by the National Academy of Engineering (14), it was stated that "contrary to widely held belief, commercially proven technology for control of sulfur oxides from combustion processes does not exist." In May 1972, a federal interagency committee responsible for evaluating state air implementation plans formed an interagency task force to evaluate flue gas desulfurization systems. The task force, designated the Sulfur Oxide Control Technology Assessment Panel (SOCTAP), issued its final report on 15 April 1973 (15). Having examined the status of stack gas cleaning in the United States and Japan, the task force concluded that the removal of sulfur oxides from stack gases is technologically feasible in installations of commercial size, and that a large number of the nation's coal-fired steam electric plants can ultimately be fitted with commercially available stack gas cleaning systems. Of many processes considered, four wet-scrubbing systems were rated as sufficiently developed for full-scale commercial application within the next 5 years; these processes were as follows: wet limestone or lime scrubbing, magnesium oxide scrubbing with regeneration, catalytic oxidation, and wet sodium base scrubbing with regeneration. Solid absorbent regenerative systems were eliminated as technically deficient or not far enough advanced for application in the near future; several regenerative wet scrubbing systems still being developed were not considered. The method of dry lime or limestone injection in utility boilers fired with powdered coal, in which sulfur oxides are recovered as dry compounds together with the fly ash, was also rejected because flue gases did not meet emission standards for sulfur oxides and the quantities of lime or limestone required were excessive. Serious operating problems also were encountered, including boiler fouling and degraded performance of electrostatic precipitators. Dry limestone injection into a fluidized-bed boiler might capture enough sulfur dioxide to meet emission standards, but the quantity of limestone required is excessive, about 300 pounds per ton of coal burned (16) [1 pound = 0.45 kilogram; 1 ton of coal (always short ton) = 0.9 metric ton]. Fluidized-bed boilers are only in the experimental stage and, because of their large size as compared to conventional boilers, are not likely to be readily accepted by utilities.

The EPA supported the SOCTAP conclusions and evaluations in testimony at public hearing (17), and added double-alkali sodium scrubbing systems to the list of commercially viable processes. The citrate process, also studied by EPA (18), was later added to the list of promising desulfurization systems.

Utility representatives at the public hearing did not agree with EPA's conclusions and testified about operating difficulties with the scrubbers that are installed. They claimed that reliability of units 100 megawatts or larger has not been demonstrated adequately enough to warrant the conclusion that the control systems are commercially available. Another major concern of the utility representatives was the disposal problem attendant with the throwaway control systems. These systems—lime or limestone wet scrubbing and double-alkali scrubbing—produce calcium sulfate and calcium sulfite, which have no market value and must be disposed of in permanent impoundment areas.

The processes considered most advanced have only been tested in a limited number of large-scale demonstration projects, if any, and the controversy continues as to whether the technology is reliable enough for widespread application to coal-fired utility boilers. Large-scale test programs now under way or being planned (17) may, in the next 2 or 3 years, solve the engineering design and operating problems to assure fully reliable sulfur oxide control systems. In the meantime, promising new processes now being developed should be available for installation before the end of this decade. Concerned parties are appraising cautiously the more thoroughly researched and advanced processes with regard to their merits and deficiencies.

Wet Limestone or Lime Scrubbing

The wet limestone and lime absorption processes are the most thoroughly studied of all sulfur dioxide control systems. In these systems (19), (i) dry lime or limestone is injected into the boiler and the partly reacted material

Table 2. National ambient air quality standards. Primary standards are those which protect public health and secondary standards protect public welfare; ppm, parts per million [from (8)].

Standards	Concentration		Description
	$\mu g/m^3$	ppm	
Sulfur oxides			
Primary	80	0.03	Annual arithmetic mean
	365	0.14	24-hour maximum*
Secondary	1300	0.5	3-hour maximum*
Particulates			
Primary	75		Annual geometric mean
	260		24-hour maximum*
Secondary	60		Annual geometric mean
	150		24-hour maximum*
Nitrogen oxides			
Primary and secondary	100	0.05	Annual arithmetic mean

*Not to be exceeded more than once per year.

Table 3. Emission performance standards for fossil fuel–fired steam generation units with heat input of more than 250 million British thermal units per hour (1 Btu = 1.06×10^3 joules; 1 pound = 0.453 kilogram) [from (9)].

Pollutant	Fuel	Maximum emission per 10^6 Btu heat input (pounds per 2-hour average)
Sulfur oxides	Liquid	0.8
	Solid	1.2
Particulates	All	0.1
Nitrogen oxides	Gaseous	0.2
	Liquid	0.3
	Solid	0.7

is removed in a wet scrubber; or (ii) slurries of lime or limestone are reacted with sulfur dioxide in scrubbing towers to form calcium sulfates and sulfites which are collected and impounded. In limestone scrubbing systems, efficiency of sulfur dioxide removal depends on intimate contact between solid and gas phases, and it is necessary to install large scrubbers, recirculate large volumes of slurry, and grind the limestone to extremely fine size (− 200 mesh) to achieve an acceptable degree of sulfur dioxide absorption. In addition, limestone utilization is poor, as much as 350 pounds per ton of high-sulfur coal burned. Absorption is more efficient with hydrated lime slurry than with limestone, but construction and operation of a kiln is required for quicklime production.

Wet limestone or lime scrubbing removes particulate matter as well as sulfur dioxide. Although the systems are designed to recycle the scrubbing fluid, the thickened sludges discharged to the impoundment area contain about 50 percent water and require large settling areas for dewatering and stabilization of the solids. Lime or limestone slurry scrubbers are capable of removing up to 90 percent of the sulfur oxides from a typical flue gas containing 0.2 to 0.3 percent sulfur dioxide.

The reliability of limestone or lime scrubbers remains questionable. One lime scrubber in Japan reportedly has operated with near 100 percent availability for 1½ years; in the United States, a scrubber using carbide sludge (calcium hydroxide) has been in reasonably trouble-free operation for 1000 hours.

Several studies have been published on the estimated costs for installing and operating limestone and lime scrubber systems (17, 20). Some data are also available on the costs of actual installations. Estimates for capital cost generally range between $27 and $46 per installed kilowatt of capacity. Annualized costs, those which the consumer can translate into the increase in the cost of electricity, range from 1.1 to 1.2 mill/kwh. The as-produced cost of electricity averages about 9 mill/kwh whereas the price to customers averages about 20 mill/kwh. The lower estimates are for new plants of large size, 1000 Mw, and the higher numbers are for retrofitting existing plants of 200-Mw capacity.

With regard to land and water pollution, the purity of the limestone or lime is of considerable concern. Pure lime-

stone is not readily available, because most contains some magnesium. Inasmuch as magnesium sulfate is water-soluble, the throwaway products generated with limestone or lime containing appreciable quantities of magnesium might present a disposal problem, particularly in areas of moderate or excessive rainfall. The soluble magnesium salts might leach and contaminate water at the surface or underground.

The cost associated with disposal of sludge varies appreciably. For some plants, the lack of a nearby sludge disposal site eliminates throwaway systems from the choices of control processes.

Despite the disposal problems, the limestone and wet lime processes are currently the most popular for U.S. power plants. About 28 utilities have selected one of these processes; in seven plants, the process is approaching operational stage (17).

Magnesium Oxide Scrubbing

The magnesium oxide scrubbing system is similar to the wet limestone and lime processes (15, 21), but it has not been as extensively tested. Magnesium sulfite and sulfate salts are formed by reacting a magnesium oxide slurry with the sulfur dioxide in the flue gas. The scrubber slurry is processed to separate the fly ash, then thickened, followed by crystallization to obtain magnesium salts. The salts are then calcined with carbon at a temperature of 980° to 1090°C to recover 15 percent sulfur dioxide gas. Regenerated magnesium oxide is recycled to the scrubber system. The sulfur dioxide can be liquefied or converted to sulfur or sulfuric acid. Because of the steps involved—thickening, fly ash separation, magnesium salt crystallization, and thermal decomposition—the regeneration is relatively costly.

Long-term reliability of this process has not been demonstrated. Only two units have been installed. One, an oil-fired boiler, was reported to be available 85 to 90 percent of the time during a 2-month period. Capital costs estimates for the process range from $33 per kilowatt of capacity for a new 1000-Mw plant up to $58 per kilowatt for retrofitting a 200-Mw existing plant. The estimated annualized costs are 1.5 and 3.0 mill/kwh for the same plants if no credit for sale of acid is assumed. Marketing the acid would reduce costs

only slightly, perhaps 0.3 mill/kwh (17). In certain situations it might be necessary to neutralize the acid with limestone or lime and impound the calcium sulfite and sulfate at additional expense.

Advantages of magnesium oxide scrubbing are that the regeneration of the magnesium oxide need not be performed at the power plant site, and a centrally located regeneration facility could service several plants. The process can remove enough sulfur dioxide from flue gases to meet emission standards, but reliability and operating costs must be verified. Current plant tests should provide this information.

Catalytic Oxidation

This process is a variation of the contact sulfuric acid process applied to the extremely dilute gases discharged by utility plants (22). The contact process produces 98 percent sulfuric acid from gas containing 3.5 percent sulfur dioxide or higher. There is no technological limitation, other than cost, in treating more dilute gases, but the gases must be thoroughly cleaned and the plants must be designed to treat large volumes.

In the catalytic oxidation process, flue gas, after thorough cleaning in cyclones and electrostatic precipitators, is passed over a catalyst to convert the sulfur dioxide to sulfur trioxide. This combines with the moisture present to form sulfuric acid of about 80 percent strength. This product has limited market value, and large quantities might pose a disposal problem.

In existing power plants, the clean flue gas from the electrostatic precipitators is not hot enough for catalytic conversion and must be reheated to 455°C. The retrofit version of this process has only been tested in pilot plants, but an acceptance test on a 110-Mw coal-fired boiler reportedly achieved 85 percent removal of sulfur dioxide. In a proposed design for new power plants, heat exchangers and hot electrostatic precipitators eliminate the need to reheat the gas. This design, however, has not been tested on a large scale.

Information is not available regarding system reliability, but performance of the particulate cleaning system will influence the percentage of time that the unit is out of operation. Costs are estimated at $41 to $64 per kilowatt, and annualized costs range from 1.5 to 2.6 mill/kwh (17). The need to clean particulate matter from the catalyst bed in the acid unit almost continuously, together with reheating and maintaining the large volumes of reaction gases at proper reaction temperatures for effective catalysis, are problems requiring further study.

Wet Sodium-Base Scrubbing

There are several sodium-base scrubbing systems; in the most advanced process, a sodium sulfite-bisulfite solution is used to absorb the sulfur dioxide and convert the sulfite to bisulfite (23). In this system, the flue gas must be cleaned thoroughly to remove particulates and must be cooled to about 55°C for effective absorption of the sulfur dioxide. A portion of the liquor is steam-stripped to recover strong sulfur dioxide and is then evaporated to recover sodium sulfite crystals for recycling. The sulfur dioxide can be used to make sulfuric acid or elemental sulfur. Since some oxidation of sulfite to sulfate occurs in the absorber, it is necessary to bleed off part of the solution and make up losses with caustic. Bleeding also controls buildup of particulate matter in the system. The process is capable of removing 90 percent or more of the sulfur dioxide from dilute gases, and has been installed at chemical plants and on oil-fired boilers. Experience in these plants probably has provided more accurate operating cost data than is available for most other advanced processes.

Process reliability greater than 95 percent for more than 2 years has been reported in one instance, for an oil-fired boiler. The process has not been tested at a coal-burning plant, but a demonstration project is planned to begin in 1975. Capital cost estimates range from $38 to $65 per kilowatt with corresponding annualized costs from 1.4 to 3.0 mill/kwh if no credit for byproduct acid or sulfur is assumed (17).

No serious technological limitations in the process are apparent. Any reluctance about widespread adoption probably stems from uncertainty about the amount of sulfite to sulfate oxidation and the high annualized costs.

Double Alkali Scrubbing

Although not as well developed as wet limestone or lime scrubbing, this process has potential because it elimi-

nates scaling problems associated with the limestone and lime systems. The scrubbing liquor is an alkaline solution of sodium or ammonium sulfates and sulfites, and efficiency of sulfur dioxide removal is high (15). Loaded scrubber effluent is treated with either limestone or lime to recover a throwaway sludge of calcium sulfates and sulfites and to regenerate the solution, which is returned to the scrubber. Development has largely been focused on the sodium system.

Cost estimates for the sodium double-alkali process as applied to utility power plants are encouraging, with capital investment cost ranging as low as $25 per kilowatt for a new 1000-Mw unit. Retrofitting a 200-Mw unit is estimated to cost $45 per kilowatt. Estimated annualized costs for these plants are 1.1 and 2.1 mill/kwh, respectively (17). An evaluation by the Environmental Protection Agency has indicated that the double alkali and citrate processes may be up to 20 percent less costly than processes such as wet limestone or sodium-base scrubbing (18).

Double alkali scrubbing has the same disadvantages as other throwaway processes, including the need for adding sodium or ammonium salt. However, because of its high efficiency and freedom from scaling in the scrubbing unit, the process is receiving increased attention.

Citrate System

The citrate process is one of the more attractive systems that has emerged in the past several years for flue gas desulfurization (7, 24). Developed by the Bureau of Mines to remove sulfur dioxide from nonferrous smelter stack gases, the process has the advantage that elemental sulfur is recovered without the need for intermediate sulfur dioxide regeneration. The system, which is considered among the least costly of the advanced processes (18), comprises (i) washing the flue gas to remove particulates and sulfur trioxide, and to cool the gas below 66°C; (ii) absorption of sulfur dioxide in a buffered sodium citrate–citric acid solution in a packed tower; (iii) reaction of the loaded solution with hydrogen sulfide in a closed vessel to form elemental sulfur; and (iv) separation of sulfur from the regenerated solution by oil flotation followed by melting. Hydrogen sulfide for the sulfur precipitation step is generated by

reacting part of the recovered sulfur with natural gas and steam.

Recently the bureau began testing the process in a pilot plant with capacity of 1000 standard cubic feet per minute (scfm) at the Bunker Hill lead smelter, Kellogg, Idaho. More than 95 percent removal of sulfur dioxide has been achieved without difficulty from a gas stream containing 0.5 percent sulfur dioxide.

Since June 1973, the process has been tested in a 2000-scfm demonstration unit at a coal-fired steam generating plant in Terre Haute, Indiana (25). Tests on gas containing 0.27 percent sulfur dioxide, generated by burning coal containing 3 percent sulfur, have largely confirmed Bureau of Mines findings. Although the citrate process has been proposed for producing elemental sulfur, it also is possible to recover sulfur dioxide for conversion to acid by incorporating a steam-stripping step.

Estimated capital cost of a citrate process desulfurization unit for a 1000-Mw plant burning coal containing 3 percent sulfur is $31 million. Annualized costs would be 1.4 mill/kwh, if no credit for the 214 long tons of sulfur produced daily is assumed.

Summary

We must expand the use of coal for electricity generation as rapidly as possible to help alleviate the immediate oil and natural gas shortage, which threatens to become more acute unless the pattern of energy use is changed.

It is not likely, nor is it proposed, that coal should completely replace oil or gas in power generation; geographic location of plants and ready availability of high- or low-sulfur coal will to some extent dictate the choice of fuel. However, replacing 50 percent of the oil and gas now used in power generation would release more than 200 million barrels of oil and 1.9 trillion cubic feet of natural gas (1 barrel of oil = 0.16 m³; 1 cubic foot = 2.8 × 10⁻² m³) annually for other uses such as home and commercial heating, transportation, chemical feedstock, and selected industrial and manufacturing uses. Even more important, use of coal instead of oil or gas in new fossil fuel–fired electrical generating plants would go far toward conserving natural gas resources and holding the line on increased petroleum imports.

In recent years, U.S. pollution regulations restricting sulfur oxide emissions from power plants have been one of the major deterrents to the use of the high-rank, high-sulfur coals of the Midwest and East. Reliable flue gas desulfurization processes that permit burning of these coals without adverse environmental effects are approaching full development and should encourage wider use of coal in electricity generation for the next 25 years. Estimates indicate that more than 40 sulfur dioxide scrubbing units will be installed on power plants totaling about 20,000-Mw capacity by late 1976 (*15*). The cost of these units will approach $750 million. Although this is not a significant amount of our coal-fired generating capacity, these installations should give impetus to construction of more and larger ones by 1980 and the next decade; this would refute the tenet that wide use of coal and a clean environment are mutually exclusive. As the choice of proved scrubbing technology broadens, no single process will dominate the market. Individual utilities, in addition to considering the economics, will be faced with making choices on the basis of the type of coal burned; water, land, and air pollution regulations; and the marketability of the end products.

The cost of flue gas desulfurization will be high, ranging from 1.2 to 3.2 mill/kwh. The average increase in electricity cost to consumers is expected to be about 3 to 6 percent, and in some instances as much as 15 percent. However, the added burden may not be as high as that of dependence on foreign oil, both in terms of price and reliability of supply. Combustion of high-sulfur coal followed by stack gas cleanup appears to be the cheapest alternative for meeting our electricity needs in the next few decades.

References and Notes

1. *U.S. Geol. Surv. Bull No. 1136* (1961); *ibid., No. 1275* (1969); *U.S. Bur. Mines Inform. Cir. No. 8531* (1971); Geological Survey, unpublished data; Bureau of Mines, unpublished data.
2. P. Averitt, *U.S. Geol. Surv. Prof. Pap. No. 820* (1973), p. 133.
3. W. G. Dupree, Jr., and J. A. West, *United States Energy Through the Year 2000* (Department of the Interior, Washington, D.C., 1972).
4. *Steam Electric Plant Factors/1967 Edition* (National Coal Association, Washington, D.C., ed. 17, 1967).
5. Data available from the Federal Power Commission and Bureau of Mines, *Bituminous Coal Data* (National Coal Association, Washington, D.C., 1973), pp. 108–109.
6. *Steam-Electric Plant Factors/1972 Edition*, (National Coal Association, Washington, D.C., ed. 22, 1972).
7. E. F. Osborn, *Science* **183**, 477 (1974).
8. *Fed. Reg.* **36**, 8185 (30 April 1971); *ibid.* **38**, 25678 (14 September 1973).
9. *Ibid.* **36**, 24875 (23 December 1971).
10. "East coast shifts to greater use of coal for electric generation, 'borrows' electricity from other utilities (press release and status report, Federal Energy Office, Washington, D.C., 6 February 1974).
11. "U.S. energy use up nearly 5 percent in 1973" (press release, Bureau of Mines, Department of the Interior, 13 March 1974).
12. T. L. Montgomery, J. M. Leavitt, T. L. Crawford, F. E. Gartrell, *J. Met.* **25** (No. 6), 35 (1973).
13. *Fed. Reg.* **38**, 25697 (14 September 1973).
14. National Academy of Engineering–National Research Council, *Abatement of Sulfur Oxide Emissions from Stationary Combustion Sources* (P.B. 192,887, National Technical Information Service, Springfield, Va., 1970).
15. Federal Interagency Committee Evaluation of State Air Implementation Plans, *Final Report of the Sulfur Oxide Control Technology Assessment Panel on Projected Utilization of Stack Gas Cleaning Systems by Steam-Electric Plants* (Report No. APTD-1569, Environmental Protection Agency, Research Triangle Park, N.C., 1973).
16. J. McLaren and D. F. Williams, *Combustion* **41** (No. 11), 21 (1970).
17. F. Princiotta, "EPA presentation on status of flue gas desulfurization technology," testimony at national power plant hearings sponsored by the Environmental Protection Agency, 18 October to 2 November 1973 (hearing records available for consultation at the Environmental Protection Agency, Washington, D.C.).
18. G. T. Rochelle, paper presented at the flue gas desulfurization symposium of the Environmental Protection Agency, New Orleans, 14 to 17 May 1973.
19. A. V. Slack, H. L. Falkenberry, R. E. Harrington, Preprint 39d, 70th national meeting, American Institute of Chemical Engineers, Atlantic City, N.J. 29 August to 1 September 1971.
20. J. K. Burchard, paper presented at the technical conference "Sulfur in utility fuels: the growing dilemma," sponsored by *Electrical World Magazine*, 25 to 26 October 1972.
21. I. S. Shah and C. P. Quigeley, Preprint 39e, 70th national meeting of the American Institute of Chemical Engineers, Atlantic City, N.J. 29 August to 1 September 1971.
22. W. R. Horlacher, R. E. Barnard, R. K. Teague, P. L. Haylen, paper presented at the 71st national meeting of the American Institute of Chemical Engineers, Dallas, Tex., 20 to 23 February 1972.
23. J. L. Martinez, C. B. Earl, T. L. Craig, in *AIME Environmental Quality Conference, Washington, D.C., June 7–9, 1971, Preprint Volume* (American Institute of Mining, Metallurgical, and Petroleum Engineers, Washington, D.C., 1971), pp. 409–420.
24. J. B. Rosenbaum, W. A. McKinney, H. R. Beard, L. Crocker, W. I. Nissen, *U.S. Bur. Mines Rep. Invest. No. 7774* (1973).
25. F. S. Chalmers, L. Korosy, A. Saleem, paper presented at the Industrial Fuel Conference, West Lafayette, Ind., 3 October 1973.

Nuclear Eclectic Power

David J. Rose

Enough work has been done to permit a reasonable assessment of the major issues of nuclear power. Most of the recent fluctuations in energy patterns tend to reinforce what seemed evident even several years ago: a massive switch to nuclear power for electric energy generation, and perhaps later for other purposes. The total installed electric utility generating capacity in the United States is expected to be 480,000 megawatts by the end of 1974 (*1*); the average generation rate in March 1974 was 212,000 Mw (*2*). The present nuclear installed capacity is about 30,000 Mw. Serious predictions of 1,000,000 Mw of nuclear power installed by A.D. 2000 may come true; the total cost of those nuclear plants would be more than $600 billion. The grand total, including factories to produce the equipment and facilities to enrich uranium, process fuel, and handle wastes, may come to $1 trillion, plus the cost of transmitting and distributing the energy. Also, as alternate fuel costs rise, nuclear heat will become interesting for large-scale industrial and commercial applications. If events turn out this way, nuclear power will constitute the largest coherent technological plunge to date, with long-lasting consequences.

Any assessment of nuclear power, to be useful, must be comparative; the question is, compared to what? Until about A.D. 2000, the major choices are nuclear power, fossil fuels (of various sorts), or nothing, in varying proportions. In the 21st century, they are advanced nuclear power, increasingly sophisticated chemical fuels, probably derived from coal or oil shales, perhaps hydrogen (but made with nuclear power), perhaps solar power (more likely for many small-scale applications, in my opinion), or nothing. Beyond that era, resource limitations increasingly exclude fossil fuels. The

The author is a professor in the Nuclear Engineering Department, Massachusetts Institute of Technology, Cambridge 02139.

benefits of nuclear power are lower production costs, vastly larger resources, and (I will try to show) substantially less total adverse environmental impact compared with fossil fuels. Costs and hazards include not only the usual economic ones of the facilities themselves, but also those associated with (i) illegal diversion of nuclear fuels, (ii) accidents, (iii) radioactive waste storage, and (iv) other environmental and societal impacts.

In this article, I will not seriously entertain the notion of opting for less electric power, believing that economic, demographic, and other social forces already present will lead to substantial increases in demand over the next several decades. The precise amount of growth turns out not to affect this discussion. Thus, while recognizing the necessity, importance, and consequences of limiting growth and of conserving energy wherever possible, one can debate the issue of nuclear power during the next 50 years separately.

Nuclear Plant Properties,
Economic Costs, and Demand

This is not an article on reactor principles, but a few remarks will facilitate the debate that follows.

Virtually all present-day nuclear power reactors work on the basis of fissioning the relatively rare isotope uranium-235 (0.77 percent of natural uranium) to produce fission products (chiefly intermediate-weight elements), about 2.5 neutrons per event, and energy (200 million electron volts per event). Some neutrons go on to initiate further ^{235}U fissions; controlling the neutron fate by initial design and by adjustment of neutron-absorbing materials controls the reactor. Also, some neutrons are absorbed in the predominant uranium isotope ^{238}U to make a substantial amount of plutonium (^{239}Pu). The conversion ratio (^{239}Pu formed/ ^{235}U fissioned) is about 0.5 for reactors being installed today. Thus, current reactors bring with them plutonium handling and hazard problems, which are incorrectly thought by some to apply only to future breeder reactors. Some of the ^{239}Pu actually fissions in the reactor; most is removed at fuel reprocessing time, then stored for later use in the first breeder reactors, for which it is the fissionable fuel. Also, ^{239}Pu can be recycled as fuel in present-day reactors, but that has not been done yet.

Table 1. U.S. uranium reserves (7). The amount of U_3O_8 available comprises reasonably assured plus estimated additional reserves; ppm, parts per million.

Concentration: U_3O_8 in ore (ppm)	U_3O_8		Electricity producible (10^3 megawatt-years)	
	Cost (dollars per pound)	Amount available (10^3 tons)	Light water reactor	Breeder reactor
> 1600	Up to 10†	1,127	6,600	880,000
> 1000	Up to 15†	1,630	9,500	1,270,000
> 200	Up to 30†	2,400	14,000	1,860,000
> 60	Up to 50‡	8,400	49,000	6,500,000
> 25	Up to 100‡	17,400	102,000	13,500,000
3*	Several hundred	10^6–10^7		

* Natural crustal abundance.   † Includes copper leach residues and phosphates.   ‡ Includes Chattanooga shale.

Turning now to more specific types, the reactors most commonly used and ordered in the United States contain fuel and ordinary (light) water in large pressure vessels, the so-called light water reactors (LWR's). They operate at 1000 to 2200 pounds per square inch ($\sim 15 \times 10^6$ newtons per square meter) and 315°C; the safety of this arrangement and its associated piping has been the subject of recent lively debate. The relatively low operating temperature limits the net efficiency of these plants to 32 percent. There are two subspecies: the pressurized-water reactor, where the water does not boil, but passes into a heat exchanger that produces steam for the turbines in a separate loop; and the boiling-water reactor, where the steam from the pressure vessel passes directly through the turbines. The first of these was developed principally by the Westinghouse Electric Company, partly from experience in building smaller versions for the U.S. Navy. The second was developed solely by the General Electric Company. Importantly, both companies could afford to offer loss leaders, so to speak, in order to capture a substantial early share of the reactor market; thus, LWR's have proliferated, almost to the exclusion of other types. Advantages are: relatively well-developed technology and predictable performance, well-developed fuel cycle technology, best-known cost. Disadvantages are: low efficiency, public questions about reactor safety, only moderate conversion efficiency (0.5). A somewhat neutral feature is the requirement for fuel enriched to 3 percent ^{235}U; present uranium enrichment facilities will require substantial augmentation, at a cost of several billion dollars, in the 1980's.

Other reactor species need mentioning here. In the United States the General Atomic Company has for years been developing slowly a high-temperature gas-cooled reactor (HTGR), but could not afford to offer a loss leader. Thus the HTGR, which many imagine to be a better idea, lagged until the Gulf Corporation, and later Shell also, took it over. Advantages are: higher operating temperature and efficiency (40 percent), possibly lower cost, higher conversion ratio (0.7, intermediate between the LWR converters and a true breeder), and the absence of some mechanical failure modes discussed in relation to LWR's. Disadvantages are: there is only one supplier, whose fuel must be fully enriched fissionable uranium, which is weapons-grade material and thus raises the specter of illegal diversion (but design changes could permit using lower enrichment); and the fuel cycle is incompletely developed. In this last respect, a typical problem is what to do with the large amount of slightly radioactive graphite in which the fuel will be embedded. Burning it freely seems not acceptable, but I see nothing to prevent turning it into an insoluble chemical (a carbonate?) and sequestering it safely. At present, one HTGR is about to commence operation, six more are on order, and some analyses have shown the HTGR taking over a substantial share of future markets. The present fuel for the HTGR is ^{235}U, but eventually it would work mainly on the thorium-^{233}U cycle.

Another candidate is the Canadian CANDU reactor, of which several are in operation there, with others on order for Mexico and outside North America. The CANDU is of pressure-tube construction (thought to be a safer design than the U.S. light water reactors) and permits on-line refueling. It can run on natural uranium (but does better with enriched fuel), because it is moderated and cooled with heavy water; it is an older design than most, and operates at even lower efficiency than the U.S.

light water reactors. It is probably more expensive than the U.S. reactors, but how much is hard to discover, because of differences between U.S. and Canadian costing policies. Another version is the heavy-water-moderated organic-liquid-cooled demonstration reactor at Whiteshell station, Manitoba. If the United States were starting its reactor program today, with no large commitment already made, the Canadian ideas would merit serious consideration; but under present circumstances, the need for development and prototype construction makes any such introduction to the U.S. market unlikely.

All modern nuclear power reactors are large, to capture economies of scale inherent in building larger components (up to a limit). The U.S. Atomic Energy Commission has limited all reactor approvals (until 1978 at least) to units that develop not more than 3800 Mw of nuclear heat. Thus, LWR's at 32 percent efficiency will be limited to 1200 megawatts electric [Mw(e)] and HTGR's at 40 percent to 1500 Mw(e).

These comparisons have international impact. New electric plants in France will be LWR's of the U.S. type. The United Kingdom is finishing a complex internal debate over whether to build more of its ancient but familiar (to the British) gas-cooled Magnox reactors, to adopt LWR's of U.S. type, or to adopt a version of the Canadian reactors.

Turning now to costs, an excellent study has been made of nuclear and fossil fuel possibilities for the Northeast Utilities system by Arthur D. Little, Inc. (3). A.D.L. estimates total capital cost per kilowatt of $389 for an oil-fired plant, $588 for a coal plant with sulfur and particulate removal, and $702 for an LWR, all for operation in 1981. These figures are much higher than those guessed in the 1960's for several reasons: substantially higher construction costs of all kinds, need for environmental controls on fossil fuel plants, need for more experience by the nuclear industry, increasing complexity of nuclear plants, and construction delays (which add interest and inflation charges). These capital costs appear in the electric bill at about 1¢ per kilowatt-hour for each $500 (for 7000 operating hours per year and a 14 percent rate of return on capital before taxes). Thus, at this stage nuclear power has a disadvantage of about 0.2¢/kwh with respect to coal and 0.64/kwh with respect to oil.

Operation and maintenance costs (0.09¢, 0.18¢, 0.135¢ per kilowatt-hour for oil, coal, and nuclear fuel, according to A.D.L.) give a slight further advantage to oil. But the greatest single fact influencing present demand for nuclear power is that petroleum at $10 per barrel (0.16 m³) represents 1.5¢/kwh of the cost of electricity, using the most efficient plant available (40 percent). Total nuclear fuel cycle costs will be less than 0.3¢/kwh, giving an advantage over oil of 1.2¢/kwh, and an overall system advantage of 0.5¢/kwh. Much the same situation is predicted for coal, and the gap between nuclear and fossil fuels will widen with time. Petroleum prices, now about three times higher than those prevailing in early 1973, are not likely to decline very much, being supported both by a shortage of cheap oil in oil-consuming countries and increasing economic sophistication in the oil-producing ones. The likely advent of more domestic crude oil at prices of $7 to $10 a barrel, or of synthetic crude at perhaps the same price (after the middle 1980's?) still leaves nuclear power with strong economic advantage.

Studies like this show that nuclear power has become by far the most attractive large option for electric power generation, both in the United States and abroad, with few exceptions. The energy crisis of 1973–1974 is one of fossil fuels, not nuclear ones, and nuclear power tends to benefit on that account. Development of a strong conservation ethic will not have the effect of strongly decreasing the growth rate of nuclear power; the first results would be a limitation of nonnuclear plant construction or operation.

Here are some projections. The year A.D. 2000 is a good date to focus on: Plants planned today will be halfway through their operating life. The AEC estimates 1,200,000 Mw of nuclear capacity installed by that date (4), and Dupree and West's predictions (5) amount to about 960,000 Mw. Considering the capacity of plants now operating (30,000 Mw), under construction, or planned for operation before 1985 (about 200,000 Mw), the various factors mentioned above, and the traditional growth of electric power (7 percent per year), an installed capacity of 1,000,000 Mw nuclear seems likely to be exceeded. Beyond A.D. 2000, the rate of growth is more difficult to predict: acceptable sites will be particularly hard to find, even with use of wet cooling towers, and dry cool-

ing towers are even larger and more expensive ($100/kw?); and the likelihood and timing of new major applications (such as making hydrogen from cheap nuclear heat or electricity, or powering personal electric vehicles) are unknown factors at present. The 1,000,-000 Mw of nuclear electric power is imagined to be perhaps two-thirds of the total electric capacity predicted for A.D. 2000, about four times the capacity of present installations. Western Europe and Japan, with less fossil fuel resources than the United States, find nuclear electric power even more attractive.

Resources

Various scenarios (6) predict a total cumulative requirement of about 2.5 million tons of uranium oxide (U_3O_8) by A.D. 2000 and 4 to 4.5 million tons by A.D. 2010. The precise amount depends on the mix of reactor types, on when breeder reactors are introduced, and on the actual future electric demand.

The U.S. uranium resources according to the AEC (7) are shown in Table 1. The resources available up to $10 a pound ($\sim$ 0.45 kg) would, if used in LWR's, generate 6,000,000 megawatt-years of electricity, a total electric supply for almost 30 years at present rates, but not enough for the growing nuclear demand to A.D. 2000. With LWR's, the increase in the cost of electricity would be 0.1¢/kwh for each increase of $17 a pound in U_3O_8. To wipe out the present nuclear cost advantage of at least 0.5¢, U_3O_8 would have to reach nearly $100 a pound, at which cost Table 1 shows a great deal of uranium available.

The numbers in Table 1 provide a substantial fraction of the input for the debate pro and con nuclear power and especially for the nuclear breeder debate. The AEC saw trouble ahead, from these and similar estimates made a few years ago: If used in LWR's, the low-cost reserves are modest, and rising U_3O_8 prices after (say) A.D. 2000 would place a new penalty on nuclear power, perhaps 0.1¢/kwh. Thus, it was necessary to develop the breeder reactor; by converting the common ^{238}U to fissionable plutonium, it utilizes almost all the nuclear energy of the uranium, instead of only the ^{235}U plus a small additional plutonium conversion. In effect, not only are the nuclear energy resources multiplied by a factor of

100, but (since almost all of it is used) the resource cost per energy unit drops similarly. Thus, to a good approximation, the cost of electricity from nuclear breeders becomes independent of uranium prices. Also, at least by implication, if the breeder were not developed and massively deployed in time, nuclear power might become expensive enough to drive electric utilities back to fossil fuels. Thus, a "slot" in time was imagined when breeder reactors must be introduced—late enough that plutonium would be available from existing LWR's to make initial fuel charges, but not so late that power from LWR's would have become expensive because of the rising cost of uranium. The period 1985 to 1995 was envisaged for commercial introduction.

With present oil and coal prices and environmental protection costs the slot is virtually open-ended, and the nuclear advantage is unlikely to be overcome by any large-scale fossil option, except in special locations. Also, the entire debate is likely to have been mistaken, as follows. With a real market for U_3O_8 at (say) $10 a pound, prospectors seriously searched for high-grade ore, and the 1,127,000 tons of reserves shown in Table 1 is the result. But what of the approximately equal increment represented by the third row of Table 1, supposed to include all ores with a U_3O_8 concentration greater than 200 parts per million? Those lower grades were not actively sought per se, but were found somewhat incidentally. Thus we can explain the anomalous dip in reserves at intermediate prices and concentrations—no one seriously looked for them. The outcome of the reasoning is that if a definite offer to purchase were made at more than $10 a pound, a great deal more would easily be found, and the AEC would have no scarcity argument in favor of the breeder until well into the 21st century. Three additional circumstances support this interpretation: (i) In the middle and late 1950's and 1960's, when the federal government offered incentives to discover new uranium resources, much showed up at $8 to $10 a pound. (ii) The reserves at $10 a pound are enough for nearly 30 years for domestic purposes. This is an anomalously large amount in terms of the economic optimum (at private investment rates); for decades our reserves of many minerals have represented a supply for 8 to 10 years, and this has been determined by economic

pressures to buy them and economic penalties for exploring for things that will not be used for a long time. (iii) Canada and Australia, for instance, report increasingly large resources.

A generally similar debate could be constructed for thorium, which can be used in a breeder to make ^{233}U; it is thought to be at least as plentiful as uranium.

Diseconomies and Nonmarket Costs

More important issues appear here than there is space properly to discuss, so I choose to develop three in subsequent sections—illegal acts, accidents, and radioactive waste disposal—and give brief mention to others that have already been well illuminated in public debate.

Present nuclear plants are less efficient than fossil fuel ones, and in addition do not exhaust any waste heat directly to the atmosphere through a chimney. Thus a light water nuclear plant will reject into cooling water almost twice as much waste heat as do the most efficient fossil fuel plants, for the same electric power. Siting problems then ensue, exacerbated by the large size of the power plants. But these problems seem surmountable, perhaps at a cost of visual pollution from cooling towers or design complications arising from siting off-shore; and introducing more efficient reactors will eventually ameliorate the difficulty.

Licensing is a complex issue. Two separate federal licenses are required: before construction and again before operation. At each stage, detailed studies are required, including environmental impacts, and interveners must be heard. Long delays then become possible; they are expensive—$50,000,-000 a year in interest and other charges

on a completed nonoperating plant. One might imagine, therefore, some reversion to fossil-fueled plants for which, alas, no such licensing is required; but cost penalties make that alternative unattractive.

Illegal Acts

The problem is vexatious, and even discussion can be dangerous. Two non-problems are: (i) Present security arrangements at reactors make it highly unlikely that one or a few persons, even well-prepared, can cause a large disruptive accident. (ii) Stealing new fuel for LWR's is useless, because the fuel is nonradioactive and cannot be enriched to weapons-grade ^{235}U (90 percent +) without a technology capable of doing the whole job, starting with natural uranium.

However, a number of possibilities exist for illegal acts, against which the reactor operators and public authorities (particularly the federal government) take increasingly strict precautions, whose adequacy has from time to time been questioned.

1) A large, organized raid on an operating reactor. The outer containment shell will resist the impact of moderate-size airplanes, and shells of reactors near airports are designed to resist the impact of the largest loaded airplanes. Thus, ingress would have to be made by direct attack on the entrances, and various security steps have been taken against this possibility. It would be logical to arrange reactor protective devices so that the reactor would shut down when any such hostile event occurred and could not be restarted except through time-consuming operations by experts; in that case attackers could cause financial mischief, but no public calamity. In addition,

91

Table 2. Summary of health effects of civilian nuclear power, per 1000 Mw(e) plant-year (8).

Activity	Fatalities			Injuries (days off)
	Accidents (not radiation-related)	Radiation-related (cancers and genetic)	Total	
Uranium mining and milling	0.173	0.001	0.174	330.5
Fuel processing and reprocessing	0.048	0.040	0.088	5.6
Design and manufacture of reactors, instruments, and so on	0.040		0.040	24.4
Reactor operation and maintenance	0.037	0.107	0.144	158
Waste disposal		0.0003	0.0003	
Transport of nuclear fuel	0.036	0.010	0.046	
Totals	0.334	0.158	0.492	518

reactors are so complex that the active assistance of knowledgeable persons inside seems necessary; thus, to summarize this item, an economic calamity causable by an irrational employee seems the dominant danger.

2) Theft of used fuel elements. Until recently, used fuel was shipped in technically safe casks, but with almost no guard. That has now been corrected, and the used fuel is monitored during shipment in various ways. Making a bomb from it requires technological facilities and sophistication comparable to those of the AEC itself. The most likely threat would come from the fuel being ground up and used for blackmail, a strategy which would be very hazardous to the conspirators.

3) Theft of makeup fuel for high-temperature gas-cooled reactors, which is 93 percent ^{235}U. This is weapons-grade material, and must be handled as such.

4) In the future, theft of breeder fuel, which is weapons-grade plutonium. The possibilities for mischief and handling requirements are the same as for item 3 above; but the risk to conspirators is immense, because plutonium is so lethal (see below).

It seems to me that the greatest diversionary hazard is related not to civilian nuclear power, but to weapons and their components. At increasing cost, more protection can be bought, and no one—public or private—would imagine settling for less than enough. But in dealing with irrationality, how much is enough? No one knows. It would be bitter irony if civilization had to renounce its claim to that name through inability to control these aspects of nuclear power; meanwhile, illegal use is to me the most worrisome and least resolved hazard, and a prime motivation for exploring the possibilities of controlled nuclear fusion.

Accidents and Related Hazards

An immense amount has been done; the situation is in no way as some critics of nuclear power portray it, but trouble spots persist. Before some hotly debated topics are assessed, consider Table 2, which summarizes a study made by Walsh (8) of the casualties associated with nuclear power. Events are normalized per unit of electric energy produced—per 1000 Mw(e) plant-year (8.76×10^9 kwh).

Several features of Table 2 are notable: (i) "conventional" accidents are dominant, especially in the hazardous occupation of mining; (ii) the total fatality rate is about 0.5 per reactor-year, tout compris; (iii) most of the hazards are occupational, not public. These numbers will be compared later with others for fossil fuel power.

The data of Table 2, gleaned from a large number of sources, are in reasonable agreement with those of other studies. Hub et al. (9) report 0.932 fatality and 373 total days off due to injuries, and Sagan (10) reports 0.390 and 1022, respectively. The AEC (11) settles on the range 0.161 to 0.364 for fatalities, and does not give an estimate of injuries. A variation of a factor of 2 should be expected because of the periods studied, assignment of casualties, and so forth. For example, of 11,870 short tons of U_3O_8 produced domestically in 1969, 4700 were sold for electricity production and only about 350 were actually used up that year in operating reactors (1 short ton $\sim$ 0.9 metric ton). Also, the various investigators agree fairly well that occupational accidents unrelated to radiation dominate. For example, Lave and Freeburg (12), in an exceptionally well-documented comparison of the effects on health of electricity generation from coal, oil, and nuclear fuel, cite about 0.12 fatality per 1000 Mw(e) plant-year from mining and milling accidents, compared with Walsh's 0.173.

Table 2 does not seem to contain the item most hotly debated: the probability of large nuclear accidents, for example from a pipe rupture, followed by failure of the emergency core cooling system, followed by transfer of a substantial fraction the radioactive mess to the external environment. It was just this possibility that stimulated a marathon debate between the Union of Concerned Scientists and the AEC from 1972 to 1974 (13). An intensive study of hypothetical large accidents has been made by N. C. Rasmussen and co-workers for the AEC. No such reactor failures have occurred, but the data base is nevertheless substantial—all the large high-technology, high-pressure, high-temperature chemical processors and vessels. According to Chairman Ray of the AEC (14) the Rasmussen study can be roughly summarized by assigning a chance of about 10^{-6} per reactor-year of a major accident with loss of several hundred lives, including later cancers and genetic deaths. For the

sake of argument, make this 1000 lives. The actuarial hazard would be 10^{-3} per 1000 Mw(e) plant-year, and it duly appears as a 1 percent contribution to one of the entries in Table 2.

Also present in Table 2 are the public hazards from releasing radioactive gases—principally ^{85}Kr and tritium—from boiling-water reactors during operation, from pressurized-water reactors during refueling, and from fuel reprocessing plants. Radioactive xenon presents less total hazard, because it decays quickly. New reactors built with longer gas holdup permit even lower releases.

No substantial quantitative study is in disagreement with these results. The AEC itself prepared a now-notorious report (15) predicting several thousand deaths and billions of dollars damage if a large amount of material from a modest-size reactor got into the atmosphere under adverse meteorological conditions. The authors of that work never considered the probability of any sequence of events leading to the hypothetical radioactive release; this makes it somewhat like analyzing (say) the consequences of the New York World Trade Center falling over.

If Rasmussen's estimates are believed, the fatality rate per person would be about 10^{-12} per hour in A.D. 2000, about the same as the probability of being struck by a meteorite, and a thousand times less than the probability of being electrocuted.

Having seemed to bury the reactor accident bogey, let me now resurrect it. Accidents seem so remote only because of intense, persistent, and highly competent professional effort. Will that continue indefinitely, or not, and is reactor technology that good worldwide? One can easily imagine inadequate vigilance, both here and abroad, or what is just as bad, lack of social responsibility toward these matters; then disaster would surely follow.

The accident issue cannot be closed without mention of plutonium, a principal and proximate cause for the worry. An excellent and convenient review has been given by Bair and Thompson (16); the AEC has long been concerned (17). Plutonium is an alpha-particle emitter; when introduced into the body in a soluble form, it (i) circulates as complexes in the blood in large molecules; (ii) gets into the bones; (iii) goes to the liver, where it tends to stay unless there is a stress on the body's iron stores; and (iv) as with iron, gets caught up in the body's transport and storage system, which prevents loss and promotes reuse. When introduced as particulates (usually the oxide) through wounds or by inhalation, some of it forms local tiny hot spots, and some travels throughout the body. It is thought to be about five times as toxic as radium, and present maximum occupational body burden is now set at 40 nanocuries (0.6 microgram of ^{239}Pu, but only 2.3 nanograms of ^{238}Pu). These limits, based in part on comparisons with the effects of radium, have been questioned because of the concentration in the liver, which is not the case with radium, and the problem of hot spots. On this latter point, Tamplin and Cochran (18) pick a probability of 1/2000 that a single hot plutonium particle will cause cancer, and propose a body burden limit of two such particles. That would be 1.4×10^{-13} curie, a factor of 300,000 below the present limits. So far, the evidence indicates that plutonium is not that dangerous, and that something near the present limits will eventually be well justified. In the meantime, experimental work on animals continues, and persons inadvertently exposed in the past to plutonium are carefully monitored.

It is very unsettling that present reactors contain substantial amounts of plutonium, and breeder reactors will contain a huge quantity—close to 10^6 curies. The extreme ratio between the resource available and the allowable body burden emphasizes the necessity of vigilance, which must be presumed to exist everywhere, forever. If the Tamplin and Cochran risk estimates turn out to be correct, nuclear fission power will need to be rethought, because the consequences of even a single large accident become disastrous.

Nuclear Waste Disposal

The costs of proper waste disposal are higher than were originally imagined, but still small compared to the total costs of nuclear power. The main problems seem to have been failing to appreciate the importance of public concern and failing to explore the available options with enough money and imagination. Fortunately, those shortcomings in the civilian waste disposal program are being corrected.

A more comprehensive assessment of the situation has appeared (19), and

a brief summary will suffice here. The wastes fall into two categories. First, there are fission products of intermediate atomic weight, ^{90}Sr, ^{137}Cs, and ^{85}Kr, for example, and all the main ones have half-lives of 30 years or less; thus, in 700 years less than 10^{-7} of the waste remains, which further calculation shows is innocuous. Second, there are the so-called actinides, mainly plutonium, neptunium, curium, americium, and so on, all heavy elements made by neutron absorption in the original uranium (or thorium, if the reactor works on a ^{232}Th-^{233}U breeding cycle). These typically have very long half-lives—24,600 years for ^{239}Pu, for example. All these elements are very toxic, because of their radioactivity, proclivity to settle in bone and other body sites, and so on. If merely stored they last a million years or more, beyond the time horizon of present rational planning.

At present, only plutonium and uranium values are extracted from the wastes, and that only to about 99.5 percent (the limit of profitable recovery); this narrow economic optimum is clearly not the social one; an extraction of 99.9 percent of uranium, neptunium, and plutonium and 99 percent of americium and curium reduces the long-term activity by a factor of 100 compared to present practices, leaving essentially just the fission products. The extracted actinides can be recycled in the reactor at small penalty; they all turn eventually into fission products, and the million-year problem is effectively eliminated. Kubo and Rose (19) estimated an additional cost of perhaps 0.02¢/kwh for implementing this option.

Now the nuclear waste problem becomes a 700-year one—a long time, but short compared to geologic eons. Sequestering the remainder, perhaps in the form of a borosilicate glass, in selected salt deposits, hard rock sites, or even near-surface repositories (with complete retrievability) makes sense; such sequestrations can be accomplished with great assurance (for example, in granite monoliths near the sea where any drainage paths would lead under the continental shelf).

Some options that are not appealing at present are disposal in the ocean deeps (either buried or not), in ice sheets or continental rocks, or in space; but the possibilities should be reviewed from time to time.

Certainly, the responsibility for radioactive waste disposal must eventually

lie with the government, because the time horizon of conventional economic groups cannot guarantee concern for so long; private industry can at best act as the agent of the public interest. Narrowly regional solutions are also difficult to find, because the patterns of desirable sites for nuclear reactors, fuel reprocessing plants, and waste disposal do not come anywhere near coinciding. Thus, for example, it would be highly desirable for Europe to develop an integrated nuclear waste management strategy; but a set of national decisions to accept wastes and the responsibility for them must presage workable broader agreements (20).

Breeder Reactors

A few more remarks are required on breeders, to augment material in previous sections. The liquid metal fast breeder reactor (LMFBR) has been the prime energy goal of the AEC, which budgeted $357 million for it in fiscal year 1975 and plans a total of $2556 million from 1975 to 1979. The 1974 allotment is 36 percent of the entire federal budget for energy research and development; similar or higher percentages in previous years, plus the attitudes expressed by the AEC, the Executive Office of the President, and the Joint Committee on Atomic Energy, have led to criticism of "all the eggs in one basket."

The LMFBR has substantial technical points in its favor, besides the eventual but presently slippery advantage of resource conservation. It is nonpressurized, and in that respect more completely sealed, simpler, and safer. It will operate at higher temperatures than LWR's, giving an efficiency of 41 percent, comparable to the HTGR's or modern fossil fuel plants. The high thermal conductivity and heat capacity of its coolant—liquid sodium—make it virtually immune to damage in case of mechanical failure of the cooling system external to the reactor. It may eventually be cheaper, but that depends on the outcome of the expensive development program presently under way. There are disadvantages too. The liquid sodium is at about 620°C, and becomes intensely radioactive, forcing refueling and other operations on the reactor to be carried out blind, and constituting a chemical hazard in respect to failures in circulation pumps, pipes, or heat exchangers. The plu-

Nuclear operators at Boston Edison's Pilgrim Station nuclear power plant at Plymouth, Massachusetts, prepare the 80-ton reactor vessel head for replacement on the plant's reactor at the completion of recent refueling operations. [Courtesy of Boston Edison Co., Boston, Massachusetts]

tonium hazard has already been discussed. The Soviet Union and France have prototype or demonstration LMFBR's already operating, and the United Kingdom will soon follow. The U.S. program has suffered from a plethora of rigid directions from the AEC to its field offices and contractors, which has led to excessive delay and expense. The Fast Flux Test Reactor, a prototype for the U.S. demonstration reactor, has escalated in cost from an initial $80 million to an uncertain $600 million to $800 million; the first demonstration plant, planned to be built in Tennessee, is slated to cost $700 million including development costs, and will produce 300 Mw(e).

The LMFBR is not the only breeder. The General Atomic Company, with some AEC help, is making slow progress on a helium gas–cooled fast breeder reactor; having no massive coolant, it promises to breed plutonium with much higher conversion ratio than the LMFBR; but by the same token it has very little internal thermal inertia, and overheats in seconds if the cooling gas fails to circulate. It has little internal resemblance to General Atomic's HTGR other than utilizing the same sort of prestressed concrete pressure vessel and helium circulation system, but leans substantially on the AEC's

LMFBR program, for example for fuel and fuel rod development. Another possible candidate is the molten-salt breeder, where a mixture of lithium, beryllium, and uranium fluorides circulates through the reactor space, then through the heat exchangers and pumps. There is no solid fuel. The principal advantages are that it can operate completely on the thorium-^{233}U breeder cycle, there is no need for outside fuel reprocessing (the molten salt is continuously purified on-line), and it utilizes quite different technology from the other reactors. Thus, it is a possible alternate route to fission breeders, in case the other programs fail. Its main disadvantage is chemical engineering complexity, plus the fact that hot radioactive salt must flow outside the reactor. Even the LWR and the HTGR can be technologically upgraded, to increase their conversion ratio and extend fissionable uranium resources.

The AEC has supported these alternate breeder approaches only reluctantly, and sometimes not at all, through fiscal year 1974, and now plans to allocate $11 million for them in 1975. That is better, but will do little more than keep those high-technology programs alive.

When should the breeder reactor be introduced? That cannot yet be an-

swered exactly, but the preceding discussion permits some guesses. The breeder promises to be cheaper because of its very low uranium cost per unit of energy. But fuel costs are not the dominant ones in any reactor, and the saving over LWR's will be about 0.1¢/ kwh for each $17-a-pound rise in the cost of U_3O_8. To avoid offsetting penalties of expensively reprocessing the plutonium fuel too often, the burn-up in the breeder must be high. Long fuel life means more fission products to absorb neutrons, plus mechanical limitations imposed because of dimensional changes—all of which conflicts with good plutonium breeding. If goals of (say) 100,000 Mw-days per ton of burnup and a breeding ratio of 1.24 can be achieved, a saving corresponding to about $50-a-pound U_3O_8 would accrue to the breeder, translatable into a capital advantage of $150/ kw. If the burnup is less for that breeding ratio, or if the breeder costs more, or when plutonium is recycled in present-day reactors (thus introducing competition for the fuel), then the advantage shrinks. I estimate that the breeder will almost surely be attractive when U_3O_8 reaches $50 a pound in 1974 dollars. That will not happen in the first few decades of the 21st century (see the "resources" debate). In the meantime, nuclear power is in no danger of losing out to other fuels, and there does not need to be a crash breeder program. Economic introduction at A.D. 2000 would be a sign of technological good fortune, not of resolving an energy crisis with a time limit.

Controlled Fusion

Controlled nuclear fusion may appear as a 21st-century option to (say) advanced fission reactors, but that is not yet assured. The U.S. fusion program has grown from its inception in the early 1950's, through a long level period of physics-oriented experimentation supported at $20 million to $30 million a year, to its present stage of rapid growth ($102 million for fusion via magnetic confinement, plus $66 million for laser fusion, in fiscal year 1975).

The trick is to heat up a mixture of deuterium and tritium to a temperature between 10^8 and $10^{9\circ}$K (10^4 to 10^5 ev) at a density high enough and for a time long enough that the product of the two quantities exceeds (about) 3×10^{14} cm^{-3} sec^{-1}. This is the so-called Lawson criterion. One major class of schemes depends on confining the highly ionized plasma with strong magnetic fields, say 50,000 to 100,000 gauss, at a density of 10^{14} cm^{-3} for a few seconds. The most successful example of this technique so far is the Tokamak, wherein the plasma is confined and heated in a toroidal magnetic field.

It seems fairly clear that the scientific feasibility of controlled fusion can and will be demonstrated: A large enough well-designed magnetic structure can be made to achieve the Lawson criterion. Whether laser fusion will get there is less certain: the process depends critically on the laser pulse ablating a deuterium-tritium target pellet so fast and so evenly that the reaction forces on its surface compress it by a volumetric factor exceeding 1000. Then it undergoes nuclear fusion in about 10^{-12} second.

Controlled fusion has, during this scientific stage, been the most challenging and difficult of all such assignments ever given to physical scientists, and they deserve credit for doing so well. But there is much more to controlled fusion than applied plasma physics, and now controlled fusion shows signs of becoming, in addition, the most difficult and challenging assignment given to technologists and engineers. Thin-section vacuum walls, operating at high temperatures, cooled by liquid lithium or gas, possibly under cyclic mechanical stress as well, and bathed in an immense flux of 14-Mev neutrons—what will they be made of? No one knows, or even whether materials with adequate life under those conditions are developable. Many of the fusion concepts require pulsed or cyclic operations, which introduces new complexities and constraints, further eroding the option space desired by any fusion reactor designer. While having a favorable neutron balance in the fusion reactor still does not seem to be a problem, power balance may be one: in every concept, a great deal of energy must be spent to heat the fusion plasma, overcome energy losses while building up or taking down large magnetic fields, operate lasers, or do other tasks. Thus, the deuterium-tritium fusion reaction, which has some inherent disadvantages but the great advantage of 50 times the reaction rate of any other, seems mandatory. Because of all these,

and a host of other problems connected with recovering tritium fuel, removing spent plasma, injecting new fuel, and assuring reasonable possibilities of repairing such a complicated device, the AEC's implied goal of beneficial installation after 1995 seems optimistic. If economic attractiveness then could be assured, the fission breeder would be superfluous. But such success with fusion is still problematic; so the breeder programs, which are the only assured routes to long-term nuclear energy, should not be appreciably modified now on account of fusion.

The advantages of success are substantial: (i) deuterium fuel is sufficient for 10^{10} years, and lithium (used with fusion neutrons to breed the tritium fuel component) is in somewhat uncertain supply but probably adequate for any technological age to come; (ii) the only appreciable radiation hazard is from tritium, which is less hazardous than plutonium by many orders of magnitude, per unit of weight or nuclear energy content; (iii) the reactor structure, while surely made radioactive by 14-Mev neutrons, is not liable to pose any appreciable hazard; (iv) there is no reason to steal the nuclear material: hydrogen bombs are best made by other processes, and require atomic bombs to trigger them.

Thus, a strong sense of social purpose keeps driving the controlled fusion program, with $1450 million planned for fiscal years 1975 to 1979; it is the next largest federal plan after the LMFBR and the newly upgraded coal programs.

Nuclear versus Fossil Power

With some reservations, the social costs of nuclear power are being measured, as has been shown earlier. The social costs of burning fossil fuels to generate electricity are very hard to determine: one must extract the electric power contribution from the general costs associated with extracting, processing, and burning fossil fuels, which are quite different for different modes (local pollution by home heating equipment differs from the effects of effluents from tall power plant stacks, for instance). In addition, the studies themselves have been on a relatively small scale.

Lave and Freeburg (12) in their general comparison of power from coal, oil, and nuclear fuel, conclude that

nuclear power is substantially less hazardous than coal. First, the hazard for coal mining was judged to be 18 times as high (per unit of energy) as that for uranium mining; on that count alone, coal would rank much worse than all the nuclear power hazards of Table 2. In addition, Lave and Freeburg estimate mortality and morbidity arising from power plant effluents, finding that a pressurized-water reactor appears to offer at least 18,000 times less health risk than a coal-burning power plant, and a boiling-water reactor 24 times less health risk. Comparing low-sulfur oil and nuclear fuels, they are less sure: uranium mining is more hazardous than oil drilling, but power plant effluent data would again favor nuclear power.

Preliminary results of studies under way at Massachusetts Institute of Technology tend to support the view that even low-sulfur fuels are unlikely to be as benign as nuclear ones. Lave and Seskin's earlier data (21) indicate that lowered urban air quality reduces the average life span by about 3 years. They also show that the most hazardous pollutant is SO_2, and that most of it comes from home heating systems (22). Even so, an appreciable fraction comes from electric power production, and analysis of their data and other data indicates a fatality rate on this account alone at least ten times the total nuclear one (per unit of energy), even after cleanup to the Environmental Protection Agency's SO_2 standard of 80 $\mu g/m^3$. These analyses assume a linear relation between concentration and damage, which of course will lead to overestimates of damage if a threshold exists; the same linear approximation is applied over many more orders of magnitude to effects of penetrating radiation, in the nuclear case.

Other workers tend to the same general conclusion: for example, Starr et al. (23). What seems increasingly clear is that the hazards of burning fossil fuels are substantially higher than those of burning nuclear ones, yet many debates have enticed the uncritical spectator to just the opposite conclusion. Several reasons can be put forward to explain this peculiar response. First, the hazards of reactors and radiation were perceived as "unknown," and hence very possibly large. Second, the public had come to accept the social cost of polluted air, not realizing (i) that much could be done (until recently) and (ii) that its perception of the fossil fuel hazard was faulty. But I think a third reason dominates: over the past 20 or 30 years, the federal government has invested well over $1 billion attempting to measure the public health costs associated with nuclear power, and until recently almost nothing was done to measure similar hazards of fossil fuel power—in retrospect, a scandalous omission. Thus, even with sometimes clumsy words and bad grace, a vast amount of literature appeared about nuclear hazards, providing material for a great public debate. The absence of any appreciable parallel assessment of fossil fuels ensured that the debate would be unbalanced, and only now are semiquantitative social cost figures starting to appear. This profound issue can hardly fail to be resolved in the next few years as more data accumulate, especially on effects of fossil fuels. I conclude from the evidence to date that all the costs—economic and social—will favor nuclear power, unless the problem of illegal use of nuclear materials gets out of hand, or plutonium turns out to be as bad as its worst critics believe.

Conclusion

The uranium and thorium resources, the technology, and the social impacts all seem to presage an even sharper increase in nuclear power for electric generation than had hitherto been predicted. There are more future consequences.

The "hydrogen economy." Nuclear power plants operate best at constant power and full load. Thus, a largely nuclear electric economy has the problem of utilizing substantial off-peak capacity; the additional energy generation can typically be half the normal daily demand. Thus, the option of generating hydrogen as a nonpolluting fuel receives two boosts: excess nuclear capacity to produce it, plus much higher future costs for oil and natural gas. However, the so-called "hydrogen economy" must await the excess capacity, which will not occur until the end of the century.

Nonelectric uses. By analyses similar to those performed here, raw nuclear heat can be shown to be cheaper than heat from many other fuel sources, es-

pecially nonpolluting ones. This will be particularly true as domestic natural gas supplies become more scarce. Nuclear heat becomes attractive for industrial purposes, and even for urban district heating, provided (i) the temperature is high enough (this is no problem for district heating, but could be for industry; the HTGR's and breeders, with 600°C or more available, have the advantage); (ii) there is a market for large quantities (a heat rate of 3800 Mw thermal, the reactor size permitted today, will heat Boston, with some to spare); and (iii) the social costs become more definitely resolved in favor of nuclear power.

Capital requirements. Nuclear-electric installations are very capital-intensive. One trillion dollars for the plants, backup industry, and so forth is only 2 percent of the total gross national product (GNP) between 1974 and 2000, at a growth rate of 4 percent per year. But capital accumulation tends to run at about 10 percent of the GNP, so the nuclear requirements make a sizable perturbation. Also increasing the electric share of energy provision means increasing electric power utilization, which has a high technological content and demands yet more capital. Thus, provision of capital is a major problem ahead, especially for electric utilities.

The need for people. The supply of available trained technologists, environmental engineers, and so on, especially in the architect-engineer profession, is insufficient for the task ahead, especially since the same categories of people will be in demand to build up a synthetic fuels industry and do other new things.

Beyond these specific items and beyond the technological discussion, one can feel deeper currents running in this debate. Issues that started out seeming technological ended up being mainly societal: prevention of clandestine use, either by vigilance or by public spirit; a determination to maintain quality and to safeguard wastes that transcends narrow interests; a perception of social benefits and damage much more holistic than before; the need to manage programs more openly and better than before. Questions and doubts become more acute, answers and methods less sure.

Here is a final question. We have never before been given a virtually infinite resource of something we craved. So far, increasingly large amounts of energy have been used to turn resources into junk, from which activity we derive ephemeral benefit and pleasure; the track record is not too good. What will we do now?

References

1. From a survey by the National Electrical Manufacturers Association, as quoted in *IEEE (Inst. Electr. Electron. Eng.) Spectrum* **11**, 115 (1974).
2. Edison Electric Institute, *Elec. Output No. 49* (6 March 1974).
3. "A study of base-load alternatives for the Northeast Utilities System," report to the Board of Trustees of Northeast Utilities by Arthur D. Little, Inc., Acorn Park, Cambridge, Mass., 5 July 1973. The report has had substantial circulation.
4. "Nuclear power 1973 to 2000," *USAEC Rep. WASH 1139* (1972).
5. W. G. Dupree, Jr., and J. A. West, *United States Energy through the Year 2000* (Government Printing Office, Washington, D.C., 1972).
6. For example, see *Report of the Cornell Workshops on the Major Issues of a National Energy Research and Development Program* (College of Engineering, Cornell University, Ithaca, N.Y., 1973), chapter 4 by H. A. Bethe and appendix G thereto by H. A. Bethe and C. Braun.
7. "Nuclear fuel supply," *USAEC Rep. WASH 1242* (1973); "Nuclear fuel resources and requirements," *USAEC Rep. WASH 1243* (1973).
8. P. Walsh, Environmental Engineer's thesis, Massachusetts Institute of Technology (1974).
9. K. Hub, J. G. Asbury, W. A. Buehring, P. F. Gast, R. A. Schlenker, J. T. Weills, *A Study of Social Costs for Alternate Means of Electric Power Generation for 1980 and 1990* (Argonne National Laboratory, Argonne, Ill., 1973).
10. L. Sagan, *Science* **177**, 487 (1972).
11. "The safety of nuclear power reactors and related facilities," *USAEC Rep. WASH 1250* (1973).
12. L. B. Lave and L. C. Freeburg, *Nucl. Saf.* **14**, 409 (1973).
13. D. F. Ford, T. C. Hollocher, H. W. Kendall, J. J. MacKenzie, L. Scheinman, A. S. Schurgin, *The Nuclear Fuel Cycle, a Survey of the Public Health, Environmental and National Security Effects of Nuclear Power* (Union of Concerned Scientists, Cambridge, Mass., 1973); see especially chapter 3; "Emergency core cooling systems (ECCS) hearings," AEC Docket RM50-1, AEC Public Document Room, Atomic Energy Commission, Washington, D.C.
14. Reported by AEC Chairman Dixy Lee Ray, at the National Press Club, Washington, D.C., 21 January 1974.
15. "Theoretical possibilities and consequences of major accidents in large nuclear power plants," *USAEC Rep. WASH 740* (1957).
16. W. J. Bair and R. C. Thompson, *Science* **183**, 715 (1974).
17. For example, see the report "Meeting of the advisory committee on reactor safeguards, plutonium information meeting" (Los Alamos, New Mexico, 4 and 5 January 1974), AEC Document Room, Atomic Energy Commission, Washington, D.C.
18. A. R. Tamplin and T. B. Cochran, *Radiation Standards for Hot Particles* (Natural Resources Defense Council, Washington, D.C., 1974).
19. A. S. Kubo and D. J. Rose, *Science* **182**, 1205 (1973).
20. D. J. Rose and G. Tenaglia, *Ambio* **2**, 233 (1973).
21. L. Lave and E. P. Seskin, *Science* **169**, 723 (1970).
22. ———, *Am. J. Publ. Health* **62**, 909 (1972).
23. C. Starr, M. A. Greenfield, D. F. Hausknecht, *Nucl. News* **15**, 37 (1972).

Energy Choices That Europe Faces: A European View of Energy

Wolf Häfele

Demand and Supply of Primary Energy

Up to the middle of the 1950's domestic coal was available in sufficient quantities for a number of European countries (such as Germany, England, Belgium) to make them self-reliant in energy. After the second world war the low prices of oil, the increasingly open market, and a certain aging of the coal industry together with the comparatively extreme working conditions prevalent in coal mining resulted in a major change. Since the end of the 1950's, oil has conquered an ever increasing share of the expanding primary energy market in the booming economies of Western Europe and elsewhere.

The relevant data on the primary energy needs in the Federal Republic of Germany are shown in Table 1. The share of coal has fallen from roughly 70 percent in 1957 to a value as low as 23 percent in 1972, while the share of oil has risen from 11 to 56 percent. The absolute figures show a less dramatic decrease, which is nevertheless severe. The share of oil in the Community of the Six is even higher. It was at 65 percent in 1970, while the corresponding figure for the United States was 43 percent. The important points is that in the United States only about one-third of that oil is imported (or 14 percent of the total energy demand), while in Europe practically all the oil is imported. This observation reveals a first and basic difference between the energy situation in the United States and Europe.

Table 2 gives the consumption in kilowatts per capita in various European countries as compared to that of the United States. While the per capita consumption in Europe at present is 40 percent of that of the United States, it is expected to increase to 60 percent by 1985. By and large this gives a factor of 2 between the United States and Western Europe and establishes a second difference between the energy situation in the United States and Europe. However, the gross domestic product (GDP) per capita in Western Europe is much closer to that of the United States than is indicated by the ratio of the per capita energy consumption. It is also interesting to consider the use of such primary energy. Figures 1 and 2 indicate the shares of the various uses of energy in the United States and Germany.

Limited Oil from the Middle East and Substitution by Coal

It has been estimated that the amount of crude oil in the Middle East is 350×10^9 barrels or 2 Q (1 Q $= 10^{18}$ Btu). If 430 million people (all of Western Europe plus Japan) at 10 kilowatts per capita use oil to make up two-thirds of that amount, 0.09 Q per year would be required. The reserves of the Middle East would then last for about 23 years. With U.S. participation in the harvesting of these reserves the period would be shorter. Although the actual period that these reserves might last will be somewhat different, the estimate of 23 years is indicative. A. Khene, Secretary-General of the Organization of the Oil Exporting Countries, observed (1) that such a period is too short for the countries of the Middle East. They must make use of their natural wealth for a significantly longer period. Khene therefore concludes that the oil price must be raised to a level that allows other primary energy sources to enter the scene and thereby to alleviate the oil supply situation.

Coal reserves are about 15 times, as a global average, larger than oil reserves (2). Therefore, the natural substitute for oil is coal. However, in making the substitution, we must realize that geographical differences in coal reserves are large. The United States appears to have an unusually large proportion of the total amount of coal, while Europe does not.

The data in Table 3 are based on a consumption rate of 10 kilowatts per capita. The 37 Q of the United States therefore should last for more than 600 years if all 10 kilowatts were provided by coal. This figure and the others in Table 3 are merely indicative; the actual figures cannot be predicted easily. Europe's main coal reserves are located in Germany and England. If these reserves were consumed by all countries of Western Europe, a time span of only 36 years would result—which would be in sharp contrast to the U.S. figure. If Germany alone consumes all of its available coal it would be enough for 160 years. The figures become less threatening if coal reserves at depths greater than 1200 meters are considered. These are given in Table 3 in parentheses. As a contrast to coal, Table 3 also shows the figures for domestic oil and gas. It is obvious that these domestic oil and gas resources are of significant usefulness for a much shorter time period only—or for a much smaller portion of the supply of the primary energy. It is therefore only natural for the United States to prepare for the large-scale use of coal (3).

The question arises as to whether nuclear energy can reduce the extent of coal use. One has to realize that nuclear power has been developed as a means of providing electricity that is competitive with (artificially) cheap fossil fuels [50 cents per million Btu (1 Btu $= 1.06 \times 10^3$ joules) or less]. At the same time, the development of nuclear power was intended to act as a technological innovator, rather than to solve an early energy crisis. As a result, during the current energy crisis, nuclear power can at best take care of that portion of primary energy which goes into the production of electricity. At present this is at 25 percent in Europe and 20 percent in the United States, but it is expected to steadily increase to provide as much as 40 percent or more, because of the annual

The author is a staff member of the International Institute for Applied Systems Analysis, Laxenburg, Austria, and is director of the Institut für Angewandte Systemtechnik und Reaktorphysik Kernforschungszentrum, Karlsruhe, Germany.

increase of 8 percent in electricity consumption as compared to that of 4.5 percent for primary energy. In any event, we can try to ease the transition from oil to coal by shifting the production of electricity to nuclear power insofar as possible.

The government of the Federal Republic of Germany has recently announced an energy plan for the years up to 1985. In Germany, nuclear energy is expected to take care of 15 percent of the primary energy demand, that is, 45 gigawatts of electricity. Similar percentage figures have been given for the United States. But in contrast to the United States, it will be difficult to raise the coal production in Europe: Most of the miners are gone (Table 4). The German coal production is now down from 141 million tons (metric) in 1962 to 102 million tons in 1972. The productivity per miner per shift has risen from 2.4 to 4 tons, and therefore the number of employees in the coal industry is down from 434,000 to 221,000. The figure for employees actually engaged in mining is still smaller. It has been estimated that it will be virtually impossible to raise the coal production to more than the original 140 million tons per year. In contrast, to satisfy present coal uses and to substitute for oil as a primary energy source would, in 1985, require 380 million tons of coal in the case of the Federal Republic of Germany alone. Of these 380 million tons, 330 would be for the substitution of oil

Table 1. Annual demand (as percent of total) for primary energy for the Federal Republic of Germany. [Source: "Das Energie-pogramm der Bundesregierung," Report of the Bundesministerium für Wirtschaft, Federal Republic of Germany, Bonn, 1973]

Source	1957	1967	1972
Oil	11.0	47.7	55.4
Coal	69.9	36.2	23.6
Lignite	14.8	10.2	8.7
Gas	0.3	2.1	8.6
Nuclear		0.2	0.9
Others	4.0	3.6	2.8
Total	100.0	100.0	100.0
$\triangleq 10^6$ mtce/ yr*	198	271	362
$\triangleq$ Q/yr	0.0054	0.0074	0.0099

* 1 Q $\equiv 10^{18}$ Btu $\triangleq 2.93 \times 10^{04}$ kilowatt-hours $\triangleq 2.52 \times 10^{17}$ kcal $\triangleq 3.6625 \times 10^{00}$ metric to coal equivalents (mtce).

by synthetic fuels, while only 50 million tons would be for genuine coal consumption. If it becomes necessary for the relatively coal-rich Germany to provide other European countries with coal, the coal production required would be higher, making it obligatory to go to mining depths greater than 1200 meters. The more restricted and cumbersome situation of coal mining in Europe at a scale that could alleviate the oil supply basically differs from the respective situation in the United States, and this is another very significant difference between the energy situation in the United States and Europe. Undoubtedly there is a strong incentive to look into new coal mining technologies. It remains to be seen to what extent it can be successful.

Three Phases of the Energy Problem

It has been indicated that the global resources of fossil fuel are about 200 Q (2). With 10^{10} people and 10 kilowatts per capita this gives a period of only 66 years before these resources are used up. Of course, reality is more complex and actual figures would be different but it is possible to draw one simple conclusion from this little calculation: In a not too distant future we will have to live with an energy supply that comes from nonfossil fuel resources.

There are four options for such nonfossil energy supply (4): (i) nuclear fission in the fast breeder and other reactors; (ii) nuclear fusion; (iii) solar power; and (iv) harvesting of the heat of the earth crust (geothermal in the general sense). Both the fast breeder and the fusion breeder, which is based on the (d,t) reaction, give energies that are sufficient for about 10^6 years with no qualitative difference between these two options except that the fast breeder is already technically feasible. This observation is in contradiction to a widespread belief, and I would like to refer to an article which elaborates on that issue in greater detail (5). The options of solar and geothermal energy must be explored more thoroughly before it will be possible to make assessments.

Although it must be borne in mind that eventually there could be more than one option for the long range

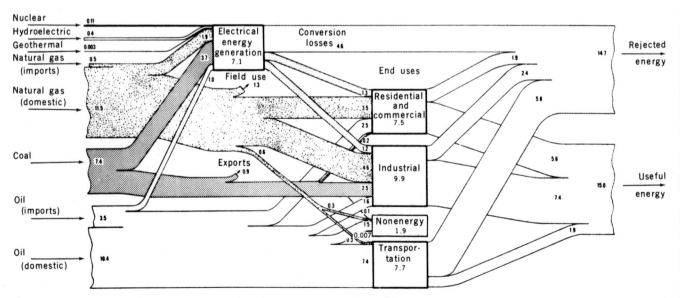

Fig. 1. Total energy flow pattern in the United States 1970. Units are in millions of barrels of oil equivalent per day. (1 ton coal equivalent per year = 0.01312 barrels of oil equivalent per day). [Source: Joint Committee on Atomic Energy, Certain Background Information for Consideration When Evaluating the "National Energy Dilemma," U.S. Government Printing Office, Washington, D.C. (1973)]

supply, nuclear fission, must now be examined further since it is the only viable option today.] As mentioned earlier, nuclear power has been developed for the competitive production of electricity only. If electricity's share is not more than 40 to 50 percent, how can nuclear fission be the source of all the primary energy demand? The answer is: By reactors that provide process heat at high temperatures. The incentive to develop such reactors now turns out to be larger than the incentive to develop and operate reactors for the production of electricity. Fortunately, the United States has the high temperature gas cooled reactor (HTGR), which has been developed by the Oak Ridge National Laboratory and the Gulf General Atomic Company. In Germany there is the high temperature pebble bed reactor, which has been developed by the Kernforschungsanlage Jülich and Brown Boveri Company at Mannheim. In the long run the most convincing scheme for the use of nuclear process heat is the splitting of the water molecule with the result that hydrogen would be used on a truly large scale. Hydrogen would then complement electricity as another secondary fuel. Much attention has already been given to this long range option (6).

Gulf General Atomic (7) and the Kernforschungszentrum Karlsruhe, Germany, have considered using the breeding gain of fast breeder reactors for providing the necessary ^{233}U fuel for the high temperature gas cooled reactors. In such a scheme, where energy consumption has leveled off, all of the secondary energy in the form of electricity would be produced by fast breeders; at the same time all of the secondary energy in the form of hydrogen would be produced by high temperature gas cooled reactors that are fueled by the breeding gain of fast breeders. More detailed investigations indicate that in such a scheme the ratio between secondary energy in the form of hydrogen and secondary energy in the form of electricity, for example, could be 3 : 2, which generally fits with market requirements. Figure 3 illustrates such an asymptotic integrated reactor scheme, with the abundant isotopes ^{238}U and ^{232}Th being the only input. The transition periods into such an asymptotic scheme have already been evaluated (8). A model consisted of a community of 250 million people, which would grow to 350 million within 40 years, and which then would remain constant. It was assumed that the share of primary energy devoted to the production of electricity was 25 percent at the beginning and would increase to 50 percent. At first, nuclear reactors were installed; these were light water reactors (LWR) built to increase the capacity by 18 gigawatts of electricity per year. After 18 years, the yearly plutonium output

Table 2. Consumption of energy (as kilowatt per capita) in Europe and the United States. [Source: "Prospects of primary energy demand in the community (1975–1980–1985)," Commission for the European Communities, 4 October 1972]

Country	1970	1975	1980	1985
Belgium	5.6	7.3	9.0	10.7
France	3.9	4.8	6.1	7.7
Federal Republic of Germany	5.1	6.3	7.8	9.8
Italy	2.7	3.7	4.7	6.1
Netherlands	4.9	6.8	8.5	10.4
Average in the European Community of the Six*	4.4	5.8	7.2	8.9
United States	10.9	12.3	13.7	15.2
European Communities/ United States	0.404	0.472	0.526	0.586

* The dates of the United Kingdom fit into the here extended pattern of energy consumption.

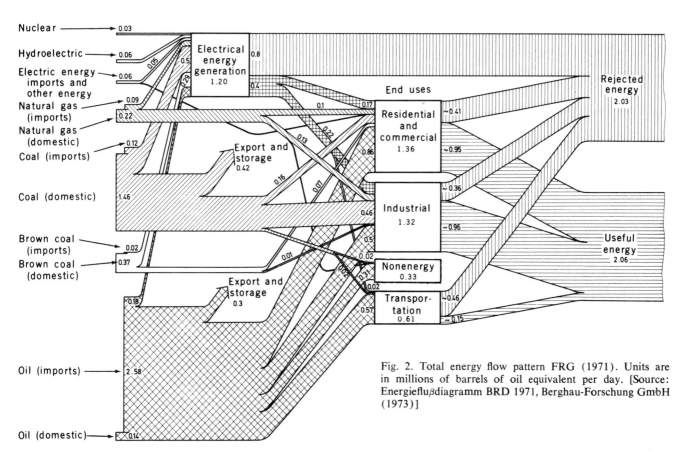

Fig. 2. Total energy flow pattern FRG (1971). Units are in millions of barrels of oil equivalent per day. [Source: Energieflußdiagramm BRD 1971, Berghau-Forschung GmbH (1973)]

of these LWR's becomes large enough to provide the plutonium inventories of fast breeder reactors (FBR), which were built at the same rate of 18 gigawatts per year. The FBR's are then assumed to replace the LWR's after 18 years. At the same time the installation of HTGR for the production of hydrogen becomes possible. Further, 18 gigawatts of electricity correspond to 45 gigawatts of heat, and because of the coupling of ^{233}U (production in FBR's and consumptions in HTGR), a rate of introduction of HTGR's of 45 gigawatts of heat per year is assumed.

The installation of FBR's and HTGR's would continue until all of the primary energy demand has been met and all LWR's have been replaced by FBR's. Until that time fossil fuel and cheap uranium for feeding the LWR's with ^{235}U are required. It should be noted that in such a scheme

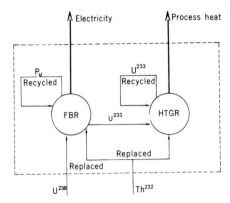

Fig. 3. Asymptotic integrated power reactor system. [Source: reference (8)]

FBR's act as a final waste box for all the plutonium produced by the limited generation of LWR's; and that at the same time FBR's produce the necessary electricity and the necessary ^{233}U that allows for the production of hydrogen. In this radically different use of

the virtues of fast breeders, no doubling of any kind has been taking place. A few of the results obtained so far are given in Table 5. Most important is that at the construction capacity considered here it takes 60 years to master the transition from today's situation into an all-nuclear energy economy. With significantly higher construction capacities, this period could be shorter. To master the transition, 3 Q of fossil fuel is required. The model society described above corresponds roughly to conditions in Europe. Fortunately the required 3 Q matches the genuine European coal reserves, as shown in Table 3. Within the constraints of the model employed here the major conclusion is that for European conditions the envisaged new coal era can last about 60 years or so if all this coal is to be burned. Further, the United States does not differ greatly from this model society. But U.S. coal reserves are larger by an order of magnitude if all U.S. coal is to be burned within the United States. Under these conditions the relevant transition period would be much longer. However, whether all U.S. coal should be consumed domestically is a question for review. Table 5 points to the relatively large consumption of cheap uranium during the transition period. Therefore the supply of cheap uranium could become a concern sooner than could the supply of coal. Evaluation of this scheme is continuing (9).

Here it must be emphasized that the coupling of FBR and HTGR is not meant to be the only scheme of interest. The potential of the heavy water reactor, the possibility of producing hydrogen by electrolysis, the option of fueling HTGR's with plutonium, and many others have to be taken into account. The discussion in this article is primarily meant to introduce a new general possibility.

Against this background of an asymptotic phase for the provision of energy on a nonfossil basis, the new uses of coal are obvious signs of a transition period, which requires, in itself, major technological preparations and change. Until such technological changes can become effective some time will elapse, and this interval characterizes the near term phase of the energy problem. Table 6 identifies these three phases of the energy problem.

Timing and the evaluation of the transition—for instance by systems analysis—turn out to be the principal

Table 3. Coal, lignite, and oil reserves in Western Europe and the United States, and periods for these reserves to last. [Source: Figures derived from data of the *Statistical Yearbook of the United Nations*, New York, 1973]

Item	F.R. Germany	Western Europe	United States
Coal and lignite reserves (Q)	2.92 (+ 4.37)*	3.50 (+ 4.37)*	36.69
Oil and natural gas reserves (Q)	0.017	0.214	0.469†
Annual consumption for 10 kw/capita (Q/yr)	0.018	0.098	0.061
Period of time, if coal (yr)	160 (+ 238)	36 (+ 44)	602
Oil and natural gas exclusively (yr)‡	0.9	2.2	7.7

* Reserves in depths below 1200 m, the use of which today is not feasible economically and sociologically.   † Tar sands and shale oil not included.   ‡ No population growth assumed.

Table 4. Coal production in the Federal Republic of Germany. [Source: "Das Energieprogramm der Bundesregierung," Report of the Bundesministerium für Wirtschaft, Federal Republic of Germany, Bonn, 1973]

Item	1962	1964	1966	1968	1970	1972
Coal production (10⁶ metric tons)	141.1	142.2	126.0	112.0	111.3	102.5
Total number of miners (thousands)	434	399	334	364	250	331
Coal per miner per shift (metric tons)	2.37	2.61	2.93	3.53	3.76	4.02

Table 5. Transition into an all nuclear energy supply for a model society. The data are based on the assumption of a model society with 250×10^6 people at the start ($t = 0$) and 360×10^6 people 40 years later, the rate being 10 kilowatts per capita in the asymptotic state.

Item	Unit
(i) Reactor construction capacity	18 gigawatts of electricity per year (LWR or FBR for electricity generation)
(ii) As (i), and in addition after 18 years	45 gigawatts of heat per year (HTGR for process heat generation)
(iii) Length of transition period—time until total reliance on nuclear energy is achieved	$\approx$ 60 years
(iv) Total energy consumption during transition period	$\approx$ 6 Q
(v) Amount of fossil fuel required during transition period	$\approx$ 3 Q
(vi) Amount of cheap natural uranium required during transition period	$\approx$ 3.10⁶ tons

points of attention in the energy problem. It is therefore advisable for the various research and development activities to be compatible with each other and with the timing of the problem. And the fairly important differences between the European and the U.S. situation can best be identified by emphasis on the different timing. Europe has much less time to master the transition into the asymptotic phase.

It is against this background that I now turn to problems of secondary energy.

Secondary Energy

As was observed earlier, 75 percent of the primary energy in Europe today is devoted to nonelectrical purposes. About 55 percent goes to stationary applications, while about 20 percent goes to transportation. In Germany Schulten conceived and promoted the idea of the pebble bed reactor (10), with a random package of balls of about 5 cm diameter making up the core. The fuel elements are balls and not rods. With appropriate fuel management [the OTTO (once through then out) scheme (11)], this pebble bed reactor is particularly well suited to high temperatures. On 27 February 1974, the Jülich AVR experimental reactor for the first time reached an outlet temperature of 950°C, thus providing heat for many chemical applications. Schulten and his co-workers have now proposed to employ such nuclear process heat for transformation into chemical binding energy. The splitting of the water molecule in three or more chemical stages as proposed by C. Marchetti and co-workers (12) is only one, but very promising, scheme for such a transformation into chemical binding energy. A more typical near term application would, for instance, be the application of nuclear process heat to the well-known chemical reaction

$$CH_4 + H_2O + 49 \text{ kcal/mole} \rightleftarrows 3H_2 + CO$$

The procedure for such an application is shown in Fig. 4. Methane with the appropriate amount of water is transformed into hydrogen and carbon monoxide by nuclear process heat. In a heat exchanger these gases are cooled off and as cold gases can be transported over any distance. On the consumer side they are led to react and give away their chemical binding energy. Methane is transported back to the power station. The chemical reactor for the production of hydrogen and carbon monoxide is called EVA (Einzelspalt-rohrversuchsanlage), and its counterpart is called ADAM, of course. ADAM is the burner of the gaseous fuel (13). The advantages of this or similar schemes are remarkable:

1) Process heat can be transported over any distance. This allows central nuclear power stations to play the role of a natural gas field far away from applications.

2) The reaction cycle is a closed one (one may send back the water if so desired). The implication is that the environment remains completely untouched by pollutants or by CO_2 which always results if coal or other fossil fuels are burnt and which may also have adverse effects (14).

3) Apart from losses no material other than nuclear fuel is consumed. No fossil fuel except for producing the initial inventory of the pipes is required.

4) It employs technology that is basically available already.

At the Kernforschungsanlage (KFA) Jülich the demonstration of that scheme over a distance of a few miles and in the megawatt range is being prepared. The consequence, of course, would be the installation of a widespread pipeline system that uses more than one single pipe at a time. In fact, a pipeline must contain two subpipes: one for hydrogen plus carbon monoxide and the other for methane. This is somewhat in parallel with electrical transmission lines. In both cases there are two (or more) conduits.

As before, I do not mean to say that it is specifically the production of hydrogen and carbon monoxide which is the solution to all problems. There may be more suitable chemical reactions. Again my point is to introduce a new general possibility.

I consider the development of a scheme like EVA and ADAM and its installation together with the installation of appropriate central power stations for nuclear process heat to be among the main energy tasks in Europe. It serves both for the transition phase and the asymptotic phase as described in Table 6. The energy costs for the EVA and ADAM scheme are estimated to be $2 per million Btu for the consumer. Let us consider this an indication of the relevant range of energy prices. It is equivalent to an oil price of $12 per barrel (to the con-

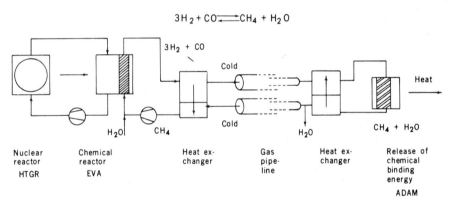

Fig. 4. Energy transmission system EVA + ADAM. [Source: reference (13); courtesy of KFA Julich, Germany]

Table 6. The three phases of the energy problem.

Characteristics	Dates	
	Beginning	End
Asymptotic phase		
Based on nuclear fission, fusion, solar, geothermal power, or a combination	2050 in Europe 2200 in the U.S.	To forever?
Transition phase		
Based on the substitution of oil by coal and on nuclear energy for the production of electricity	1985	2050 in Europe 2200 in U.S. (??)
Near term phase		
Characterized by the administration of fuel shortages and the preparations for the transition phase	1973	1990

sumer) and is now comparable to prices on the present oil market. Against this background it is interesting to look at the already existing pipeline system for gases in Europe.

Figure 5 is a map of the existing European pipelines for gases—already a fairly tight system. On the basis of $400,000 per kilometer for pipelines larger than 50 centimeters and $240,000 per kilometer for pipelines smaller than 50 centimeters, the investment costs for the existing pipeline system have been estimated to be about $15 billion. To establish a more extended modern pipeline system may cost something like $200 billion. To put this figure into perspective it is worthwhile to consider the present cost of the energy transmitted by that modern pipeline system. At 5 kilowatts of heat per capita and 327 million people with $2 per million Btu, one arrives at the linear value of 10^{11} per year; at a discount rate of 15 percent, the present value would be about $700 billion. In view of these numbers and of the global energy challenge an investment of $200 billion, large as it is, appears acceptable, especially because it would be spread over at least 10 years. For 327 million people this amounts to $60 per year per person over a period of 10 years. But this is not the only expenditure. The central power plants and other devices must also be built. Nevertheless, this above sum indicates the order of magnitude of what is at stake. I intentionally refrain from elaborating on the question of whether a market mechanism alone can bring this change about and to what extent an emergency type venture must be envisaged.

The above discussion deals with process heat for stationary applications —what about transport?

The answer is to make use of coal for synthesizing hydrocarbons. Methanol seems to be a promising fuel (15). Its heat content is 170.9 kilocalories per mole, that of carbon is 94 kilocalories per mole. The ratio between these two is 1.8 or, in other words, the value of carbon as a fuel can be multiplied by the factor of 1.8 if the difference in chemical binding energy is supplied by a nonfossil fuel source. I refer, of course, to nuclear process heat. If 20 percent of the primary energy demand is for transportation this means in effect that only 11 percent need be taken over by carbon as a source of primary energy. Other chemicals should be considered also —particularly, methane—whose lower weight makes it feasible for aviation purposes. Methane produced from coal with nuclear heat increases the fuel value of the carbon by a factor of 2.2. One must also continue to keep hydrogen in mind. Schulten and others have proposed that only this reduced percentage of coal designated for transportation purposes be used for burning. This would be indeed in sharp contrast to the situation in the United States where one envisages the burning of all coal resources. Under these circumstances European reserves would last for a period of perhaps 150 years. Here, too, my intention is to open up a general possibility.

In Europe all the components to master the energy problem are available: light water reactors, high temperature gas cooled reactors, the fast breeder, a little bit of coal, the technology for handling process heat as chemical binding energy, and the technology of pipelines and chemical engineering. If properly put together, these components could be a more or less

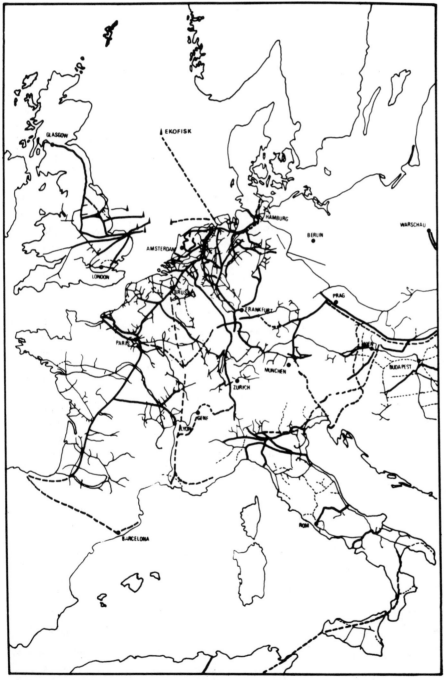

Fig. 5. Present natural gas pipeline system in Europe. [Source: Niedersächsisches Landesamt für Bodenforschung, Hannover; Jahrbuch für Bergbau, Energie, Mineralöl und Chemie, Verlag Glückauf GmbH, Essen (1973)]

final answer to the energy problem during the transition period. To a large extent this solution could reestablish Europe's "energy" self-reliance and could alleviate the oil situation.

Primary Energy Parks

A large and modern pipeline system tends to deemphasize the question of siting of large power plants that provide chemical process heat for the use in chemical reactors such as EVA. As was stated above, large central power plants could assume the function of natural gas fields. If so, we should examine the possibility of centralizing large electrical power plants. Such a project would require an extension of the electrical grid. The present European grid is already very extended and strongly interconnected. But one has to realize that the weighted average distance for the transport of electric power in Germany is only 100 kilometers. The existing high voltage lines serve to reduce standbys and the handling of peak loads. At 380 kilovolts they can transmit about 5 gigawatts over distances of 500 kilometers. An upgrading of technology into the domain of 10 to 50 gigawatts therefore is required. Ultra high voltage, direct current lines or superconducting cables (16) can probably do the job. In so doing the consistency with gases as the other form of secondary energy must be kept in mind and the entire infrastructure must be optimized.

A modern infrastructure for the handling of secondary energy, gases and electricity, tends to deemphasize the question of siting large power plants. This could be important in the long run. Let us consider, for example, the cooling water requirements for the production (conversion) of primary energy. If electricity assumes 50 percent of the primary energy production with a thermal efficiency of 0.4 and the other 50 percent of the primary energy production is for the production of chemical process heat at a thermal efficiency of 0.6, then out of 10 kilowatts per capita as much as 5 kilowatts per capita is waste heat at the sites where the secondary energies are to be produced. For a population of 3.27×10^8 Europeans, this leads to a total of 1.6×10^{12} watts of waste heat at the site of the power plants. Wet cooling towers permit the dissipation of 3×10^9 watts per cubic meter of water per second. Therefore 1.6×10^{12} watts requires 1.6×10^{10} cubic meters per year if that waste heat is to be dissipated in wet cooling towers. The rainfall in central Europe is at 0.8 meter per year, thus giving 0.8 cubic meter per year per square meter. Therefore 2×10^{10} square meters is required if all of the related rainfall be given to wet cooling towers. More realistically, if only 10 percent of all the rainfall, and that means 20 percent of all runoffs in rivers, creeks, and the like, were given to wet cooling towers, then an area of 500 by 500 kilometers would be required within which such collection of water had to take place. This crude calculation points to the difficult problem of interfaces between energy, water, the climate, and land use. This is a subject in its own right and cannot be covered in this article. It leads to the recognition of the fact that not only the production of energy is a problem, but increasingly it is also the embedding of energy in the atmosphere, the hydrosphere, the ecosphere, and the sociosphere which has to be considered (4, 17). I feel that such embedding will be the principal incentive for the energy technology of the asymptotic phase (18).

At present it appears that the concept of having large primary energy parks in the open sea could largely solve these problems of adequate energy embedding. The handling of waste heat in the open sea seems to be much less of a problem than on the continents. In case of nuclear power such primary energy parks should be large enough to embrace their own fuel cycle facilities, as has been proposed by A. M. Weinberg and R. P. Hammond (19). Many of the concerns about nuclear power could be eased in this way. If eventually solar power turns out to be a feasible source of energy, large areas will be required for the harvesting of solar energy. I feel that not more than 20 watts per square meter can be expected. If all of the primary energy demand of Europe were to be provided by solar power this would then require an area of 400 by 400 kilometers. Such a large area would best be found in the open sea; this immediately leads to problems of the Law of the Seas, but it is still consistent with the idea of large primary energy parks in the open sea.

The point is this: If Europe develops a modern secondary energy system, it deemphasizes not only the painful problem of siting power plants but also the problem of deciding early what kind of process for the conversion of primary energy into secondary energy should eventually be employed. I believe that nuclear fission and in particular the combination of FBR and HTGR will continue to play a dominant role. But if other options turn out better let us use them in primary energy parks. The continents would remain unaffected. Remarkably enough, such primary energy parks are already being developed in Europe. In Fig. 5 the pipelines are shown which connect the continent with floating platforms above the new (even though in the long run limited) gas fields of the North Sea. This suggests a later transformation of such platforms into energy parks.

Conclusion

In conclusion, I feel that the energy challenge, tough as it is, does not pose unsurmountable technological problems, even in Europe. At least in principle, the necessary technology is already there. This article is meant to make that statement plausible. It is not the intention to insist on certain ideas. It is important, however, to have a consistent approach, and this means to obey the timing of the problem. Therefore the most important aspect during the transition phase probably is the buildup of a modern secondary energy system. In the long run it will be energy embedding and not the production of energy which will be the principal driving force for the development, because in principle at least there is more than one option to provide almost unlimited amounts of energy. In order to meet the demand for an appropriate embedding of energy, the concept of primary energy parks in the open sea seems to be most promising.

References and Notes

1. A. Khene, a shortened version of a speech given at the Friedrich-Ebert-Foundation, Bad Godesberg, Germany, 28 September 1973, has been published by Gesamtverband des deutschen Steinkohlenbergbaus, Essen, Glückaufhaus, entitled: "Aktuelle Ölprobleme aus der Sicht der OPEC."
2. M. K. Hubbert, *Sci. Am.* 225 (No. 3), 61 (1971).
3. C. L. Wilson, *Foreign Affairs* 51, 657 (1973).
4. W. Häfele, *Am. Sci.*, in press.
5. ——— and C. Starr, *J. Br. Nuclear Energy Soc.*, in press.
6. D. P. Gregory, *Sci. Am.* 228 (No. 1), 13 (1973).
7. P. Fortescue, *Nucl. News,* 15, No. 4 (April 1972).
8. W. Häfele and W. Schikorr, IAEA (International Atomic Energy Agency) Study Group on Reactor Strategy Calculations, Vienna,

5 to 9 November 1973 (proceedings in press).

9. W. Häfele and A. S. Manne, paper to be presented at ORSA-TIMS Meeting, San Juan, Puerto Rico, 16 to 18 October 1974.

10. See, for instance, W. Häfele and H. Krämer, in "Technischer und wirtschaftlicher Stand sowie Aussichten der Kernenergie in der Kraftwirtschaft der BRD," Report Jül-775-RG, KFK-1430 (1971).

11. V. Maly, R. Schulten, E. Teuchert, in *Einwegbeschickung Atomwirtschaft* **17**, 216 (1972).

12. Progress Report, Euratom Joint Nuclear Research Center, Ispra, Italy, EUR 5059e (1973).

13. Private communication of KFA Jülich, Germany, Institute for Reactor Development Report, in preparation.

14. W. H. Mathews, W. W. Kellogg, G. D. Robinson, Eds., *Man's Impact on the Climate* (MIT Press, Cambridge, Mass., 1971), p. 247.

15. T. B. Reed and R. M. Lerner, *Science* **182**, 1299 (1973).

16. W. Heinz, *Atomwirtschaft* **17**, 579 (1972).

17. *Proceedings of IIASA Planning Conference on Energy Systems* (The International Institute for Applied Systems Analysis, Laxenburg, Austria, July 1973).

18. W. Häfele, *Minerva*, in press.

19. A. M. Weinberg and R. P. Hammond, *Proceedings of the Fourth International Conference on Peaceful Uses of Atomic Energy, Geneva* **1**, 171 (1971).

20. The data were compiled and the article was prepared for this issue in a very short time. It is for this reason that mainly tables referring to the German situation have been incorporated. This work would have been impossible without the assistance of a whole team. I thank in particular: R. Avenhaus, R. Patzak, Mrs. T. Koopmans, C. Marchetti, and M. Grenon, all at Laxenburg; D. Faude, W. Sassin, and G. Friede, all at Karlsruhe. I am also greatly indebted to Direktor S. Pirklbauer, Salzach-Kohlenbergbau Ges.m.b.H., Direktor W. Renner, Österr. Verbundgesellschaft, and Direktor W. Zauner, Österr. Mineralölverwaltung A.G., for providing me with important background data.

Developing Technology

Geothermal Electricity Production

Geoffrey R. Robson

This article is an attempt to evaluate the institutional and economic factors that will play a part in determining the future scale of geothermal development in the short term. To be complete, it would be necessary to evaluate technical factors also, such as probable developments in exploration techniques, the prevention of scale formation in hot water fields, the disposal of mineralized water, the use of geothermal energy in nonpower applications such as space heating and cooling and water desalination, and (for the long term) to evaluate the technology for the extraction of thermal energy from hot rock at depths of several kilometers. This article, however, is concerned only with the future scale of geothermal development, and since, in general, technology is developed and technical problems are solved when institutions which can command the finances required choose to solve them, a passing reference only to some of the technical problems mentioned above will be made here.

Over the past 2 years there has been an increasing concern over the continued availability of natural resources, the demand for which is growing and is expected to continue to grow at a high rate. At the same time, awareness of the environmental effects of unregulated use of natural resources has led in many countries to the establishment of legislation designed to control environmental damage and restrict the way in which natural resources, and in particular energy resources, can be developed and used. In the United States, for example, environmental considerations, coupled with the need to import increasingly large quantities of oil and natural gas, have led to re-evaluation of the potential of indigenous energy resources, including geothermal energy resources. Since the present state of development of geothermal resources and their future prospects on a world scale are in many respects reflected in the situation in the United States, an analysis of that situation can be instructive for those who are also interested in geothermal development in other countries.

The development of geothermal energy on a significant scale has been the subject of much inquiry in the United States, and several estimates of the potential by the year 1985 or the year 2000 have been published, for example, by the U.S. Geological Survey (1), the National Petroleum Council (2), the Hickel Geothermal Resources Research Conference (3), and others concerned with geothermal resources development (4, 5). There is general agreement about the total quantity of heat stored in the earth down to any particular depth, but there is very little agreement about how much of this heat can be exploited, and by what date any particular rate of exploitation can be achieved. In the present state of technological development, we can say that exploitable geothermal resources consist of steam or hot water contained in permeable rock at a depth which can be reached by drilling. As this definition implies, there are two kinds of geothermal resource; one produces only steam at the wellhead and is said to be a "dry steam" or "vapor dominated" geothermal field; the other produces either hot water alone or a flashing mixture of hot water and steam and is said to be a "wet steam" or "hot water" geothermal field.

Dry Steam Geothermal Fields

The first geothermal field to be developed was a dry steam field at Larderello, Italy, where the present generating plant, operated by the National Electricity Board, has a capacity of 380 megawatts. Another dry steam field has also been developed in Japan, at Matsukawa, where a 20-Mw plant which serves the Tohoku Electric Power Company began operation in 1961.

In the United States, the first geothermal power production began from a dry steam field at The Geysers near San Francisco. At The Geysers, expansion of steam production by the Magma Energy and Thermal Power companies together with the Union Oil Company as operator is now progressing at a rate equivalent to 110 Mw each year; the Pacific Energy Corporation was reported recently to have agreed to supply the Pacific Gas and Electric Company with steam for an initial 55-Mw plant, and the Signal Companies have undertaken the sale of further steam supplies at a rate equivalent to 135 Mw each year to Pacific Gas and Electric. The total installed capacity at The Geysers field will be 900 Mw in 1976 (6). The ultimate capacity of this field has been estimated to be more than 1000 Mw.

The cost of a geothermal production well drilled to 8000 feet (2400 meters) is about $250,000, excluding mobilization costs. Production from such a well in a dry steam field can range to over 100 tons of steam per hour at a pressure of 10 atmospheres and a temperature over 200°C. The price paid for such steam at The Geysers field, for example, was about $0.30 (United States) per ton ($0.003 per kilowatthour) in 1970. The cost of disposing of the condensed steam after use was an additional $0.05 per ton of steam produced, also paid for by the power company. If the alternative source of power is an electric power plant burning fuel oil, then the opportunity cost of geothermal steam at 200°C is about $1 per ton when fuel oil costs $7 per barrel.

The three fields already mentioned, one each in Italy, the United States, and Japan, are the only dry steam fields to have been developed so far, and this type of field therefore appears to be less common than the hot water type. From the point of view of electric power production, it will be unfortunate if further exploration confirms that this is so, since dry steam field operation is relatively simple, and in economic terms highly competitive with alternative sources of electric power.

The author is an Economic Affairs Officer at the United Nations, New York 10017. He has been concerned with the United Nations Development Programme work in geothermal resources development.

Hot Water Geothermal Fields

[The first hot water or wet steam field to be developed for the production of electric power was the Wairakei field in New Zealand, where a 192-Mw generating plant is operated by the New Zealand Electricity Department. Other hot water fields now producing electric power are in New Zealand at Kawerau, in Japan at Otake, in the Soviet Union at Pauzhetska and Paratunka, in Iceland at Namafjall, and in Mexico at Cerro Prieto.

Operation of a wet steam field for electric power production differs from that of a dry steam field because a geothermal well in a hot water field, while producing steam in quantity comparable to that from a well in a dry steam field, also produces hot water which may be three times the weight of the steam produced. All wet steam fields that are used to generate electric power by using steam turbines therefore have centrifugal separators to separate the steam and water.] The steam is then handled in the same way as the steam produced in dry steam fields, and the water is taken by pipe or by channel to a disposal point. If the geothermal water has been "double-flashed"—that is, if the water from the first steam-water separation is allowed to flash at some suitable lower pressure and the steam and water are again separated—then the water to be disposed of will have a temperature close to 100°C and will amount to about 70 percent by weight of the water originally produced. This hot water can then be used for heating or cooling at a cost which is lower than those of alternatives, if demand is concentrated in a market located within a few miles of the geothermal field. If there is no such demand for heating or cooling, and the mineral content of the geothermal water is not of value, then the residual water must be discarded. Three methods of disposal have been adopted or tested in the past. In New Zealand, where the salinity of the geothermal fluids is about one-tenth the salinity of seawater, and is therefore relatively low, the geothermal water is simply discharged into a large neighboring river, with negligible environmental effects. In El Salvador, Central America, the occurrence of a geothermal brine with a salt content about half that of seawater, and the relatively small flow of the neighboring river during some seasons, have led to the study of a

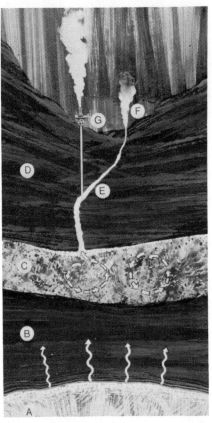

Fig. 1. Geothermal field. (A) Magma (molten mass, still in the process of cooling). (B) Solid rock; conducts heat upward. (C) Porous rock; contains water that is boiled by heat from below. (D) Solid rock; prevents steam from escaping. (E) Fissure; allows steam to escape. (F) A geyser; fumarole, or hot spring. (G) Well; taps steam in fissure. [Source: Pacific Gas and Electric Company, San Francisco]

plan to carry the rejected water some 30 km by channel to the sea. A third method of disposal, some aspects of which were tested experimentally in El Salvador, is to reinject the water beneath the surface. In El Salvador geothermal water at a temperature of 160°C was continuously reinjected for 6 months. The maximum rate of reinjection achieved without pumping was of the order of 800 tons per hour into a single well which had a production casing 9⅝ inches (~ 24½ cm) in diameter and was drilled to a depth of roughly 900 m. The tests carried out in El Salvador were in all respects successful, but further tests are needed to establish that disposal by reinjection of large quantities of geothermal water can be achieved on a 20-year or 50-year basis. In particular, tests are required to establish criteria for siting reinjection wells so that they can contribute recharge water to the reservoir under exploitation without degrading

the thermal quality of the geothermal water being produced from the area of steam production.

An average production well in a hot water field drilled to 3000 feet (915 m) costs about $150,000. Production from a geothermal well in a hot water field with a reservoir temperature near 230°C may be about 400 tons of steam and water per hour. If this water is allowed to flash in two stages, then 72 tons of steam at 5 atm and 154°C and 48 tons of steam at 0.8 atm and 93°C can be obtained. Depending on the turbine and the inlet pressures used, this steam can generate about as much power as the well in a dry steam field which delivers 100 tons of dry steam per hour at 200°C. Since the wells are commonly more shallow and therefore drilling costs are lower, it may appear that the cost of electric power from wet steam fields should be less than that from dry steam fields. However, other factors have to be considered, such as the increased turbine costs involved in using larger quantities of low-pressure steam [the turbine section using steam at 1 atm and below costs twice as much as the section using higher-pressure steam (7)] and the cost of disposal of the relatively large quantities of geothermal water. The cost of disposal by reinjection, for example, was estimated in one case to be from $0.029 to $0.047 per ton of water produced, which would add roughly $0.097 to $0.157 per ton to the cost of producing the steam. But even with the higher disposal costs for wet steam fields, the electricity produced still remains competitive with that produced in thermal stations.

Economics and Rate of Development

[The National Petroleum Council has estimated that U.S. geothermal resources can be developed to supply 1,900 to 3,500 Mw of electric power by 1985. The Hickel Conference, on the other hand, has estimated the developable potential as 132,000 Mw by 1985. Other estimates are 2,400 to 16,000 Mw, assuming a 25-year life for the resource (4). According to the largest of these estimates, geothermal resources could supply almost 20 percent of the power needed in the United States in 1985, and according to the smallest of them only about 0.5 percent, a difference of almost two orders of magnitude. This is a very considerable difference, but at the present time, unfortunately, there appears to be no certain way to determine which estimate is more nearly correct. Given existing technology, the presence or absence of hot water or steam at depth can be proved only by drilling. So far, there has been relatively little exploration drilling in the United States, or indeed in any other country.

If the average geothermal production well yields steam at a rate equivalent to 5 Mw, then 26,000 productive wells will be needed to produce 132,000 Mw in 1985. Koenig (8) reported that, at the end of October 1969, geothermal drilling to a depth of more than 3,000 feet (900 m) had taken place at ten locations in the United States and that fluid at a temperature higher than 180°C was encountered at four of these, but because of scaling and environmental problems only one of them, The Geysers field, where dry steam was encountered, has been developed for electric power production. The total number of wells drilled in these ten locations was 119, of which 78 were located at The Geysers field. Most of the wells at The Geysers are producers. In the United States, then, at ten locations where drilling has taken place, discoveries were made at four (although electric power production is under way at present at only one of these) and about 60 percent of the wells drilled can be classed as producers. If the same success ratio is maintained, then the total number of wells required in the United States by 1985 to produce 132,000 Mw will be about 42,000, or 3,800 per year starting in 1974. This can be compared with the yearly total of onshore oil well completions in the United States, which in 1969 was about 30,000, or about eight times the yearly number of geothermal wells needed. If the cost of the average geothermal well is estimated, conservatively, at $150,000 and lease, rental, and exploration costs are assumed to be in the same ratio to drilling costs as they were for the onshore oil industry in 1969, then a total expenditure on geothermal exploration and drilling of the order of $10 billion will be required to produce steam equivalent to 132,000 Mw by 1985. This implies an annual investment of risk and development capital equal to roughly 15 percent of such expenditure by the oil industry in the United States in 1969.

Table 1. Capital investment in fuel production.

Fuel	Initial investment (per kilowatt)	Reference
Persian Gulf oil	$ 2.80	(9, 10)
U.S. onshore oil	81.40	(9, 11)
U.S. geothermal steam	75.40	(12)
North American U_3O_8	4.00	(13)

An obvious question to ask is whether geothermal drilling, if it continues at the present rate, will achieve the steam production projected by the Hickel Conference. Sources close to the industry estimate that there may be ten drilling rigs at work continuously in the United States at present, indicating an average drilling rate of 60 to 100 geothermal wells per annum; this is only about one-fortieth of the rate required to meet the Hickel projections. Or, to look at it another way, to drill 42,000 wells by 1985 beginning with an annual rate of 100 in 1973 will require an annual increase of 50 percent in the number of wells drilled continuing through 1985.

Institutional Factors and Development

If geothermal power is as competitive economically as suggested above, then it may be asked why relatively little geothermal drilling is now taking place in the United States. Several answers to this question have been given. It has been pointed out that the major geothermal resources of the United States are located in the western states, where 60 percent of the geothermally prospective areas are federal land which has not yet been released for geothermal exploration and development. Federal leasing requirements are more onerous for known geothermal resources areas (KGRA's) than for other prospective areas, and since many nonfederal prospective areas are adjacent to federal lands, there is a reluctance on the part of geothermal operators to carry out exploration drilling and prove geothermal resources in these areas because the adjacent federal lands may then be reclassified as KGRA's.

In the past, two industries have mobilized and deployed risk capital for natural resource development on the scale now required for geothermal de-

Fig. 2. Generating units at The Geysers geothermal power plant, Sonoma County, California. In the foreground are steam pipes with expansion loops. The loops allow the pipe to contract when the plant has to be shut down and to expand on start-up. The steam condensate rising from the row of five low stacks at the left marks the location of blowdown valves. When the plant has to be shut down, the steam escapes through these valves. The steam at the upper left comes from a natural fumarole. [Source: Pacific Gas and Electric Company, San Francisco]

velopment. These are the mining and oil industries. It might be expected that the oil industry in particular could now easily move an appreciable part of its resources from oil to geothermal exploration and development. Yet this has not occurred, at least on the scale needed to meet the Hickel projections. The reason may be that, while oil (and also minerals) may be traded nationally and internationally, geothermal resources cannot be, but must be used close to where they are produced for the generation of electric power or to supply thermal energy. In the United States only a public utility may sell electric power, and so the oil companies should seek the utilities in some form of partnership in geothermal development if power production is the objective, yet this kind of association is not customary for the oil companies and may tend to inhibit their activities in the geothermal field.

At the risk of some oversimplification, it can be said that our main sources of energy now and in the short term future are the hydrocarbons, with, in the background, the possibility that nuclear fission may be developed into a significant energy source. It is instructive to examine the investment costs and relative profitability of these energy sources. The approximate average capital investments required to extract energy sources from the ground without refining are given in Table 1.

It is interesting to note that the initial capital investment in fuel production per kilowatt for uranium is almost as low as that for Persian Gulf oil, but the relatively high cost of nuclear generating plants and operating and environmental problems appear to have held down demand, prices, and profitability for uranium ore producers.

If it may be presumed that the production of onshore oil in the United States is a profitable industry, then the costs quoted in Table 1 indicate that, even if the profit margin per barrel for Persian Gulf oil is smaller than for U.S. oil, companies with access to Persian Gulf or comparable overseas oil and U.S. markets (in general, the major companies) may find it more profitable to invest in the production of that oil rather than alternative domestic energy sources such as geothermal steam. On the other hand, oil companies without access to the Persian Gulf or similar sources of oil may find geothermal steam produc-

Fig. 3. Part of a 53,000-kilowatt generating unit at The Geysers geothermal power plant, Sonoma County, California. The big pipe is carrying steam to the turbine generators. Completion of this unit in 1973 brought the capacity of the plant up to 396,000 kilowatts. [Source: Pacific Gas and Electric Company, San Francisco]

tion worth considering if a suitable arrangement can be made with one of the electric utilities. The cost of electricity produced from geothermal steam was about $0.0053 per kilowatt-hour at The Geysers field in 1970. For comparison, the cost of electricity from an oil-fired thermal generating plant in California was $0.01 per kilowatt-hour when fuel oil cost $3.50 per barrel, and from a nuclear generating plant it was about $0.012 per kilowatt-hour.

The utilities, if they are to generate substantial quantities of geothermal power, will need to adjust to the concept of building generating plants in multiples of small units (55 Mw is the output of the largest geothermal unit now in operation) close to the geothermal field rather than close to the center of demand, with the disadvantage that long transmission lines may be required in some cases. The utilities themselves, if they chose to mobilize and deploy risk capital, could enter the field as steam producers. However, if the utilities did choose to diversify into the development of primary energy sources, it would remain for them to assess the relative profitability of offshore oil and

gas compared to geothermal steam.

Some industries, such as aluminum, which are now facing electric power shortages in the United States, could develop geothermal power resources for their own consumption in order to achieve security of supply.

Two factors that have not been discussed in relation to geothermal energy development are matters which are of concern at the national level—these are security of supply and foreign exchange costs for imported fuels. Since geothermal energy must be consumed domestically and involves no recurrent foreign exchange costs, these two factors might lead to government policies favoring the development of geothermal resources. Such policies might be implemented either by some form of legislation favoring geothermal energy or by direct government action in exploring for and developing the resources, which then would be exploited by the utilities.

Many of the factors influencing the development of geothermal resources in the United States affect other countries also. Any country which is a net importer of energy would do well to examine its geothermal energy potential, and even countries which export oil and gas might consider whether geothermal energy could substitute for oil or gas at a lower cost and whether there may be some special application, such as space heating or cooling, or the production of desalted water or of hydrothermal minerals, where geothermal resources have a role to play. That geothermal energy is cheaper than alternatives in many cases is certain, and the prospect of rising prices for oil and gas and other energy sources in the future means that its competitive position is unlikely to change. That geothermal resources will continue to be developed successfully and profitably seems certain, but what is uncertain is whether in the United States the industry will receive the massive investment it needs to achieve the Hickel projections.

The likely scale of geothermal development in the United States is difficult to determine. There is no tradition of exploration for and development of fuels by the state, and the oil and mining companies, in the past the investors of risk capital in natural resource development, may not find investment in geothermal energy as profitable as investment in Middle Eastern or other oil resources. The outcome will depend on the policy decisions of governments as well as on institutional and financial factors and, in the United States, on how the oil and mining companies and the utilities react to the problems and challenges of geothermal energy development. In other countries, particularly developing countries, where the separation between the sectors of the economy engaged in resource development and in electric power generation may not be so clear-cut, or where the state is itself more active, geothermal resources may have a part to play in substituting at lower cost for oil, coal, or nuclear fission to meet future energy needs.

The author is director of the Laboratory of Chemical Biodynamics, and University Professor of Chemistry, University of California, Berkeley 94720. This article is adapted from an address presented at the Stanford University Energy Seminar Series, 28 January 1974, Stanford, California.

References and Notes

1. P. K. Theobald, S. P. Schweinfurth, D. C. Duncan, *U.S. Geol. Surv. Circ. No. 650* (1972), p. 24.
2. Committee on U.S. Energy Outlook, *U.S. Energy Outlook, a Summary Report of the National Petroleum Council* (National Petroleum Council, Washington, D.C., 1972), p. 52.
3. J. C. Denton, Ed., *Geothermal Energy, a Special Report by Walter J. Hickel* (Univ. of Alaska, Fairbanks, 1972), p. 95.
4. D. E. White, in *Geothermal Energy*, P. Kruger and C. Otte, Eds. (Stanford Univ. Press, Stanford, Calif., 1972), pp. 69–94.
5. L. J. P. Muffler, *U.S. Geol. Surv. Prof. Pap. No. 820* (1973), pp. 251–261.
6. *PG and E Week* (24 August 1973).
7. B. Wood, in *Geothermal Energy*, H. C. H. Armstead, Ed. (Unesco, Paris, 1973), p. 112.
8. J. B. Koenig, *Geothermics* (Special Issue No. 2) (1972), p. 1.
9. M. A. Adelman, *The World Petroleum Market* (Johns Hopkins Univ. Press, Baltimore, Md., 1972).
10. This is the average investment per initial daily barrel delivered to a loading terminal in the Persian Gulf. An investment of roughly $38 per kilowatt in tanker capacity is required to deliver oil to the United States, but this investment need not be made by the company which produces the oil.
11. This is the average investment per initial daily barrel of U.S. onshore oil. Prices are from Adelman (9).
12. It is assumed that the average geothermal well costs $150,000 and delivers a steam production equivalent to 5 Mw, that the ratio of drilling to total development costs is 1/1.6, and that 60 percent of the wells drilled are producers.
13. W. M. Gilchrist, *Mining Eng. (N.Y.)* 21, 30 (1969). The investment cost in mine development and mining plant construction is taken to be $20,000 per annual ton of U_3O_8 produced. A burnup of 3,000 megawatt-days per ton of uranium, a ratio of 1.7 tons of uranium per megawatt electric of generating plant, and a generating plant load factor of 0.75 are assumed. The cost of supplying the initial charge of unenriched uranium, in a form suitable for use in a reactor, is about $50 per kilowatt. See, for example, L. R. Haywood, J. A. L. Robertson, J. Pawliw, J. Howieson, L. L. Bodie, *Proc. U.N. Int. Conf. Peaceful Uses At. Energy 8th* (1972), pp. 185–214.

Solar Energy by Photosynthesis

Melvin Calvin

As we run out of the stored energy which oil, natural gas, and coal represent (1), the question arises as to whether we can make use of solar energy. In order to make some estimate of this possibility, we must evaluate the magnitude of the solar energy resource. The highest yearly averaged impingement is in the region of the Sahara Desert [~ 280 watts per square meter (2)], and there is another high-intensity region in the southern United States and Northern Mexico (about 260 watt/m²). Let's relate that to the solar energy constant, that is, the total energy of the sun coming in at normal incidence outside the earth's atmosphere, which is about 2 calories per square centimeter per minute or 1 kilowatt per square meter. Only about half of that reaches the earth's surface, and this amount varies considerably, depending upon the weather conditions. The annual average insolation in the United States, taking into account the variability over day and night, winter and summer is shown in Fig. 1. The region within the contour line at 260 watt/m² consists of most of New Mexico and Arizona with parts of Nevada and Southern California. The other high points are in southern Florida and in southern Louisiana. The potential contribution of photosynthesis to the collection of solar energy merits consideration. Let us examine the photosynthetic process as such and the technologically constructed systems modeled on what we know of the natural photosynthetic apparatus. I suggest two such model systems for the direct photoconversion of the quantum into useful energy, one of them to produce storable energy (probably in the form of hydrogen), and the other to use a synthetic system based on the concepts of the structure of biological membranes, the converted quantum being taken off as electrical potential.

While the hydrogen proposal and experiments are not biological photosynthesis, they are based on what we know about the photosynthetic process (3). It is a "synthetic" system, in which we expect to sensitize the photodecomposition of water to hydrogen and oxygen. The hydrogen can be a fuel that can be used in various ways. The harnessing of solar energy by a natural quantum collection process includes the generation of hydrogen or the reduction of carbon dioxide. The normal way for the quantum to be used in photosynthesis is in the reduction of carbon dioxide.

Roughly 6 percent of the energy use in the United States is for the production of chemicals or materials. For this purpose, power generation or hydrogen production can be only adjuncts: only reduced carbon can contribute directly in making materials and chemicals. I therefore distinguish between the materials and fuel. The photochemical system, as now conceived, can produce only hydrogen, whereas photosynthesis itself can produce either hydrogen or reduced carbon.

Biological (Agricultural) Photosynthetic Conversion of Solar Energy

The biological model that is the conceptual source of these two processes (4) is both the green plant and bacterial photosynthesis as we have learned to understand it in the last 20 years, a generalized scheme of which is shown in Fig. 2. The green part of the plant, represented in the center, is absorbing the sunlight and separating the positive and negative charge. The positive and negative charge can be used by the

Table 1. Fermentation of alcohol: efficiency and price. ΔH, heat of combustion; pound ~ 0.45 kg; gallon $\sim 3.8 \ 10^{-3} \ m^3$; Btu $\sim 1.06 \times 10^3$ joules.

Sugar $C_6H_{12}O_6$	Ethanol $2 \ C_2H_5OH + 2 \ CO_2$
180 g	92 g
ΔH 673 kcal	655 kcal

12.88 pounds $\longrightarrow$ 1 gallon (84,356 Btu)
at 5 cents per pound $\longrightarrow$ 64 cents per gallon
$+ \sim 20$ cents process cost
Petroleum $\longrightarrow$ ethanol
(domestic) 55 cents per gallon (controlled)*
foreign > $1 per gallon

* Not available in San Francisco area.

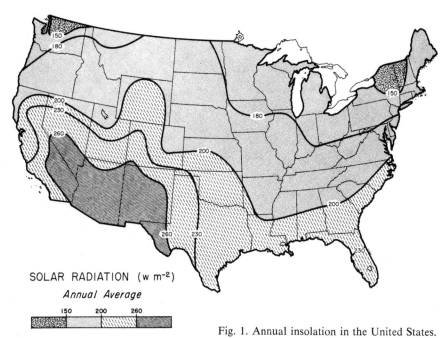

SOLAR RADIATION (w m⁻²)

Annual Average

150   200   260

Fig. 1. Annual insolation in the United States.

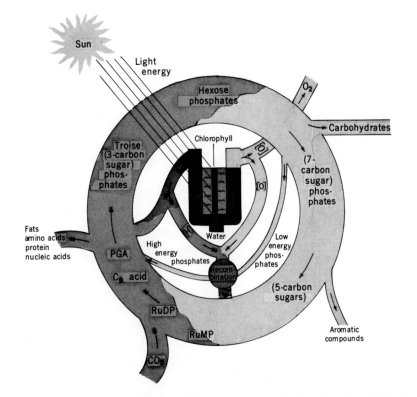

Fig. 2. Photosynthetic conversion of sunlight to energy and reduced carbon. Abbreviations: PGA, 3-phosphoglyceric acid; RuDP, ribulose 1,5-diphosphate; ribulose 5-monophosphate; [H], chemical reducing power; [O], chemical oxidizing power.

enzymatic apparatus of the green plant. The hydrogen atoms representing the negative charge can be used to reduce carbon dioxide and generate sugar; and the positive side represented by oxygen atoms can be used to oxidize water and generate molecular oxygen. The center of the diagram is the quantum converting apparatus. The carbon reduction cycle (the large circle on the outside) uses the primary reducing power produced in the chlorophyll-containing part of the plant to reduce the carbon dioxide (3). After the entry of carbon dioxide into the photosynthetic carbon cycle all the various plant components are synthesized (fats, hydrocarbons, proteins, carbohydrates, amino acids, nucleic acids, and others). One can use the information about the two parts of the photosynthetic process—the photochemical generation of [H] (which indicates chemical reducing power) and [O] (which indicates chemical oxidizing power) and carbon reduction—in two separate ways.

The photosynthetic carbon reduction cycle can be used as an energy source and as a material source (5). It does not seem possible to use the photoelectric system directly for a material source. It generates electric power, or hydrogen, neither of which are substances from which needed *materials* can be constructed. These materials represent primarily the chemicals and other nonenergy items that constitute about 6 percent of our total energy requirement (the equivalent of about 2 million barrels of crude oil per day).

One way of beginning to examine the photosynthetic cycle as an energy and material source is to inquire about the natural photosynthetic productivity in terms of reduced carbon that is spread over the earth's surface. The greatest production of reduced carbon is mainly along the equator; not the areas of the earth where the highest insolation occurs, but, rather, where the best conditions for year-round growth exist. The equatorial areas grow a very large amount of natural vegetation because of the presence of water. The overall annual production is of the order of 1 kilogram of carbon per square meter per year, mostly in the form of sugar. I say "mostly in the form of sugar" because the principal product (generally about 50 percent) of plant photosynthesis is carbohydrate.

When that fact is realized, we should then ask ourselves which plants are capable of raising that productivity from 1 kilogram of carbon per square meter per year to something more useful. The natural efficiency is very low, a few hundredths of a percent. There is little doubt about which type of plants to use. The principal plant known today which has the highest yield of yearly, averaged photosynthesis is sugarcane (6). The overall efficiency is about 0.6 percent and this will be compared with several other types of plants later.

I want to suggest the use of sugar as an industrial raw material and also to suggest its end uses. You could burn sugar—it is carbohydrate, as is cellulose, and has the same caloric content. However, there are more efficient methods than burning, and one is to convert the sugar and cane cellulose into alcohol. In this process (shown in Table 1), the thermal efficiency is very good, with practically no loss in going from sugar to alcohol. It takes 12.9 pounds (1 pound ~0.45 kilogram) of sugar to make 1 gallon of alcohol, that is, 64 cents worth of sugar at 1971–1972 price of sugarcane to make 1 gallon of alcohol. It costs about 20 cents to convert the sugar, making a total of 84 cents per gallon for alcohol by fermentation. Today (January 1974) the controlled price of the petroleum source alcohol is 66 cents per gallon, if you can find any. However, the actual offshore price for petroleum source alcohol is more than $1 per gallon. The reason for presenting these numbers is that at a price of 85 cents per gallon for fermentation alcohol, even on a thermal basis, if nothing else, we are already nearly economic in the use of alcohol, at least as an additive to fuel gasoline. These sources are coming closer economically.

As an illustration of how the economics of this kind of chemistry has affected the sources of alcohol in the last 50 years, the industrial ethyl alcohol production since 1940 is shown in Fig. 3. From 1940 to 1945 (during World War II) the alcohol was made mostly by fermentation from molasses, sulfite liquors, and grain (natural sources of carbohydrate). When petroleum became available as a cheap source of alcohol around 1950, it took over, entirely, the alcohol market. Ethylene is obtained by cracking liquid hydrocarbon and hydrating the ethylene to make ethanol. The fermentation sources of ethanol disappeared entirely after 1960 because ethylene was only

Table 2. Annual productivity for *Hevea* (rubber), cane, and beet crops.

Crop	Yield
Hevea	1 ton of rubber per acre
Cane	4 tons of sugar per acre
	2 tons of ethanol
	1.2 tons of ethylene
	68 × 10⁶ Btu (0.23 percent of incident sun)
	4 tons of bagasse per acre
Beet	2 tons of sugar per acre
	0.7 ton of pulp per acre

2 cents per pound, and the conversion cost was very small.

The price of ethylene is roughly of the order of 10 cents per pound and rising, whereas a year or two ago it was around 2 cents per pound. Thus, the economic facts of high price and scarce supply have brought back the possibility that fermentation alcohol could become a significant source of hydrocarbon (Table 2).

Sugarcane makes 4 tons of sugar per acre (1 acre ~4.05 × 10³ square meters) per year, from which is obtained 2 tons of ethanol and 1.2 tons of ethylene, with an overall efficiency of 0.23 percent of incident sunlight, if only the sucrose is counted. There is, however, an equal amount of cellulose in the cane, in the form of bagasse (the cellulose residue of the sugarcane), with a yield of 4 tons of bagasse per acre per year. The total therefore appears to be 8 tons of carbohydrate per acre of cane, raising the efficiency of solar energy conversion (agricultural solar energy conversion)

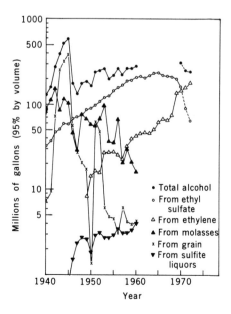

Fig. 3. Industrial alcohol production (1971).

for cane to about 0.5 percent. Sugar beets give 2.3 tons of sugar per acre, with 0.7 ton of pulp per acre, per year; but beets, unlike sugarcane, do not grow all the year round.

It occurred to me that we are going to a great deal of trouble to convert a carbohydrate (sugar) into a hydrocarbon (ethanol-ethylene-polyethylene). Would it not be possible to find a plant source that would make hydrocarbon directly (Fig. 4)? There is at least one, already available, very well known source: the *Hevea* rubber plant which was first found wild in Brazil and now is grown almost exclusively in plantations in Malaysia and Indonesia. Today the yield of rubber (which is already a hydrocarbon with no oxygen in it) is about 1 ton per acre per year, which is about half the yield of cane, and only about 20 percent less in terms of ethylene potential. The rubber growers are very optimistic that they can, and will, be able to raise the yield of rubber from 1 to 3 tons per acre per year (7). If they are able to harvest 3 tons of rubber per acre per year (that is, 3 tons of hydrocarbon), this type of plant may also become a seriously considered possibility for a direct photosynthetic source of hydrocarbon for use in chemicals and materials.

The rubber story is very similar to the industrial alcohol (ethanol) story, and, in a sense, is even a little more spectacular. After World War II, synthetic rubber (that is, butadiene and styrene) made from petroleum practically eliminated rubber plantations as a source of this material. The rubber growers then began to improve the yield, which at the end of World War II was only about 400 pounds of rubber per acre per year (8). The figure today is about 2300 pounds of rubber per acre per year. About one-third of the rubber used today comes from natural sources, and two-thirds from synthetic sources.

If the price of petroleum continues to rise, and the yield of natural rubber can be raised another twofold, we will again have reached another crossing point where a natural photosynthetic system for converting carbon dioxide and sunlight into hydrocarbon can be used. There are also many other types of hydrocarbon resources such as gutta, terpenes, and the like, which have not yet been explored as such. It is quite possible that breeding programs, such as have been devised to improve the *Hevea* rubber plant yield from 400 to

2400 pounds per acre per year, could be used to develop other souces of natural hydrocarbon. This could perhaps be done in a shorter period of time than was required for *Hevea* (a 7-year crop), provided that some of the annual plants were explored and that elasticity is not a special requirement.

Probably the first natural photosynthetic process which will be developed economically as a hydrocarbon source will be the conversion of carbohydrate. If the sugar planters in Hawaii, where gasoline is now rationed, would convert about one-third of their molasses directly into fuel alcohol, they would

not have to purchase the 15 million gallons of petroleum which they now do to run their agricultural machinery. Another special situation seems to be developing in Nebraska which has about 7 million bushels of spoiled grain per year. This should yield more than 20 million gallons of alcohol, which, as a 10 percent additive to gasoline, would give 200 million gallons of "gasohol." This is the name used by the Nebraska legislature to designate a composition which would qualify for a 3 cent state tax credit (*9*).

As a final comment on the natural photosynthetic sources of hydrocarbon, let me remind you of our use of about 2 million barrels per day of oil equivalent as a source of chemicals and materials. If we were to try to supply this entire need from sugarcane we would require about 60 million acres of cane if we used only the sucrose and only about 30 million acres if the cellulose could be used as well, a capability soon to arrive (*10*). In 1971 there were 0.7 million acres under cane cultivation and about 1.4 million acres in sugar beets in the United States.

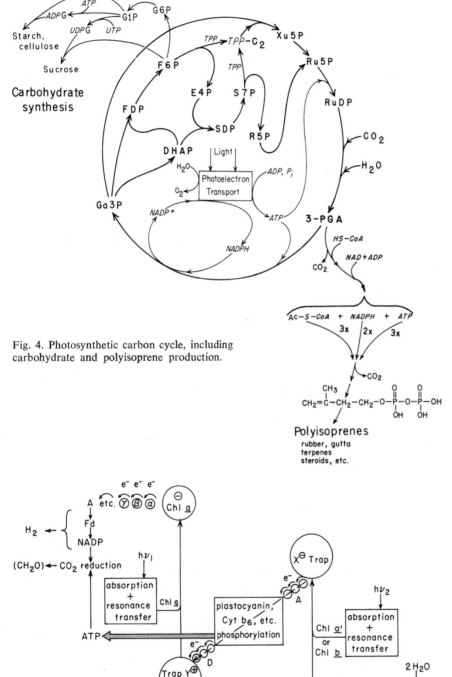

Fig. 4. Photosynthetic carbon cycle, including carbohydrate and polyisoprene production.

Fig. 5. Scheme for photosynthetic electron transport system.

Model Systems of Photosynthetic Solar Energy Conversion

A great deal is known about how the plant makes carbohydrate, and we also know how the plant makes hydrocarbon (polyisoprene, for example, rubber). We are learning more about the way in which the plant captures the quantum of energy (*11, 12*). The knowledge of the plant's quantum conversion system is not nearly so complete as the knowledge of the photosynthetic carbon reduction cycle and subsequent processes. The primary quantum conversion process is still uncertain. But using what knowledge we have of the quantum conversion process, we can ask if the concepts generated in photosynthesis research—how the plant actually captures the quantum and converts it into useful potential, or electron flow—can guide us in simulating some parts of that process by purely synthetic methods. We then might be able to use that quantum conversion (solar energy conversion) process to help solve some of the energy problems with which we are faced.

The same photosynthetic carbon cycle that is shown in Fig. 2 is more elaborately displayed in Fig. 4. The entry of carbon dioxide into the photosynthetic carbon cycle and the exit of carbon into sucrose, starch, and cellulose, as well as hydrocarbon, is shown in some detail. The energy which drives the carbon cycle is represented by the photoelectric cell shown in the center of Fig. 2. Here, in Fig. 4, light enters the black box, which takes oxygen from the water and expels it into the atmosphere, and uses the remaining hydrogen to generate the reduced pyridine compound (NADPH) which, together with the adenosine triphosphate (ATP), drives the carbon reduction cycle. All of the driving chemicals— the ATP and NADPH—come from the light source.

How much do we know about this black box? We know a good bit about what is occurring inside the "photoelectric cell" of the green plant (Fig. 5). There are two successive quantum absorptions; the first one (photosystem 2) produces a strong oxidant and an intermediate reductant energy state, that is, raising the energy of the electron so that it may pass through electron transfer agents back to another previously oxidized chlorophyll molecule at a lower oxidation potential (12). After it has reduced the second chlorophyll to its normal state, it is again raised by another light action (photosystem 1) to a still higher reduction potential and then it comes down through a series of carriers, of which NADPH is one, and eventually goes into the carbon dioxide reduction process. Whereas Fig. 4 emphasized the carbon reduction cycle, Fig. 5 emphasizes the quantum conversion (electron transfer) scheme of photosynthesis.

An analysis of this photosynthetic electron transfer scheme can give us some clues as to how we might be able to construct a system which might be a device for converting solar energy into some useful form. One method might simply be to try to isolate a particle which would contain the entire system asymmetrically arranged with an acceptor, perhaps ferredoxin (Fd), on one side and an oxygen generator on the other, and use that particle (if it exists) in an asymmetric membrane. Light would then transfer electrons from the oxygen-generating side (donor) of the system to the acceptor (or hydrogen-generating) side. Suitable electrode-active redox couples could be placed in the solutions on either side of the membrane to couple this electron transfer process to electrodes, and so generate a current for use. While

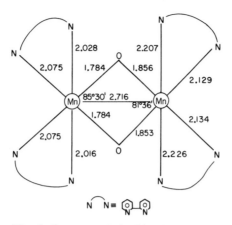

Fig. 6. Structure of the binuclear manganese photocatalyst di-μ-oxotetrakis(2,2'bipyridine)dimanganese (III, IV) perchlorate.

the successful construction of such a system would be very illuminating, it is not likely to be easily constructed or to be very stable if, as now appears, it must depend on complex structures isolated from plants and placed in an unnatural environment.

Photochemical Hydrogen Production

In some green plants and bacteria it is possible to modify the end result of this type of photochemistry. Instead of the active hydrogen reducing carbon dioxide to make sugar, it is possible to limit the amount of carbon dioxide available to the plant and, by keeping the oxygen level very low, induce the plant to use the light energy to generate molecular hydrogen (13). The oxygen must be swept out, or used up, because the enzyme system which generates the molecular hydrogen is sensitive to oxygen. This is one of the problems. However, it appears possible to alter the conditions in such a way that the photosynthetic apparatus will generate hydrogen instead of reducing carbon. Thus we know that it is possible to have catalytic systems in the plant which can use sunshine (solar energy) to generate hydrogen from the water (14). This fact has been known for more than 20 years (13), but recently a system was described in which a blue-green alga, Anabaena—which contains in it the entire photosynthetic apparatus and, additionally, a heterocyst cell that has no oxygen-producing apparatus— but has in it the hydrogen-generating apparatus (15). The reduced compounds are made in the green part of the plant (the oxygen-producing cells)

and then diffuse into the nongreen part (heterocyst) with resultant evolution of hydrogen.

The fact that the plant has in it an apparatus capable of capturing the quanta and liberating molecular hydrogen was sufficient to make me feel that if I knew more about the details of the quantum conversion (16) and about the enzymatic systems involved I might be able to devise a simpler set of chemicals which would perform the same function, that is, generate hydrogen and oxygen from water. It would not be necessary, then, to reduce carbon, or have the whole skeleton of construction of a green plant which is required to make another green plant. I wanted to derive a system which would not be as complex as the one the green plant has in order to reproduce itself. To do that, however, it was necessary to have a concept of how the hydrogen is evolved and how the oxygen is evolved, and put the two processes together conceptually and, ultimately, synthetically.

The right side of Fig. 5 shows that the oxygen comes from the water, and the water molecule has only one oxygen atom in it, while the oxygen molecule has two. A total of four electrons is involved in converting two molecules of water into a molecule of oxygen and four hydrogen atoms. In order to generate oxygen molecules from the water molecules it is necessary to bring two oxygens together and remove four electrons. It is known that manganese is involved in this part of the system (17), but a single manganese ion by itself seems unable to remove four electrons. However, it appeared to me that if two manganese atoms, each of which would have oxidation number changes from 2+, to 3+, to 4+, were put together in the same complex, there would be a source of the required electrons without the necessity of generating free oxygen atoms or hydroxyl radicals. This process could be performed entirely in the double manganese complex. Thus arose the notion of a binuclear manganese complex, which contains two water molecules and which could be used in the quantum conversion process (18). The light, sensitized or direct, could induce a ligand-to-metal charge transfer, thus generating reduced metal ions and virtual hydrogen peroxide on the way to molecular oxygen. The reduced metal ions could then be the source of electrons for another quantum act, giving rise to molecular hydrogen. This was the theoretical basis on which the next experiment was performed. The idea was that we needed at least two manganese atoms in one complex. Could we find a system that could generate oxygen or hydrogen in separate quantum acts? The structure of a dimanganese complex which might be used is shown in Fig. 6 (19).

The overall scheme representing the action of light on a polynuclear manganese catalyst that generates oxygen and reduced catalysts is shown as reaction 1 in scheme 1. The reduced catalyst can move to the place where the hydrogen-liberating enzyme exists (presumably near ferredoxin) and another quantum act could then move the electron into an acceptor (the ferredoxin) and reoxidize the catalyst (reaction 2). The reduced ferredoxin plus protons with either one of the hydrogen-liberating enzymes, hydrogenase or nitrogenase, would then liberate hydrogen and recover the oxidized ferredoxin (21) (reaction 3).

$$\frac{1}{2} H_2O \xrightarrow[\text{[cat]}_{ox}]{h\nu_{(2)}} \frac{1}{4} O_2 \uparrow + [H]_{\text{[cat]}_{red}} \quad (1)$$

$$[H]_{\text{[cat]}_{red}} + Fd^{3+} \xrightarrow{h\nu_{(1)}} Fd^{2+} + [cat]_{ox} \quad (2)$$

$$2 Fd^{2+} + 2 H^+ \xrightarrow[\text{(ii) hydrogenase}]{\text{(i) nitrogenase or}}$$

$$H_2 \uparrow + 2 Fd^{3+} \quad (3)$$

Scheme 1

What I have shown you so far are some concepts for the first reaction only. We are also in the process of deciding how to achieve the second step. For this purpose we have had to examine the structure of ferredoxin from green plants and of the hydrogen-liberating enzymes. It appears that these two substances have certain elements of structure in common, if they are not identical. Both their functional groups are iron atoms completely coordinated by sulfur atoms of various kinds. The bacterial ferredoxin contains the unit of four iron atoms and four sulfur atoms, arranged at the alternate corners of a distorted cube, the entire cube being supported or contained in a polypeptide framework by the four mercaptide sulfur atoms of cysteine molecules in the peptide chain (22). A somewhat simpler structure consisting of two iron, two sulfur, and four cysteine mercaptides is suggested for

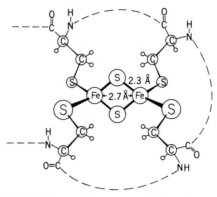

Fig. 7. Proposed structure of plant ferredoxin and hydrogenase, showing the suggested $Fe_2S_2(CyS^-)_4$ center of green plant Fd and for hydrogenase.

both plant ferredoxin and hydrogenase (Fig. 7) (23). At the binuclear iron center each iron is tetrahedrally surrounded by four sulfur atoms, two of which are sulfide bridges between the two iron atoms. The remaining four are mercaptides, from a presumed surround of peptide. This latter structure (Fig. 7) has simple analogs that can be synthesized. By tying all the mercaptides together into a macrocyclic structure it should be possible to add two electrons to such a system of iron and sulfur atoms without causing the separation of the iron and sulfur atoms. The reduced complex, with the two sulfur atoms so close together, could provide the centers for the addition of protons and the ejection of molecular hydrogen, and thus return to the oxidized form.

If we can succeed in this construction we will then have available the components of a totally synthetic system that sensitizes the photochemical decomposition of water into hydrogen

and oxygen in two different places. There are various methods of engineering this process, and I am not much concerned about that problem. Once the two separate reactions are achieved as two separate reactions, the construction of the system will go forward.

Photoelectric Membrane

Another type of notion has evolved from an examination of the nature of the primary quantum conversion act in the green plant. As was shown earlier, the primary quantum conversion apparatus in some ways simulates a solid state device in which impinging light separates charge—positive and negative, electrons and holes. We have used this concept for the last 15 years, trying to learn if and how such a system might work in the green plant (20). In the last couple of years we have found that it is possible to demonstrate that the intact chloroplasts of the green plant, when light of the proper wavelength is shone on them, do indeed behave as though there were "conduction electrons" developed by incident light (24). We were able to demonstrate a Hall effect in illuminated chloroplasts. By placing the chloroplasts in a magnetic field and shining the light on them, two different carriers are evolved, one positive and one negative, having different lifetimes and moving in opposite directions in the magnetic field.

This result encouraged us to design sensitized systems for separating charge, using various dyestuffs whose photoactivity resembles that of chlorophyll (25, 26). Figure 5 shows some of the details of such two quantum processes. Instead of allowing the evolution of oxygen, and hydrogen, or carbohydrate, it may be possible with this quantum conversion system to take the holes and electrons off as current, across a suitable device. The device I am about to propose is an example (18). I have seen the designs of other such devices (27, 28). It is a photoelectrochemical cell (25) modeled on the photosynthetic membrane itself, which incorporates the idea of photoelectron transfer, generating voltage and a current (Fig. 8) (29). There is a sensitizer (S) on one side of the synthetic membrane which, upon the absorption of a quantum, transfers its excited electron by tunneling 10 to 20 Å (27) to a carotenoid (C) which resembles a wire inside the membrane. The electron delocalized in the caro-

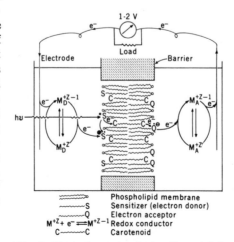

Fig. 8. Photoelectrochemical cell modeled on photosynthetic membrane.

tenoid travels through the membrane and is captured by an electron acceptor (Q) on the other side, which then goes through the cycle of a dyestuff (M_A) to deliver the electrons to the electrode. Similarly, the hole remaining (S^+) is fed an electron from another pair of dyestuffs (M_D) at a different potential. The dyestuffs are electroactive on the electrodes, thus generating a voltage and a current which can be taken off, and dependent on incident light which transfers the electron from one side of the membrane to the other. Components of such systems have been made, for example, in which the bilipid membrane has a donor system on one side and an acceptor on the other, without the conductor, only two lipid layers thick (about 60 Å). The idea of a conductor is to produce various conducting channels through a thicker membrane which will allow only the excited electron to pass through but be thick enough to be stable (30).

This kind of a totally synthetic system which emulates and stimulates in some ways the chloroplast membrane activity of the green plant may very well, in the more distant future, be another means of capturing the energy of the sun and producing electricity directly from it.

Summary

Photosynthesis, both natural and as a model process, can be examined for its potential as a possible annually renewable resource for both material and energy. The conversion of carbohydrate from cane, beets, and other sources through fermentation alcohol to hydrocarbon may soon again become economic in the light of increasing costs of recovery of hydrocarbon from fossil sources and improved fermentation technology. Even the direct photosynthetic production of hydrocarbon from known sources (for example, *Hevea*) or newly bred ones seems possible. Finally, more distantly, synthetic systems constructed on the basis of growing knowledge of the photosynthetic processes, may produce both fuel and power.

References and Notes

1. M. K. Hubbert, *Sci. Am.* **224** (3), 60 (1971).
2. One kilocalorie per square centimeter per year is 1.33 watts per square meter.
3. M. Calvin, *Science* **135**, 879 (1962).
4. A. Hollaender, K. J. Monty, R. M. Pearlstein, F. Schmidt-Bleek, W. T. Snyder, E. Volkin, report on workshop held October 1972 at Gatlinburg, Tennessee (Univ. of Tennessee, Knoxville, December 1972), and references cited.
5. F. A. Greer and T. J. Army, Eds., *Harvesting the Sun: Photosynthesis in Plant Life* (Academic Press, New York, 1967).
6. *Cane Sugar Refining in the United States: Its Economic Importance* (U.S. Sugar Refiner's Association, Washington, D.C., 1971). for a technical discussion of sugarcane yields, see: "Photosynthesis in sugar cane," Proceedings of an Internaional Symposium, June 1968, London, England, sponsored by the Imperial College of London and Tate & Lyle, Ltd.
7. Annual Report of the Rubber Research Institute of Malaya (Kuala Lumpur, 1971).
8. P. D. Abraham *et al.*, *J. Rubber Res. Inst. Malaya* **23** (2), 85 (1971), and other papers in this series by the same authors and in the same journal.
9. See *Chemical Week*, 30 January 1974, p. 33; *Chemical Marketing Reporter*, 11 February 1974; G. B. Castor, *Science* **183**, 698 (1974).
10. G. Mitra and C. R. Wilke, Lawrence Berkeley Laboratory report LBL-2334 (Berkeley, California, February 1974).
11. R. K. Clayton, *Annu. Rev. Biophys. Bioeng.* **2**, 131 (1973); *Light and Living Matter: A Guide to the Study of Photobiology* (McGraw-Hill, New York, 1971); vol. 2; M. Calvin, in *Proceedings of the 6th International Photobiology Congress, Bochum, Germany, 1972*, G. O. Schenk, Ed. (Deutsche Gesellschaft Lichtforschung, Hamburg, Germany, 1973).
12. R. K. Clayton, *Proc. Natl. Acad. Sci. U.S.A.* **69**, 44 (1972).
13. H. Gaffron and J. Rubin, *J. Gen. Physiol.* **26**, 219 (1942).
14. J. R. Benemann, J. A. Berenson, N. O. Kaplan, M. E. Kamen, *Proc. Natl. Acad. Sci. U.S.A.* **70**, 2317 (1973).
15. J. R. Benemann and N. M. Weare, *Science* **184**, 174 (1974).
16. M. Calvin, *J. Theor. Biol.* **1**, 258 (1961); G. M. Androes and M. Calvin, *Science* **138**, 867 (1962); M. Calvin, *Adv. Catal.* **14**, 1 (1963).
17. B. Kok and G. M. Cheniae, in *Current Topics in Bioenergetics*, D. R. Sanadi, Ed. (Academic Press, New York, 1966); vol. 1, pp. 1–47.
18. M. Calvin, "Solar energy," Colloquium at U.S. Atomic Energy Commission, Germantown, Maryland, 1 February 1973.
19. P. M. Plaskin, R. C. Stoufer, M. Mathew, G. J. Palenek, *J. Am. Chem. Soc.* **94**, 2121 (1972).
20. S. R. Cooper and M. Calvin, in preparation.
21. W. H. Orme-Johnson, *Annu. Rev. Biochem.* **42**, 159 (1973).
22. E. T. Adman, L. C. Silkin, L. H. Jensen, *J. Biol. Chem.* **248**, 2987 (1973); H. Herskovitz, B. A. Averaill, R. H. Holm, J. A. Ibers, W. D. Phillips, F. J. Weiher, *Proc. Natl. Acad. Sci. U.S.A.* **69**, 2437 (1972).
23. W. R. Dunham, G. Polsna, R. H. Sands, A. R. Bearden, *Biochim. Biophys. Acta* **253**, 373 (1971); J. J. Mayerle, R. B. Frankel, R. H. Holm, J. A. Ibers, W. D. Phillips, J. F. Weiher, *Proc. Natl. Acad. Sci. U.S.A.* **70**, 2429 (1973); G. Nakos and L. E. Mortenson, *Biochemistry* **10**, 2442 (1971).
24. R. A. Bogomolni, thesis, University of California, Berkeley (1972); LBL report 1972.
25. H. Tributsch and M. Calvin, *Photochem. Photobiol.* **14**, 95 (1971).
26. H. Tributsch, *ibid.* **16**, 261 (1972).
27. H. Kühn and D. Möbius, *Angew Chem. Int. Ed. Engl.* **10**, 620 (1972).
28. H. T. Tien, *Nature (Lond.)* **219**, 272 (1968); —— and S. P. Verma, *ibid.* **227**, 1232 (1970); H. T. Tien, *Photochem. Photobiol.* **16**, 271 (1972).
29. This concept was initially discussed at the colloquium of the U.S. Atomic Energy Commission, Germantown, Maryland, February 1973.
30. For an explanation of the structure and function of biological membranes, see M. K. Jain, *The Bimolecular Lipid Membrane* (Van Nostrand-Reinhold, New York, 1973).
31. Sponsored by the U.S. Atomic Energy Commission.

Solar Energy Utilization by Physical Methods

Martin Wolf

An interesting feature of solar energy is that it can be utilized through a multitude of differing methods. Solar energy utilization does not require a great deal of technology development, since technical feasibility has been proved for most approaches, so that the work remaining to be done extends generally to proving or achieving economic feasibility and to applications engineering. Economic feasibility not only includes adequately low cost to facilitate introduction into the marketplace, but also the assurance that the new energy source will become economically significant by being utilized in large scale. This means that it should not only be cost competitive with other internally or externally available energy resources but should be usable in adequate quantity at realistic price, should the old energy sources not be procurable in sufficient quantity at acceptable prices. In this case, the new resource can prevent the general economic development from being stymied, and can exert a stabilizing influence on the economic availability of the other energy sources. Two preliminary conditions to achieving this status, the adequate availability of solar energy in the United States and the potential utilization without significant ecological problems, have been extensively discussed (1). The discussion can therefore turn to the state of technological development and, particularly, to the potential for meeting both the economic requirements for quantity and the cost of the various approaches to the utilization of solar energy. The question then becomes one of time scale which may conveniently be broken: (i) the short range with prime emphasis on overcoming ecological and social problems and on local or temporary energy supply shortages (up to 1980); (ii) the medium range, characterized by increasing general shortages of natural gas and petroleum (up to 2000); and (iii) the long range in which these two resources will be essentially exhausted, and, if consumption should have increased as frequently predicted, concern about large-scale thermal pollution may start to mount.

The various approaches to solar energy utilization can be divided into four groups: indirect methods using meteorological or geophysical effects; utilization of biological effects; direct use for heating; and conversion to electricity. The approaches, with exception of the second, are discussed in the following sections.

Indirect Utilization of Solar Energy

Hydropower, among the first sources of mechanical energy for man, has also been utilized for the generation of electricity before the introduction of steam power plants. It is efficient (~ 90 percent), economical, and supplies at present approximately 17 percent of the total electricity generated in the United States. Apart from high capital costs, there are ecological reasons for avoiding the construction of numerous further dams. Approximately one-third of the total hydropower potential of the United States is already developed, so that a large increase in hydropower utilization will not be possible.

Wind power has, in the past centuries, been extensively used to provide mechanical energy. Now, however, the wind power plants with their intermittent output have become obsolete through the availability of power on demand from cheap fossil fuels. With the coming shortage in fossil fuels, and the design of larger and more efficient aeroturbines, a new interest in the use of wind power is manifest. A conceptual design with aeroturbines stationed off the Atlantic coast to produce 160 billion kilowatt-hours of electricity a year has been completed for the New England region (2). Limiting factors in the large-scale utilization of wind power are a combination of available wind energy and the possibility of weather modification. Thus, according to conservative estimates, 1 percent of the electricity consumption or 0.43 percent of the total energy consumption in the United States could be supplied by wind power in the year 2000 (3). This schedule depends on government support for technology de-

Fig. 1. The seven-story laboratory building at Odeillo, with the parabolic reflector mounted on its north wall and the target building to the right. [Courtesy of *Life*]

The author is research associate professor of electrical and mechanical engineering and is associated with the National Center for Energy Management and Power, at the University of Pennsylvania, Philadelphia 19174.

118

velopment and proof of feasibility, with industry carrying out the development of this resource after feasibility of the approach has been established. It is interesting to note here the recent announcement of a joint NSF-NASA effort to develop a 100-kilowatt wind generator.

Ocean thermal gradient power plants are based on the utilization of vertical temperature profiles which are established in the ocean waters by absorption of sunlight in the upper layers of the ocean, combined with density separation by depth. In certain areas, the resulting temperature gradients are enhanced through the action of ocean currents, such as the Gulf Stream off the East Coast of the United States. Although the temperature differences are relatively small, it is expected that conversion to electrical power can be accomplished with an efficiency that approaches 2 percent. Since this thermal energy is continuously available without fuel cost, and since its utilization creates no thermal pollution if carried out on a moderate scale, the approach looks basically attractive. The temperature difference between the Gulf Stream

surface water and that at a depth of 2000 feet ranges from 15° to 22°C. A collection system of units moored at 1 mile spacing along the length and breadth of the Gulf Stream off the coast of Florida is thought to be capable of energy production equal to the total 1970 U.S. energy consumption (3). From a conceptual design for such an ocean thermal gradient power plant using low-temperature vapor turbines it has been estimated that such units can produce electric power at competitive cost (4). If sufficient support is given to development, it has been estimated that 1 percent of the electricity consumed in the United States in the year 2000 could be provided from ocean temperature differences.

ref?

Solar Energy for Heating

Use of solar energy in the form of heat has been made for more than 2000 years. Such heat has been used for the distilling of liquids—for example, of perfume in the ancient and medieval times, and of fresh water, which is now being produced from the

seawater surrounding Mediterranean and Caribbean islands; for the drying of materials, particularly agricultural products such as hay, raisins, and lumber; for the heating of water for household consumption—which is very common in Israel and in Japan, and which is also used in Florida; for the heating of houses for which a few experimental units are in operation in the United States; for the experimental operation of absorption refrigeration systems for cold storage as well as air conditioning purposes; for the generation of high-temperature heat by means of optical concentrators, which were used for the ignition of wooden ships in warfare 2100 years ago, as well as for metallurgical purposes for which the largest system ever built is in operation at Odeillo in the French Pyrenees (Fig. 1), producing more than a megawatt of power and reaching temperatures of 3300°C.

These systems for the direct use of heat generated from solar energy operate at high efficiency (~ 50 percent reachable in simple systems), are technologically the best developed of any solar energy utilization systems, and are

Fig. 2. Solar collector driving steam engine, exhibited by Mouchot at the World's Fair in Paris, 1878.

Table 1. Energy consumption in the United States in 1967 (*11*).

User	Energy used (10^{12} kilowatt-hours)					
	Space heating	Other heating	Electricity*	Motive power	Other	Total
Residential	2.08	0.69	0.87			3.64
Commercial	0.35	0.69	0.52			1.56
Transportation	0.17			3.47		3.64
Industry	0.35	3.47	1.73		0.69	6.24
Other	0.17	1.04	0.52		1.21	2.94
All users	3.12	5.89	3.64	3.47	1.90	18.02

* The figures for electricity are thermal energy input to all utilities.

closest to providing energy competitively to energy from other sources (*5*). They also address an area of greatest use of energy (Table 1). Solar domestic water heaters are available in Florida (*6*), where they provide energy at lower cost than that provided by electric power, and at not more than twice the present costs of gas. These systems are produced in very small quantities, essentially in hand operation, and mass production methods should result in cost reductions to levels where these solar collectors can provide energy competitively with any other source.

A similar approach to that used for domestic water heating can be applied for the heating of houses. Such systems can, if combined with thermal energy storage of a capacity corresponding approximately to 1 day's use, economically produce 50 to 75 percent of the annual energy consumption for heating, cooling, and hot-water preparation in a building (*5*). This figure applies in many parts of the United States, including the highly populated northeast coast. Since the collectors would normally be mounted on walls or roofs of building structures, no additional land area would be required for this source

of energy, thus causing no ecological effects beyond those of the building itself. Even visual pollution would be minimal. It has been estimated that these systems would provide, in the year 1985, up to 1 percent of the total energy consumption in buildings, or 0.15 percent of the total national energy consumption, and 10 and 35 percent of the energy consumption in buildings by the years 2000 and 2020, respectively, which would then amount to 1.2 and 3.5 percent of the total national energy consumption (*3*).

The other areas of conversion of solar energy into heat are at present not considered to be of similarly great significance and are therefore not included in the forecast, except for the generation of heat for the conversion to electricity.

Electric Power Generation

For the generation of electric power from solar energy, two basic routes are available: (i) the sequential conversion from sunlight to heat, to steam, to

Fig. 3 (above). The "solar power farm" built by the Philadelphia engineers Shuman and Boys in 1912 at Meadi, Egypt, providing steam for a 100-horsepower piston engine (visible in shed at right). Fig. 4 (left). One of the sun-tracking collectors of the Shuman-Boys plant with the boiler tube in the focal line of the cylindrical paraboloid reflector.

mechanical power, and ultimately to electric energy; and (ii) the direct conversion of sunlight to electricity by the photovoltaic process. The first route has been experimented with quite extensively. A working system, where a water pump was driven in lieu of the electric generator, was demonstrated by A. Mouchot at the Paris World's Fair in 1878 (Fig. 2). Also, the Philadelphia engineer F. Shuman built a 100-horsepower (1 metric horsepower is ~ 7.4 × 10² watts) solar power steam engine plant in Egypt, 11 kilometers south of Cairo, in 1912 (Figs. 3 and 4). It is interesting to note the similarity of some of the proposed designs for solar plants to that of this early plant. However, the general technology has considerably advanced, and improved materials and methods are now available which can result in significantly higher efficiencies (15 to 20 percent is a reasonable expectation, and 30 percent has occasionally been mentioned) and lower systems costs (7). The work remaining to be done will therefore be focused on the application of this new technology to achieve acceptable cost-performance data, to determine the optimum system size and approach, and to prove technical and economic feasibility of large solar power stations. At present, the cost of electric power generated by this approach is predicted to be higher by a factor of 4 than power from fossil or nuclear power plants.

Photovoltaic solar energy conversion by means of silicon solar cells has provided the power for nearly all the spacecraft, launched by any nation, which were designed for missions exceeding 2 to 3 weeks duration. These cells have proved to be a reliable source of power, more suitable for spacecraft than any other. For terrestrial applications, the current price of solar power arrays is much too high to permit consideration of large-scale application (the efficiency is 13 to 14 percent on commercially available units, and is 16 percent on laboratory units). This high price has partially been the result of very small production (50 to 70 kilowatts per year) for a very restricted market, which provided no incentives for the development of very low cost processes. Thus, considerable impovements in process methods, partially also based on materials other than silicon—for instance, cadmium sulfide—will be necessary to permit large-scale terrestrial applications.

An advantage of the photovoltaic sys-

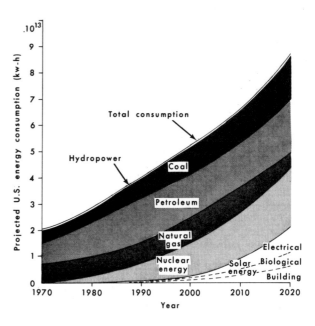

Fig. 5. The potential share of solar energy in the future energy supply, as contributed by the various sources. Data for the nonsolar energy contributions are from (10), but are adjusted for solar energy contributions according to the penetration percentages given in (10) and distributed over the other energy sources according to energy use and energy source distribution for these uses.

tem is that its size is not limited and that it therefore can easily be used at the site of energy consumption, potentially matching the distributed nature of sunlight to the distributed pattern of energy consumption. Photovoltaic solar arrays can be mounted on roofs or walls of buildings—eliminating the use of additional land area—and can even be combined with solar collectors that are used for space heating or hot-water preparation, to form a particularly efficient and economical system.

Both approaches to electric power generation, that via heat and the photovoltaic route, basically provide power only during times of incoming solar radiation. To supply energy at all times of demand, they require storage—which can be heat storage for the steam systems, but has to be either electrical, mechanical, or chemical storage for the photovoltaic system.

Provided that government support for technology development and proof of feasibility is available, it has been estimated that 1 percent of the total electricity generation in the nation could be provided by solar energy through either one of the two routes in the year 2000; this would be 0.43 percent of the total energy consumption. In addition, through photovoltaic systems on buildings, 0.45 percent of the total national energy consumption could be provided in the year 2000 (3).

An unusually advanced concept to electric power provision utilizes a space station in synchronous orbit, carrying huge arrays (32 square kilometers) for the photovoltaic conversion of solar energy to electricity (8). This energy

would be beamed by a microwave link to receiving antennas on the ground (10,000 megawatts available on the ground). The approach has the advantage that solar energy can be converted to electricity for 24 hours per day, eliminating the requirement for energy storage. Although this proposal is very ambitious, it seems quite probable that, with little more than the available technology, technical feasibility can be demonstrated. And, assuming the availability of six to ten times more solar energy in synchronous orbit than on the earth's surface, there exists also the potential for economic feasibility. If there is government support for development, which will have to be most substantial in this case, it has been estimated that these space systems could provide 0.43 percent of the total national energy consumption in the year 2000 (3).

Conclusion

On the basis of the estimated contributions of these differing methods of the utilization of solar energy, their total energy delivery impact on the projected U.S. energy economy (9) can be evaluated (Fig. 5). Despite this late energy impact, the actual sales of solar energy utilization equipment will be significant at an early date. Potential sales in photovoltaic arrays alone could exceed $400 million by 1980, in order to meet the projected capacity buildup (10). Ultimately, the total energy utilization equipment industry should attain an annual sales volume of several tens of billion dollars in the United States, comparable to that of several other energy related industries.

Varying amounts of technology development are required to assure the technical and economic feasibility of the different solar energy utilization methods. Several of these developments are far enough along that the paths can be analyzed from the present time to the time of demonstration of technical and economic feasibility, and from there to production and marketing readiness. After that point, a period of market introduction will follow, which will differ in duration according to the type of market addressed. It may be noted that the present rush to find relief from the current energy problem, or to be an early leader in entering a new market, can entail shortcuts in sound engineering practice, particularly in the areas of design for durability and easy maintenance, or of proper application engineering. The result can be loss of customer acceptance, as has been experienced in the past with various products, including solar water heaters. Since this could cause considerable delay in achieving the expected total energy impact, it will be important to spend adequate time at this stage for thorough development.

Two other aspects are worth mentioning. The first is concerned with the economic impacts. Upon reflection on this point, one will observe that large-scale solar energy utilization will not cause a greater impact than other new energy sources, based on the reasoning that a self-consistent set of conditions will have to be fulfilled in order to achieve such large-scale use. Without cost competitiveness, other energy resources would fill the requirements, or, if their resource and cost structure also would create severe problems, the economic forecasts simply cannot be fulfilled. We also should not think of a "solar-only" energy future. First, there is still enough coal to last for several hundred years. Second, there should be enough fissionable fuel available to operate breeder reactors for a similar time span, and geothermal energy could satisfy some requirements for a long time. And finally, there may be fusion. It would be unlikely that any one of the available options should play a really dominant role. Rather, we should expect to be using an energy mix, just as we do now, with each energy source supplying the requirements which it can satisfy in the most suitable way, and solar energy should play an important role in this long-range future.

References and Notes

1. A. M. Zarem and D. D. Erway, *Introduction to the Utilization of Solar Energy* (McGraw-Hill, New York, 1963); I. Bennett, *Solar Energy* **9**, 145 (July 1965); G. O. G. Löf, T. A. Duffie, C. D. Smith, *ibid.* **10**, 27 (January 1966); M. Altman, M. Telkes, M. Wolff, *Energy Conver.* **12**, 53 (1972).
2. W. F. Heronemus, private communication.
3. "Solar energy as a national resource," report of the NSF/NASA Solar Energy Panel to the Office of Science and Technology; available from the Department of Mechanical Engineering, University of Maryland, College Park, Maryland.
4. J. H. Anderson and J. H. Anderson, *Mech. Eng.* (April 1966), p. 41; C. Zener, *Phys. Today* (January 1973), p. 48.
5. H. G. Lorsch, *Energy Conver.* **13**, 1 (1973).
6. R. A. Tybout and G. O. G. Löf, *Natl. Resources J.* **10**, 268 (1970).
7. R. C. Jordan, private communication; A. B. Meinel and M. P. Meinel, *Phys. Today* (February 1972), p. 44.
8. P. E. Glaser, Proceedings of the Intersociety Energy Conversion Engineering Conference (SAE), Boston, August 1971, p. 38; private communication.
9. "Reference energy systems and resource data for use in the assessment of energy technologies," *Report AET-8 for the Office of Science and Technology under contract OST-30* (Associated Universities, Upton, N.Y., 1972).
10. M. Wolf, "Cost goals for silicon solar arrays for large scale terrestrial applications," in *Proceedings of the 9th IEEE Photovoltaic Specialists Conference*, 2 to 4 May 1972, Silver Spring, Md. (Energy Conversion).
11. S. F. Singer, *Sci. Am.* **223**, 174 (September 1970).

Power, Fresh Water, and Food from Cold, Deep Sea Water

Donald F. Othmer and Oswald A. Roels

The sun's radiation is both the essential requirement of all life and the great source of man's energy. Besides keeping us warm, it supplies, directly or indirectly, (i) most of the energy we use, (ii) all of our food through photosynthesis in plants and many links of the food chains, and (iii) our fresh water supply from the cycle of evaporation from the sea, to clouds, to rain, to rivers.

The oceans contain 98 percent of the earth's water, over 1.3 thousand million cubic kilometers of that other great necessity of all life. With 71 percent of the earth's area, the oceans receive most of the sun's radiation to the earth. This radiation is absorbed on the hundreds of millions of square kilometers of the oceans and stored in vast amounts of living organisms stemming from photosynthesis and in the remains of this life—as organic and inorganic nutrients—and as vast amounts of heat in the surface waters of the tropic seas. These two resources —heat to supply energy and nutrients for food chains from single cells through all edible plants and animals up to man—are our greatest resources, as yet practically untapped. In the utilization of the heat, the third product, also from the usual radiation from the sun, fresh water, may be produced, often where needed most.

Sea water is always cold in the deeps, and often it approaches the temperature of its maximum density, near the freezing point. It is cooled in the Arctic and Antarctic where it settles to the depths and, by a grand thermosyphon system, moves on the bottom toward the tropics, where it is warmed,

and moves again in tremendous currents toward the poles, to recycle. Photosynthesis in the upper layer penetrated by the sun produces single-cell organisms, thence bigger marine growths, and, by steps, up to the earth's largest plants and animals. Surface waters in the tropics may be crystal clear because photosynthesis has utilized all nutrients; and larger living things have consumed all of the small organisms which cause haze, and thus have stripped the water of carbon, nitrogen, and phosphorus, the principal nutrients for life.

But this life, largely in surface water, dies, as does that in deeper water; and the remains settling slowly, as befits a burial, return to "dust," that of the ocean depths. Slowly these remains disintegrate; and, in solution and as particles, residues are carried in the deep currents back to particular areas of upwelling—only about 0.1 percent of the total area of the oceans. Here the great amount of nutrients causes an explosion of marine life. Just one major one, the upwelling of the Humboldt Current off Peru, supplies one-fifth of the world's total fish harvest.

Availability of Thermal Energy

Again with reference to energy (here heat), its concept implies the temperature of the "hot" substance being higher than that of another "cold" substance. Heat is only usable by its transfer to a colder body. Deep sea water may be from 15° to 25°C colder than surface water; but there is little conduction of heat, top to bottom, and

little mixing because of density differences, except in notable upwellings.

While this temperature difference between surface and deep waters is small, considering usual sources of energy, the available heat is the product of this difference multiplied by the available masses of sea water which are infinite for all practical purposes. Means for the conversion of this available heat to electrical energy would give continuously very much more than mankind has found capability to use.

For example, the Gulf Stream, first studied scientifically by Benjamin Franklin, carries the heat absorbed in the Caribbean and the Gulf of Mexico past the coast of Florida. Some 2200 cubic kilometers of water per day may be as much as 25°C warmer than the cold, deep water which it was. To heat just 1 cubic kilometer of sea water per day 25°C would take six or eight times as much energy as all of the electrical energy produced in the United States. The reverse is staggering; it has been estimated that this heat in all of the Gulf Stream, if discharged to water colder by 25°C, could generate more than 75 times the entire electric power produced in all of the United States (1).

Both coasts of Africa, the west coast of both Americas, and the coasts of many islands, particularly in the Caribbean area, have places within a few miles of land where sea water has a surface temperature of 25° to 30°C, while at 750 to 1000 meters below the surface, the temperature may be 4° to 7°C (2). In some places, the ocean floor drops off from the shore line very steeply to an ocean deep within some hundreds of meters of land. The ideal location for a land-based power plant, using warm surface water on one side of a peninsula, would have a great sea depth close to shore on the other side of the peninsula. The contour of the bottom should be favorable to the installation of a large suction pipe to supply cold water.

Dr. Othmer is Distinguished Professor of Chemical Engineering at the Polytechnic Institute, Brooklyn, New York 11201. Dr. Roels is professor of oceanography at the City University of New York, and chairman, Biological Oceanography, Lamont-Doherty Geological Observatory of Columbia University, Palisades, New York 10964.

Potential Values

Both this energy and these nutrients are available, and they could supply all the world's power, light, and much of the protein food it uses; but so far they are locked away from us by the difficulty of their recovery from such dilute sources, compared to the relative ease of the utilization of other, more concentrated resources. With shortages of energy and food in the world, this utilization is a job for the present, and one well within the capabilities of technology now available. The dilution is indeed not prohibitive. The water brought up from the depths of tropical seas will absorb surface heat energy equal to the mechanical energy available from a 120-meter waterfall. Compared to other systems proposed for using solar energy, this utilizes a vast reservoir at any one of many places. Always the equipment for utilizing solar energy is large and expensive. And the mariculture using the nutrients can produce $125,000 of product per year from each hectare of land converted to ponds [$50,000 annually per acre].

Thus, if very large amounts of cold, deep sea water can be brought to the surface, warmed in receiving the heat discharged by a suitable power station, and passed to tropical ponds wherein its nutrients are used in photo- and biosynthesis by marine plant and animal food chains, the ultimate product is not fish meal or an artificial substance, but choice shellfish. The water is warmed in the pools to a temperature higher than surface sea water and is passed to the high temperature side of the power cycle. The simplest is direct production of very low pressure steam, turbine-generation of electricity, and condensation of the steam in warming the cold, deep sea water, giving fresh water as condensate.

Power Cycle and Process Engineering

Great minds backed by large sums of money, somewhat less large when the potential benefits are considered, have worked throughout almost a century to develop systems of utilizing the small difference of temperatures of surface and deep sea water to produce power (3). Claude made the most optimistic contributions 40 years ago (4), and the great problems which he recognized were principally two—the installation of the enormous pipeline to carry water from the depths and the removal of air from the evaporating warm water (5).

However, theoretically mechanical energy—and from it electrical energy —can be developed from heat from any body at any temperature being passed to any other body which can receive it, because of its lower temperature. Such energy is always more difficult and less efficient to produce, the lower this temperature difference is. Carnot showed the maximum efficiency to be $(T_1 - T_2)/T_1$ where T_1 is the temperature of the hot body and T_2 is the temperature of the cold body. These are measured above absolute zero.

This temperature difference for efficient heat engines may be many hundred or even a thousand degrees. The closer the temperature of the heat input approaches that of the output, the less the efficiency becomes. Here warm water is at 30°C and it is cooled, in producing very low pressure steam, to 25°C, the temperature of the steam. If this steam is condensed at 15°C by heating cold water from 5° to 10°C, with a 5°C loss in the condenser tubes, this temperature of 15°C may be regarded as the low temperature at which all heat is discharged.

Hence, if the steam supply is at 25°C, or $273° + 25° = 298°K$, above absolute zero, and the corresponding temperature of the heat rejection is 15°C, or $273° + 15° = 288°K$, then the maximum thermodynamic efficiency is $(298 - 288)/298$, or about 3.3 percent. Practically, because of many energy requirements in related machinery, and because of many losses, the efficiency obtainable could not be more than about 2 to 2.5 percent. Of equal importance usually, the amount and cost of equipment required always *increases* greatly with a decrease of the temperature difference. Thus, the heat in a cubic kilometer of warm sea water may be passed to colder sea water to develop mechanical energy, then electrical power. Necessarily, the heat available at this low temperature can be converted to power only with a large, costly plant, at a very low efficiency, and by the handling of extremely large amounts of the cold sea water to absorb the heat. However, the total amount of water to be handled may be less than the amount of water required to produce the same amount of power in a hydroelectric plant. Dams, penstocks, and machinery of a hydro-electric plant are also expensive in developing a "free kilowatt"; that is, free of cost of energy.

The cold water does not have to be lifted from the great depth by the pump; only the friction head must be considered, plus the small static head caused by the difference in density of the cold water and the average density of the water from the surface to the bottom of the pipe.

Various designs for floating power plants have been made with vertical suction pipes suspended from the vessel and with submerged power cables and fresh water lines carrying the products to the shore. However, these would make controlled mariculture more difficult.

Any plant for handling these large volumes of water and converting the available thermal energy to mechanical and then to electrical energy will be huge and expensive; and even the smallest one which would be worthwhile for demonstration purposes will involve many millions of dollars worth of equipment.

The simplest of many possible systems that have been studied depends on flash evaporating, in an evacuated chamber, a small amount of the warm water as it is partially cooled. This gives a maximum of 1 percent of the weight of the water as a very low pressure steam. This low pressure steam turns a turbine in cooling further and then is condensed on tubes through which the cold water from the deep is passing and being warmed. The condensate is fresh (distilled) water, almost always a valuable commodity on tropical coasts; and its sale adds to the revenue from the power produced by the generator turned by the steam turbine.

Because of the very low temperature and pressure of the steam, the turbine must be specially designed; and the condenser must be large. Some systems have not provided a surface condenser, but have depended on "open" condensation by sprays of the cold sea water. This produces no condensate fresh water, the sale of which is a valuable revenue for any system, unless a cooled fresh water spray were used (6).

A substantial plant using low pressure steam with a condenser for fresh water has been engineered (7). Several other designs were studied and discarded. The design for a 7180-kilowatt (net) power plant also showed an output of 6 million U.S. gallons of fresh water per day at a total installed cost of $18.4 million.

Several factors were considered in the economic analysis; and charts were made to show the interrelation of (i) the capacity factor, that is, actual production compared to maximum capacity, and (ii) the cost of power generation. Thus, for an investment of $18.4 million, a calculated maintenance and operating cost of $100,000 per year, at an assumed fixed cost of capital of 12 percent per year and a capacity factor of 0.9, fresh water would be produced for $1 per 1000 U.S. gallons, and electric power for 6 U.S. mills per kilowatt-hour; and, in general, total costs can be divided between the two products as desired, since total amounts of both are produced.

As another example, if the capital or fixed charges are taken as 16 percent per year at a capacity factor of 0.90; and if the cost of producing power is taken as 6 mills per kilowatt-hour, fresh water costs are $1.38 per 1000 gallons, or if power cost is taken as 1 cent per kilowatt-hour, then fresh water is $1.26 per 1000 gallons.

Under the economic conditions prevailing at the particular site, which changed during the program, the rate of return on private risk capital was not regarded as sufficiently attractive to private investors to warrant this investment to compete with power and fresh water from a combustion plant. The warm water was regarded as the more valuable stream—it contained the heat that was discharged to the equally necessary stream of cold water, brought up by the very expensive pipeline and pumping system.

In the case of a mariculture program, the valuable stream is that from the depths, with the nutrients therein. The warm water stream does nothing for the mariculture, except that its vapors condense and heat the cold water somewhat in passing through the condenser, and the higher temperature increases the rate of growth of marine life. However, it should be noted that, in passing through the sun-heated enclosed basins for mariculture, the effluent, when it is discharged back to the sea, may be warmer than the surface water from the open sea. If so, this effluent would be cycled through the flash evaporator or boiler of the electric power–fresh water system, and only one stream would be drawn from the sea. The process engineering, mechanical engineering design, and civil engineering

design were completed along with the economic analysis which showed that this project was economically profitable. However, under other particular conditions pertaining at the site, it would be desirable to delay the construction of the plant for fresh water and electric power production. Some details may be of interest.

Plant Layout and Equipment as First Designed

Because of an existing highway at the proposed site, the power and desalinating units were laid out about 140 feet from the shore line. Hydraulic losses and steam friction losses were minimized by short conduits with a minimum of bends. The warm surface water intake, a large subsurface conduit, supplies the boilers through trash racks and fine screen, then deaerators. Special design adapted from desalination evaporator practice minimized losses during flash-boiling of about 1 percent of the warm water supplied. A boiler discharge pump removes the cooled surface sea water.

A turbine with horizontal rotor is directly above each boiler and was designed to operate at a low speed because of its large diameter.

The two pipes for cold sea water intake were designed with a nominal diameter of 4.13 meters and to withstand the stresses imposed by the carefully planned system of installation and by the irregular sea bottom, the contour of which was explored from a small submarine. The section was located 4100 meters offshore at a depth of 975 meters.

Improvements in Design of Plant and Equipment

Improvements have been made in the newer design planned for installation as an integrated component with the mariculture unit at a demonstration plant. Various improvements and advantages will be included in the new design.

1) The water effluent from mariculture operations will be used, and it will be warmer than open sea water, thus a better efficiency should be achieved. Also there will be a considerable economy in almost eliminating the warm surface sea water circuit.

2) A greater ratio of surface water

to deep sea water will use the latter more efficiently.

3) Improved design of the hydraulics of deep water systems should reduce installation and power costs.

4) Condenser cost will be greatly reduced if plastic tubes are used.

5) Boilers will use the controlled flash evaporation (CFE) system to reduce losses in pressure and temperature drops which will increase production of both water and power (6, 8). The CFE system also will reduce substantially the deaeration costs, which require 20 percent of power produced in previous plants.

6) In some locations where fresh water is unusually expensive, all of the available heat will be used for this production, with no power.

Mariculture in Cold, Deep Sea Water

Deep sea water which has absorbed the heat from warm surface water in producing power and fresh water has been brought to a temperature more favorable for biologic growth. It is rich in nutrients which often are exhausted almost completely by the high rate of photosynthesis in the sparkling clear surface tropic waters; and is practically free of organisms which produce disease in humans, predators and parasites of shellfish, fouling organisms, and man-made pollutants. By contrast, shellfish culture has had major pollution disasters in the past years along the continental Atlantic coast.

An experimental station has been operated on the north coast of St. Croix, one of the U.S. Virgin Islands, near Puerto Rico. Here the ocean floor slopes sharply to the Virgin Islands Basin (4000 meters deep) and reaches a depth of 1000 meters, 1500 meters offshore. Three [69-millimeter inside diameter (3 inches nominal)] polyethylene pipe lines, each 1800 meters (6000 feet) long, supply water from a 870-meter (2900 feet) depth in an amount of 159 liters (42 U.S. gallons) per minute. This water is warmed in being drawn up through the small pipes so that its cooling effect would be negligible but it is satisfactory for the mariculture work.

This water in January 1973 averaged (microgram atoms per liter) nitrate nitrogen, 32.1; nitrite nitrogen, 0.13; ammonia nitrogen, 1.1; phosphate phosphorus, 2.15; and silicon in silicates, 21.7. The salinity was 34,841 parts per million. While these amounts equal only a relatively small weight of synthetic nutrients which could be added, this clean, unpolluted water is free of parasites and hostile microorganisms which could endanger the cultured animals, or remain in their bodies to be passed to humans. Also the water, if used in a power and desalination cycle must be pumped up to gain its cooling value. It may also be fortified with additional amounts of added nutrients having components carefully chosen to give the greatest value in the particular mariculture used.

A development program is now in progress to determine the most desirable plant and animal species for a food chain to give optimum value of the produce species at the top of the chain with minimum cost in production. Two varieties of diatoms have been particularly satisfactory; and after inoculation the water develops up to 1 million diatoms per milliliter, when it is metered into the shellfish tanks.

Early work showed a 27-fold increase in unicellular algae (diatom) grown in water from a depth of 800 meters compared to that from the surface; and peak yields of 230 grams per cubic meter (1900 pounds per 1 million U.S. gallons) have been obtained. This amounts to 2.8 grams of algal protein per cubic meter of water.

Various types of shellfish feed on these unicellular animals by filtering them from the water they continually process; from previous work it appeared possible to obtain at least a 60 percent conversion of the diatoms to commercial foods. Thus, from an overall material balance, these nutrients of the deep sea water, basically the nitrogen, which would be utilized through the food chain to be explained, should give 1 kilogram of fresh clam meat per 300 cubic meters of deep sea water (27 pounds per 1 million gallons).

From the available marine life in nature, the most promising species are being chosen; there are hopes of improving the natural strains, as has been done by animal husbandry in every animal which has ever been bred for food. Greatly improved yields appear through proper control of (i) natural nutrient concentration—and possibly that of artificial nutrients, or other additives; (ii) solar radiation—by adjusting the depth of the ponds; (iii) water temperature; and (iv) still other variables as these first or axiomatic ones are optimized.

Algal Cultures

Many species of microscopic algae have been isolated, cultured, and studied as cultivated food for shellfish. Those preferred are fast-growing strains, readily accepted by shellfish and causing their rapid growth; they should be hardy against competitive organisms, against high summer temperatures, 32° to 33°C of the pools, and against the excessive sunlight radiation which prevails in shallow pools. Some have developed weight increases of young oysters (3 millimeters) of more than 75 percent in 3 weeks.

Extensive experiments in all sizes of tanks and pools up to 45 cubic meters (12,000 gallons) of 1.2 meters (40 inches) depth, with many variables, have indicated that dependable production of large amounts of algae satisfactory for shellfish food can be maintained. This work to improve the breed and production of algae continues because of the promise of considerable improvements in the development of better, more stable, and hardier strains. Also the geometry of the pools is being optimized; and continuous operation has been developed.

Shellfish

Oysters and clams from cultures stemming from Long Island (New York), Japan, and various tropical locations have been worked with as brood stock and for growth studies.

Experimentation with the shellfish has indicated that certain species grow very rapidly indeed in this "artificial upwelling" system: thus, hybrid clams were grown to market size in 6 months. Similarly, the European oyster and the bay scallop were grown from spat to market size in 6 months (9). This is considerably faster than generally occurs in nature. Clams, European oysters, and bay scallops of commercial size grown in this system were submitted to a panel of seafood experts for taste testing, and judged to be of excellent taste and superior to those harvested in natural waters. Thus, hybrid clams averaging 8 grams, on introduction, increased in weight almost five times to 38.5 grams in 6 months so they could be marketed in the littleneck size.

Scallops multiplied their weight 60 times in 145 days, from an average single weight of 0.24 gram at an age of 8 days to 14.42 grams. Average lengths of the scallops were, respectively, 9 and 40.7 millimeters.

Oysters have grown from 3 millimeters to market size in a little more than 8 months; and one species of oysters grew from an average live weight of 1 gram when introduced to 70 grams in 74 days.

Shellfish filter the microorganisms from the water for food; their filtering efficiencies for gathering and retaining the food cells from the pools have varied from 49 percent without culling of the shellfish to over 90 percent when the small shellfish have been periodically harvested to stimulate the growth of the larger ones remaining. These harvesting techniques are now being optimized.

Crustaceans

A great variation in the growth rates of shellfish has been observed; one long-term objective is to improve the strain by selective breeding of the fastest growing individuals, which also have other desirable characteristics. Thus a large number of small clams at different ages would always be culled to minimize competition of the faster growing animals; and the culls may be used as a very acceptable food for crustaceans. First tried were adult spiny lobsters, native to St. Croix in the Virgin Islands. The best of these showed an average weight gain (in an 89-day period between moltings) of 55 percent, while eating 5.2 times as much food weight as its gain in weight.

Similar experiments are under way with cold water lobsters from the Massachusetts coast which are growing at a greatly accelerated rate in the warm waters of the mariculture ponds.

Seaweed

If the effluent from the shellfish and lobster growing operation were returned directly to the sea, the animal wastes might constitute a source of pollution. Therefore, experiments are under way with commercially useful seaweeds which can be processed to obtain either agar or carrageen. These seaweeds are grown in the effluent from the animal tanks, to optimize the nutrient utilization in the system, and to purify the discharged waters before returning them to the sea.

Chain of Nutrient Utilization

The water from the deep will have been substantially warmed in the plant for production of energy and fresh water; and the optimum utilization of its nutrients appears now to be via (i) single cell algae; (ii) filter-feeding shellfish, such as oysters and clams, which feed on the algae; (iii) lobsters, shrimp, and possibly other crustaceans which feed on culls of the shellfish; and (iv) specialized seaweed, which grows in effluent water containing the solubilized body wastes of the shellfish and crustacea, and has several important markets.

Mariculture Ponds and Operation

The mariculture will be done in a series of shallow concrete pools of optimized depth. The deep sea water flows through slowly to permit residence times, not widely different, for (i) algal growth, (ii) shellfish growth, (iii) crustacean growth, and (iv) seaweed growth. The apportionment of the time periods for the different growths has not been established exactly to date but will be optimized insofar as possible to give the greatest financial return with the minimum of land and pool area.

For the demonstration plant now being planned, it is expected that 25,000 gallons (95 cubic meters) of deep sea water per minute will be available and that there may be a total of 6 hectares (15 acres) of ponds required with a total time of water in transit of about 2 days. This area may be divided approximately as follows: (i) 50 percent for algal growth, (ii) 10 percent for shellfish growth, (iii) 10 percent for crustacea growth, (iv) 20 percent for seaweed growth. It is impossible as yet to estimate the optimum operational yields of different products; but it is expected that, at an average annual yield, an average value at the plant will be about 340,000 pounds of shellfish at $2.25 to $2.50 per pound of meat. This works out to be an average of over $50,000 annual revenue per acre of ponds without credit for values that cannot yet be optimized.

For a larger plant, handling 870,000 gallons (3390 cubic meters) per minute, a somewhat lower unit price for shellfish may have to be taken; and the total annual revenue has been projected to be between $20 and $25 million.

Summary

Many times more solar heat energy accumulates in the vast volume of warm tropic seas than that produced by all of our power plants. The looming energy crisis causes a renewal of interest in utilizing this stored solar heat to give, in addition to electric power, vast quantities of fresh water. Warm surface water, when evaporated, generates steam, to power a turbine, then fresh water when the steam is condensed by the cold water.

A great increase in revenues over that from power and fresh water is shown by a substantial mariculture pilot plant. Deep sea water contains large quantities of nutrients. These feed algae which feed shellfish, ultimately shrimps and lobsters, in shallow ponds. Wastes grow seaweed of value; and combined revenues from desalination, power generation, and mariculture will give substantial profit.

References and Notes

1. D. F. Othmer, in *Encyclopedia of Marine Resources*, F. E. Firth, Ed. (Van Nostrand, Reinhold, New York, 1969), p. 298.
2. R. D. Gerard and O. A. Roels, *Marine Technol. Soc. J.* **4** (No. 5), 69 (1970).
3. S. Walters, *Mech. Eng.* **93** (No. 10), 21 (1971).
4. G. Claude was developing support in the United States in 1925–26 for the pilot plant which he then built in Cuba. He gave a demonstration lecture in the laboratories of the University of Michigan where D. F. Othmer was then a graduate assistant. Claude's equipment included a small tank for warm water and one for cold, a vessel to which the warm water was admitted to undergo flash evaporation (about 1 percent), a small steam turbine driven by the low pressure steam that was forming, a condenser having the cold water in direct contact with the turbine exhaust steam, and a vacuum pump for air removal. A small generator was driven by the turbine and was wired to a small electric bulb, which lit as the house lights went off—and the audience cheered.
5. G. Claude, *Mech. Eng.* **52** (No. 12), 1039 (1930).
6. The vapor reheat system of multistage flash evaporation uses a separately cooled fresh water stream to condense vapors for fresh water production and has been described [R. E. Kirk and D. F. Othmer, *Encyclopedia of Chemical Technology* (Wiley, New York, ed. 2, 1970), vol. 22, pp. 39–48].
7. The sea water power and fresh water plant was engineered by Alemco, Inc., now a division of Viatech, Inc., Syosset, New York. One of us (D.F.O.) is a consulting engineer to and director of both corporations. The plant was designed for another island site in the Caribbean which was then regarded as eminently suitable.
8. R. C. Roe and D. F. Othmer, *Mech. Eng.* **93** (No. 5), 27 (1971).
9. J. S. Baad, G. L. Hamm, K. C. Haines, A. Chu, O. A. Roels, *Proc. Nat. Shellfish. Ass.* **63** (No. 6), 63 (1973).
10. Supported by Sea Grant 1-36119. This article is Lamont-Doherty Geological Observatory contribution No. 2016 and City University of New York Institute of Oceanography contribution No. 21. The first engineering design was made by Alemco, Inc., a subsidary of Viatech, both of Syosset, New York.

Windmills: The Resurrection of an Ancient Energy Technology

Nicholas Wade

The windmill seems fair set to make a comeback from the trash heap of technical history. Once a derisible symbol of archaic technology, the environmental reawakening and the sudden wane of the cheap energy era have left the windmill looking more like the feasible alternative power source that its enthusiasts claim it to be.

A recent sign of the windmill's potential as an unfueled provider of electricity was to be tilted at by the oil industry. "But what do you do when the wind dies down?" one company's television ad asked its audience last year. To advocates of the windmill, the question misstates the problem. The basic technology, they believe, is already there. The remaining task is primarily economic: to make the capital costs of windmill energy competitive with what the oil industry and other rivals have to offer. With that achieved, for an energy device that runs on air and doesn't pollute, it should be plain sailing.

Interest in windmills is picking up fast. Two years ago only a dozen or so people in the United States were studying the devices; now there are a few hundred, working at universities, in large companies such as Boeing or Grumman, and in smaller firms such as R. Buckminster Fuller's Windworks. A few weeks ago the National Science Foundation (NSF) asked the research community for proposals on how best to use and construct windmills. The agency plans to spend $7 million on windmill research in the next fiscal year (this fiscal year's budget is $1.5 million, last year's was $200,000).

NASA also intends to harness the winds with a giant mill to be built at Sandusky, Ohio (Fig. 1). The NASA machine, a pair of blades measuring 125 feet from tip to tip and mounted on a tower 125 feet tall,

will be capable of generating 100 kilowatts of electricity. The rivalry between the two bureaucracies is being contained by making NSF keeper of the budget and NASA the chief beneficiary.

Large scale generation of electricity is the principal use envisaged for the windmills of the future. NASA predicts that mills "could supply between 5 to 10 percent of the country's total electric power needs by the year 2000." William E. Heronemus, a former designer of nuclear submarines who will be recognized as the prophet of windmill power if his visions ever come true, believes that by 2000 wind-

Fig. 1. NASA windmill to be built at Sandusky, Ohio.

mills could be pumping an annual 1.5 trillion kilowatt-hours of electricity into national power grids, which is nearly as much as the total yearly amount of electricity generated in the United States at present.

The estimate depends on the fruition of no Lilliputian a scheme. Heronemus, now a civil engineering professor at the University of Massachusetts, envisages chains of windmills stretching up across the Great Plains from the Texas coast to the Canadian border. An earlier version would have consisted of some 300,000 towers, each 850 feet tall and bearing 20 turbines. Now, to conserve land, he would build 800-foot-tall kingposts straddling the highways at half mile intervals with the turbines slung from cables in between. Two or three years ago few would have given such a conception serious thought. Today Heronemus has an audience, and his ideas are embodied in a recent study of solar (and wind) energy prepared by the NSF and NASA.

The windmill seems to be Persian in origin but the ancient form—still in use today in the eastern provinces of Khurasan and Seistan—has a vertical axis instead of the more familiar horizontal arrangement. The wind is caught by sails rigged between the spokes radiating from the top and bottom of the shaft, which itself is attached to a stone for grinding wheat (see Fig. 2).

The vertical windmill spread throughout the Islamic world after the Arab conquest of Iran, and to China during the world peace imposed by the Mongols. When the windmill appeared in Europe, during the 11th century, the axis was no longer vertical but inclined at an angle of 30° to the horizontal. Some historians cite this as evidence for independent European invention; others consider that, as with so much other technology at the time, the windmill was a transfer from the Islamic world.

By the 17th century the Netherlands had become the world's most industrialized nation by extensive use of wind power in ships and windmills. The machine continued to be improved and refined. The sails gave way to hinged shutters, like those of venetian blinds, and the shutters in turn gave way to the propeller or airscrew.

Windmills helped in the development of the western United States, being used for pumping water and

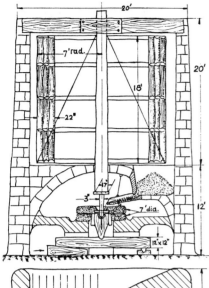

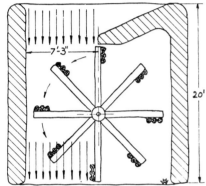

Fig. 2. Persian vertical windmill with grindstone, in sectional views. This version has bundles of reeds instead of cloth for its sails. [From *Traditional Crafts of Persia*, Hans Wulff (MIT Press, Cambridge, Mass., 1966)]

running sawmills. Up until 1950, some 50,000 small windmills converted wind energy into electricity in the Midwest. These backyard generators were put out of business by the activities of the Rural Electrification Administration.

As for large scale generators, giant windmills have at various times in the last 60 years been built in Britain (see Fig. 3), the Soviet Union, and the United States, but none has proved a commercial success. The American windmill, 110 feet high and with blades 175 feet from tip to tip, was built in 1941 on a hill called Grandpa's Knoll outside Rutland, Vermont. The machine cost about $1 million at prevailing prices and provided power on a commercial basis for less than 1 month before one of its 8-ton metal blades snapped off from metal fatigue in 1945.

Though the Grandpa's Knoll machine was in many ways a technical, if not a commercial success, the company that constructed it decided not

to persevere, and the development of large scale windmills in the United States—despite the personal interest of science power broker Vannevar Bush —came to a fairly conclusive halt.

Application of the technology of the last two decades in a large scale research effort should produce a much improved windmill, says NSF windmill project manager Louis Divone. The perfect windmill has not yet been found, but the laws of physics and economics dictate many of its features. An ideal windmill could extract a theoretical limit of 16/27, or about 59 percent, of the kinetic energy of the wind passing through the area swept by its blades. Windmills of good aerodynamic design in fact generate about 75 percent of the theoretical maximum. The power developed by an ideal windmill is

$$\frac{16}{27} \times (\frac{1}{8}\pi\rho D^2 V^3)$$

the interest of which expression is its demonstration that a windmill's power depends on the square of D, the diameter of the swept area, and the cube of V, the velocity of the wind (ρ is the wind's density). For greatest power, therefore, a windmill should have blades as long as material strength will permit and stand in the fastest winds available. The greatest length envisaged for a blade is at present about 100 feet, giving a diameter of 200 feet, and the best wind regimens in the United States are found on the Great Plains, the eastern seaboard, and the Aleutian chain.

Wind speed increases in strength and constancy the higher up you go; so too does the cost of tower construction. Trade-offs envisioned at present suggest a tower height of 100 to 150 feet. For efficient power generation the windmill shaft must rotate at constant speed, a condition achieved by feathering the blades so that they present a flat face to low winds and turn more edgewise as wind speed increases.

Electric power in the United States is generated at a frequency of 60 cycles per second, which means that to avoid a large number of efficiency reducing gears, the windmill should rotate as fast as possible. In practice this means having two, or at most three, slender blades.

Controlling the pitch of windmill blades, ensuring protection in galeforce winds, and choosing the right material for the blades are among the

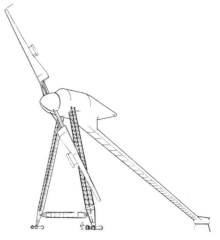

Fig. 3. British design, 1950, for a 1500-kilowatt windmill generator. [From *Wind Power Development in the United States*, Robert K. Swanson *et al.* (Southwest Research Institute, San Antonio, 1974)]

problems that make windmill design three times more difficult that that of helicopters, says Wayne Wiesner, an aeronautical engineer with Boeing Vertol in Philadelphia. Boeing Vertol and the Southwest Research Institute of San Antonio plan to build a windmill system in which during off-peak hours the windmill would pump air into an abandoned mine; in periods of high electricity use the compressed air would be released through gas turbines.

Probably the most formidable problem in designing an economic windmill system is that of coping with the consequences of the wind's variability. The windmill can be used just as a supplementary adjunct to a large power system, or it may provide the whole power, in which case a means must be found of storing energy for delivery when the wind fails. In either case, or in any intermediate situation, the capital costs of the system include considerably more than just those of the windmill and its generator. Nonetheless, capital costs seem to be within striking distance of those of competitive systems. According to Robert K. Swanson of the Southwest Research Institute, large scale wind generators (excluding a back-up system) could be constructed now for about $350 to $400 per installed kilowatt, compared with costs of $250 for gas fired steam turbines, $400 for nuclear plants, and $400 for coal plants with air pollution scrubbing equipment. Divone considers the $400 per installed kilowatt estimate could be reached in 2 years' time. Besides the compressed air system, other suggested means of storing windmill energy include pumped hydraulic storage (for example by using Lake Superior as an upper reservoir), superflywheels made of light composite materials instead of steel, conventional batteries, and the electrolysis of water to create hydrogen for use as fuel. The hydrogen fuel concept is favored in particular by Heronemus, who would have farms of windmills set up along the Aleutian chain with tankers to carry the liquefied gas to California.

If the economics of such systems have yet to be proved, there are already some applications for which windmill generators are cheaper than any alternative. When Henry M. Clews moved to a remote house in Maine, the local power company quoted $3000 to run him a line. A domestic diesel generating set would produce electricity for 30 cents per kilowatthour, or about ten times the power company rate. So Clews invested in a windmill system which, together with batteries and inverter, ran him a total of $2800 and, assuming a 20-year life for the windmill, provides electricity for a total cost of 15 cents per kilowatt-hour. Winds in the location average only 8 to 10 miles an hour.

Clews's system consists of a Quirk's wind generator, manufactured in Australia, with 19 lead-acid storage batteries. He has formed an agency, the Solar Wind Company in East Holden, Maine, to distribute the Quirk's generator in the United States, as well as a range of windmills made by the Swiss company Elektro GmbH.

Another small scale windmill, still in the development stage, is the Sailwing, a propeller-type device but with semisolid blades that deform in the wind, thus providing a self-regulated feathering function. Designed by Princeton aeronautical engineer Thomas E. Sweeney, the Sailwing is licensed to the Grumman Corporation which expects to market the system complete with batteries and generator for between $3500 and $4000.

Other types of windmills under development include two modern adaptations of the Persian vertical windmill, the Darrieus rotor and the Savonius rotor. The special advantage of vertical machines is that they operate equally well regardless of wind direction and don't need extra devices to keep them facing into the wind.

Improvements in the design of cheap, locally made windmills could be a godsend to oil-short countries of the third world. A 25-foot sailwing windmill for use in rural India has been devised by the New Alchemy Institute, of Woods Hole, Massachusetts, in collaboration with the Indian Institute of Agricultural Research and the Wind Power Division of the Indian National Aeronautical Laboratory. A prototype, used for pumping water, was constructed last year on an Indian farm. The machine is made of locally available materials such as a bullock cartwheel for the hub, cloth and a bamboo frame for the sails, and an automobile axle for the shaft.

Present systems of energy production are for the most part massive machines, dependent on man for their fuel and active embodiments of the dominion over nature. Windmills, by contrast, are passive devices, often made with natural materials, and expressive of external forces that represent nature's dominion over man. Their ecological chic is antithetical to the materials consuming style of western economies. As that style shifts, the windmill is moving back into its rightful place in the sun.

Methanol: A Versatile Fuel for Immediate Use

Methanol can be made from gas, coal, or wood.
It is stored and used in existing equipment.

T. B. Reed and R. M. Lerner

In the short period of a decade we have developed a healthy concern about our pollution of the environment and an awareness that we will soon face a shortage of convenient forms of energy. Hydrogen has been suggested (1, 2) as a universal, nonpolluting fuel, since it can be produced from water and burns cleanly to water. Although we may some day see a "hydrogen economy," we have yet to find ways of making hydrogen cheaply, of storing and transporting it, of adapting it to the automobile, and of using it safely. In several recent, comprehensive studies of potential fuels, hydrogen has been compared with other synthetic fuels such as methanol, ethanol, hydrazine, and methane (3–5). In these studies methanol has been described as being superior to hydrogen in many ways, and as providing an especially attractive alternative fuel to gasoline. In this article we discuss the advantages of using methanol as a fuel and suggest ways in which it could be introduced immediately into our fuel economy.

Methanol, CH_3OH, can be thought of as two molecules of hydrogen gas made liquid by one molecule of carbon monoxide. It thus shares many of the virtues of pure hydrogen. Last year in the United States, 3.2×10^9 kilograms (10^9 gallons or 1 percent of present gasoline production) of methanol were manufactured and sold at an average price of $0.06 per kilogram ($0.183 per gallon) (6). It can be made from almost any other fuel—from natural gas, petroleum, coal, oil shale, wood, farm and municipal wastes—so that a methanol economy would be flexible and could draw from many energy sources as conditions change. Methanol is easily stored in conventional fuel tanks and can be shipped in tank cars, tank trucks, and tankers; it can be transported in oil and chemical pipelines. Of most importance is the fact that up to 15 percent of methanol can be added to commercial gasoline in cars now in use without it being necessary to modify the engines. This methanol-gasoline mixture results in improved economy, lower exhaust temperature, lower emissions, and improved performance, compared to the use of gasoline alone. Methanol can also be burned cleanly for most of our other fuel needs, and it is especially suited for use in fuel cells for generating electricity. The sources, distribution, and uses of methanol are shown diagrammatically in Fig. 1.

Properties of Methanol and Related Fuels

Methanol, which is also called methyl alcohol, wood alcohol, or methylated spirits (7), is a colorless, odorless, water-soluble liquid. It freezes at −97.8°C, boils at 64.6°C, and has a density of 0.80. It is miscible with water in all proportions, and spillages are rapidly dispersed. Methanol burns with a clean blue flame and is familiar to most people as the alcohol used for heating food at the table or as the alcohol in Sterno. Mixtures with between 6.7 percent and 36 percent of air are flammable. The autoignition temperature of methanol is 467°C, which is high compared with 222°C for gasoline (5). This may account for the high octane number, 106, of methanol; a typical gasoline has an octane number of 90 to 100 (8).

The energy content of a number of fuels is shown in Table 1. Hydrogen produces the most energy on a weight basis; hence its use in rockets where volume and cost are secondary considerations. Petroleum products such as gasoline have the highest energy of the fuels listed on a volume basis and are second highest on a weight basis; hence gasoline will long be preferred for airplanes where lowest weight is at a premium. However, of all the liquid fuels, methanol produces the second highest amount of energy on a volume basis.

Although methanol is not the cheapest fuel (see Table 2), its properties make it competitive with the other fuels. Ethanol, which has many of the desirable fuel properties of methanol and could be used in most of the applications discussed herein, costs, in this country, about three times more than methanol. In less industrialized countries, however, ethanol may be an attractive fuel because it can be produced from agricultural products by fermentation.

In the manufacture of methanol, the output of the plant can be increased by 50 percent if small amounts of other alcohols can be tolerated in the product (9, 10). Such a mixture is called "methyl-fuel," and it contains more energy than pure methanol because of the presence of ethanol, propanol, and isobutanol. It can be produced in larger quantities at a lower price than pure methanol, and, in general, has superior properties as a fuel. In this article, we consider methanol and methyl-fuel to be synonymous.

Dr. Reed is a member of the solid state division and Dr. Lerner is a member of the communications division at the Lincoln Laboratory, Massachusetts Institute of Technology, Lexington, Massachusetts 02173.

Historical Uses of Alcohol for Fuel

During the last 50 years in the United States, methanol and other alcohols have not competed successfully with the abundant supplies of petroleum. Before this time, however, alcohols were used extensively as fuels. Alcohol, for example, became a popular fuel for lighting in about 1830, when it replaced malodorous fish and whale oils. In about 1880, kerosene replaced alcohol as a lighting fuel because of its sooty flame which gave more light; a clean flame produces no light without special additives. During the middle of the last century, France was partially on a methanol fuel economy. Wood was distilled in the provinces to give alcohol, which was burned in Paris for heating, lighting, and cooking. This was more economical than transporting wood to Paris and then disposing of the ashes.

During World Wars I and II, when gasoline shortages occurred in Germany and France, vehicles of all sorts, including tanks and planes, used wood burners in the rear or in trailers. Wood chips were distilled to make alcohol vapors that included carbon monoxide and hydrogen; these vapors would (barely) drive the vehicle. In 1938, 9000 wood-burning cars were used in Europe. "Power alcohol" (ethanol) was also used by France and Germany to supplement gasoline supplies and stimulate alcohol production for anticipated use in munitions production (11).

In about 1920, manufacturers in the United States began to produce metha-

Table 1. The energy content of some fuels, shown on the basis of weight and volume.

| Fuel | Formula | Heat of combustion (low) * | |
		Kjoule/ g	Kjoule/ cm³
Liquids			
Hydrogen	H₂	124.7†	8.7
Methanol	CH₃OH	20.1	15.9
Gasoline	C₈H₁₈	44.3	30.9
Solids			
Hydrides	VH₂‡	4.7	28.4
Coal	C.₂₈H.₄₂	32.2	41.8
Wood	C.₃₂H.₄₆O.₂₂	17.5	14.2
Gases			
Hydrogen	H₂	124.7	0.0010
Methane	CH₄	61.1	0.0044

* Combustion to CO_2 and H_2O (gas). † Conversion factors are: 0.948 kjoule = 1 Btu; 2.10 kjoule/g = 10³ Btu/lb; 0.27 kjoule/cm³ = 10³ Btu/gallon; 33.4 × 10⁴ kjoule/cm³ = 10⁶ Btu/ft³. ‡ Vanadium hydride is given as an example.

nol for use as a solvent, for plastic manufacture, and for fuel injection in piston aircraft. In 1972, 3.2×10^9 kg (10^9 gallons) of methanol were produced (6, 7), equal to about 1 percent of the amount of gasoline produced.

Methanol in the Internal Combustion Engine

It has been claimed that hydrogen is an ideal fuel for the internal combustion engine (12). It certainly causes little pollution, but is difficult to store, high in price, and difficult to burn efficiently in the engine without it knocking and backfiring (13). These problems arise because of the very wide flamma-

bility limits and the very high flame velocity of hydrogen. Perhaps an engine can be invented which takes advantage of these unusual properties.

Methanol used as an additive or substitute for gasoline could immediately help to solve both energy and pollution problems. We will first discuss its use in place of gasoline and then present new results to show that 5 to 15 percent of methanol added to gasoline could produce disproportionate improvements in the fuel economy, pollution levels, and performance of cars now in use.

A number of studies (14, 15) of methanol and ethanol have been conducted in the last 50 years to test their suitability as substitutes for gasoline in the internal combustion engine. Existing engines can be converted to use pure methanol by decreasing the ratio of air to fuel consumed from about 14 for gasoline to 6 for methanol, by recycling more heat from the exhaust to the carburetor, and by providing for cold starts. The conversion is estimated to cost about $100 per vehicle (16). A municipal vehicle converted in this way has been operating satisfactorily in Santa Clara, California, for the past year. Compared with gasoline, the use of methanol in a standard test engine (without catalytic treament of exhausts) yielded one-twentieth of the amount of unburned fuel, one-tenth of the amount of carbon dioxide, and about the same amount of oxides of nitrogen NO_x as gasoline (3, 17). Table 3 shows that a 1972 Gremlin fueled with methanol almost met the 1976 federal standards for emissions and had five times lower emissions than a similar car operated with gasoline (3, 4, 18). In these studies the reduced emissions were attributed to methanol being able to burn without misfire at an air-to-fuel ratio 25 percent higher than gasoline; exhaust temperatures with methanol were 100°C cooler; more spark retard was possible with methanol because of its higher flame speed (18). It was suggested that greater performance and economy could be expected in an engine designed specifically for methanol, and that such design should encompass higher compression ratios and a fuel injection system. In another study, on a one-cylinder research engine, it was found that 10 to 20 percent leaner mixtures could be tolerated with methanol than with gasoline. The amounts of unburned hydrocarbons, CO, and NO_x, produced were lower with methanol than with gasoline,

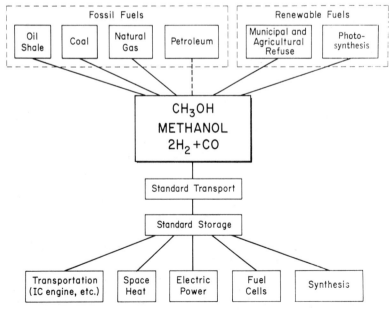

Fig. 1. Sources, transport, and possible applications of methanol.

while the amounts of aldehydes produced were higher (*19*).

From these results it seeems clear that if gasoline becomes scarce or too expensive, we can design cars that will operate on pure methanol and cause less pollution. Specific fuel consumption will certainly be higher on a weight or volume basis (see Table 1), necessitating a larger fuel tank; but specific energy consumption (energy per kilometer) will certainly be lower because higher compression ratios and simpler pollution controls can be used.

The principal drawback to the immediate use of pure methanol as a gasoline substitute is that not enough is available. We have recently tested the possibility of adding 5 to 30 percent of methanol to gasoline (*20*). A number of unmodified private cars (year models 1966 to 1972) were tested and operated over a fixed course with varying concentrations of methanol. It was found that (i) fuel economy increased by 5 to 13 percent; (ii) CO emissions decreased by 14 to 72 percent; (iii) exhaust temperatures decreased by 1 to 9 percent; and (iv) acceleration increased up to 7 percent. The results obtained on a 1969 Toyota (1900 cm³ engine, 85 brake horsepower, 8 : 1 compression ratio) are shown in Fig. 2. This car has now been driven about 8000 kilometers fueled alternately with gasoline and with mixtures of gasoline and 10 to 30 percent methanol. There have been no mechanical problems. A most striking feature observed with two unmodified cars was the elimination of knock and "Diesel operation" (continued operation after the ignition is

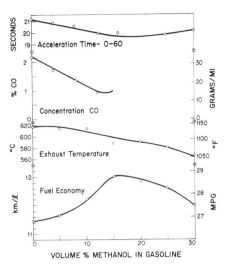

Fig. 2. Performance of a 1969 Toyota Corona with methanol-gasoline mixtures. *MPG*, miles per gallon.

turned off) when gasoline containing 5 percent methanol was used.

An octane rating of 106 for pure methanol hardly seems sufficient to explain these improvements. The methanol is said to have a "blending octane value" (BOV) of 130 (*9*, *10*) defined by

$$BOV = [O_b - O_g(1 - x)]/x$$

where O_b and O_g are the octane numbers of the blend and the gasoline (*8*), and x is the volume fraction of methanol in the gasoline. From this, 10 percent of methanol added to gasoline with an octane rating of 90 would be expected to yield a fuel with an octane rating of 94, equivalent to the addition of 0.13 gram of tetraethyl lead per liter of gasoline (*9*). Ethanol has a BOV of 110 to 160, depending on the octane of the gasoline (*15*).

To account for the disproportionate effects of methanol on the octane value and other properties of gasoline, we propose the following mechanism (*20*). When methanol is synthesized from CO and $2H_2$ at 50 to 300 atmospheres and 200°C, −90.8 kilojoules of heat must be removed (see Eq. 1). In the compression stroke of the internal combustion engine, methanol can dissociate at very low temperatures and reabsorb this energy, cooling the charge and quenching premature combustion. For example, at 10 atmospheres methanol is 18, 85, and 99.7 percent dissociated at 100°, 200°, and 300°C, respectively [calculated from data in (*7*)]. The CO and H_2 formed on dissociation increase the flame velocity of the charge, giving more complete and efficient combustion.

Other Aspects of Methanol Utilization

Although methanol is suggested here principally as a fuel for automobiles, it could also be used advantageously in most other fuel applications if it becomes sufficiently plentiful. It is a safe, clean fuel for home heating and can also be burned in power plants to generate electricity without polluting the atmosphere. In a recent set of pilot-plant and full-scale power boiler demonstrations, methyl-fuel was tested against No. 5 fuel oil and natural gas (*9*). In the tests with methyl-fuel it was observed that (i) no particulates were released from the stack; (ii) the amount of NO_x in flue gases was less than the amount emitted from natural gas and much less than that emitted from the oil; (iii) the CO concentration was less than that from oil and gas; (iv) no sulfur compounds were emitted; (v) the amounts of aldehydes, acids, and unburned hydrocarbons produced were negligible; and (vi) soot deposits in the furnace from previous oil firing were burned off with methyl-fuel, thereby allowing higher heat-transfer rates and higher efficiency.

Methanol is one of the few known fuels suited to power generation by fuel cells (*21*). In principle, the fuel cell can convert chemical energy to electricity with much higher efficiencies than heat engines such as turbines. Although methanol is not as simple to use in a fuel cell as hydrogen, it can be stored and shipped more easily. Recently a fuel cell has been developed that gives more than 30,000 hours of continuous operation on methanol and air. It uses tungsten carbide and charcoal as electrodes and sulfuric acid as electrolyte (*22*).

The costs of storage and shipment of methanol and other fuels are shown in Table 4. The storage of methanol mixed with gasoline may present cer-

Table 2. Production cost of the energy contained in some fuels. The costs are for large plant capacities, assuming that 15 percent of the plant cost is spent annually on profit, interest, depreciation, and maintenance [data from (*3*, p. 12)].

Fuel	Source	Cost ($/10⁶ kjoule)
Gasoline	Crude oil*	1.00
Methanol	Natural gas†	1.49
	Coal‡	1.40
	Lignite§	1.18
Methane gas	Wellhead	0.14–0.37
	LNG imported‖	0.76–0.95
	Coal	0.76–0.95
Hydrogen gas	Natural gas	0.92
	Coal	1.25
Liquid hydrogen		2.37

* Gasoline produced at $0.118 per gallon.   † Natural gas at $0.040 per 10³ ft³.   ‡ Coal at $7 per ton or $0.25 per 10⁶ kjoule.   § Lignite at $2 per ton or $0.14 per 10⁶ kjoule.   ‖ LNG, liquefied natural gas.

Table 3. Emissions from a 1972 Gremlin (i) that uses gasoline and (ii) that was modified for use with methanol fuel and equipped with a catalytic converter (*18*). Projected (as of 1973) federal standards (for 1975 to 1976) are included for comparison.

Fuel	Emissions (g/mile)		
	Unburned hydrocarbons	CO	NO_x
Gasoline	2.20	32.5	3.2
Methanol	0.32	3.9	0.35
Federal standards	0.41	3.4	0.40

tain problems because of the solubility of methanol and water in gasoline. Only about 0.01 percent of water is soluble in pure gasoline, and therefore excess water from condensation sometimes accumulates in storage tanks and causes corrosion. Gasoline containing 10 percent methanol will dissolve ten times as much water and so can keep the tanks dry; in fact proprietary gas-tank drying agents generally contain methanol. However, water in larger quantities will remove almost ten times its own weight from gasoline containing 10 percent methanol, so that unless a storage tank is first dried out, problems may arise when a mixture of gasoline and methanol is first put in it (15).

Although methanol is miscible with gasoline at room temperature, less than 10 percent is soluble in some gasolines at 0°C. However, the volatile constituents added to gasoline in cold weather to aid ignition increase this solubility. Also, the higher alcohols in methyl-fuel increase the solubility of methanol. For instance, 2.4 percent of isobutanol in one gasoline increased the solubility of methanol from 3 to 10 percent at 0°C (15).

Methanol, although not highly toxic, can be lethal if ingested. It would therefore be prudent to avoid the names **methyl alcohol** and **wood alcohol** in any labeling of methanol containers. Methanol vapors are also poisonous, but no more so than those of many other common substances. For example, the maximum allowable exposure to methanol vapor is 200 parts per million (ppm), while the value for ethyl alcohol is 1000 ppm; for benzene, 10 to 25 ppm; octane, 400 ppm (octane and benzene are typical constituents of gasoline); trichloroethylene, 100 ppm; and carbon tetrachloride, 10 ppm (23).

Methanol Manufacture

Methanol can be made from many sources, as shown in Fig. 1. Until about 1925 it was made (along with acetic acid and tars) by the destructive distillation of wood. Since that time, most methanol has been synthesized from CO and H_2 (7) according to Eq. 1:

$$CO + 2H_2 \rightarrow CH_3OH(gas);$$
$$\Delta G = -90,800 + 229T \ (joule/mole) \quad (1)$$

where ΔG is the free energy change and T is the temperature.

In the original high-pressure process, pressures of 300 atmospheres at 200°C

Table 4. Costs of storage and transportation of methanol, gasoline, and liquid and gaseous hydrogen (3).

Fuel	Cost ($/10^6 kjoule)	
	Storage	Transport over 100 km
Methanol	3–21	0.027
Gasoline	2–15	0.018
Liquid hydrogen	300–1000	1.55
Gaseous hydrogen	350	0.035

were used in the presence of a zinc-chromium oxide catalyst, and yields of over 60 percent were obtained. In 1968 the Imperial Chemical Industries (ICI) developed a low-pressure process using 50 atmospheres at 250°C and a highly selective, copper-based catalyst. This process produces much purer methanol. A number of processes in which intermediate pressures are used have since been developed (6, 9).

The CO and H_2 (synthesis gas) for manufacturing methanol can be obtained by partial oxidation of any carbonaceous fuel with oxygen or water. At present it is obtained almost exclusively from methane by partial oxidation with water. This source of methanol will not long be useful in this country, because there is not now enough natural gas available for our domestic heating needs. However, in the Near East the energy value of the methane flared off at the oil wells would be sufficient to supply much of our energy needs. Plans are now under way to construct methanol plants so that this gas can be converted to methanol at the wellhead and shipped in conventional tankers to this country (24).

In a recent study (25) it was estimated that methanol could be produced on the Persian Gulf and landed on the East Coast of the United States at a cost of $1 per 10^6 kjoule ($0.061 per gallon; $1.05 per 10^6 British thermal units). The construction of refrigerated tankers for methane is also being considered. Liquefied gas in refrigerated tankers would cost $1.46 per 10^6 kjoule. These estimates, which include the cost of construction of new plants or refrigerated tankers, would vary according to the distance of transportation.

Methane gas is also produced biologically by the decomposition of natural wastes, such as pig and chicken manure and sewage. It has been claimed that such methane can be used for powering automobiles, where it has an operational cost equivalent to a cost of $0.03 per gallon for gasoline (26).

It is also claimed that enough fuel could be made from this source to meet all present fuel needs in the United States, and that the use of such a process would reduce by half the problem of sewage and animal-waste disposal (27). In experiments with cars and trucks converted to use methane, the U.S. General Services Administration has reported clean, reliable operation (28). However, the type of cylinder required to contain compressed gaseous methane severely limits the amount of fuel that can be carried; a six-cylinder sedan has a range of 80 km (50 miles), each cylinder measuring 6.7 m^3 and weighing 100 kg (29). Conversion of the organic wastes to methanol rather than methane would make this fuel source much more practical.

For the next few decades, coal is the most attractive candidate for methanol production. Coal has long been used for the production of synthesis gas, according to the endothermic reaction (with ΔH being the heat change):

$$C + H_2O(gas) \rightarrow CO + H_2;$$
$$\Delta H = +131.4 \ kjoule \quad (2)$$

Although synthesis gas contains CO, which is poisonous, it is used for industrial power and for heating homes in many European cities without further conversion. It represents a clean, gasified coal (30). Much work is in progress to develop methods to obtain methane and hydrogen from coal for use as pipeline gas. The same technology can be applied to the manufacture of methanol from synthesis gas. It is estimated that the cost of making methanol from coal would be $1.40 per 10^6 kjoule ($0.085 per gallon) for a plant making 20,000 metric tons per day (3). If lignite is used as the starting material instead of coal, the resulting ash may contain 0.40 percent uranium, equivalent to commercial uranium ore, as well as other valuable minerals such as molybdenum, vanadium, arsenic, germanium, selenium, cobalt, and zirconium (3). Efforts are being made to develop practical methods of gasifying coal in the ground, eliminating the need for strip mining and consequent landscape destruction.

Some day we will run out of fossil fuels. By coupling the manufacture of methanol with the disposal of wastes, we could supplement our fuel supply and thereby prolong the existence of fossil fuels, and simultaneously clean up the landscape. A recent patent (31) describes an "oxygen refuse converter" that can dispose of our refuse and at the same time generate useful energy. In a shaft furnace shown in Fig. 3, unseparated trash or sewage sludge is fed into a hopper at the top. Low-cost oxygen (0.2 kg of O_2 per kilogram of refuse) is fed into this furnace near the bottom, creating a 1500°C zone that melts the metals and glasses found in refuse. These melts, drawn off as slag and metal, have 2 percent of the original refuse volume, while all other products are gaseous or water soluble. Carbon, burning in the high-temperature zone, produces CO, which rises through the furnace. The hot CO creates an intermediate-temperature zone where carbohydrates and plastics are broken down to a gas containing, typically, 47 percent CO, 28 percent H_2, 17 percent CO_2, and 5 percent CH_4 by volume. Finally, in the uppermost section the incoming refuse is dried as the gas mixture cools to about 100°C.

This gas mixture stores 8.0 kjoule per gram of refuse (7×10^6 Btu per ton), or 76 percent of the original refuse energy. Because oxygen rather than air is used in burning, the output gas is high in heat content, low in volume, and relatively easy to scrub to remove fly ash and chlorine.

The United States produces about 1.8×10^{11} kg of solid refuse each year. The energy in the gas from this refuse is 1.4×10^{15} kjoule, or 2 percent of the 7.4×10^{16} kjoule (7.0×10^{16} Btu) consumed each year (32). If this gas were converted to methanol, it could supply about 8 percent of the fuel for our transportation needs. Although initially developed for refuse, converters of this type could also be used to convert farm waste and the waste from lumbering into more useful forms of energy such as methanol.

Forests, which are one means of capturing solar energy, formed the principal energy source for this country until about 1875. Commercial forests now cover about 23 percent of the land area of the United States, or 2.1×10^{12} m². These forests intercept from the sun about 5.8×10^6 kjoule/m² per year, or a total of 1.2×10^{19} kjoule per year (33). If the conversion of solar energy with an efficiency approaching 1 percent could be achieved by improved forest management (34), the annual energy harvest might be 1.2×10^{17} kjoule per year, more than our present energy needs of 7.4×10^{16} kjoule per year. The advantage of utiliz-

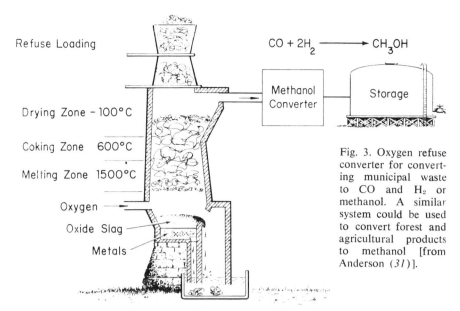

Fig. 3. Oxygen refuse converter for converting municipal waste to CO and H_2 or methanol. A similar system could be used to convert forest and agricultural products to methanol [from Anderson (31)].

ing forests for the production of methanol is that whole trees can be used, not merely those fractions that make good lumber or pulp. It has been calculated that between 5 and 20 percent of our commercial forests operated as "energy plantations," could supply all of our electrical power (35).

Recommendations

The management of energy resources is the management of the lifeblood of our economy, and whatever future energy sources evolve should be those that best blend environmental and technical solutions with economic reality. Therefore we look forward in the next few years to vigorous, public, and possibly polemic debate on the virtues of various fuels.

Recently it has been recommended that "the various energy planning agencies should now begin to outline the mode of implementing hydrogen energy delivery systems in the energy economy" (2). On the contrary, we see methanol as a more benign solution to our fuel problems. The use of methanol would produce the least dislocation of our economy and industry, and would solve environmental as well as energy problems. Since it is compatible with gasoline and existing automobiles, it can be introduced gradually as a fuel as production increases. We will not then have to scrap refineries, automotive facilities, or our cars.

The course of these debates should be influenced by the results of research on all of the various fuels that might

be used to supply our energy needs. We suggest that there are three main areas for research into the large-scale production of methanol. First, since a plant must operate under different and less exacting constraints in producing methyl-fuel than in producing the present industrial grade of alcohol, the existing methods of methanol production should be reexamined and optimized for the production of methyl-fuel. Second, while methanol is now being produced primarily from natural gas, likely to be augmented by production from coal (31), other processes should be developed for utilizing all major sources of carbonaceous materials for methanol synthesis. Third, methanol is now produced primarily by partially oxidizing other fuels to CO and H_2 and by rebuilding these to methanol with some loss of the potential energy value of the original fuel. We should look for methods of direct conversion that do not entail this energy loss.

Finally, we recommend that the various energy planning and regulatory agencies for fuels should strongly consider altering existing regulations to accommodate the introduction of new fuels. For instance, the blending of methanol with gasoline could be encouraged by considering it an environmentally beneficial additive, rather than as a fuel to be taxed. This would certainly make methanol-blend gasolines cheaper than gasoline and encourage production all over the world. We think also that it would be in the national interest to reexamine the tariff now imposed on imported methanol if it is to be used for fuel.

135

Summary

We believe that methanol is the most versatile synthetic fuel available and its use could stretch or eventually substitute for, the disappearing reserves of low-cost petroleum resources. Methanol could be used now as a means for marketing economically the natural gas that is otherwise going to waste in remote locations. If methanol were used as an additive to gasoline at a rate of 5 to 15 percent, for use in internal combustion engines, there would be an immediate reduction in atmospheric pollution, there would be less need for lead in fuel, and automobile performance would be improved.

With increasing production of fuel-grade methanol from coal and other sources, we foresee the increasing use of methanol for electrical power plants, for heating, and for other fuel applications. We hope that a practical methanol fuel cell will be commercially available by the time that methanol becomes plentiful for fuel purposes.

Methanol offers a particularly attractive form of solar-energy conservation, since agricultural and forest waste products can be used as the starting material. Indeed, at 1 percent conversion efficiency the forest lands could supply the entire present energy requirements of the United States.

References and Notes

1. D. P. Gregory, D. Y. C. Ng, G. M. Long, in *The Electrochemistry of Cleaner Environments*, J. O'M. Bockris, Ed. (Plenum, New York, 1972); C. Marchetti, *Euro-Spectra* **10** (No. 4), 117 (1971); J. R. Bartlit, F. J. Edeskuty, K. S. Williamson, Jr., in *Proc. 7th Intersoc. Energy Conversion Eng. Conf.* (1972), paper 729205, p. 1312; F. C. Tanner and R. A. Huse, in *ibid.*, paper 729207, p. 1323; D. P. Gregory and J. Wurm, in *ibid.*, paper 729208, p. 1329; F. A. Martin, in *ibid.*, paper 729029, p. 1335; R. H. Wiswall, Jr., and J. J. Reilly, in *ibid.*, paper 729210, p. 1342; see also other papers in this volume [Proceedings of the Intersociety Energy Conversion Engineering Conferences are available from the American Institute of Aeronautics and Astronautics, 1290 Avenue of the Americas, New York, N.Y. 10019; see also references (*12, 13, 17, 22, 30,* and *35*)]; D. P. Gregory, *Sci. Am.* **228** (No. 1), 13 (1973); see also collected papers in *International Symposium and Workshop on The Hydrogen Economy*, S. Linke, Ed. (Cornell Univ. Press, Ithaca, N.Y., in press).
2. W. E. Winsche, K. C. Hoffman, F. J. Salzano, *Science* **180**, 1325 (1973).
3. Synthetic Fuels Panel, "Hydrogen and other synthetic fuels; a summary of the work of the synthetic fuel panel" (U.S. Atomic Energy Commission, Report TID-26136, September 1972).
4. National Academy of Sciences, *Report by the Committee on Motor Vehicle Emissions* (National Academy of Sciences, Washington, D.C., February 1973).
5. D. P. Gregory and R. B. Rosenberg, "Synthetic fuels for transportation and national energy needs" (paper presented at the Society of Automotive Engineers National Meeting Symposium on Energy and the Automobile, Detroit, May 1973).
6. Stanford Research Institute, *Chemical Economics Handbook* (Stanford Research Institute, Menlo Park, Calif.), sections 674.5021–674.5023.
7. R. D. Kirk and D. S. Othmer, Eds., *Encyclopedia of Chemical Technology* (Interscience, New York, 1967), vol. 13, p. 370.
8. The octane number of a fuel represents its rating for antiknock properties, measured as the percentage by volume of isooctane in a reference fuel consisting of a mixture of isooctane and normal heptane and matching in knocking properties the fuel being tested. The higher the octane number, the less likely is the fuel to detonate. The octane number of methane, 106, was determined by the re-research method.
9. D. Garrett and T. O. Wentworth, *Methyl-Fuel—A New Clean Source of Energy* (Division of Fuel Chemistry, American Chemical Society, Washington, D.C., August 1973), paper 9; T. O. Wentworth, *Environ. Sci. Technol.* **7**, 1002 (1973).
10. D. Garrett, personal communication.
11. S. Egloff, *Ind. Eng. Chem.* **30**, 1091 (1938).
12. K. H. Well, in *Proc. 7th Intersoc. Energy Conversion Eng. Conf.* (1972), paper 729212, p. 1355.
13. R. E. Billings and F. E. Lynch, *History of Hydrogen-Fueled Internal Combustion Engines* and *Performance and Nitric Oxide Control Parameters of the Hydrogen Engine* (Energy Research Corp., Provo, Utah, papers 73001 and 73002, 1973); R. R. Adt, Jr., D. L. Hirschberger, T. Kartage, M. R. Swain, in *Proc. 8th Intersoc. Energy Conversion Eng. Conf.* (1973), paper 739092, p. 194.
14. J. A. Bolt, *A Survey of Alcohol as a Motor Fuel* [Society of Automotive Engineers (2 Pennsylvania Plaza, New York, N.Y.); conference paper SP 254, pp. 1–13, June 1964] (65 references are included); E. S. Starkman, H. K. Newhall, R. D. Sutton, *Comparative Performance of Alcohol and Hydrocarbon Fuels* (Society of Automotive Engineers, conference paper 254, pp. 14–33, New York, June 1964).
15. American Petroleum Institute, *Use of Alcohol in Motor Gasoline—A Review* (American Petroleum Institute, Publ. No. 4082, Washington, D.C., 1971).
16. R. K. Pefley, personal communication.
17. ——, M. A. Sand, M. A. Sweeney, J. D. Kilgroe, in *Proc. 6th Intersoc. Energy Conversion Eng. Conf.* (1971), paper 719008, p. 36.
18. G. Adelman, D. G. Andrews, R. S. Devoto, *Exhaust Emissions from a Methanol-Fueled Automobile* (Society of Automotive Engineers, paper 720693, August 1972).
19. G. D. Ebersole and F. S. Manning, *Engine Performance and Exhaust Emissions: Methanol versus Iso-octane* (Society of Automotive Engineers, paper 720692, August 1972).
20. R. E. Lerner, T. B. Reed, E. D. Hinkley, R. E. Fahey, in preparation.
21. G. Siprios, in *Proc. 20th Annu. Power Sources Conf.* (1966), p. 46.
22. L. Baudendistel, H. Böhm, J. Heffler, C. Louis, F. A. Pohl, in *Proc. 7th Intersoc. Energy Conversion Eng. Conf.* (1972), paper 729004, p. 20
23. N. I. Sax, *Dangerous Properties of Industrial Materials* (Reinhold, New York, ed. 3, 1968); Occupational Safety and Health Association, *Federal Register* **36**, 10504 (1971).
24. J. Schons, personal communication; G. Smith, *New York Times*, 29 September 1973; Anonymous, *Chemical Week*, 19 September 1973.
25. B. Dutkiewicz, "Methanol competitive with LNG on long haul," paper presented at the 52nd Annual Meeting, Natural Gas Producers Association, Dallas, 26–28 March 1973; *Oil Gas J.*, 30 April, p. 166 (1973).
26. *Clean Air Water News* **4**, 38 (1972); B. Grindrod, *Mother Earth News No. 10*, 14 (1971).
27. H. L. Bohn, *Environment* **13**, 4 (1971).
28. "GSA expands duel-fuel vehicle experiment," *Clean Air Water News* **3**, 494 (1971).
29. E. Gross, *Sci. News* **97**, 73 (1970).
30. R. A. Graff, S. I. Dobner, A. M. Squires, in *Proc. 7th Intersoc. Energy Conversion Eng. Conf.* (1972), paper 729172, p. 1153.
31. J. E. Anderson, U.S. Patent 3,729,298 (1973); *New York Times*, 21 April 1973.
32. H. C. Hottel and J. B. Howard, *New Energy Technology* (MIT Press, Cambridge, Mass., 1971), p. 4.
33. W. R. Cherry, *Astronaut. Aeronaut.* **11** (No. 8), 30 (1973).
34. P. Tonge, *Christian Science Monitor*, 5 October 1973, pp. 13–14.
35. G. C. Szego, J. A. Fox, D. R. Eaton, in *Proc. 7th Intersoc. Energy Conversion Eng. Conf.* (1972), paper 729168, p. 1131; G. C. Szego and C. C. Kemp, *Chem. Technol.* **3**, 275 (1973).

Hydrogen: Its Future Role in the Nation's Energy Economy

Hydrogen fuel derived from water could extend nuclear power and reduce dependence on imported oil.

W. E. Winsche, K. C. Hoffman, F. J. Salzano

In the near future, large scale economical sources of energy derived from nuclear fission or from other domestically available primary sources such as solar or geothermal energy will be needed. Because of its complex nature, and for reasons of safety, nuclear energy clearly cannot be utilized directly in small scale transportation systems such as the automobile. Thus the original promise that nuclear power will eventually supply all the nation's energy needs can only be effectively fulfilled by supplying the energy in the form of electricity or some storable, portable fuel.

Electricity is obviously a clean and convenient form of energy for the consumer and will always fulfill a unique and necessary role in the energy system; however, it is not the best and most practical, or even the most economical form of transportable energy for all domestic and industrial applications. The cost of transmission and distribution to the residential consumer is high—that is, in excess of 50 percent of the total cost at the point of end use. In places where environmental considerations require that cables be placed underground, the cost of transmission and distribution will be even higher. Economical storage of electricity by such means as pumped storage

is not possible in most plant locations. Therefore, the output of a power plant must be continually adjusted so that it meets the varying demands of the consumers; this causes the average power plant load factor to be about 0.5. The convenience and flexibility of general-purpose fuels is reflected in the current fuel mix in the energy economy where approximately 80 percent of the energy resources consumed are for uses other than electric generation. Thus, the present industrial and domestic technology is geared to combustible chemical fuels. Therefore, the future supply of nuclear energy to all sectors of the energy economy depends on the development of portable and storable synthetic fuels which can be derived from nuclear energy and some abundantly available or recyclable resource.

Hydrogen has the necessary properties and can fulfill the role of a secondary source of energy that can be derived from the primary source by the decomposition of water (1). It can be substituted for petroleum and coal in almost all industrial processes which require a reducing agent, such as in steel manufacturing and other metallurgical operations. Further, hydrogen can easily be converted to a variety of fuel forms such as methanol, ammonia, and hydrazine. The use of hydrogen as a fuel would allow the industrial establishment to retain its present structure and would cause the least economic burden in the process of changeover from fossil to synthetic fuels, that is,

in the transition from fossil fuel to nuclear energy which will come in the future.

Thus, for the future, a hydrogen fuel economy is of major interest as an alternative to a predominately electric economy; in either case the primary energy sources would be nuclear and possibly solar, supplemented by coal. In the immediate future, hydrogen can serve as a clean fuel for special purposes, such as urban transportation systems, and it offers significant benefit to the quality of the urban environment. A most important characteristic of hydrogen is its versatility in being able to serve both the electrical energy demands, by the use of either fuel cells or more conventional "total energy systems" (2), and other thermal energy demands. A significant amount of operating experience has been acquired with hydrogen fuel cells; such cells have already been used successfully in automotive systems (3). The feasibility of operating an internal combustion engine on hydrogen fuel has been demonstrated at Oklahoma State University and at other locations (4). The use of hydrogen in the two winning entries in the National Urban Vehicle Design Competition, August 1972 (5) was an impressive demonstration of the potential of hydrogen-fueled automobiles; however, the key problem in the application of hydrogen as an automotive fuel is storage. Storage as liquid hydrogen may be practical in some types of vehicles; however, a better alternative may be to store hydrogen as metal hydrides (6). These materials have hydrogen densities comparable to that of liquid hydrogen and release hydrogen when heated to their dissociation temperature. Hydrogen may also be used in several industrial processes including the reduction of metal ores (7). It is compatible with a variety of supply systems and may be produced electrolytically (8, 9) or by the gasification of coal or oil (10). The by-product oxygen that is obtained from electrolytic production is a valuable commodity for industrial use, for sewage treatment, and for the oxidation of other urban waste (11).

A gaseous fuel such as hydrogen

Dr. Winsche is chairman of the department of applied science, Dr. Hoffman is an assistant division head, and Mr. Salzano is a staff member in the same department at the Brookhaven National Laboratory, Upton, New York 11973.

Table 1. Estimated total cost of equipment for five different energy systems including the LMFBR (liquid metal fast breeder reactor).

Energy system	Cost* (dollars per kilowatt of capacity)	Reference
LMFBR electric generating station	385	
Coal fired electric generating station	280	
Electrolytic hydrogen plant	56	(8)
Fuel cell electric generator	100	(20)
Reformer to convert methane to hydrogen	50	

* The cost in dollars per 10^6 Btu is given by dollars/10^6 Btu = ($/kw) (0.1) (3.413)$^{-1}$ (8.760)$^{-1}$ (l.f.)$^{-1}$ where l.f. is the load factor and (0.1) is the capital recovery factor for 30 years at 9.3 percent interest. There are 8760 hours per year and 3413 Btu per kilowatt hour.

can be transported and distributed to individual consumers by pipeline at a lower cost than electricity, and hydrogen has the added advantage in that it can be stored. Recent estimates suggest that the transmission cost for hydrogen would be in the range of $0.02 to $0.04 per 10^6 British thermal units per 100 miles (12), as compared to the cost of natural gas which is $0.01 per 10^6 Btu per 100 miles (13). It is estimated that future underground electric transmission costs will be in excess of $0.20 per 10^6 Btu of electrical energy per 100 miles. As the problem of finding sites for generating facilities that are centrally situated near urban load centers becomes more severe, transmission costs of electricity from more remote sites may dictate the energy form that is to be delivered. A nationwide pipeline grid transporting a clean fuel such as hydrogen may provide a more flexible and economical system than an eletctrical delivery system of similar scope. Such a hydrogen grid could act as a load leveling device for the projected nuclear systems. Thus, these generating stations could be base-loaded (that is, running at maximum capacity) and supply either electricity directly or hydrogen for storage in the pipeline system, or both.

In this article we present the results of a preliminary evaluation of the economics and environmental benefits of hydrogen energy delivery systems in the residential and transportation sectors. We examine the future cost of energy delivered to residential consumers by several different delivery systems, and we assume that the technology required, which is theoretically feasible, can be developed and implemented.

It is evident that the systems we describe could only be implemented with a vigorous engineering research and development program; however, since the nation is now entering a period when massive amounts of capital—some $374 billion—will be spent over the next 15 years to upgrade

and improve the quantity and quality of the energy delivery system (14) it is important at this time that alternatives such as the hydrogen fuel economy be thoroughly evaluated and discussed.

Table 2. Estimated long-distance transportation costs per 100 miles to a local substation, including capital, operating, and maintenance costs (21).

Transportation	Cost (dollars per 10^6 Btu)
Methane by pipeline	0.030
Hydrogen by pipeline	0.033
Electricity by high voltage transmission	0.21
Gasoline by tanker	0.10

Table 3. Distribution costs from the local substation to a residential household including capital, operating, and maintenance costs. These costs are based on a multiple of the U.S. national average distribution costs estimated from (22). The multiple factor of 3 that holds for gas is assumed to hold for electricity as well.

Distribution	Cost (dollars per 10^6 Btu)
Methane by pipeline	0.60
Hydrogen by pipeline	0.66
Electricity by overhead wire	2.55
Gasoline by truck	0.70

Table 4. Estimated total costs of fuels.

Fuel	Cost (dollars per 10^6 Btu)
Coal at the mine mouth	0.15
Nuclear fuel	0.05
Gasoline at the filling station	0.80

Table 5. Estimated costs of operation and maintenance of energy supply, not including the cost of fuel.

Energy supplies	Cost (dollars per 10^6 Btu)
Liquid metal fast breeder reactor	0.15
Coal fired electric system	0.15
Fuel cell electric generator	0.15
Electrolytic hydrogen plant	0.06

Reference Systems and Options

A preliminary evaluation has been made of the use of hydrogen fuel to satisfy the annual energy requirements of a typical household including the automotive fuel requirements. Comparisons are made with all-electric supply systems and systems that are based on coal gasification. Industrial and commercial demands were not considered in this preliminary evaluation because they involve complex interactions between supply, demand, and the substitutability of electricity and fuels in these sectors.

The residential and automotive energy demands specified for these comparisons are estimates of future national averages for a single household (15). A central air-conditioning system is assumed in specifying that energy demand, and it is assumed that gaseous fuels and electricity have the same efficiency for water heating and cooking. The efficiencies of utilizing energy for the other demands are indicated on the energy flow diagrams (Figs. 1 to 7).

When electrical heating is used, a heat pump with a coefficient of performance of 3 is specified and is sized for the air-conditioning load. The balance of the space heating is provided by electrical resistance heating. When hydrogen or methane gas is delivered to the consumer, it is burned directly for space heating and operates an absorption cycle system for air conditioning.

The estimated total costs for fuel, transportation, distribution, and maintenance and operations are summarized in Tables 1 to 5. It is assumed that the facilities have the same useful life and their capital costs are amortized over a 30-year period at a 9 percent interest rate and at load factors listed in the figures.

It is assumed that it will be more expensive to transmit and distribute hydrogen than natural gas because of the higher relative pumping energy required to deliver 10^6 Btu of hydrogen compared with natural gas and the higher degree of leak tightness that is required for hydrogen. The costs for transmission of hydrogen and local distribution are assumed to be $0.042 per 10^6 Btu per 100 miles and $0.66 per 10^6 Btu, respectively. The cost indicated for hydrogen produced by electrolysis does not include any credit for by-product oxygen since the exact market for this material is uncertain.

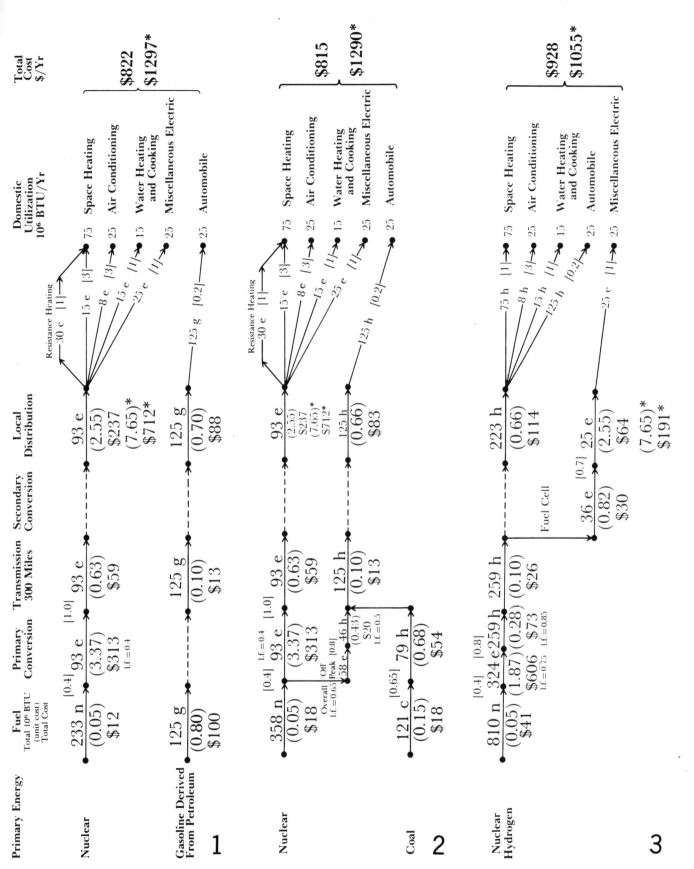

Fig. 1. Energy flow diagram of a reference system, system 1, in which the primary sources of energy are nuclear power and gasoline derived from petroleum. The number above each arrow is the total amount of energy used annually, expressed as 10^6 Btu, the cost per 10^6 Btu is shown in parentheses below each arrow. The total annual cost of each operation in the energy system is shown below the unit cost and is expressed as dollars per year. Numbers in square brackets are efficiency factors; costs marked with an asterisk are for underground distribution. Abbreviations: n, nuclear; e, electrical; g, gasoline; c, coal; m, methane; l.f., load factor.   Fig. 2. System 2, in which hydrogen derived from nuclear energy and coal is used only for automotive propulsion. For further details see Fig. 1.   Fig. 3. System 3, in which hydrogen derived from nuclear energy is used to supply all domestic energy needs except the electricity required for small appliances. For details see Fig. 1.

139

Energy Delivery Systems

We now compare the cost and environmental impact of hydrogen energy systems with some reference systems in which conventional energy sources and delivery systems are used. To simplify the problem we consider only the total annual energy needs of the average domestic residence. The energy needs of industrial and commercial sectors should be factored in a more detailed study of this type to determine the impact of those demands on total installed electrical capacity, load factors, and the availability of off-peak power. The study we describe serves primarily as an example of the application of hydrogen to a given sector, the analysis required, and the cost and benefits to be realized. The residential energy needs considered here are for space heating, air conditioning, water heating and cooking, electricity required for small electrical appliances, and the automobile. The total cost per unit of energy including amortization is made up of the following elements. (i) The cost of the primary energy source or fuel; (ii) primary conversion of the fuel to whatever form of energy is transported; (iii) the cost of long distance transportation of the energy form to the local area; (iv) the cost of secondary conversion in the local area to an alternative energy form, for example, the conversion of hydrogen to electricity in a fuel cell; and (v) the cost of local distribution to the domestic consumer.

The cost of the utilizing device or system in the household has not been included. We could not consider all possible combinations of energy sources and delivery systems, but selected seven basic systems in which a cost comparison could be made between hydrogen energy delivery systems and some alternatives. The seven systems are described below.

In making the cost comparisons we assume that in each example the entire system is newly installed. This implies that the comparison applies to either a new city or to a long-range evaluation where the existing system is completely replaced. The air pollutants, waste heat, and other waste products produced in each system are summarized in Table 6. Wastes and emissions produced in centralized operations are stated separately from those produced at or near the place of consumption.

System 1. This is a reference system in which we assume that the primary sources of energy are nuclear power and gasoline derived from petroleum (see Fig. 1). Nuclear electricity is assumed to supply all the domestic energy needs and gasoline is used for transportation. The average long distance transmission of the energy is taken to be 300 miles. Local distribution of electricity can be done either by conventional overhead transmission or by underground electrical cables and the costs for each are shown in Fig. 1. Conservative estimates (*16*) indicate that underground transmission will cost three times that of conventional overhead systems used presently for local distribution of electricity.

System 2. In this system the primary source of energy is nuclear power and coal (see Fig. 2). Nuclear power is used to generate electricity which is transported by conventional means to satisfy all the domestic energy needs except the automobile. Off-peak electrical power at the central station is used to produce hydrogen to supply 37 percent of the hydrogen required for automotive propulsion (*17*). The remaining hydrogen requirements are supplied by converting coal to hydrogen by means of conventional technology.

System 3. Nuclear energy is used to generate hydrogen by electrolysis of water (see Fig. 3) by means of an improved technology that has been shown to be feasible. All of the electricity is converted to hydrogen which is transported by pipeline to the local area. A major fraction, 86 percent, of the hydrogen is used to supply all the domestic energy needs including the automobile, but excluding electricity required for small appliances. The remaining fraction, 14 percent, of the hydrogen is used in a fuel cell operating at a load factor of 0.5 to generate the electricity required for small appliances. We have assumed that the fuel cell is located at a local electrical substation; however, the fuel cell could be located in the domestic residence with a lower load factor. Although this might increase its cost, the cost of distributing the electricity in the local region would be reduced. The cost of transporting gas by pipeline is significantly less expensive than transporting an equivalent amount of electrical energy by wire.

System 4. This is similar to system 3 except that the primary source of

Table 6. Summary of emissions and waste production; T, tritium; Kr, krypton; CO_2, carbon dioxide; CO, carbon monoxide; SO_2, sulfur dioxide; NO_x, oxides of nitrogen; Part., particulates; HC, hydrocarbons.

	Concentrated waste production in centralized plants, per household, per year										Distributed waste production at fuel cell sites and points of end use, per household						
Wastes (curies)			CO_2 (10^8 lb)	Wastes (lb)					Heat (10^6 Btu)	CO_2 (10^9 lb)	Wastes (lb)					Heat (10^6 Btu)
T	^{85}Kr	Solids*		CO	SO_2	NO_x	Part.	HC			CO	SO_2	NO_x	Part.	HC	
System 1. Nuclear-electric energy and gasoline																
0.084	0.31	0.34							140	18.6	113	8.8	12.5	8.8	11.3	218
System 2. Hydrogen derived from nuclear energy and from coal																
0.13	0.48	0.53	27.1						261				12.5			218
System 3. Nuclear energy conversion to hydrogen																
0.29	1.08	1.19							551				17.5			259
System 4. Coal conversion to hydrogen																
			89.1						139				17.5			259
System 5. Coal conversion to methane																
			42.5						146	27.2	115		17.5	4.3	12.0	271
System 6. Nuclear-electric energy only																
0.12	0.45	0.49							203							135
System 7. Coal conversion to electricity and gasoline																
			52.2	4.7	280	163	47	1.9	140	18.6	113	8.8	12.5	8.8	11.3	218

* Solid high-level radioactive wastes.

energy is coal and the electricity is generated at the mine mouth (see Fig. 4). The cost of gasifying coal to hydrogen is assumed to be 10 percent less expensive than the production of methane (18).

System 5. This is similar to system 4 except that the coal is used to generate methane rather than hydrogen (18) (see Fig. 5). The fuel cell is located at the substation and requires a reformer to convert the methane to hy-

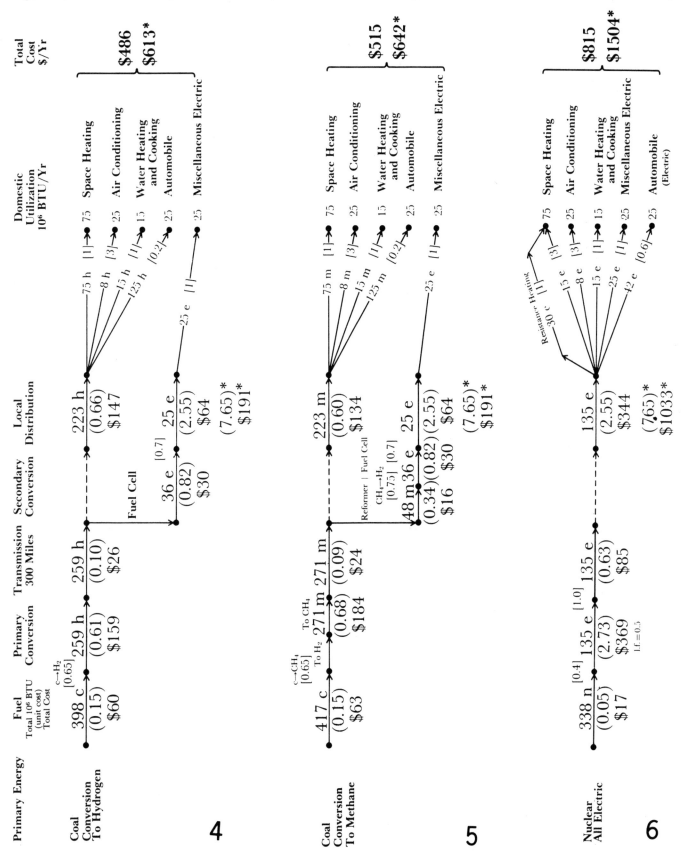

Fig. 4. System 4, in which hydrogen derived from coal supplies all domestic energy needs except the electricity required for small appliances. For further details see Fig. 1.   Fig. 5. System 5, in which methane derived from coal supplies all domestic energy needs except the electricity required for small appliances. For further details see Fig. 1.   Fig. 6. A reference system, system 6, in which electricity derived from nuclear energy supplies all domestic energy needs. For further details see Fig. 1.

drogen which in turn is converted to electricity in the fuel cell. As in systems 3 and 4 the reformer and fuel cell could be located in the residence.

System 6. This is another reference system. The primary energy source is nuclear which is used to produce electricity (see Fig. 6). The electricity is transported to the local region and is used to supply all the domestic energy needs. This includes the automobile which is assumed to be all-electric and to operate on storage batteries.

System 7. This is another reference system which is similar to system 1 in all respects except that the primary source of energy is coal.

Discussion

Data from the seven systems are summarized in Table 7 and are shown in the form of energy flow diagrams in Figs. 1 to 7. In each energy flow diagram, the number above each arrow is the total amount of energy used annually, expressed as 10^6 Btu per year. The unit cost of the energy in dollars per 10^6 Btu is shown in parentheses below each arrow. The total annual cost of that operation in the energy system is shown below the unit cost and is expressed as dollars per year. For example, in system 1, 233×10^6 Btu per year of nuclear fuel are required; this fuel costs $0.05 per 10^6 Btu and the total cost of the fuel used to supply energy to one household is $12 per year. The efficiency factor for converting the primary fuel to the ultimate energy form (hydrogen or electricity) is shown in square brackets. In the case of air conditioning or heat pumping, the efficiency factor becomes a utilization factor and is therefore greater than unity.

For local electrical distribution, two cost figures are given. The first two numbers below the arrow correspond to the unit cost and total cost per year of local electric transmission by means of overhead cables. The numbers below these that are marked with an asterisk correspond to the unit cost and the total cost per year of underground electrical distribution, the cost being increased by a factor of 3 in comparison with overhead distribution (16). The costs at the extreme right of each energy flow diagram show the total annual costs of energy supplied to the domestic user; the costs marked with an asterisk indicate the use of underground cables for local electrical distribution.

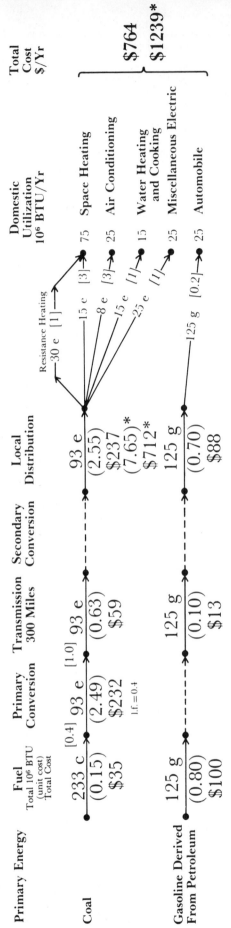

Fig. 7. A reference system, system 7, that resembles system 1 except that the primary sources of energy are coal and gasoline derived from petroleum. For further details see Fig. 1.

The data for these seven systems show that the delivery of hydrogen energy is economically competitive with the delivery of conventional energy sources (for example, compare systems 2 and 3 with the reference systems 1 and 7). This is primarily because of the lower cost of transmission and distribution of a gaseous fuel compared with electricity, and the fact that only a small fraction, 15 percent of the total domestic energy need is electrical. Thermal energy can satisfy the major fraction of the domestic energy needs including refrigeration and air conditioning. To supply the total domestic energy need with electricity is expensive even when the automobile uses gasoline as a fuel (see reference systems 1 and 7). This is due primarily to the high cost of electrical transmission and distribution.

Coal is an especially economic source of energy when used as the primary source in a hydrogen energy system, as shown by a comparison of systems 3 and 4. The costs of energy from conventional systems using coal or nuclear power are similar, as shown in systems 1 and 7. It is more realistic to consider a mixed system in which a number of primary energy forms are used, such as nuclear power and coal as in system 2. In this system also the use of hydrogen derived from coal and off-peak electricity is competitive with the reference system 1.

Methane derived from coal is also economically attractive; however, hydrogen can be produced as easily as methane. The cost difference in systems 4 and 5, for example, are probably insignificant because of the relatively arbitrary assumptions made for the cost of transporting hydrogen. The merits of hydrogen as opposed to methane must be compared on some basis other than cost.

An important element in the energy utilization system is the automobile which now accounts for over half of the total energy consumed by a household. Development of the technology of hydrogen utilization in automobile engines would make a hydrogen energy distribution system an economically competitive alternative to the present energy delivery systems. It is of interest to determine how the price of electrolytic hydrogen relative to gasoline is affected by the cost of electricity. In Table 8 we show results derived from system 3 in which the cost of electricity is 6.8 mills per kilowatt hour (12). In this case the cost of hydrogen is slightly greater than twice the cost of gasoline. However, if the cost of electricity were reduced to 1.5 mills per kilowatt hour, hydrogen would be competitive with gasoline as an automotive fuel. Off-peak electric power can be available at such low rates, as shown in system 2.

If we focus only on the automotive sector in the energy system, hydrogen is not competitive with gasoline unless off-peak power is used. If we examined the total energy need, including the automotive sector, hydrogen energy delivery systems can be competitive with conventional systems involving electricity and gasoline, as in system 1. Even if the hydrogen must be converted to a more easily stored fuel for automotive use, such as methanol, ammonia, or even propane, some form of hydrogen energy distribution system is an attractive alternative which should be examined in more detail.

A significant advantage in the application of hydrogen to the automotive sector is the reduction in the amount of automotive emissions such as carbon monoxide, hydrocarbons, and lead. Although nitrogen oxides are emitted in the combustion of hydrogen it should be much simpler to control these emissions than those of hydrocarbon fuels because of the cleaner exhaust gases. If the hydrogen is produced from nuclear energy there will be an increase in the production of radioactive fission products. For example, in the year 2000, the available off-peak power (nuclear and fossil) could supply hydrogen to 50 percent of the private automobiles. This would increase the total radioactivity produced by 23 percent. Additional fossil fuel would have to be burned; however, if the energy were all nuclear and supplied the same need, the amount of radioactive fission products would not increase by more than 59 percent over the amount projected to be produced in the year 2000.

Summary

In examining the potential role of hydrogen in the energy economy of the future, we take an optimistic view. All the technology required for implementation is feasible but a great deal of development and refinement is necessary. A pessimistic approach would obviously discourage further thinking about an important and perhaps the most reasonable alternative for the future. We have considered a limited number of alternative energy systems involving hydrogen and have

Table 7. Summary of annual cost of energy to residential sector.

System	Distribution cost (dollars per year)	
	Overhead	Underground
1. Nuclear-electric energy and gasoline	822	1297
2. Hydrogen derived from nuclear energy and from coal	815	1290
3. Nuclear energy conversion to hydrogen	928	1055
4. Coal conversion to hydrogen	486	613
5. Coal conversion to methane	515	642
6. Nuclear-electric energy only	815	1504
7. Coal conversion to electricity and gasoline	764	1239

shown that hydrogen could be a viable secondary source of energy derived from nuclear power; for the immediate future, hydrogen could be derived from coal. A hydrogen supply system could have greater flexibility and be competitive with a more conventional all-electric delivery system. Technological improvements could make hydrogen as an energy source an economic reality. The systems examined in this article show how hydrogen can serve as a general-purpose fuel for residential and automotive applications. Aside from being a source of heat and motive power, hydrogen could also supply the electrical needs of the household via

Table 8. The influence of the cost of electricity on the relative cost of electrolytic hydrogen and gasoline of equal energy equivalents at the pump. The ratio of the cost of electrolytic hydrogen to gasoline is given by

$$\frac{\text{Cost of electrolytic } H_2}{\text{Cost of gasoline}} =$$
$$0.65 + 0.23 \ g \left(\frac{\text{mills}}{\text{kwhr}}\right)$$

where g is the cost of electricity in mills per kilowatt hour. The value 0.65 represents the cost of transportation and distribution.

Cost of electricity (mills per kilowatt hour)	Electrolytic hydrogen/ gasoline* (ratio of costs)
0.0	0.65
0.2	0.69
0.4	0.74
0.6	0.78
0.8	0.83
1.0	0.88
1.5†	0.99
2.0	1.1
4.0	1.6
6.0	2.0
8.0	2.5
10.0	2.9
12.0	3.4

* No credit has been given for the by-product oxygen. The cost of the hydrogen fuel tank, that is, hydrogen stored in a Mg_2NiH_4 alloy, will be $70 to $100 per year. This assumes that the tank costs two to three times the price of the alloy and is amortized over 10 years at 10 percent interest.   † This is the break-even point where electrolytic hydrogen at the pump is competitive with gasoline which is assumed to cost $0.19 per gallon at the pump exclusive of state and local taxes.

fuel cells (19), turbines, or conventional "total energy systems."

The total cost of energy to a residence supplied with hydrogen fuel depends on the ratio of the requirements for direct fuel use to the requirements for electrical use. A greater direct use of hydrogen as a fuel without conversion to electricity reduces the overall cost of energy supplied to the household because of the greater expense of electrical transmission and distribution. Hydrogen fuel is especially attractive for use in domestic residential applications where the bulk of the energy requirement is for thermal energy.

Although a considerable amount of research is required before any hydrogen energy delivery system can be implemented, the necessary developments are within the capability of present-day technology and the system could be made attractive economically. Techniques for producing hydrogen from water by electrolysis, from coal, and directly from thermal energy could be found that are less expensive than those now available; inexpensive fuel cells could be developed, and high-temperature turbines could be used for the efficient conversion of hydrogen (and oxygen) to electricity.

The use of hydrogen as an automotive fuel would be a key factor in the development of a hydrogen energy economy, and safe storage techniques for carrying sufficient quantities of hydrogen in automotive systems can certainly be developed. The use of hydrogen in automobiles would significantly reduce urban pollution because the dispersed fossil fuel emissions would be replaced by radioactive wastes generated at large central stations. The conversion of internal or external combustion engines for combustion of hydrogen fuel would probably have less economic impact on the automotive industry than the mass introduction of electric automobiles. However, this is a subject that requires more detailed study.

All of the safety aspects of hydrogen utilization will have to be examined, especially the problems of safety in the domestic use and the long distance transport of hydrogen in pipelines at high pressures.

It is our opinion that the various energy planning agencies should now begin to outline the mode of implementing hydrogen energy delivery systems in the energy economy. The initial transition to hydrogen energy derived from available fossil fuels such as coal should be considered together with the long range view of all the hydrogen being derived eventually from nuclear energy. By the year 1985 when petroleum imports may be in excess of the domestic supply, these plans could set the stage for the transition period from fossil to a predominantly nuclear energy economy able to supply abundant synthetic fuels such as hydrogen. Synthetic fuels will obviously be more expensive than fuels now derived from petroleum; however, there may be no other viable choice. Thus, it is essential that the analysis and technological feasibility of a hydrogen energy system be considered now. It is of vital importance to the nation to develop some general-purpose fuel that can be produced from a variety of domestic energy sources and reduce our dependence on imported oil.

References and Notes

1. L. W. Jones, *Science* **174**, 367 (1971); G. De Beni and C. Marchetti, *Euro Spectra* **1970**, 46 (1970); D. P. Gregory, D. Y. C. Ng, G. M. Long, in *The Electrochemistry of Cleaner Environments*, J. O'M. Bockris, Ed. (Plenum, New York, 1971); D. P. Gregory, *Pub. Util. Fortn.* **89**, 21 (1972); L. O. Williams, *Astronaut. Aeronaut.* (Feb. 1972), p. 42.
2. B. W. Vincent, K. W. Webb, P. Don Vito, "A report on preliminary findings on innovative utility technologies of operation breakthrough" (Working paper 118-1, Urban Institute, Washington, D.C., 5 May 1971).
3. K. V. Kordesch, *J. Electrochem. Soc.* **118**, 812 (1971); G. Evans, "Hydrogen-air fuel cell for vehicle propulsion," presented at Symposium on Power Systems for Electrical Vehicles, April 1967.
4. R. J. Schoeppel, "Design criteria for hydrogen burning engines, final report" (Oklahoma State Univ. contract EHS 70-103 with the Environmental Protection Agency, October 1971); P. Underwood and P. Dieges, "Hydrogen and oxygen combustion for pollution free operation of existing standard engines," Proceedings of the Intersociety Energy Conversion Engineering Conference 1971 (Society of Automotive Engineers), p. 317; R. O. King, S. V. Hayes, A. B. Allen, R. W. P. Anderson, E. J. Waler, *Trans. Eng. Inst. Can.* **2**, 143 (1958).
5. National Urban Vehicle Design Competition, held in Detroit at the General Motors Proving Ground, August 1972.
6. K. C. Hoffman, W. E. Winsche, R. H. Wiswall, J. J. Reilly, T. V. Sheehan, C. H. Waide, "Metal hydrides as a source of fuel for vehicular propulsion," International Automotive Engineering Congress, Detroit, Mich., 13–17 January 1969, sponsored by the Society of Automotive Engineers.
7. Proceeding of a symposium on Abundant Nuclear Energy, held at Gatlinburg, Tenn., 1968 (U.S. Atomic Energy Commission, Division of Technical Information, Oak Ridge, Tenn., 1969).
8. R. L. Costa and P. G. Grimes, *Chem. Eng. Progr.* **63**, 56 (1967).
9. J. E. Mrochek, in *Ammonia, A Fertilizer*, A. V. Slack and G. R. James, Eds. (Decker, New York, in press).
10. *Encyclopedia of Chemical Technology* (Inter-science, New York, ed. 2, 1966), vol. 10, p. 353.
11. W. E. Winsche, T. V. Sheehan, K. C. Hoffman, "Hydrogen—a clean fuel for urban areas," Proceedings of the Intersociety Energy Conversion Engineering Conference, August 1971, p. 38.
12. One British thermal unit is equivalent to 1055 joules; 1 mile is equivalent to 1.6 kilometers; a mill is a unit of monetary value equal to 1/1000 dollars; 1 lb. is equivalent to 0.45 kilogram.
13. D. P. Gregory, Institute of Gas Technology, private communication.
14. Committee on U.S. Energy Outlook, *U.S. Energy Outlook; An Initial Appraisal 1971–1985* (National Petroleum Council, Washington, D.C., 1971), vol. 2.
15. These demands are our estimates and represent the national average for a single household at the present time. It is assumed that in the future the pattern of domestic energy use will not change significantly.
16. U.S. Department of Interior and the Edison Electric Institute, *Underground Power Transmission* by Arthur D. Little, Inc. Electric Research Council of Edison Electric Institute, Publ. No. 1-72 (1966).
17. We have estimated that in the year 2000, off-peak power could be available to supply 50 percent of the energy required by private automobiles.
18. See Committee on U.S. Energy Outlook (*14*), pp. 53–54 for the cost of coal gasification to methane.
19. The Pratt and Whitney Aircraft Company is conducting limited tests of fuel cells produced for the "Target Project" which are intended for commercial residential applications.
20. Office of Coal Research, *Final Report Project Fuel Cell* (Research and Development Report No. 57, Office of Coal Research, U.S. Department of the Interior, Washington, D.C., 1970).
21. U.S. Federal Power Commission, *The 1970 National Power Survey* (Government Printing Office, Washington, D.C., 1971), parts 2 and 3.
22. U.S. Bureau of the Census, *Statistical Abstract of the United States; 1970* (U.S. Bureau of the Census, Washington, D.C., ed. 91, 1970), p. 515.
23. This work was performed under the auspices of the U.S. Atomic Energy Commission.

Energy Storage: Using Electricity More Efficiently

Arthur L. Robinson

"What do you do when the wind dies down?" asks a widely shown television commercial as the inhabitants of a windmill-powered house are left with a suddenly darkened home. One answer not suggested in the commercial might be: Store the energy generated while the wind is blowing for use when it is not.

Energy storage is becoming increasingly important for utilities that face fluctuating demands for power. And solving storage problems is the key to wider use of electrically powered vehicles and intermittent energy sources, such as the sun and wind. There is no shortage of ideas for energy storage, but most storage technologies are in an early stage of development and will not be ready for use in the near term.

Probably the largest existing need for energy storage is related to the way electrical power is generated and consumed. The demand for electrical power depends on the time of day, on the day of the week, and on the season of the year. On a hot and humid summer day in the eastern half of the United States, for example, the peak power demand can be more than twice the minimum demand on the same day, and the trend is toward ever larger costs of peak power relative to the base load. Utilities companies meet this quasi-periodic fluctuation in the demand for power by generating power in three different ways. That part of the total power needed throughout the day, namely, the base load, is generated by large steam turbines powered by fossil fuels, by water turbines (hydroelectric power), and, increasingly, by nuclear-powered steam turbines. The power consumed only during the daylight hours (intermediate power) is generated by older and smaller units powered by fossil fuels. In times of exceptional or peak demand for power, additional steam units or gas turbines are used for the short time they are needed. Brownouts or worse result when even these power generating units are insufficient to meet the peak demand. There is also a reserve capability (spinning reserve) to provide power system stability in the event of power fluctuations (transients).

If electrical energy could be generated during times of low demand (at night, for example) and stored for later use during times of high demand, there could be two beneficial results, points out Fritz Kalhammer of the Electric Power Research Institute, Palo Alto, California. Now, when we have only marginal ability to satisfy peak power demands, storage units could effectively increase the capacity of the power system with energy generated in off-peak hours. In the future, when presumably there will be a sufficiency of generating capacity, storage units could enhance the overall economics of the power plant by allowing the larger and more efficient steam base load units to account for more of the total power generated than is possible in the absence of energy storage. Such a benefit would be especially important if nuclear power generation became widespread. (One utilities' spokesman termed energy storage "the handmaiden of nuclear power.") Primarily because of the high capital cost of nuclear power plants, the economic benefits are realized only when the plants are operated at as high an output as possible. Energy storage could also reduce the requirement for increasingly expensive fossil fuels used for intermediate power generators by coupling storage with nuclear generation. A further benefit for utilities would be that energy storage could form part of the utilities system's spinning reserve, if the stored energy can be delivered at sufficiently high rates.

Pumped Storage Economical

The only economical mode of storage now available to utilities is pumped hydroelectric storage. Pumped hydroelectric storage operates like the hydroelectric power generation common in the northwestern part of the United States, except that the water to operate the turbines must first be pumped uphill (by means of electricity generated during off-peak hours) and stored in a reservoir before it can be used to generate power during periods of high

Fig. 1. The upper reservoir of the pumped hydroelectric storage plant near Luddington, Michigan. The reservoir embankment is 110 meters above Lake Michigan (upper right). The reservoir holds up to 102 million cubic meters of water.

demand. This method of storage is only about 66 percent efficient; that is, it takes 3 watt-hours of energy (1 watt-hour equals 3600 joules) to pump the water to the upper reservoir for 2 watt-hours of energy generated when the water runs back to the lower reservoir. However, the cost of electricity generated in this way is often less than if additional gas turbines or older, fossil-fueled steam turbines were used to meet peak demands.

The first pumped hydroelectric storage facility in the United States was built in western Connecticut in the 1930's and had a power capacity of about 32 megawatts. Now several much larger plants are in operation or are planned. The largest (nearly 1,900 megawatts maximum power and 15,000 megawatt-hours of stored energy) is operated jointly by the Consumers Power Company and Detroit Edison Company at Luddington, Michigan (Fig. 1). The Luddington plant uses Lake Michigan as the lower reservoir, while the upper reservoir is a manmade lake more than 3 kilometers long and nearly 1.5 kilometers wide. The plant was 10 years in the planning stage and it took 4½ years more to complete construction, at a cost of more than $340 million.

While pumped hydroelectric storage is an attractive concept, it is not without its difficulties. There are only a limited number of sites for storage facilities with the elevation difference needed for large storage capacities. Thus pumped hydroelectric storage is not a viable concept for many parts of the country. Even where sites are available, local opposition is often considerable, the objections pointing toward interference with aquatic life and otherwise spoiling the natural environment. The Consolidated Edison plan for a 2000-megawatt pumped hydroelectric storage plant (the Storm King project) on the Hudson River near Cornwall, New York, had been successfully blocked for 10 years by environmentalists, and contracts to begin construction have only recently been signed. Pumped hydroelectric storage facilities are often far from the areas they serve, thus necessitating long-distance power transmission lines, which are becoming more and more costly. Finally, the large size, the long lead time for planning and construction, and the high capital cost involve an inherent inflexibility and inability to respond to changing needs, according to some critics.

A number of new storage technologies that may be more widely applicable than pumped hydroelectric storage are being developed. One such energy stor-

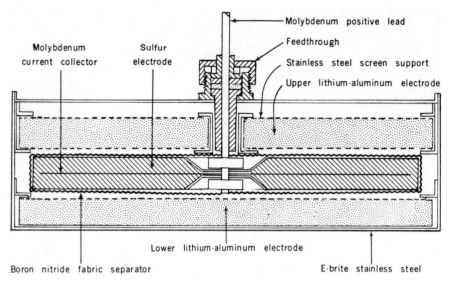

Molybdenum current collector
Sulfur electrode
Molybdenum positive lead
Feedthrough
Stainless steel screen support
Upper lithium-aluminum electrode
Lower lithium-aluminum electrode
Boron nitride fabric separator
E-brite stainless steel

Fig. 2. Diagram of a lithium-sulfur cell. Full-sized cells might be from 12 to 15 centimeters across and 1.6 centimeters high when used in automotive power plants. [Source: Paul Nelson. Argonne National Laboratory]

age technique is compressed air storage. In a normal gas turbine, fuel is mixed with air compressed in the compressor stage and combusted to generate mechanical power. About two thirds of the power produced by the turbine is needed to run the compressor. In compressed air storage, however, the compressor and the turbine stages can be alternately connected and disconnected from the motor-generator unit. Thus, in off-peak hours when the demand for power is low, the turbine stage can be disengaged, and electrical energy from a base load unit can be used to run the compressor stage with the result that the air is compressed and then pumped into an underground cavern and stored. During hours of peak demand, the compressed air can be used in the combustion stage to run the turbine. All the turbine power can be used for generation of electricity, because the air is already compressed. A considerably enhanced power output per unit of fuel consumed by the turbines results.

The compressed air storage method has some disadvantages. The gas turbines are powered by No. 2 fuel oil, and suitable sites must be found. Although some disagree, many energy storage investigators regard the economics of compressed air storage as unfavorable unless suitable natural caverns can be used. Excavation is considered too expensive. Researchers at United Aircraft Research Laboratories, East Hartford, Connecticut, however, believe that specially mined caverns can enable higher operating ef-

ficiencies and overall lower capital costs than is possible with natural caverns. In some cases a water reservoir might be used to maintain a constant pressure in the cavern. Since the air may be compressed to 40 atmospheres, the cavern would have to be more than 300 meters deep. The size of the reservoir would be less than 15 percent of that of an equivalent pumped hydroelectric storage facility.

Although the basic technology exists for compressed air storage, a hard engineering study, beyond exploratory design studies, has yet to be made in the United States. Nor has a demonstration facility yet been built, although Stal-Laval, a Swedish turbine manufacturer, reportedly is much closer to such a plant than anyone in the United States (1).

If only because the largest part of the research dollar for energy storage is spent on them, storage batteries may be one of the likeliest energy storage technologies to reach fruition. But so far no battery exists whose performance and costs are adequate to compete with either pumped hydroelectric storage or gas turbines (2). If they could be perfected, observers point out, storage batteries would have some desirable features that are absent in pumped hydroelectric storage. Batteries would have minimal siting problems. They make no noise, emit no pollutants, and, being modular in nature, would be rapidly assembled in factories in any desired size. Batteries can also be placed much closer to the power load as compared to pumped hydroelectric facilities, thus

reducing the load on power transmission lines.

Although there is no fixed performance goal to be met, it is believed that a battery that delivered a specific energy of 220 watt-hours per kilogram, a specific power of 55 watts per kilogram, a lifetime of 4 years, a cycle life of 1000 (the number of charges and discharges), and a storage efficiency of 70 percent would be attractive for utilities (3). A 100–megawatt-hour storage facility, a substation size, made of such batteries might occupy a cube 8 meters on a side.

The lead-acid battery is used to start automobiles and to power industrial and recreational vehicles. In its present state of development, however, the lead-acid battery is not designed for electrical energy storage for utilities. In particular, lead-acid batteries cannot sustain the cycling between fully charged and discharged states which would occur in utility storage facilities. Thus they would have a short life and most investigators discount the use of lead-acid batteries except in circumstances where the high cost of specifically designed heavy-duty batteries can be tolerated. However, scientists at Westinghouse Research Laboratories, Pittsburgh, Pennsylvania, believe economical lead-acid batteries for storage can be developed. And the Atomic Energy Commission is planning a demonstration storage facility that will, at least initially, use lead-acid batteries.

High temperature batteries (that is, batteries that must be heated to a few hundred degrees Celsius in order to operate) promise improved performance, lower cost, and good prospects for the availability of the required raw materials. The two high temperature batteries receiving the most attention are the lithium-sulfur and the sodium-sulfur batteries (4). Of the two, the sodium-sulfur battery is thought to be in a somewhat more advanced stage of development, although there is general agreement that it will be 10 years before any high temperature battery is widely available. The earliest work on the sodium-sulfur battery was done at the Ford Motor Company, Dearborn, Michigan, but several laboratories in the United States, England, France, and Japan are now developing them also.

A sodium-sulfur cell operates from 300° to 350°C with molten sodium and sulfur electrodes. The unique feature of these cells is the electrolyte, which is a solid ceramic material called beta alumina ($Na_2O \cdot 11Al_2O_3$). The beta alumina electrolyte is fabricated by proprietary hot pressing and sintering techniques. The high operating temperature is necessary to achieve an appreciable sodium ion conductivity of the electrolyte. The ceramic electrolyte permits a simplicity of design because the electrolyte can also be a container and separator of the electrodes and because its properties prevent battery self-discharge. The beta alumina tends to crack during recharging at a high rate, however, which shortens the battery life. Although on their guard about releasing specific figures, scientists say that the performance of individual cells is approaching that desired for storage applications. Still to be accomplished, however, is the fabrication of individual cells into multicelled, long-lived batteries that can be hermetically sealed. (In the laboratory, cells are often operated in inert atmospheres, but are not sealed.) Identification of component materials that are inexpensive, yet corrosion-resistant, is also required.

Lithium-sulfur batteries differ from sodium-sulfur in that their electrolyte is a molten salt (such as a lithium chloride–potassium chloride eutectic mixture) (Fig. 2). They operate at a slightly higher temperature (375° to 400°C) and theoretically have a higher performance capability. The leading proponent of lithium-sulfur cells has been the Atomic Energy Commission's Argonne National Laboratory, Argonne, Illinois, although there is also ongoing research on these cells in other U.S. laboratories, in England, and in the U.S.S.R. Problems with lithium-sulfur batteries include containment of the electrodes, corrosion, and sealing the high temperature cells.

A battery that does not require high temperatures is being developed at Energy Development Associates, Madison Heights, Michigan. In this battery, the electrodes are zinc and chlorine, and the electrolyte is a zinc chloride solution. The unique feature of this battery is that the chlorine evolved during charging of the battery is stored in a solid chlorine hydrate ($Cl_2 \cdot 6H_2O$), so that the chlorine gas is not a problem. Researchers at Energy Development Associates expect to have a prototype battery in operation within 2 years.

Vehicles, including cars and buses, also have an energy storage problem. Up to now, this has been solved by carrying energy in the form of liquid fuels, such as gasoline or diesel oil. Although the performance (acceleration, speed, load, range, and refueling convenience) of liquid-fueled vehicles will be hard to match, air pollution resulting from internal combustion engine emissions and the prospect of a decreased availability of fuel (and that at a high price) has stimulated interest in other ways to store energy for vehicles.

Electric vehicles powered by storage batteries could be one solution but, as with storage for utility load leveling, there is still no adequate battery for powering automobiles. At present, the lead-acid battery is inadequate because of its short lifetime, its weight, and its cost. (Lead-acid battery-powered vans are now being tested by the U.S. Postal Service; and, in Great Britain, a full-sized bus using lead-acid batteries will soon be in operation.) Many of the batteries suitable for load leveling could also power conventional automobiles, provided that the specific power achievable could be increased to 220 watts per kilogram from the lower specific power projected for batteries used in load leveling (2). Several hours would still be required each night for recharging the vehicle. Even if batteries with a specific energy of 220 watt-hours per kilogram cannot be achieved, availability of batteries with specific energies of 50 to 100 watt-hours per kilogram would make practical electric vehicles of two to five times greater range than present vehicles powered by lead-acid batteries. This capability would cover a large part of the present use of cars, especially for urban and suburban driving, say proponents of electric vehicles.

Most observers agree that it is much harder to build a good battery to power an automobile than to store power for utilities. So far, the Electricity Council Research Center in England has produced a sodium-sulfur battery to power a van (but the performance is still less than optimum). Scientists at Energy Development Associates have produced a laboratory zinc-chlorine battery to power an experimental 2-ton vehicle. However, this battery could not be recharged while in the vehicle. Workers at Standard Oil of Ohio (Sohio) in Cleveland are developing a high temperature lithium battery that uses tellurium tetrachloride ($TeCl_4$) positive electrodes. Prototype batteries to power fork-lift trucks are expected in 3 years.

Other types of energy storage systems are also being studied, and some are being actively developed, including magnetic energy storage, mechanical storage in flywheels, chemical storage in hydrogen, and thermal storage. A second article will examine some of the many proposed storage technologies.

References

1. "First pumped air storage plant nears reality," *Engineering News Record*, 17 February 1972.
2. M. L. Kyle, E. J. Cairns, D. S. Webster, *Argonne National Laboratory Report ANL-7958* (Argonne National Laboratory, Argonne, Illinois, 1973).
3. E. J. Cairns, *Bull. Am. Phys. Soc.* **19**, 57 (1974).
4. ——— and R. K. Steunenberg, in *Progress in High Temperature Physics and Chemistry*, C. A. Rouse, Ed. (Pergamon, New York, 1973), vol. 5, p. 63.

Energy Storage: Developing Advanced Technologies

Arthur L. Robinson

The concept of energy storage—storing energy generated when demand is low for use when it is needed later on—is rapidly coming of age (see page 144). Electric power utilities, faced with a demand for electricity which fluctuates with the time of day and season of the year, estimate that, by the end of the century, up to 25 percent of the total power generated during the day could be stored and subsequently used. One spokesman rated energy storage as the best technological and economic investment after advanced nuclear power. In addition to serving the needs of utilities, energy storage is needed for electric vehicles. While experiments with vehicles powered by storage batteries, one alternative to petroleum-fueled internal combustion engines, are well under way, advanced energy storage systems could make such vehicles much more useful than they are now. And energy storage will be essential to the development of presently unexploited energy sources, such as the sun, the wind, or the tides, which are intermittent in character.

A number of proposed storage technologies are emerging from the stage of preliminary feasibility studies and entering the stage of engineering study and prototype development. For example, energy can be stored in a magnetic field. In the familiar electromagnet, however, the resistance of the magnet windings results in power losses, and power must be constantly supplied in order to maintain the field. If the windings lacked resistance—that is, if they were superconducting—then once the desired magnetic field was obtained, it would require no further power, and the energy originally supplied to the magnet would be stored in the magnetic field. Later the stored energy (proportional to the square of the current) could be recovered by drawing off some of the current in the magnet. The storage efficiency (the fraction of stored energy that is recoverable) could be about 95 percent.

Such an idea for storing electrical energy has been advocated by researchers at the University of Wisconsin, Madison (1), and at the Los Alamos Scientific Laboratory, Los Alamos, New Mexico (2). Both groups have pointed out that storing energy for utilities via superconductors is economically thinkable only for large storage capacities, in the range 1,000 to 10,000 megawatt-hours (1 watt-hour equals 3600 joules). A typical magnet might be a solenoid with a radius of 50 meters and a height of 50 meters, and would probably be set in bedrock in order to contain the large forces on the conductors of such an immense magnet. Because of the relatively low energy density (measured in watt-hours per cubic meter) of superconducting magnetic storage, this type is inappropriate for vehicles.

Both the Madison and Los Alamos groups have made preliminary engineering and economic studies of the feasibility of storing energy in this way, and are hoping to build model systems from which to obtain data for extensive analysis. The Wisconsin group is aiming for a 10–megawatt-hour model (in the form of a solenoid) to be completed by 1980 or 1981. The solenoid would be made of niobium-titanium composite superconductors (*Science*, 25 January, p. 294) and would operate at 1.8°K with a field of 0.5 tesla. The Los Alamos researchers are planning first on a 30–kilowatt-hour model (in the shape of a torus), to be followed by a 10–megawatt-hour prototype later on. The largest superconducting magnets now operating (in terms of energy storage capacity, not magnetic field strength) are those used in bubble chambers, such as the big European bubble chamber (BEBC) magnet at CERN in Geneva. The BEBC magnet has a storage capacity of about 220 kilowatt-hours.

The large size of the superconducting magnetic storage plant means that there may be a need for extra power transmission lines, if large storage facilities are located far from the areas they serve. There could be superconducting storage facilities close to cities, however, since there is some flexibility in locating the storage site. Except for the possible influence of the magnetic field, which should be minimized by placing the storage unit underground, environmental effects ought to be small. The often expressed fear of what happens to the stored energy if the superconductor fails (goes normal) apparently can be assuaged if cryogenically stabilized superconductors are used. The term "cryogenically stabilized" means that even if the superconductor fails, the adjacent metal, usually copper or aluminum, can safely carry the current in the magnet. As was expressed by R. W. Boom of the University of Wisconsin, one builds an aluminum magnet, then short-circuits it with a superconductor. The heat that would be generated by the passage of the magnet current through the copper or aluminum in the event of failure of the superconductor can be dissipated via the structures supporting the magnet.

A number of questions still remain to be answered, however, and magnetic storage is rated by many as an exotic technology whose impact will not be felt for some time.

A proposal to store energy in rapidly rotating flywheels is eliciting much attention (3). The principle of the flywheel is thought to have been known for several thousand years, and the potter's wheel is the example given to support this contention. Flywheels are now being used in such diverse applications as automotive engines and synchrotrons.

The energy stored in a rotating flywheel is given by $W = \frac{1}{2}I\omega^2$, where W is the stored energy, I is the moment of inertia of the flywheel, and ω is the angular frequency (radians per second). Thus the stored energy can be increased both by increasing the mass of the flywheel and increasing its angular velocity, and, in principle, flywheels of any desired capacity could be built, if it were not for the limits implied by the finite strength of the flywheel material. When the stresses in the flywheel exceed its strength, the wheel will fail, with possibly catastrophic results. Up to now, most flywheels have been made of steel, but because of the fear of the results of large chunks of steel loosed from a failed flywheel, they have been operated at such low speeds that their usefulness has been limited. Even so, experiments with such flywheels to power trolleybuses in San Francisco and for braking and acceleration of subway cars in New York (regenerative braking) are under way.

The real future for flywheels, however, appears to depend on a new class of materials that have unidirectional mechanical properties (4). These materials often are made in the shape of long thin fibers or they are fibers embedded in a lower strength matrix. David Rabenhorst of Johns Hopkins University's Applied Physics Laboratory, Silver Spring, Maryland, has been an enthusiastic proponent of these superflywheels, as he terms them. A wide variety of materials, including steel wires, boron filaments, fiberglass, Kevlar (a new organic material from the DuPont Company), carbon fibers, bulk glass, and wood, could be used. Because of the relatively exotic nature of many of these materials, costs could be high. Future superflywheels might, however, become more competitive in cost through the use of low-cost ballast materials, according to Rabenhorst. (Ballast materials are used to add weight to the flywheel, but do not contribute any strength.)

Unlike previous flywheels, which have been solid disks, the likely configuration of the superflywheel would be either the fanned circular brush configuration (Fig. 1) or a multirim configuration in which the fibers are arranged in consecutive hoops of successively larger radii. Both configurations take advantage of the unidirectional properties of the fibers.

A utility peak power storage facility composed of superflywheels could offer a number of advantages, say flywheel proponents. Electric power generated during off-peak hours could be used to increase the rotational speed of the storage flywheel. During peak demand hours, energy could be withdrawn from the flywheel. Flywheels make little noise, emit no pollutants, and can be made with any desired storage capacity. They can therefore be put close to the load. The estimated storage efficiency of a flywheel system is 80 to 90 percent. Flywheels could also be a power source for automobiles and other vehicles. Vehicle-sized flywheels may be able to be recharged in a matter of minutes, whereas batteries require several hours; they are projected to achieve a much higher specific power (a few hundred watts per kilogram) than batteries, so that vehicle acceleration would be improved. However, flywheels probably will not be able

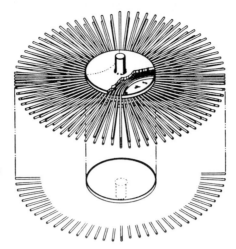

Fig. 1. Proposed superflywheel in the fanned circular brush configuration. The flywheel is not solid, but is made up of many long, thin fibers or rods. A flywheel 8 meters in diameter might be composed of rods less than 1.2 centimeters thick and weighing about 2.2 kilograms. [Source: David Rabenhorst, Johns Hopkins University]

to achieve the specific energy of advanced batteries, thus limiting vehicle range. Even so, it may be necessary to use a small flywheel in series with a battery to achieve the required specific power.

So far, no superflywheels have been built. Although some testing of materials has begun and flywheel development is under way at the Johns Hopkins laboratory, the ultimate costs, efficiencies, and engineering designs of flywheel systems are still theoretical. Hence, some observers suggest that widespread use of flywheels is still far in the future.

Hydrogen has received a good deal of attention in the context of the "hydrogen economy" in which, for example, hydrogen could be generated by electrolysis with the use of electricity generated by nuclear power plants; then the hydrogen could be stored or transported to appropriate sites via pipelines; and at the load site the hydrogen could be used directly as a fuel, or could be converted back to electricity via fuel cells or high temperature turbines (Science, 24 November 1972, p. 849). It is possible, however, to envisage a less grand scheme that would permit hydrogen to act as a storage medium both for utility load leveling applications and as a fuel for vehicles. Scientists at the Brookhaven National Laboratory, Upton, New York, are studying one such concept (5). Hydrogen can be stored with the use of metals. When pressurized hydrogen gas comes in contact with the metal surface, it

readily diffuses into the metal and forms a metal hydride compound. Although a number of metals, usually alloys, have been and are being investigated, a 50 atom percent iron–50 atom percent titanium alloy appears to be the most attractive so far, primarily because of its lower cost. The hydride formation is exothermic, so the heat generated during the reaction must be carried away. Later, when hydrogen is desired, heat can be applied to the metal hydride, and hydrogen is evolved. The temperatures involved, both when the hydrogen is stored and when it is released from the hydride, are close to the ambient temperature. (Storage of hydrogen in liquefied form or compressed in storage tanks also has been proposed.)

Hydrogen stored as hydrides could be used in an electric power storage plant if the power generated during off-peak hours were used to electrolyze water into hydrogen and oxygen. During the peak-demand hours, the hydrogen could be recovered and used to power fuel cells. The Brookhaven workers will soon be designing just such a prototype storage facility, although how to reconvert the hydrogen to electrical power has not yet been decided. The present objective is to construct a 2–megawatt-hour prototype storage plant, with a 50– or 100–megawatt-hour facility being a later goal. Already a prototype hydrogen reservoir capable of storing 6.4 kilograms of hydrogen has been constructed at Brookhaven and will be undergoing testing by the Public Service Electric and Gas Company of New Jersey to study the feasibility of storing off-peak electrical energy.

One difficulty with hydrogen for storing electrical energy is that the overall efficiency of systems based on available fuel cells is only about 40 percent. Fuel cells are also expensive and short-lived (Science, 22 December 1972, p. 1273). Improvements in fuel cells operating on pure hydrogen are projected to permit system efficiencies of the order of 65 percent, which would make them more attractive. The alternative—converting hydrogen to electrical power via high temperature turbines—also is awaiting advances in technology. But minimizing the cost and maximizing the efficiency of the hydrogen production process may still pose problems, according to some observers.

The possibility of using solar energy (or some other intermittent energy source) brings with it its own energy storage problem. Here the question is one of matching the energy available only during sunny daylight hours to the demand that continues during cloudy days and at night. Solar energy has been proposed both for space heating or cooling individual homes, and for generating electricity in central power plants (*Science*, 22 September 1972, p. 1088). Except for those solar energy schemes that rely on photovoltaic cells, energy storage is most naturally accomplished via storage of thermal energy, since heat is the usual quantity that is collected. Facilities based on collection of solar energy via photovoltaic cells, which generate electricity directly, would require electrical storage systems, such as storage batteries or any of the several other alternatives.

Two Ways to Store Heat

Thermal storage can be accomplished in one of two ways. The sensible heat method works by simply heating up some object which can be thermally insulated from its surroundings. When the heat is required, a suitable working fluid is passed by the heated object, and the heat is carried away. Heat can be more easily stored if the temperature of the object in which the heat is stored is not too different from that of the surroundings; thus it is desirable to use objects with a large heat capacity as the storage medium. Among the many materials used for sensible heat storage are water, rocks, and metals, such as sodium (in liquid form). Disadvantages of this way of storing thermal energy are that the storage medium takes up a lot of space and that heat cannot be stored for long periods effectively. For example, Mason Watson of the Aerospace Corporation, El Segundo, California, noted that a study of the feasibility of a solar energy plant to generate power in the Southwest, with liquid sodium being both the storage medium and the heat transfer fluid, included estimates that about 1 million cubic meters of sodium would be required to accommodate 10 hours of storage. Because storage periods longer than 10 hours were found to be impractical, solar power plants using sensible heat storage might best serve as a supplemental daytime source of power (intermediate power) rather than as a primary or base load source.

A second method of thermal storage makes use of the latent heat associated with a phase change, such as the transition from a solid to a liquid (melting). Thus, collected solar heat can be stored by melting the solid storage medium, and can be recovered by allowing the liquid storage medium to solidify. The primary advantage of this method of thermal storage as compared to the sensible heat method is that a great deal more heat can be stored in the same volume of material. For example, Glauber's salt ($Na_2SO_4 \cdot 10H_2O$), a much-studied heat-of-fusion material, when storing the same amount of thermal energy as water, requires only one-eighth the volume. In addition, storage occurs within a narrow temperature range near the phase transformation, rather than over the wider range of temperatures required by the sensible heat method.

Despite the much greater ability of heat-of-fusion materials to store heat, a number of problems have yet to be overcome. Many heat-of-fusion materials are expensive. They are usually corrosive, thus presenting containerization problems similar to those of high temperature batteries. Some of them have short lifetimes because they tend to decompose in various ways as they are thermally cycled. Many materials exhibit a large degree of supercooling so that they do not freeze at the expected temperature. And the problem of efficient heat transfer (from the working fluid to the storage medium) limits the effectiveness of the storage. Thus, heat-of-fusion storage is often regarded as being farther off than sensible heat storage, especially when intended for use in large electrical power plants. Sensible heat storage systems are already in use in a number of solar-heated buildings.

Probably thousands of heat-of-fusion materials have been looked at for thermal storage. Maria Telkes of the University of Delaware's Institute of Energy Conversion has extensively studied salt hydrates, such as Glauber's salt, for thermal storage in home-sized units (6). Another salt hydrate, sodium thiosulfate pentahydrate ($Na_2S_2O_3 \cdot 5H_2O$), is being used in the University of Delaware's Solar I experimental solar house. At the University of Pennsylvania's National Center for Energy Management and Power, where there is also interest in solar energy for use in individual homes (7), researchers are studying, among other materials, organic materials, such as paraffin waxes, for storage where a long cycle life is required. For the higher temperatures needed in solar energy central power generating plants, several laboratories are studying eutectic salts, such as sodium nitrate–sodium chloride.

A number of other storage options are also emerging, and observers say there will likely be several more. For example, steam generated in central power plant boilers might be stored in tanks or caverns until it is needed to run turbines. Coal gasifiers, when operational, are expected to be most efficient when operated continuously. The gas produced might similarly be stored at high pressure in caverns. A rate structure for energy that reflected the cost of energy (base load electricity is cheaper to make than peak electricity) might reshuffle consumption patterns so that the demand for energy was more uniform. Or a new storage scheme may enter the scene with the potential of becoming dominant in its field. For example, recently, J. A. Van Vechten of the Bell Laboratories, Murray Hill, New Jersey, described a thermal storage scheme where molten semiconductors were used as a heat-of-fusion storage material (8). Van Vechten suggested that substantial improvements in storage efficiencies (because of larger heats-of-fusion and better heat transfer) and lower costs could result from the use of semiconductors.

Despite the importance of energy storage, the activity as indicated by funding can only be described as modest. The largest advanced storage research program in the federal government belongs to the Atomic Energy Commission, which is spending about $1.8 million this year, the largest part going toward batteries. Overall, probably less than $10 million is being spent throughout the United States on advanced energy storage (that is, excluding pumped hydroelectric and commercial batteries). A possible consequence is that some time will pass before any of the advanced energy storage systems become available.

References

1. R. W. Boom *et al.*, in *Advances in Cryogenic Engineering*, K. D. Timmerhaus, Ed. (Plenum, New York, in press), vol. 19.
2. W. V. Hassenzahl, B. L. Baker, W. E. Keller, *Los Alamos Scientific Laboratory Report LA-5377-MS* (Los Alamos Scientific Laboratory, Los Alamos, N.M., 1973).
3. R. F. Post and S. F. Post, *Sci. Am.* **229**, 17 (December 1973).
4. D. W Rabenhorst, paper presented at the 14th Annual Joint Symposium of the New Mexico Sections of the American Society of Mechanical Engineers and American Society for Metals, and the University of New Mexico on Engineering for the Materials/Energy Challenge, Albuquerque, N.M., 1974.
5. J. J. Reilly, K. C. Hoffman, G. Strickland, R. H. Wiswall, in *Proceedings of the 26th Power Sources Symposium* (PSC Publications Committee, Redbank, N.J., in press).
6. M. Telkes, in *National Science Foundation Report NSF/RANN-73004* (National Science Foundation, Washington, D.C., 1973).
7. G. Belton and F. Ajami, *Report No. NSF/RANN/SE/GI27976/TR/73/4* (University of Pennsylvania National Center for Energy Management and Power, Philadelphia, 1973).
8. J. A. Van Vechten. *Bull. Am. Phys. Soc.* **19**, 54 (1974).

Index

Pollution, 41, 95
Air, 3, 54, 73, 74, 101, 131, 132, 136, 140, 147, 149
  Carbon dioxide, 132, 333
  Carbon monoxide, 101, 143
  Hydrocarbons, 143
  Lead, 9, 119, 136, 143
  Nitrogen oxides, 84, 132
  Particulates, 84
  Sulfur oxides, 3, 72, 73, 76, 84–87, 95, 133
Controls, 13, 24–25, 84
Pesticides, 45
Water, 6, 86, 125, 126
Polyisoprenes, 114
Potassium, 42, 43
Potatoes, 53
"Power gas." *See* Industrial gas
Prien, Charles, 72
Process heat, 103. *See also* Hydrogen, production. *See also* Nuclear energy
Process steam, 13, 14, 31
Project Independence, 3, 34, 66, 69, 73, 74, 76
Propane, 143
Protein, 45, 46, 51, 54, 112
Public Service Electric and Gas Company of New Jersey, 149
Pyrite, 84

Q and R

Quirk's wind generator, 129
Rabenhorst, David, 148
Rasmussen, N. C., 92
Ray, Dixy Lee, 92
Reactors, chemical, 103
Recycling
  Metals, 16, 56
  Organic wastes, 36, 37, 131, 132, 134, 135, 137
  Solid wastes, 23
Refrigeration, 13, 14, 48, 49, 50, 56, 119
Rice, 52, 53
Rubber, 113–114
Rural Electrification Administration, 128
Russia, 7, 52, 79, 108
  Gasifiers, 79

S

Scotland, 77
Seaweed, 126
Secord, C. H., 79
Sedimentary rock, 68, 69
Seismic detection technology, 68
Shale. *See* Oil shale
Shell Oil Company, 89
Shellfish, 125–127
Signal Companies, 107
Simon, William E., 74
Slag, 79, 80
Smith, Gene, 27
Sodium, liquid, 93
Solar collectors, 35, 119, 120, 121
Solar energy, 8–9, 20, 44, 55, 83, 88, 98, 118–122, 123, 137
  Cost, 118
  Efficiency, 119, 121
  Forests, 135
  Generation of electricity, 9, 118, 120–121, 149
  Ocean thermal, 119, 123–124
  Photosynthesis, 49, 111–117, 123
  Photovoltaic process, 121
  Potential, 9, 111, 118, 121
  Problems, 118
  Storage, 120, 121, 149
  Utilization, 9, 16, 118–122, 149
Solar house, 35

Solar stills, 35
Solar water heaters, 35, 120
Solar Wind Company, 129
South Africa, 77, 78
Southwest Research Institute, 129
Soybeans, 45, 53, 54
Stal-Laval, 146
Standard Industrial Classification, 48
Standard Oil of Ohio, 147
Steam power plants, 31, 118
Sugar beet, 113
Sugarcane, 112, 113, 114
Sulfur dioxide, 72, 73
Sulfur Oxide Control Technology Assessment Panel, 85
Sun Oil Company, 67
Swanson, Robert K., 129
Sweeney, Thomas E., 129
Synthesis gas. *See* Coal
Synthetic fuels, 73, 74, 75, 77, 78, 98, 131–136, 137
Szikla-Rozinek boiler. *See* Boilers

T

Tars, 81
Telkes, Maria, 150
Tennessee Valley Authority, 18, 85
Thermal energy, 19, 123–125, 143, 150
Thomason, Harry, 35
Thorium, 89, 91
Trans-Alaska pipeline, 6
Tritium, 95
Turbines
  Aeroturbine, 118
  Gas, 78, 145
  High temperature, 143, 149
  Low-temperature vapor, 119
  Nuclear powered, 145
  Steam, 108, 110, 124, 125, 133, 145
  Water, 145
Turkey, 77

U and V

Union of Concerned Scientists, 92
Union Oil Company, 70, 72, 107
United Aircraft Research Laboratories, 146
United Mine Workers of America, 74, 75
U.S. Geological Survey, 62, 63, 66–69, 107
U.S. Postal Service, 147
University of Colorado, 72
University of Delaware Institute of Energy Conversion, 150
University of Pennsylvania National Center for Energy Management and Power, 150
University of Wisconsin, 148
Uranium, 13, 89, 90–91, 93, 100, 110, 134
Urban Mass Transportation Act, 18
Van Vechten, J. A., 150

W–Z

Ward, John C., 72
Waste disposal, 49, 50, 72, 81, 85, 140, 143. *See also* Recycling
Watson, Mason, 150
Weeds, control of, 45, 54
Wellman-Galusha producer, 77
Westinghouse Electric Company, 89
Westinghouse Research Laboratories, 146
Wheat, 42, 52
Wiesner, Wayne, 129
Wind power, 19, 34, 36, 37, 55, 83, 118, 127–130, 145
Winkler gasifier. *See* Gasifiers
Yugoslavia, 77
Zapp, A. D., 68